Hope at Last
for
At-Risk Youth

Robert D. Barr

Boise State University

William H. Parrett

University of Alaska Fairbanks

Allyn and Bacon

Boston • London • Toronto • Sydney • Tokyo • Singapore

Senior Editor: Raymond Short
Marketing Manager: Ellen Mann
Production Administrator: Marjorie Payne
Editorial Assistant: Christine Shaw
Cover Administrator: Linda Knowles
Composition Buyer: Linda Cox
Editorial-Production Service: Chestnut Hill Enterprises

Copyright © 1995 by Allyn & Bacon
A Simon and Schuster Company
Needham Heights, Massachusetts

Library of Congress Cataloging-in-Publication Data

Barr, Robert D.
    Hope at last for at-risk youth /
  Robert D. Barr, William H. Parrett.
        p.   cm.
    Includes bibliographical references and index.
    ISBN 0-205-16267-3
    1. Problem children—Education—United States.   2. Problem youth—
  Education—United States.   3. Socially handicapped children—
  Education—United States.   4. Socially handicapped youth—
  Education—United States.   I. Parrett, William.   II. Title.
  LC4802.B37   1995
371.93'0973—dc20   94-18807
                                                                              CIP

This book is printed on recycled, acid-free paper.

Printed in the United States of America
10 9 8 7 6 5 4 3 2 1   99 98 97 96 95 94

Contents

Preface

During the early hours of a misty February morning, a policeman spotted a suspicious looking car parked in the shadows at the side of the street. After pulling over, the young policeman tugged down his bulletproof vest, climbed out of his patrol car, and walked back to take a look. As he bent down to talk to the driver, he was shot at least three times in the face and fell dead. What makes this event so chilling is that the scene was not played out in Los Angeles or South Chicago, Detroit or Dallas, and the accused murderer was not a gang member or some drug-crazed addict. The policeman was gunned down in the small rural town of New Plymouth, Idaho, surrounded by the rich, fertile farmlands of the irrigated high desert just outside of the state capital, Boise. The person arrested for the murder was a 14-year-old boy out for a joyride in a stolen car with two of his pals. The newspaper quoted his single mother as saying, "I just couldn't do anything with him." Even though juvenile authorities had received a tip that the youth was carrying a weapon, they were far too busy to check out just another anonymous phone call. School officials explained that the boy almost never came to school. "We really didn't know him," they said.

Similar tragedies are turning up everywhere these days. News stories have reported that Oregon doubled the number of prison cells in the state in a recent five-year period. During the past 18 months, youth gangs all but overwhelmed schools in Salt Lake City, Utah. There were television stories about a rash of teen suicides in Plano, Texas, and in another Texas community, an entire squad of high-school cheerleaders became pregnant. A national magazine reported that 20 percent of the first graders in a small town outside Columbus, Ohio, had been held back a grade because they could not read. It is increasingly evident that life in the United States has changed and a grim future is suddenly upon us.

Choose almost any community in the nation. Walk into one of the local schools, sit down and talk to the teachers. The story these days is almost always the same: too many kids arriving at school unprepared to learn; too many failing their courses; too many dropping out of school; overwhelming numbers of students living in poverty or in dysfunctional homes; growing numbers of students who rarely come to school, and when they do, disrupt the orderly learning of the others. Too many students are increasingly violent; too many carry weapons each day; too many are becoming pregnant; too many are influenced by drugs and alcohol.

Teachers throughout the United States tell the same stories. Their classrooms include more and more children and youth who are dangerously at risk of not gaining an adequate education and who are doomed to live out their lives underemployed, unemployed, or unemployable. Technology, international competition, and the information age have quietly closed the door of opportunity on all of these tragic youth. These at-risk kids confront public schools with some of the most difficult and complex problems our educational system has ever faced. Dealing with these problems poses for schools and communities a complex array of moral, ethical, and educational dilemmas.

In addressing these problems, schools often turn to special education for help, and as a result there has been a huge increase in the number of students identified as learning disabled, hyperactive, suffering from attention deficit disorder, attachment disorders, or a host of other disabilities. Some schools simply cannot tolerate these youth and have segregated them into slow learning tracks or expelled them. The vast majority of schools, lacking any other strategy, simply retain them in hopes that a second time through will prove more successful than the first.

This book offers a dramatic, essential message to schools and communities: help is finally available for addressing the difficult, complex issues associated with children and youth at risk. At last we know what to do and how to do it. This book represents a major effort to find, describe, and integrate what we know about effective programs for at-risk youth. It represents a careful effort to provide schools and communities with specific, practical, down-to-earth information about what works and what does not. This book will prove useful to schools and communities in their quest to teach at-risk students at every level. It should help teachers and administrators to decide what to do today, next Monday, and next year. It includes suggestions for parents, descriptions of specific programs that teach all children to read, where to go for help, and the best we know about combatting youth violence. The book also provides specific directions for reforming the educational process to ensure success for at-risk youth.

Guaranteeing Success

This book provides, perhaps for the first time, a comprehensive review of evidence regarding effective programs for at-risk youth that makes it finally possible to speak with authority and assurance that effective programs can indeed be developed. Now, all children can be guaranteed succeess in school, even those who have been considered to be severely at risk. This guarantee has only recently become possible as an emerging body of evidence documents in the most forceful way that our educational structure does indeed posses. the resources to promise school success for all children.

Others have offered a guarantee. Robert Slavin states that with the exception of severely mentally impaired youth, schools can now teach all children to read. He further argues that it is the entitlement of every child in the United States to learn to read. Slavin and his colleagues at Johns Hopkins University have documented that the Success for All Schools approach is, in fact, effectively teaching severely at-risk youth to read, youth who for decades have been considered unable to learn. The Reading Recovery program represents yet another approach which has demonstrated that we do possess the knowledge and programs to teach all youth to read, most within a 16-week period. Add to these successes the fact that some schools, like the Hawthorne Elementary School in Seattle, an inner-city elementary school serving primarily African-American children, do promise to parents that their children will learn to read. They even guarantee it.

Stop at any bookstore selling current educational materials and you will notice a number of publications that document and declare that we now possess the ability to teach all students. Recent titles such as *Every Child Can Learn, Every Child Can Succeed, What Works, Schools That Work,* and *Public Schools That Work* represent a growing number of books, articles, and reports identifying schools and programs throughout the United States where all children and youth are succeeding. During the past 25 years, thousands of alternative public schools, magnet schools, experimental schools, and other non-traditional programs have been developed and documented to be effective in teaching reluctant learners.

The 1993 Louisiana School Effectiveness Study, a 10-year qualitative and quantitative research effort involving schools in all types of communities, went even further. The study reported that certain schools, even regular local elementary schools, were effectively teaching all types of children and documented that these schools were successful regardless of the home situation or the socioeconomic status of the family. Similar results have been reported from in-depth, long-term case studies of junior-high, high-school, and K-12 alternative and magnet schools. Such definitive evidence provides the foundation for ensuring, guaranteeing if you will, the success of all children, particularly those who have been considered at risk. If some schools can be successful with all children and youth and if we identify and understand the program characteristics that are essential to that success, then it is finally possible that other schools can do the same. This recent development indeed presents a landmark opportunity and challenge to public education throughout the United States.

There is a "catch" to all this optimism. None of this is easy. To be successful with all children and youth demands that schools must start as early as possible, work extensively with parents and the larger community, provide long-term comprehensive support, and significantly change the teaching and learning process that has traditionally been used in public schools. To ensure success, schools and communities must relentlessly pursue excellence in their programs. A review of the material found in this book is also quite clear regarding school reform. To be successful with at-risk youth, schools must be significantly restructured at every school level. Public schools, as they have been traditionally organized and structured, not only do not work for at-risk youth, they often contribute to many of the problems at-risk students encounter. Schools must eliminate programs and practices that discriminate against at-risk youth, and they must redesign and restructure the traditional teaching and learning approach that has been used for so long in public education. To do less is unacceptable.

Why Read This Book

Hope At Last For At-Risk Youth delivers an unprecedented synthesis of the research efforts of others, evaluations of effective school programs and practices from throughout the country, descriptions of promising practices that have yet to be fully evaluated, and a collection of the authors' personal anecdotes and experiences with teachers and at-risk students in schools and communities throughout the nation.

This book started as a highly focused effort to collect, analyze, synthesize, and interpret the research on at-risk children and youth. While the authors were at times overwhelmed by the sheer volume of research, reports, publications, scholarly papers, and monographs on the topic, much of what was found proved to be far too narrow or esoteric to be of great value to the real, complex world of schools, teachers, and students. As the authors began to spread out before them what could be gleaned from this rich array of research about at-risk youth, it was evident that huge pieces to the puzzle were missing. There were still as many questions as there were answers.

To fill these gaping holes and try to find specific answers to the hard questions facing schools or even indicators that could guide decisions, the authors turned to school and program evaluations, student assessment data, and program descriptions which seemed to hold promise for at-risk youth. It was out of this composite blend of data and insight that comprehensive patterns began to emerge. Out of the confusion regarding at-risk youth, a gestalt of order began to fall into place. As each new piece to the puzzle was added, as programs at each school level were identified and analyzed, we began to think of our work as a comprehensive, detailed, fine-lined structure of an educational blueprint. It was finally possible to begin to plan with confidence, to predict results.

The book begins with a review of the crisis which has resulted from so many youth who have failed in school. The first two chapters analyze the crisis in terms of the larger context of national and international developments in technology, changes in the economic marketplace, and social changes in the family that have created an escalating set of complex problems for schools everywhere. Criteria are presented to help schools and communities identify and anticipate at-risk students and their needs. Chapters 3 and 4 review efforts toward improving and reforming public schools and specifically document how traditional school programs, even those with the best of intentions, have failed the very students that they were attempting to help.

Chapter 5 provides a synthesis of what we know about children and youth at risk and includes a detailed description of the essential characteristics of effective programs for at-risk youth. Descriptions of effective programs and conceptual models for kindergarten, elementary, middle/junior high, and high schools are presented in Chapters 6, 7 and 8. This review offers the most comprehensive effort available to date, identifying effective programs at each of the school levels.

Chapters 9 and 10 offer distinctly new ideas about how to restructure and improve public schools. The final chapter provides a comprehensive resource guide which includes a bibliography of print and media, a list of technical assistance and university research centers, and a guide to foundations that have established at-risk youth as a funding priority. The book concludes with a self-evaluation checklist for K–12 educators, parents, and community members designed to assist school improvement efforts to help students at risk.

Hope At Last presents a precise, step-by-step set of descriptions and options that should guide schools toward the development of successful programs for at-risk youth. This book represents the first comprehensive effort to synthesize an era of study, experimentation, and practice toward improving educational opportunities for at-risk youth. The result presents a landmark opportunity for schools and communities to finally develop schools that effectively teach all youth.

Acknowledgments

There is an old Texas "poor boy" depression-day story that we have all heard dozens of times. Most recently the story appeared in the periodical, *Texas Monthly*, as told by the senior United States senator from the state, Phil Gramm. The Senator from Texas explains that he had already failed the third, seventh, and ninth grades. The story always begins with a student who is doing poorly in school. Somewhere along the line the school calls the parents in for a meeting and explains that their child will never be a doctor or an engineer and should, in fact, be transferred to some type of vocational training or trade school program. "Your child," the school official says, "lacks the ability to ever graduate from high school." At this point, the mother leans across the table and in a voice quivering with anger, explains to the teacher or administrator in no uncertain terms, "In our family, I'll have you know, we don't believe in ability!" Mrs. Gramm, like so many parents, knew that one educator's opinion regarding a child's lack of ability was not acceptable.

This book is dedicated to all of those at-risk students, both past and present, who were believed to not have the ability to succeed in school but did. The authors have known and taught many of these students. A number of these students are anonymously described in one section or another of this book. They include the youth who have graduated from Foxfire, the St. Paul Open School, Portland's Vocational Village and Metropolitan Learning Center, Pan Terra in Washington, the schools in the Louisiana School Effectiveness Study, the Alternative Schools in East Harlem, and other programs throughout the United States. This is their story.

The authors have many people to thank for their help in researching and writing this book. The reason so many people were involved in the project is because the book has been researched and written in fits and starts during a five-year period. Portions of the book were written while one or the other of the authors were working in Indonesia, Japan, Alaska, Oregon, Idaho, Washington, Florida, Minneapolis, Washington, D.C., Chicago, or Atlanta. During the past year of writing, when the majority of the book was completed, the authors were never once together. Through the use of facsimiles, overnight mail, small package airline express shipping, telephones, and the Internet, work progressed on a day-to-day basis. Wherever one or the other of the two authors was traveling, there were always phone messages, facsimiles, and overnight packages awaiting his arrival at the next hotel. Laptop computers and portable printers enabled a small production center to accompany each author to complete this book.

The book was researched and written in several distinct stages. The project was started at Oregon State University in 1987 when Ron and Sonya Darling walked into the office of Robert Barr, then dean of the College of Education, and donated $50,000 to fund efforts to address the problems of at-risk youth. With this generous gift and an additional matching grant from Oregon State University and the Oregon State System of Higher Education, the At-Risk Youth Technical Assistance Center was created. William Parrett helped to launch the center.

The authors are deeply indebted to Beverly Hobbs who, while completing her Ph.D. at Oregon State University, led a small team of undergraduate assistants who initially started collecting and compiling research data regarding at-risk youth, identifying and contacting other centers throughout the country, beginning a comprehensive gathering of information about at-risk youth. Marjorie C. Knittel of the Oregon State University Library also provided extensive assistance with associated bibliographic work.

During this time an advisory group was established to guide the development of the book. Members included a number of creative educators from the Portland, Oregon public schools: Paula Kinney, director of the Jefferson High School for Performing Arts; Mike Harris, at that time principal of the Metropolitan Learning Center; Paul Erickson, principal of Vocational Village; and Nate Jones, the District Director of Alternative Education. Other advisory board members included Judy Miller, Assistant State Superintendent of Schools in Oregon and her associate, Leon Fuhrman; Barbara Ross, who was at that time director of the state's teen parent program; and John Ball, the Oregon Commissioner of Children and Youth Services.

Through their work on this book, the authors also provided extensive technical assistance, conducted school evaluations, and participated in accreditation site visits in schools throughout the nation. During a five-year period the authors worked in over 200 schools, conducting teacher, student and parent interviews that later became a part of this book in the form of short, personal vignettes. Many thanks go to all of these people who sat with the authors and shared their feelings, frustrations, hopes, and dreams.

Special thanks are in order for the Alaska team who worked on all phases of this project and carried forward the draft stage of the manuscript production. Susan

Mitchell, of the Center for Cross-Cultural Studies Publications Center, provided crucial editing, support, and advice throughout the project. Her associate Paula Elmes also offered valuable technical assistance and graphics assistance. Draft manuscript preparation was further assisted by Evy Walters, Wu Jian Huai, Yin Jian Jun, and Diane Butler. Graduate student Lisa Brosseau tracked down numerous citations and helped with research Chapter 11. Allan Glatthorn, Acting Director of the University of Alaska Fairbanks School of Education, provided the authors with invaluable direction during the early phase of manuscript development, as did several local educators including Richard Cross, Superintendent of Fairbanks Schools, and principals, Jerry Hartsock, Sandy McGill, and Ernie Manzie.

In Idaho, the project came to rely on two outstanding graduate students: Janine Brookover who conducted data searches and later Donna Vakili who assisted with research and obtaining permissions for reprints. Donna also conducted a national phone survey of effective schools, contributed up-to-date data regarding many of the schools described in the book, and became the Idaho resident authority on "renegade" citations, eltations, and worked extensively on the book's index. Also, assisting at Boise State University was the dean's right-hand administrative assistant and confidant, Ernie Roberson and the undergraduate, award-winning, word-processing wizard Linda Alvarado. Linda is another of those remarkable people that schools initially felt had little chance of success, but who has persevered and today is a senior engineering student who stepped forward and provided a significant contribution to this book.

A number of people provided the authors with ideas and suggestions and reviewed early drafts of the manuscript. Special thanks are in order to Bob Cole at the Center for Leadership in School Reform in Louisville, Joe Nathan of the University of Minnesota's Hubert Humphrey Institute, Ruth Vinz of Columbia University, Vern Smith of Indiana University, Stephen Jackstadt of the University of Alaska Anchorage, Devon Metzger of California State University at Chico, Nora White of the University of Alaska Fairbanks, Jan Zulich of the University of Hawaii at Hilo, and several Boise State University professors: Phyllis Edmundson, Holly Anderson, and Lamont Lyons. Later reviewers, William E. Davis of the University of Maine and Sharon McGuffie and Marta Harrinston of the Deer Isle (Maine) school district, provided many valuable suggestions. The production staff of Allyn and Bacon, particularly senior editor Ray Short, provided valuable support throughout this project for which we are most appreciative.

The heroes of this book are of course the many scholars, policy makers, teachers, and administrators whose work we have attempted to collect, understand, and interpret. These pioneers of school improvement include James Comer, Robert Slavin and his colleagues at Johns Hopkins University, Hank Levin and his associates at Stanford, and Gary Wehlage and Fred Newman and their associates at the University of Wisconsin in Madison's Center on Organization and Restructuring Schools. We also drew heavily on the works of Lisbeth Schorr, who speaks and writes so eloquently and with such hope for at-risk youth.

A small planning grant from the New American School's Development Corporation and the Minnesota Community Learning Centers enabled one of the authors to work with Joe Nathan and Wayne Jennings, to study contract and charter schools and educational experimentation and research in the Minneapolis area.

The authors are deeply appreciative of the understanding and encouragement provided by our families. Finally and most important of all were Beryl Barr and Ann Dehner, who lived through this ordeal with their husbands and served as critics extraordinaire and final editors of the manuscript.

C h a p t e r 1

The Crisis of At-Risk Children and Youth

"I just don't know what I'm going to do. Every year, my first grade class has more and more of these kids. They don't seem to care about right or wrong, they don't care about adult approval, they are disruptive, they can't read and they arrive at school absolutely unprepared to learn. Who are these kids? Where do they come from? Why are there more and more of them? I used to think that I was a good teacher. I really prided myself on doing an outstanding job. But I find I'm working harder and harder, and being less and less effective. A good teacher? Today I really don't know. I do know that my classroom is being overwhelmed by society's problems and I don't understand it. What's happening to our schools? What's happening to society? I don't understand all of this and I sure don't know what we're going to do about it."
—(ELEMENTARY TEACHER, ATLANTA, GEORGIA, 1993)

Today, the United States faces a crisis that threatens our future. Not a foreign war or an impending invasion and even more destructive than our out-of-control deficit, this crisis originates from our own neglect. The crisis will continue to erode our social and economic well-being until we as a nation confront its origin and remedy its disastrous effects. The crisis grows out of our unwillingness to educate all children and youth. It is a crisis that has placed our nation at risk.

There is a renewed hope and vision for the solution of this crisis as the spotlight of national attention has begun to focus on those youth who have not been successful in public education. Many times our nation has attempted to address this problem. Twenty years ago, it was part of the "war on poverty"; more recently, it has been part of the war on drugs. Today, it might be better defined as a battle for survival in the international marketplace. It is a crisis that has always been with us, but now it is getting worse, threatening the survival of our civilization. Yet today there is a key difference to our continuing dilemma. Researchers have finally provided solutions that can address the problems of the at risk effectively and immediately. At last there is hope for our at-risk children and youth.

Twenty years ago, the problem centered on poor and minority youth, but social and economic changes in the world have greatly expanded that target group. At first these youth were referred to as socially and culturally "deprived"; later on, as racial consciousness raised, the terminology changed to that of "disadvantaged." More recently, these students are described as the "disengaged" or "disconnected" youth of the United States.

Even more disturbing, there has been a growing realization that it is not just the poor or minority student who is of concern. Today, we recognize that any young person may become at risk. At various times in the life of all youth, there are episodes of disappointment and sometimes depression; there are encounters and pressures relating to alcohol, drugs, and the growing possibility of teenage parenthood. With the occurrence of widespread sexually transmitted disease and a startling increase in teenage suicide, the risks now facing our youth have become a matter of life and death. It is now clear that students who are at risk are not limited to any single group. They cut across all social classes and occur in every ethnic group. And while many at-risk youth can be identified, often with frightening accuracy, a vast number of youth, in contrast to all the predictive research, may frequently be endangered by their own behavior by placing themselves in the "risky business" of sex, drugs, and alcohol or by reacting negatively to upheavals in their home and family.

Yet to recognize that all youth can, at one time or another, become at risk cannot cause educators to overlook the fact that we can identify with high predictability a large group of students who arrive at school each year with little or no hope of success in school or productivity in later life. It is this growing group that we can no longer afford to ignore; it is this group that has placed us all at risk.

The term *at risk*, originally coined a decade ago in Washington, D.C., has found its way into the national vocabulary. But regardless of what others might call them, teachers have always known these kids. They have known them as disinterested and disruptive, as those students who refused to learn, and as those who they thought could not learn. And they have known these students as those who, by their presence, have made teaching and learning so difficult for all the rest.

Over the past two decades the nation's perspective toward and understanding of these youth have begun to change. In the 1960s, responsibility for failure in school seemed to be assigned to the student and his or her tragic social situation. Everyone knew that "something was wrong with them"; they were deprived, disadvantaged, or just plain "dumb." If these students did not learn in school, it was their fault, not the fault of the schools. We now know that we were wrong, and we know how destructive this attitude has been.

Regardless of what the in-vogue terminology happens to be, we now know far better who these youth are and the extent of their worsening problems. It is not just that some students may be Spanish speaking or illiterate or disruptive or pregnant or in danger of dropping out or have already left school. Now, we are beginning to understand that the problems associated with these youth threaten to overwhelm our schools, diminish our economy, and eventually paralyze our society. Evidence of the crisis is visible in many of the inner-city schools and communities in our nation's urban areas. Inside these schools, absenteeism and failure rates overwhelm successes; in the communities outside the school, unemployment, crime, drugs, and despair have all but destroyed the social fabric. Too many adults continue to believe that these problems are occurring only to tragic youth in Milwaukee or Miami or Los Angeles. Increasingly, we recognize that they are happening in all communities and may in fact include that kid stretched out in our own front room watching MTV.

Why Be Concerned About At-Risk Youth?

I asked the seventh-grade boy how he was doing. He shrugged his shoulders and mumbled, "Okay, I guess." "I understand that your mom is a single parent," I said, "and that she works as a waitress every night." He shrugged again and nodded his head. "That must be kind of tough?" I said. "Well, not really," he said. "I get my little brother to bed around 9:30 or 10:00 and then I can kick back, have a smoke, and catch a little tube. It's not so bad."
—(MIDDLE SCHOOL STUDENT, BOISE, IDAHO, 1993)

The problem is not simply that some students are doing poorly in school. The problems relate to all youth who are in danger of not just failing and dropping out of school, but of entering adulthood illiterate, dependent upon drugs and alcohol, unemployed or underemployed, as a teenage parent, dependent on welfare, or adjudicated by the criminal justice system. Fred Newman, director of The Center on Organization and Restructuring of Schools at the University of Wisconsin, Madison, has argued that these students "are being 'disconnected' from the functions of society, not just from economic productivity, but from the functions of citizens in a democracy" (Newman, 1987, p. 3). The essential knowledge and skills needed to participate adequately in contemporary life have expanded far beyond the grasp of a large number of young Americans.

There exists an expanding underclass of youth who will live their lives in the United States and never work. Many of them will fill our prisons, others will demand growing health, welfare, and social services. We will support them and their children in a widening generational cycle of despair. Teenage parents tend to have a second child, and when that occurs, they tend to be on welfare for a minimum of 10 years (Barr & Ross, 1989). Over 80 percent of the inmates of America's prisons are high-school dropouts (Barr & Ross, 1989). During the last decade the number of prison cells has doubled in many states such as New York, where prison spending tripled between the years of 1982 and 1991. During the same period, drug-related crime grew by 350 percent while public school expenditures grew by only 80 percent (State of New York Executive Budget, 1993–94).

It is now apparent that, throughout our country, we are building prisons rather than schools. Surveys of state legislatures in 1993 documented a significant shift of resources from education to the escalating cost of health, welfare, and corrections (State Policy Research, 1993a). This shift from educational support to the increasing cost of social programs vividly portrays the cost of not dealing with at-risk youth during the school years. Clearly the age-old adage is correct: *either we pay now or we pay later.* Either communities invest in educational prevention and intervention at the preschool, elementary, and secondary years, or they must confront the escalating cost of dealing with the lifelong needs and problems of these individuals through health, welfare, police, and prison interventions.

The shift away from increases in educational funding also reflects the growing taxpayer revolt over the funding of public schools. The revolt started in California more than two decades ago with the enactment of Proposition 13. The resistance to taxes continues to gather momentum to this very day, as evidenced by the property tax limitation (Measure 5) passed in the State of Oregon in 1990 and, more recently, legislative action in Michigan toward abolishing state property tax as a means of funding public education. In the fall of 1992, California placed a statewide voucher plan on the ballot that would allow parents to "invest their vouchers" in either the public or private education of their children. While voters overwhelmingly rejected the plan, the issue is likely to surface again in California and other states. These developments reflect a continuing citizen concern regarding the rising costs of funding public schools—the same schools where the majority of our at-risk children are enrolled.

While challenges mount and controversy continues over the funding of public education, the number of at-risk youth is increasing dramatically in our nation's schools and communities. Educators no longer talk about the one or two percent of their students who are troublemakers. Discussion has shifted to the 30 to 50 percent of the school population who are dropping out. Dale Parnell, former president of the National Community College Association, argues that the schools are really serving only that 17 percent of American youth who will someday graduate from college (Parnell, 1982). Albert Shanker of the American Federation of Teachers agrees with Parnell. He stresses that the American public schools have never "really educated more than 15 to 20 percent of the kids of this country" (Miller, 1988, p. 48). Most would agree that school curriculum and graduation requirements continue to be focused primarily on the needs of those students who will someday go off to college. For the rest of the school student body, which Parnell calls the "neglected majority," the school curriculum may be virtually unrelated to their needs and the needs of the marketplace. We now are beginning to understand that those who are at risk are all youth who are unable to function effectively in the modern world. The proportion of these youth continues to increase as a result of what some critics refer to as a "plague of ignorance" (Bell & Elmquist, 1991, p. 1).

Shifting Demographics

Each year our classrooms contain increased numbers of poor, non-English speaking, mainstream handicapped, culturally different, and single-parent children. Five states will soon have minority majorities (California, Arizona, New Mexico, Texas, and Florida) and in over 30 of the largest school districts in the United States, Caucasian students have become the minority (U. S. Department of Commerce, 1992; Hodgkinson, 1985).

Public education as a middle-class phenomenon appears to be vanishing. In most urban areas, the concept is already a memory. Increasing numbers of the parents (without regard to ethnic background) who can afford it are leaving public education and enrolling their children in private and parochial schools; others are providing home schooling. The affluent middle class is also having fewer children. We have heard of the typical "yuppie" couple being described as DINKs—Double Income, No Kids. Even the middle-class parents who do have children in school tend to be single parents who work. The vast majority of the mothers of school-age children now work, and as a result, many of these children have become latchkey children who return home at the end of the day to an empty home or apartment (Hodgkinson, 1985).

A review of recent demographic data concerning U.S. society documents an incredible new world that is emerging in our midst:

- For the first time people over 65 years of age now outnumber teenagers.
- The median age of the U.S. population is 30 years today, in a decade it will be 35, and in less than three decades it is estimated that it will be 40.
- Fewer than half of all married couples have children.
- The fastest growing category of households is the childless one.
- Almost half of all households in the United States since 1980 consist of a single person living alone.
- After World War II, up to 70 percent of the adult population had children in school; today only 28 percent have children. Sixty-four percent of all households have no children at all (Martin, 1988).
- It is estimated that by the year 2000, 42 percent of the students enrolled in public schools will be black or Hispanic (Kuykendall, 1992).
- By the year 2000, approximately 47 percent of the U.S. workforce will be women.
- By the year 2000, African Americans and Hispanics will make up one-third of the new entrants into the workforce (Wilson, 1993).

These data depict a new society of haves and have-nots, a society growing older and older, with fewer people having a direct vested interest in supporting schools with adequate taxes to upgrade equipment and facilities, and provide necessary school programs and services.

The result of these shifts in our nation's demography is that today's public school classrooms are characterized by diminished parental involvement and support. Classrooms are filled with a growing percentage of students who are at risk of failing, dropping out of school, and disconnecting from society. Public schools report all-time highs in violence and vandalism, alcohol and drug problems, and problems of discipline and disruption. Nearly every major city in America has begun to experience the type of youth gangs previously known only in Los Angeles. Drugs and drive-by shootings have become common in more and more cities and even the suburbs. Youth violence has literally exploded within the American society. Suddenly children are carrying guns and killing each another as well as adults at an escalating rate that simply stuns belief. Violence in schools has catapulted into the nation's consciousness as the number-one urban problem in schools (Kantrowitc, 1993, p 45). Metal detectors are becoming commonplace in urban schools just as they are in airports throughout the world. Never before has the rate of teenage pregnancy been so high. Never before have so many youth attempted suicide; never have so many been so tragically successful (Barr & Ross, 1989).

There may have been a time, a generation or so ago, when dropping out of school posed no great problem and carried little or no stigma. At the turn of the century, over 90 percent of school-age youth dropped out of school but found almost unlimited opportunities to work in the forests, fields, and factories of America. As recently as the 1950s, when the national dropout rate decreased below 50 percent, there were still good jobs available to the dropout, many with upward career opportunities. Unfortunately, those opportunities are rapidly disappearing, and today they exist only for a very small percentage of our youth. The primary reason for this is that there are fewer and fewer job opportunities for people with poor educational skills. With increased international competition and a growing trade deficit, more and more companies are moving their factories and the less-skilled jobs that they provide outside the United States. Unskilled or low-skilled jobs are now being filled by workers in Mexico, Taiwan, Hong Kong, Korea, and a host of other developing nations.

Demands of the Changing Marketplace

Technology today is demanding more sophisticated skills and abilities at an accelerating rate. There are dramatically diminishing opportunities for U.S. workers in the production of steel, automobiles, agriculture, wood products, and petroleum—once the backbone of the U.S. economy and of the middle class. Increasingly, the jobs available to those with little sophisticated education and training are service-oriented minimum-wage jobs with little or no opportunity for advancement, health care, or retirement benefits. Even the U.S. military, which traditionally offered career opportunities and job training for many dropouts, will no longer accept applicants, even if they possess the general equivalency diploma. Like business and industry, the U.S. armed forces wants only the best and brightest.

The military does not want at-risk youth, and the same is true of business and industry. In the past, the federal government has discovered that employers cannot be paid to take these youth as employees. No one wants to employ these youth.

So often, even special school programs do not want these youth. Even public school vocational education programs, originally created to serve the noncollege bound student, serve an unusually small percentage of at-risk youth. The message from business, industry, and the military has been loud and clear: if the schools can't deal effectively with these kids, can't teach them to read and write and develop a healthy work ethic, don't expect us to solve their problems. That attitude may, however, be changing.

Sudden changes in the marketplace have attracted the interest of business and industry in relation to the at-risk youth of our society. David Kerns, former chairman of the board and CEO of Xerox Corporation, has stated that "the American work force is running out of qualified people. . . . if current demographic trends continue, American business will have to hire a million new workers a year who cannot read, write or count. [To train these workers] will cost more than 25 billion dollars a year" (Miller, 1988, p. 48).

Even in the recent past, those who dropped out of school had unusually good opportunities in America. With determination and hard work, men and women with little education could achieve the good life for themselves and their families. Throughout America there were opportunities for mill hands, deck hands, farm hands, roughnecks, and assembly-line workers. To a very real extent our nation was built by a mass of people who dropped out of school and through hard manual labor and little or no formal education earned a decent wage, served in the armed forces, bought their family a home, owned a car, a truck, and sometimes an RV and boat, and one day sent their kids off to college. This is the stuff of the American dream, and it has disappeared. The optimism of the past is being replaced by declining opportunities for uneducated workers. Today the promise of America to the high school dropout is not the comforts of the middle class; it is a life without the opportunities for meaningful work and advancement. Too often it is a life of despair and discontent.

In the past, it has mattered little that 30 to 50 percent of U.S. youth dropped out of school. It has not mattered that 23 million adults and almost 20 percent of all 17-year-old youth were functionally illiterate. It has not mattered that a large percentage of youth could not interpret a bus schedule, could not compute the cost of a meal in a restaurant or find the Pacific Ocean on a map. In the past, none of this has really mattered, for U.S. industry has always been able to generate a sufficient number of jobs for nearly everyone willing to work. For the future, it is now certain that this will not be true. In a recent Ford Foundation Report entitled *Toward A More Perfect Union: Basic Skills, Poor Families and Our Economic Future*, Berlin and Sum argue that the growing number of illiterate and poorly educated youth who are entering the American workforce threatens our nation's competitive edge. "The skills of our nation's workforce are becoming an increasingly important detriment to America's competitive position, workers' real wages, and our overall standard of living" (Hollifield, 1988, p. 2).

It is now clear that the solution to the crisis of at-risk youth, or for that matter at-risk adults, is education. Regardless of whether the at-risk person is a malnourished and abused kindergarten student, a third-grader far below grade level in reading and math, a disruptive, illiterate middle-school kid, a punk-rock dropout drowning in a sea of drugs, or a 50-year-old displaced, middle-class petroleum worker, the only solution is education. We can even be more specific. The solution is not just the traditional high-school education. It is an education that enables employment, that accesses a meaningful job. It is education that creates literacy. It is education that leads to productive participation in our society.

Unfortunately, many high-school graduates lack these basic skills. The education that is demanded today requires more than reading Silas Marner, memorizing sections of Julius Caesar, and learning the causes of World War II; it may be more than wood shop and earning graduation credit in physical education. A recent Ford Foundation study investigated 11,900 youths between 1979 and 1986. The one common problem of at-risk youth was a lack of basic academic skills and functional illiteracy (Hollifield, 1988). Schools must provide students, regardless of their age and their background, with the essential basic skills necessary to accommodate additional learning and an education that leads to jobs and opportunity for social participation. Our schools and communities must meet this challenge for there are few others who will respond. It is for just this reason that there is an urgent need for schools to develop programs that will be effective for all children and youth.

Chapter 2

Who Are the At Risk and Why?

*The principal laughed and shook his head. "Do you remember the
good old days when we had parent conferences? Well, let me tell
you, the world has changed. Last week I asked the secretary to
schedule a meeting with this really screwed up 15-year-old kid and
everyone who had some type of responsibility for him. When I
walked into the conference room I nearly fell over because the room
was packed. There was the kid, his probation officer, his mother, his
grandmother, his foster parents, his attorney, his case worker from
Health and Welfare, and God knows who else. There must have
been a dozen people in the room. Let me tell you, so many of these
kids are just a mess. When you really find out what's going on in
their life, the really remarkable thing is not that they drop out of
school, but that they ever bother to come to school at all."
—(SUPERINTENDENT, LINCOLN COUNTY SCHOOLS,
NEWPORT, OREGON, 1987)*

During recent years, research on at-risk youth has been successful in identifying
and documenting factors that place a child or youth at risk. This research focus has
been so successful that it has achieved a chilling level of predictability. Using only
a few identified factors, schools can predict with better than 80 percent accuracy
students in the third grade who will later drop out of school. So powerful are these
factors that researchers now maintain that if a poor child attends a school composed largely of other poor children, is reading a year behind by the third grade
and has been retained a grade, the chances of this child ever graduating from high
school are near zero (McPartland & Slavin, 1990) (See Figure 2-1). At least one state,
Indiana, plans future prison cells based on projections that are developed by
studying second graders ("Mark of Cain," 1990). Unfortunately, such scientific accuracy does not provide hope or any real peace of mind, for it now confronts
schools with knowledge that can no longer be ignored.

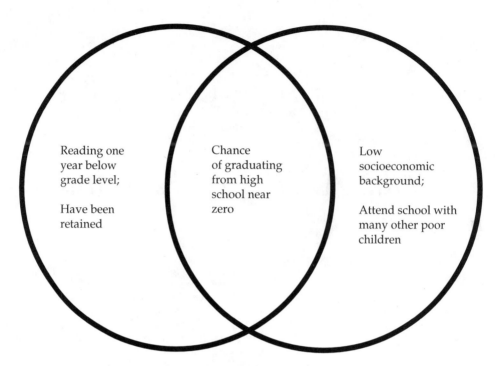

FIGURE 2-1   Research on Third-Grade Students

(McPartland & Slavin, 1990, p. 7)

The factors that place children and youth at risk can be divided into two primary areas: those related to the individual, family, and community and those related to school. While it is difficult to expect immediate change or improvement in the home and community, it is not only possible but realistic to believe that schools can immediately eliminate many of their practices that contribute to placing children at risk. Over 20 years of research and study have provided a compelling body of data that can assist schools and communities in their quest to identify and serve youth at risk. To begin to address the dilemma, schools and communities must initially understand and identify the contributing factors which place youth at risk.

Lisbeth Schorr and Daniel Schorr, in their classic work *Within Our Reach*, argue that we currently know enough about risk factors associated with leaving school and the number of students imperiled by this crisis that we have ample reason to formulate new social policies attending to this national concern. They present the following analogy to make their case.

The 17th-century maritime insurers knew that the risk factors of a winter sailing presaged a more likely loss, just as today's life insurance companies know that a high cholesterol level and little exercise raise the risk of premature death. In the same way, we know that a child with school problems in the third grade is at risk of dropping out of high school and becoming a teenage parent. The experts may not be able to forecast which of seven youngsters is most likely to commit a heinous crime on being released from detention and which will henceforth lead a life of virtue. Great strides have been made in identifying factors that place whole categories of children at risk of disastrous outcomes and in determining which of these factors are most amenable to intervention. We now have proof that disastrous outcomes are much more likely when several risk factors interact. (Schorr & Schorr, 1989, p. 24)

Determining the Causes

The Charles Stewart Mott Foundation funded a study in the late 1980s entitled "Who's Looking Out For At-Risk Youth?" The executive summary of this work, entitled *America's Shame, America's Hope: Twelve Million Youth At Risk,* speaks to the urgency of the problem.

A crisis exists in the back rows of America's public school classrooms. It has so far eluded the full attention of the much bruited educational reform movement of the 1980's. Yet its threat to our economic future, and to the lives of millions of American youth, is present, grave, and sure to become more costly to meet, the longer we delay in meeting it. (Smith & Lincoln, 1988, p. 2)

The crisis is the undereducation of a segment of our students presently constituting one out of three students in today's classrooms. Dominant in this group are the children of poverty—those impacted by economic and cultural disadvantage. They have come to be called youth "at risk" because they are at risk of emerging from school underprepared for further education or the kinds of jobs available. Often they are only ready for lives of alienation and dependency. The Mott study continues:

They are said to be failing in school, and yet it is clear that it is we who are failing to educate them. The danger this failure of education poses to these youth and to all of us grows apace. It is best described first in terms of the realities of today's and tomorrow's job market and then in terms of the young Americans who will be expected to fill those jobs. (Smith & Lincoln, 1988, p. 2)

It is estimated that approximately one million youth per year leave school without completing their basic educational requirements. The majority of these students leave without essential literacy skills and other basic abilities, which renders them virtually unemployable. In addition, it is estimated that 700,000 students graduate yearly with skills as deficient as those of students who do not complete their schooling. Others have estimated that over 80 percent of our graduating seniors depart school with inadequate writing skills, with less than 50 percent of them being able to carry out moderately complex tasks (Davis & McCaul, 1990).

Scholars who have studied issues related to at-risk youth generally agree on the fundamental focus of the at-risk crisis. These include:

> *Those who are likely to leave school at any age without academic, social, and/or vo-cational skills necessary to lead a productive and fulfilled life. (Institute for At-Risk Infants, Children and Youth and Their Families, 1991, p. 8).*

While others may argue minor semantic variation, the problem involves school-age youth leaving school without adequate skills.

Risk Factors

A number of factors characterize youth at risk. Some of the factors are associated with individual personality; others relate to the home, community, and school. Slavin and Madden identify low achievement, retention in grade, behavioral problems, poor attendance, low socioeconomic status, and attendance at schools with large numbers of poor students. They conclude, "each of these factors is closely associated with the drop-out-rate; by the time students are in the third grade we can use these factors to predict with remarkable accuracy which students will drop out of school and which will stay to complete their education" (Slavin & Madden, 1989, p. 4).

The Vocational Studies Center of the School of Education at the University of Wisconsin-Madison attempted a far-reaching analysis and description of risk factors. The analysis presents families, students, family-related issues, cultural differences, and gender issues as the organizing principles around which individual factors of at-risk youth aggregate (Nash, 1990). Davis and McCaul of the Institute for the Study of At-Risk Students at the University of Maine have taken a slightly different approach. They subdivide risk factors around more general issues of society, students, and school environment and teacher-student interactions (Davis & McCaul, 1990).

Stressing the existence and evidence of the interrelation of risk factors, Pallas, Natriello, and McDill list five key indicators: (a) minority, racial, or ethnic group identity; (b) living in a poverty household; (c) living in a single-parent family; (d) having a poorly educated mother; and (e) having a non-English language background (1989, p. 4).

At least one study has identified student mobility, i.e., moving from school to school and from community to community, as a major unrecognized cause for dropping out. This study tracked a group of eighth graders until a year after they would have graduated from high school, had they graduated on schedule. Of the 615 students that they were able to follow, only 83 had attended a single elementary school, a single middle school, and a single high school. The graduation rate for these nonmovers was 95 percent. For those who had moved once, the graduation rate was 68 percent; for those who had moved three times, only 30 percent. The effects of moving were strongest between grade 7 and grade 9. Of those who did not move during those years, 72 percent graduated (Bracey, 1989).

Michelle Fine's attempt to discover students' reasons for dropping out was characterized in her study of inner-city youth in Philadelphia. Using an ethnographic approach, she identified five central reasons that alienated youth reported as the causes of their departing school. They include:

1. *Low value of high-school diploma*
2. *Competing responsibilities*
3. *Undermined self-esteem*
4. *Push-out policies of schools*
5. *Pregnancy*
   (Fine, 1986)

Fine joins virtually all scholars who have investigated risk factors for dropping out of schools by agreeing that an interaction of these factors is almost always present when a youth decides to leave the formal education process.

The interaction of the various factors involved in dropping out are far from simple. Dale Mann describes the range of circumstances for dropping out of school as "impressive, even daunting." He states further:

> *Most students quit because of the compounded impact of, for example, being poor, growing up in a broken home, being held back in the fourth grade, and finally having slugged 'Mr. Fairlee,' the school's legendary vice principal for enforcement. These young people need a range of things, just as any system's at-risk population will need services to fit their hurts. If the problem is complex, so will be the solutions. (1986, p. 307)*

Mann uses the phrase "a collision of factors" to characterize what generally precedes an unfortunate decision by students to drop out.

The most comprehensive study to date focusing on risk factors associated with youth at risk established even wider parameters. Directing the work of Phi Delta Kappa's national study of at-risk youth, Frymier and Gansneder (1989) developed a matrix of 45 at-risk factors and ranked them from most serious (attempted suicide during the past year) to least serious (changed place of residence during the past year).

This study was one of the most ambitious and comprehensive studies of at-risk youth ever attempted. But the 45 at-risk factors that the study identifies proved almost too much for schools to deal with. Some schools reported that almost every one of their students had one or more of the factors that placed them at risk. The result of this study seemed to overwhelm schools with a staggering mass of details. Frymier and his colleagues later condensed the original 45 factors into a 36 factor description (See Table 2-1). In a follow-up analysis of this work, Frymier

TABLE 2-1   Factors That Place Students At Risk

- Attempted suicide during the past year
- Used drugs or engaged in substance abuse
- Has been a drug "pusher" during the past year
- Sense of self esteem is negative
- Was involved in a pregnancy during the past year
- Was expelled from school during the past year
- Consumes alcohol regularly
- Was arrested for illegal activity
- Parents have negative attitudes toward education
- Has several brothers or sisters who dropped out
- Was sexually or physically abused last year
- Failed two courses last school year
- Was suspended from school twice last year
- Student was absent more than 20 days last year
- Parent drinks excessively and is an alcoholic
- Was retained in grade (i.e., "held back")
- One parent attempted suicide last year
- Scored below 20th percentile on standardized test
- Other family members used drugs during past year
- Attended three or more schools during past five years
- Average grades were below "C" last school year
- Was arrested for driving while intoxicated
- Has an IQ score below 90
- Parents divorced or separated last year
- Father is unskilled laborer who is unemployed
- Mother is unskilled laborer who is unemployed
- Father or mother died during the past year
- Diagnosed as being in special education
- English is not language
- Lives in an inner city, urban area
- The mother is only parent living in the home
- Is year older than other students in same grade
- Mother did not graduate from high school
- Father lost his job during the past year
- Was dropped from athletic team during past year
- Experienced a serious illness or accident

(Frymier, Barber, Denton, Johnson-Lewis, & Robertson, 1992,

analyzed and synthesized the 36 factors into five general problems that have proven far more helpful to educators (Frymier, 1992). He described these five problem areas as

- Personal pain
- Academic failure
- Socioeconomic situation of the family

- Family instability
- Family budgeting

Of the five factors, Frymier believes that three are beyond the control of the school: family socioeconomic situation, family instability, and family budget. The two remaining factors, personal pain and academic failure, he identified as factors that the school could deal with. It is in these two areas where schools can generate programs that could hold great promise in alleviating factors that place children and youth at risk. Frymier also discovered in his analysis that youth who were at risk because of one factor tended to be placed at risk by a large number of other factors. As Frymier expressed, "Children who hurt, hurt all over; children who fail, failed in everything they do" (Frymier, 1992, p. 258).

With a growing arsenal of research-based factors, it is now possible for schools to identify at-risk youth long before they arrive at school and by the end of the second or third grade be able to predict with great accuracy those children who will fail in school and ultimately drop out. Many school districts have developed systematic efforts to identify the at-risk or potentially at-risk child (see Table 2-2). If this information is used in a positive manner to connect kids with services and support, the identification of at-risk youth is most valuable. However, there exist compelling arguments against the identification of children and youth as at risk.

A Word of Warning: To Identify or Not to Identify

She was a surprisingly attractive student. Even attractive did not quite capture an adequate description of this young woman. Perhaps stunning was closer to the truth. She was also defiant. And she was aiming that defiance right straight at me. "Okay, so I'm a hooker. I'm not trying to give you any jazz bullshit. I know who I am. I am black, I am broke, and I am bad. I walk the streets for a living. But you listen to me! This school has just about saved my life. These people are really helping me. I know I'm going to graduate from high school. I'm already enrolled in the nursing program at the community college. Get this! I am going to be a nurse! I'm going to be the first person in my family to ever get an education. I'm definitely going to be the one to break loose from this depressing, destructive life cycle of poverty and shame. Listen to me! I'm going to make it. I'm going to be a nurse."
—*(HIGH SCHOOL STUDENT, VOCATIONAL VILLAGE, PORTLAND, OREGON, 1989)*

Schools and communities must be very careful regarding the identification of at-risk youth. There is a body of research that has documented that labeling students may serve as a self-fulfilling prophecy, i.e., to label a student as "learning disabled" and to treat the student as learning disabled often leads to a youth with serious learning deficiencies. Some very successful programs insist that schools should not attempt to identify at-risk youth. They argue that schools should develop effective

TABLE 2-2   Student Information Summary

Date Completed _____

Student ID# _____

School _____   Grade _____   Age _____

The factors listed below are generally identified as characteristics of the potential school dropout. Early identification of a child who might be at risk is essential.
THREE OR MORE = AT-RISK CONCERN
* One or more grade retentions
* Low math or reading scores (at least one year below grade level)
* History of absenteeism, tardiness, or truancy
* Repeated discipline or behavior problems resulting in disruption or referral
* Free or reduced fee lunch program eligibility
* School not meeting student's needs
* Low self-esteem or self-concept
* Student appears dissatisfied, expresses dissatisfaction with school and teachers
* Frequent health and hygiene referrals
* Drug or alcohol issues may be affecting school
* Friends outside of school
* Family status issue (divorce, unemployment, family crisis)
* High mobility (changed residence three or more times in past two years)
* One (or more) parent did not complete high school
* History of child abuse or neglect
* Little or no home or parent response to school-initiated contact
For Middle School and High-School Students
* Low G.P.A. (below 2.0)
* Behind in credits (2 or more)
* Pregnancy/teen parent

TOTAL NUMBER OF ITEMS CHECKED _____

programs, provide all students the opportunity to participate in the programs, and ensure that they all learn. Others emphasize that existing characteristics should be ignored in favor of a careful, ongoing performance assessment of all students, with greater attention and emphasis being placed on the needs of any child or youth who is not progressing satisfactorily. The primary value in understanding the factors that tend to predispose a child to become at risk is to anticipate future problems and to develop appropriate prevention and intervention programs.

This emphasis on not identifying at-risk youth is supported by three important issues. First, any child or youth, regardless of family circumstances or socioeconomic background, can at any time become at risk. Second, recent research has identified characteristics of individual resiliency that seem to enable children and youth, regardless of their life situations, to overcome severe problems and become successful students and adults. The third is that some students who are academically able may choose not to learn.

Any Child May Become At Risk

Research has helped educators to understand that virtually any student may begin to perform marginally or poorly, regardless of factors related to economics, gender, ethnicity, or family structure (Sinclair & Ghory, 1987). The researchers further caution against the use of set indicators to identify at-risk youth, urging instead that schools begin addressing overall school structural characteristics and practices that negatively impact marginal youth.

Given the attention to the analysis and identification of prevailing conditions and factors related to a young person becoming at risk, it is of paramount importance that schools and teachers recognize the existence of these youth and initiate assistance. Regardless of differences and debates concerning ratings and definitions of at-risk factors, it is imperative that schools be alert to sudden changes in student behavior. Teachers and school counselors must be careful in identifying students whose grades begin to fall, who begin to miss school, and who exhibit dramatic or even subtle changes in their behavior. Often divorce, teenage pregnancy, violence and abuse in the home or community, death, drugs and alcohol, or even the breakup of a teenage romance can intrude into the life of children and youth and suddenly imperil their success in school. The tragic increase in teenage suicide has caused educators to become more attentive to the impact of disruptions in a teenage life and has helped schools to develop programs that anticipate problems.

Resilient Children and Youth

Research at the Johns Hopkins University Center for the Study of Disadvantaged Youth and elsewhere has focused on identifying the characteristics of children and youth who seem to succeed in school and life in spite of having all the characteristics of being at risk. These protective factors or characteristics of resiliency seem to enable many young people to succeed despite severe situations in their home and community. Recently, the Northwest Regional Educational Lab has synthesized research on these factors of resiliency and has urged that schools should attempt to reinforce and cultivate the personal factors that strengthen these protective factors in individuals, families, schools, and communities (Benard, 1991). The resilient child has been identified as having the following attributes:

Social Competency

Resilient children tend to have qualities of "responsiveness, flexibility, empathy and caring, communication skills, a sense of humor and other prosocial behavior" (Benard, 1991, p. 3). Resilient children tend to be more responsive, more active, and more flexible (Werner & Smith, 1982; Demos, 1989). Because of their flexibility and interpersonal skills, especially a sense of humor, the resilient child seems to develop more positive relationships and stronger friendships (Berndt & Ladd, 1989; Werner & Smith, 1982).

Problem-Solving Skills

Resilient children tend to have skills that include the ability to think abstractly, reflectively, and flexibly and to look for and attempt creative, alternate solutions to both cognitive and life problems. Such characteristics have been identified in street children who are able to survive in the midst of extremely difficult life situations.

Autonomy

Resilient children tend to be far more independent, have a greater sense of personal power, and have a stronger self-esteem.

Sense of Purpose and Future

Resilient children tend to have realistic, healthy, goal-directed, and optimistic expectations regarding the future.

Research supports the conclusion that the characteristics common to resilient children could well be developed and cultivated. The Northwest Regional Educational Lab is exploring the possibility of developing programs for the home and school that will focus on these characteristics as desirable educational outcomes (Benard, 1991).

Resistant Learners

Herbert Kohl, in his provocative book *I Won't Learn From You* (1991), explores the lives of a number of students who decide, for a variety of reasons, that they will not learn. Sometimes the student may feel that his or her self-respect, self-esteem, or racial identity may demand that he or she will not learn; other times, it may be a point of personal honor among peers that causes a student not to learn. Teachers should read this small book and be alert to the reality that some students who are failing may indeed be quite capable. Kohl suggests that these students may be effectively taught if a teacher develops a closer relationship which permits a deeper understanding of the students' reasons for not learning.

A Different Approach to Identifying At-Risk Youth

A growing number of highly successful schools throughout the United States have begun to gather data on key aspects of school life and observe these areas over time. Such careful long-term monitoring can lead to consensus building and schoolwide goal setting. By continuing to monitor certain areas, the school gains a sense of how successful it is in achieving its goals. Rather than attempting to identify individual students as being at risk, this approach serves to unite the entire school and community to work together to improve their overall success in problem areas that are directly related to at-risk youth.

Schools and their communities interested in this approach should closely review the long list of factors associated with at-risk youth and then collectively identify key criteria that they feel are relevant to their settings. For example, groups may be alarmed about increases in teenage pregnancy, drug use, absenteeism, violence, the number of students being retained in elementary school or dropping out of school, or the number of children who have reading problems. What is important is for the school and community to agree on problem areas that they feel need to be addressed, to establish goals and to develop a plan for attacking these problem areas. The school should then systematically gather data to monitor the success of their efforts.

This approach involves the entire school and community in working together to address schoolwide and communitywide issues. If this process is developed carefully, it often becomes a self-fulfilling process, i.e., if the school and community collectively identify problems, establish goals and monitor their work, goals often are achieved without identifying or stigmatizing individual students as being at risk. This approach is used as part of a growing number of successful programs that are described in later chapters of this book.

Why Have the Needs of At-Risk Youth Not Been Addressed?

Despite an enormous amount of credible research that has focused on identifying the students and remedying the many problems confronting at-risk youth, it is surprising that schools have not moved with vigor to better serve the needs of these tragic students. Three reasons appear to explain this lack of response. First, schools lack the will to act to ensure that all students receive a quality education; second, schools have proven to be unusually resistant to change, and third, communities are increasingly unwilling to adequately fund public education.

The Will To Act

Many educators have referred to the needs of serving at-risk students as similar to the services of hospital emergency rooms that provide intensive care. Research is quite clear that students possessing combinations of factors that lead at some point in their lives to a disassociation with school are in need of immediate and comprehensive diagnosis, assistance, and support if they are to have any opportunity for reentry into or success in our public school system. Toward this end, early prevention programs have been judged to be far more effective than intervention programs for older children. This concurrence of research and scholarly analysis compels immediate national attention and action toward intervention. Yet, as in many instances where a chasm between research and practice exists, developing appropriate interventions and taking immediate action appear beyond the grasp of our educational structure. Anthony Alvarado, former New York Superintendent of Schools, in testimony to the Senate Children's Caucus, stressed that our schools must start their dropout intervention effort far earlier than we presently do. "It's strange," he stated, "we know what to do. We just don't do it" (Schorr & Schorr, 1989, p. xxvi). As many scholars argue, it is clear that we now understand the significance of this crisis and furthermore are quite aware of effective interventions that can positively address detrimental factors. The problem of inaction, as discussed by Superintendent Alvarado and others, is central to our nation's current crisis. We know who the at risk are. We know what has caused their personal crisis. We know how they act. We know what must be done to affect their current crisis. The question remains, will we act?

The Difficulty of School Reform

Unfortunately, the problem of addressing the needs of at-risk youth involves more than a will to act and the financial ability to act. It must also involve knowing how to act. In the following chapter, a detailed description of effective responses to at-risk youth will be explored. The problem, however, is complicated because schools have proven to be unusually difficult to change. Even modest improvement projects have proven extremely difficult to achieve. More profound, comprehensive efforts at reform and restructuring to address the needs of at-risk youth have proven all but impossible using traditional efforts at school reform. Compounding this problem is the unacceptable divergence which exists between research and practice. Noted curriculum authority Bruce Joyce has studied this dilemma and concluded that the time required for a proven, research-based educational practice to move from theory to accepted practice in our nation's schools is 30 years (Joyce, 1986). The problem of school reform will be explored more thoroughly in a later chapter.

School Funding

Increasingly, public education's response to at-risk children and youth has been directly related to school funding. In state after state and in community after community there has been a growing reluctance to provide increased funding for public education. Far too few communities have been willing to support public education at little more than the basic minimum level, and too often these tend to be the most affluent school districts. Originating from changing demographics, extended life expectancy and fewer adults having school-aged children, the growing resistance to school funding has focused on such basics as teachers' salaries, buildings and equipment, administrative costs, and special programs designed to serve at-risk youth.

The recent success in school board elections by what has been termed the radical right has led some communities to consider eliminating special funding for at-risk programs. In Vista, California, fundamentalist Christians recently were elected to a majority on the local school board. In one of its initial actions the conservative majority has made it clear that it wants to limit support programs for disadvantaged students by rejecting a $400,000 state grant to provide health counseling to low-income kids and their parents (McGuillie, 1993).

The inequity in school funding that reflects the local tax base of rich communities and poor communities continues to penalize and punish the children of the most impoverished neighborhoods (Howe, 1991). While there are many inexpensive programs that can have a positive long-lasting impact on the at-risk student, no one can deny that many programs for these students inevitably cost more. The old adage of "cash, computers, and commitment" represents far too simplistic a formula for educational reform, yet there exists an underlying truth to this saying when it comes to at-risk youth.

The combination of these three factors—how to create the will to act, how to adequately fund public education, and the difficulty of actually changing schools—continues to frustrate public education's ability to meet the needs of all kids, particularly the at risk. The good news is that there is indeed hope at last for at-risk youth. In the coming chapters, schools and communities will be provided with the detailed components of a comprehensive blueprint for making schools effective for all youth.

The next chapter will review historical efforts at school reform, provide an analysis of why many of these efforts have proven so ineffective, and examine the disastrous effects of many traditional responses to at-risk youth. Later chapters will include descriptions of essential components of effective programs, descriptions of real life school programs that have been documented as successful with at-risk youth and finally a description of three approaches to school reform that work.

Chapter *3*

Why Reform Has Failed to Address the Crisis

The principal looked like a poster boy for a high blood pressure campaign. He looked swollen and uncomfortable. His stomach rolled over his belt and his neck wallowed over his collar. His face was a mottled, bright red. He jerked a paper from his inside jacket pocket and handed it to me. "Read it," he said. The paper proved to be a short, handwritten note from a 10th grade student. The note said, "I have not had a drink for 27 days, but it is so hard. I just crave a drink all the time: morning, noon and night. I need some help. I wonder if we could start a group with other kids to talk about our problem. I bet there are a lot of other students like me who would participate.' I put away my glasses and handed the principal back his letter. "This is what I mean about wanting the school to be everything to everybody," he said. "I've got English teachers, history teachers, coaches, and special educators. And now the damn kids want support groups. Can you imagine this?" With that the principal, a former coach, crushed the paper in his hands and slam dunked it in a trash can as he walked off down the hall.
—*(HIGH-SCHOOL PRINCIPAL, INDIANA, 1993)*

With the growing national concern for at-risk youth and the increasing sophistication of research in this area, many are surprised and often angry that schools have not adjusted their programs to serve these youth. Yet schools have proven extremely difficult to change. For years, researchers have documented the failures of schools and communities that have tried to improve. Too often, conscientious educators, even when they have been substantially funded, have been unable to significantly change a public school. More disturbing, many school programs that have been implemented to assist at-risk youth have only exacerbated the problems of these students. This section will review the major attempts at reform of schools and provide an analysis of why most of these efforts have proven so ineffective.

Failed Efforts Toward Changing Schools

During most of this century, improving and reforming public schools has been a continuing national agenda. Although most of the concern has focused on improving the education of the best and the brightest of our students, there has been a recurring interest in why schools seem to fail to educate so many American youth. Over the decades, there has been a long and impressive array of blue-ribbon committees, national commissions, legislation, and reports dedicated to improving the public schools of the nation. Some of these efforts have been funded by the federal government; others have been sponsored by professional associations, nonprofit foundations, and even private corporations. Over the past 30 years organizations as diverse as the New York Times, the American Historical Association, the National Education Association, the Progressive Education Association, the Council for Basic Education, the Carnegie and Ford Foundations, along with a legion of scholars and education writers have studied public education and sought to transform it.

These efforts have documented with shocked dismay that far too many U.S. public school students do not acquire an adequate knowledge of history, math, science, geography, economics, and even the ability to read. Many high school graduates are unable to interpret a bus schedule, or make change at the corner market. A disturbing number of our public school students have also been documented as having antidemocratic values and attitudes. More recently, an abundance of comparative international studies have found that the majority of our students score significantly lower on mathematical and science examinations than students in other developed nations. Many of these studies have been accompanied by recommendations for improving instruction, parental involvement, textbooks, assessment, teacher education, and a host of other factors.

Reform efforts in the late 1950s were ignited by the success of the USSR Sputnik space program. Reform efforts of the 1960s were sparked by compassionate critics who claimed the schools were ineffective, mindless, boring, inhumane, and destructive. Schools have been criticized as having antiquated curricula; more recently schools have been criticized for a lack of choice, lack of technology, and the growth of violence, vandalism, and adolescent suicide. Recent decades of declining SAT scores have likewise fueled the fires of reform.

Nearly three decades of school reform literature have taken on a frightening and almost macabre tone: *No More Public School, Death at an Early Age, Savage Inequalities, School is Dead, Crisis in the Classroom, Murder in the Classroom, The Neglected Majority,* and the infamous *A Nation At Risk,* which accused public school educators of "intellectually disarming a generation of American youth." The reform efforts that have been generated by a century of studies, reports, and recommendations are impressive. The following is a thumbnail review of reform efforts over the past four decades.

The Comprehensive High School

Following the studies and recommendations of James Conant in the 1950s, efforts successfully occurred throughout the United States to consolidate small, often rural public schools into single, comprehensive high schools (Conant, 1950). In spite of the fact that comprehensive high schools have been developed throughout the country, few learning gains were ever documented, even in the areas of math and science, where new laboratories and accelerated academic programs were expected to produce impressive improvement. Recent research has further documented the negative effects of large schools on at-risk youth.

Research and Development

A number of important efforts have attempted to use the techniques of research and development to improve public education. Perhaps the most significant early effort was the Eight-Year Study. Conducted during the late 1930s and early 1940s, students graduating from 30 select high schools in the United States were released from traditional college entrance requirements, and the schools were encouraged to create new curricula and new approaches to teaching and learning (Hemming, 1948).

Using concepts developed by John Dewey and the Progressive Education Association, each school developed a new approach to education. Many of the schools replaced required courses with competencies or projects. Students in the Eight-Year Study were carefully assessed during their high-school years, with special attention focusing on standardized test scores and college entrance examinations. They were then studied during the four years following graduation. Although the results are regarded as controversial, the Eight-Year Study did document that students in the experimental schools performed better on college admission exams than students from regular high schools and tended to be more successful after graduation than students from regular schools. Unfortunately, the Eight-Year Study was viewed with suspicion by most educators and failed to influence mainstream public education.

During the 1970s, a number of public schools, including the St. Paul Open School and the Minnesota Community Learning Centers, were created based on the concepts and research of the Eight-Year Study. By replacing graduation requirements with outcome-based performance competencies the St. Paul Open School has been able to replicate the impressive learning gains found earlier in the Eight-Year Study (Jennings & Nathan, 1977).

More recently, research and development have focused on identifying effective teaching and effective schools, the effectiveness of Alternative Public

Schools, and privatizing public schools. All of these efforts hold promise for significant educational reform. These efforts will be explored in a later section of this book.

Curriculum Revolution

The 1960s were a time of a national curriculum revolution, though few if any specific projects or innovations focused on the needs of at-risk youth. Almost every professional association initiated comprehensive curriculum reform initiatives, many of which were supported by massive funding from the federal government, private foundations, professional organizations, and universities. The curriculum revolution developed what proved to be a collection of the most creative and sophisticated educational materials that had ever been available (Barr, Barth, & Shermis, 1977). A new "modern mathematics" was developed, along with a "new science," a "new social studies," and other new instructional materials. Curriculum materials that were developed in the social sciences tended to emphasize an inquiry-oriented approach and often were developed as multimedia learning kits, sometimes including a wide variety of films, photographs, reproduced artifacts, and simulation games. Some projects developed and marketed "teacher-proof" materials which were carefully designed to prevent teachers from "undermining" the new curriculum.

Most of the curriculum projects focused on the structure of knowledge in academic disciplines and were developed by teams of academic scholars, educators, and learning theorists. The curriculum revolution was driven by the ideas of Jerome Bruner, who believed that any child could learn any concept at any age, as long as the instructional program was developed carefully (Bruner, 1960). Unfortunately, few of these curriculum materials, many extremely expensive and packaged as large, complicated sets, were ever used extensively in public schools. By the early 1970s, a number of studies reported that the public school curriculum had changed little from the curriculum found in schools at the turn of the century.

Instructional Revolution

During the 1970s and 1980s, an arsenal of new instructional and organizational techniques and approaches were developed and tried. These included everything from team teaching, behavioral objectives, structured lesson planning, assertive discipline, values clarification, learning styles, phase electives, modular scheduling, open education, middle schools, and even more recently cooperative learning, developmentally appropriate learning, whole language, and dozens of other approaches. A large number of these creative and often franchised concepts have contributed to the feeling that public education is "just one damn fad after another" (Barr, 1973, p. 7). And while research on these approaches have often been promising, most have come and gone, often to re-emerge later under a new design and a new name. Unfortunately, few significant long-term improvements have been noted in public education in spite of decades of experimentation with these various instructional and organizational approaches, especially for at-risk youth.

Model School Approach

Another approach to school reform involved the development of experimental showcase schools that would model aspects of educational innovation: new curricula, new instructional approaches, new organization, new techniques, and the latest technologies. This approach to educational reform was based initially on the belief that if educators could only observe and experience a truly reformed school, change would be easier to stimulate in other schools. The model schools were to serve as lighthouses of educational reform. Almost every state and most large school districts have tried the model school approach. A major national effort was funded by the Ford Foundation in the late 1960s and early 1970s. Unfortunately, the evaluation of the Ford Foundation's model school program, entitled *A Foundation Goes to School*, concluded that after the external funds ran out, the principals of these schools tended to be promoted into other positions or recruited away to other school districts, and the schools ultimately returned to their previous approach (Nachtigal, 1972).

State and National Mandates and Legislation

School reform has been attempted through the adoption of state mandates, statutes, and legislation. This approach has been frequently used since the early 1980s in an effort to improve public schools. Many of these changes have focused on increasing school graduation and college entrance requirements and have also established minimum competencies to be applied to both students and teachers, extending the school year or the school day, and a variety of student attendance rules. Especially during recent years, as governors and state legislators have discovered the political power of educational reform, almost every state has legislated some aspect of reform in public education. Perhaps most significant, nearly every state has increased the graduation requirements in math and science, but once again there have been few indicators that the state-mandated requirements have positively affected the learning of children and youth in any significant way.

Although public education is clearly controlled locally, the federal government on occasion has intruded into public education. A few of these federal programs have proven to be most significant for at-risk youth. The federally-funded Head Start program, the free lunch program, special education legislation, Upward Bound, and even court-ordered school desegregation have had dramatic impacts on at-risk children and youth. Though often controversial, most of the programs have proven to be significantly successful in addressing the needs of at-risk youth in a positive manner. Head Start may well be the most successful education program ever implemented (Schorr & Schorr, 1989). However, none of these programs has received the comprehensive support to ensure their availability for all youth who need them.

Recent examples of statewide action are occurring in Kentucky and Oregon. The Kentucky state legislature has passed KERA, the Kentucky Education Reform Act, which has moved to decentralize public education by creating local boards of control designed to reduce administrative requirements and increase efficiency. The state is insisting that every school be required to achieve up to a set minimum expectation. Should a school fail to achieve this minimum expectation, they become at risk of closure by the state (Steffy, 1993). In Oregon, the state has developed a plan to require two years of preschool education, to establish nongraded elementary schools, to implement barrier testing at the 5th, 8th, and 10th grades, and to create a complex of applied technology learning centers to serve students during the 11th and 12th grades. Only time will determine whether or not these statewide efforts will succeed in addressing the needs of at-risk youth.

Assessment

While there is a long history of testing student achievement, the assessment of student learning has emerged in recent years with almost a religious fervor. The controversial use of standardized tests to assess learning has become the focus of debate in almost every state. For more than a decade, the National Assessment of Student Learning has carefully documented the educational achievement and lack of achievement of U.S. students. In addition, almost every state has developed or is developing statewide outcome assessment programs. There is also a growing national interest in using student assessment to provide evaluative "grades" for teachers, schools, school districts, and states. Some districts use student assessment data to set teachers' salaries and school budgets. There is also a growing momentum to replace graduation requirements with outcome performance assessments and couple these assessments with aligned curricula. During recent years, reports of the National Assessment of Student Learning have begun to document consistent though modest improvement in student achievement. The research literature on school reform has consistently documented the importance of accurately assessing student learning. Unfortunately, little significant improvement of student learning, especially for at-risk students, has been reported to date (National Center for Educational Statistics, 1991).

Technology

Over the years, technology has been perceived by many as one of the key aspects of educational reform. At one time, films, media, and even the overhead projector were identified as essential to the learning process and were believed to hold great promise for dramatically improving learning. Today there is even greater enthusiasm for computers and related computer technology, distance learning, networking, videos, and even commercial television in the classroom. Many have concluded that computers will eventually revolutionize public education or perhaps even replace public schools as we now know them (Bell & Elmquist, 1991). Some schools are attempting to provide one computer for every three to five students. While it is still too early to speculate on the power of technology to ultimately improve learning and transform schools, most agree that the long-term impact of technology holds the greatest single promise for educational reform. Unfortunately, early expectations regarding the impact of technology have not yet materialized, and the costs of hardware, software, networks, and teacher retraining have proved to be too expensive for most public schools and the taxpayers who support them. There have also been few studies which have confirmed the positive impact of technology on at-risk youth.

Teacher Education

It was once thought that public schools could be reformed through teacher education. The idea has always been compelling: with wave after wave of new, better trained teachers entering the schools each year, it was thought that the cumulative impact over time would ultimately result in reforming schools. Research over the last two decades has all but destroyed that concept. Research has documented that new teachers do not change schools; in fact the opposite is true, that schools seem to change new teachers. Over time, even after a few weeks of student teaching, teachers tend to conform to the expectations of the school in which they teach (Zeichner, 1983). Most states now require some type of minimum competency teacher testing, often requiring both a basic skills test and a professional knowledge test. Some states require content knowledge tests. During recent years there has also been a move by the Holmes Group and several individual states to move teacher education to the graduate level, requiring preservice teachers to complete a fifth-year program of study (*Tomorrow's Teachers*, 1986). Others, like John Goodlad, are working to create professional development schools where teacher education programs become partners with the local schools to prepare teachers as well as join in reform efforts (Goodlad, 1990). Although these efforts are promising, there is still little evidence that any of these efforts have led to significant increases in reforming K–12 public education.

Choice

The most recent national effort at educational reform has focused on choice. The idea is to break up the public monopoly of public education by giving parents and students the opportunity to select the school of their choice. In Minnesota, the concept has been implemented for the first time. Parents are now allowed to choose any public school and school district. In California, citizens recently rejected a voucher plan which, if passed, would have enabled parents to choose between public schools and private schools, thus transferring a substantial amount of state education dollars to private schools. Both the Bush and Reagan administrations supported the concept of choice and included both private and parochial schools as available options. Many states now permit home schooling, and for those families who can afford it there has always been the choice of private and parochial schools. There also seems to be a growing interest in developing "franchise" private schools throughout the United States. Although private and parochial schools have often documented learning achievement that is significantly better than public schools, there is considerable doubt as to whether or not this achievement would be sustained if nonpublic schools enrolled increased numbers of students representing the cultural and socioeconomic mosaic that is found in today's public schools. Many fear that choice will permit the parents of the more affluent students to choose either new restructured public or private schools, leaving the at-risk youth in their local schools without the benefit of their more successful classmates (Boyer, 1983).

Why Reform Efforts Have Failed

During our lifetime, school reform has been like air-lifting survival kits to people who live in the swamps. We made life a good deal better in the swamps, but I don't think that we ever seriously tried to drain the swamp.
—*(INDIANA UNIVERSITY PROFESSOR, BLOOMINGTON, INDIANA, 1980)*

Perhaps the most positive outcome from the recent decades of reform efforts is that educators have finally begun to understand why schools have proven so resistant to change. During the last 10 years, researchers have significantly contributed to a growing body of educational knowledge that has provided new insights into effective strategies for institutional change, as well as a better understanding of why, after decades of reform efforts, schools are by and large the same as they were 70 years ago. Institutions are all but impossible to change, whether the institution is the Roman Catholic Church, the Electoral College, or the neighborhood elementary school. There are three major reasons for this intransigence: systemic pressures, institutional cultures, and internal forces of resistance.

Systemic Pressures

Institutions, especially schools, develop an elaborate web of interrelationships that contribute to an incredibly rigid stability (Fenstermacher, 1992). For schools, these interrelationships developed rather quickly after the turn of the century and continue to exercise a powerful influence on public-school curriculum, instructional approaches, and organization. One of the earliest and continuing influences on public schools is college admission requirements. Almost every change in college admission requirements has precipitated a mirror reaction in high-school graduation requirements. Teacher certification in each of the states regulates teacher preparation through the provision of licensure to individuals to teach those specific required courses found in the public-school curriculum. Offering new courses in such fields as anthropology, Asian languages, communications, and computer science creates difficulties since a state may not have a licensure program for specific disciplines not previously found in the public-school curricula.

Textbook publishers also exert a powerful influence on curriculum stability, as companies prepare and publish textbooks for the courses required for graduation, designing their books to be approved and sold in the largest markets of Texas and California. Most conclude the result is often a mediocre product which accommodates all critics and often proves to be less than stimulating to students. National professional associations have likewise influenced curriculum stability in schools. The associations representing math, science, history, language arts, and other teaching areas regularly revise their own standards for the curriculum to be taught and exercise considerable pressure toward maintaining or expanding their proportion of the school curricula. As interest in other academic disciplines has grown—political science, economics, psychology, computer science and communications, and others—these disciplines have discovered that it is all but impossible to wedge their fields of study into the public-school curriculum.

While some argue that an entirely new public-school curriculum is needed for the 1990s, the combined influence of college admission, graduation requirements, textbook publishers, teacher certification regulations, and tradition make substantial change extremely difficult. Public education continues to operate on a course-driven curricular model, and to significantly transform this approach has proven to be an all but insurmountable challenge.

Throughout their existence, national professional associations of teachers, including the National Education Association and the American Federation of Teachers, have been responsible for massive improvements in the majority of areas related to the teaching profession and the education of our nation's youth. These powerful national associations have exerted a cautious approach toward recent school reforms including merit pay, career ladders, advanced study requirements for teachers' certification, site-based management, and student assessment. At the national, state, and local level, teachers' organizations have often made class size their single, most important goal, along with improved teacher pay and associated economic benefit packages. The approach of conceptualizing education around a single teacher in a contained classroom tends to conflict with a variety of the most significant educational reform recommendations, especially those which call for improved technology. Even though research has clearly documented the effectiveness of and critical need for the adoption of many new approaches, such as one-to-one tutoring, early interventions for at-risk youth, and a multitude of applications for computer technology, teaching continues to be practiced in the vast majority of schools in a directed instructional approach using a single teacher. Few schools have been willing to consider adjusting class size in order to employ other individualized instructional approaches.

Other systemic forces in the school or school district include transportation and bus schedules, grading practices, a host of federal rules and regulations, state regulations regarding legal liability and funding formulas. School districts' contracts reflect state laws which dictate the number of school days per year, the length of the school day, and even the number of minutes that must be devoted to particular subjects during the elementary grades. Such networks of regulation can render significant reform efforts all but impossible to implement. Too often teachers have learned that there is a reason, often a rule or law, that prohibits, prevents, or discourages them from doing almost anything unique, distinctive, or different.

It is this network of interrelated institutional forces that makes public schools so much alike. This is the reason it is difficult to find schools with graduation competencies rather than graduation course requirements. It is why public schools teach their courses every day rather than using an alternating schedule like colleges and universities and why so few schools have tried a four-day week with one day for student projects or to explore individualized, self-paced approaches to education. It is also why so few schools have been able to implement a shared decision-making or site-based management approach. It is why almost no school in the United States could be provided a budget and permitted to redefine the personnel into differentiated staffing with fewer teachers and administrators and more aides and tutors. It is why it is so difficult for professionals from business, the performing arts, government, and even the university to teach or offer their services to public schools.

Institutional Cultures

In his landmark book, *The Culture of the School and the Problem of Change,* Seymour Sarason explained the power of "patterns or regularities of behavior" in institutions (1971). He describes these behavioral patterns as providing a "cultural setting" for any institution. While institutional and human cultures have been studied in a wide variety of public entities and corporations, Sarason focused his attention on schools. It is just this culture, this set of behavioral regularities of students, teachers, and administrators, that combines to create an eerie sameness of all schools. People, especially new teachers, do not change schools; schools change the people who work in them. The behavior regularities of schools create a powerful conforming force throughout any educational institution (Sarason, 1971; and Zeichner, 1983). Studies have found that within a few weeks, student teachers abandon their personal beliefs regarding education and also the approaches and concepts taught in their teacher education programs and begin to conform to the beliefs, norms, and expectations of the school (Sarason, 1971). Studies of first-year teachers and fifth-year teachers found more of the same. Many teachers either become more and more like the behavioral norms of the school, or they grow so frustrated that they transfer to another school or leave teaching altogether. Understanding the phenomena of school culture helps to explain why beginning teachers often criticize teacher education programs as being so unrelated to the "real world" of schools.

Internal Forces of Resistance

Research concludes that it is all but impossible to impose change on teachers unless they support the change. If teachers oppose an educational innovation, a new rule, or even a new curriculum requirement, they will find ways to resist or

undermine the reform. This rather simple concept has proven difficult for legislators, governors, principals, school superintendents, school boards, and professional associations to understand. Year after year, decade after decade, the inti-
mate experience called teaching has resisted reforms that were not supported by
teachers.

The lesson from this brief review of efforts toward school reform is that historically schools have been very difficult to change, and to restructure them to address the needs of at-risk youth may be even more difficult. Any effort to improve
the education of at-risk youth in public schools must take into account the powerful influence of prevailing systemic forces and school cultures and must avoid the
negative implications of imposition. Because of the difficulty inherent in educational reform, schools throughout the United States continue to attempt to teach at-
risk students in traditional ways that have long been documented as ineffective, or
even worse, that may only contribute to the problems of these troubled youth.

How Schools Fail At-Risk Youth

"Well, I just couldn't believe it. In fact," the U.S. history teacher said, "I am embarrassed to say, I never even thought about it. This kid in my third-period history class came by after school and asked if he could talk to me. And look, the kid was doing okay in my class. Not great, but believe me he was more than passing the course. God! I guess I'll admit it; he had a C average, and it was already late November. Well, I don't know why he came to me, but there he was. And what it was all about: he told me that he didn't know how to read. Of course I thought he was teasing. It just blew me away. He was serious. Well, you know, I didn't know what to say. At the time I didn't even know what he meant; what he was talking about. Here I am with an 11th grade student with a C average and he is confiding in me that he doesn't know how to read? Like, think about it; what would you do? Don't kids learn to read in elementary school, then take their subject courses in junior and senior high schools? I was at a total loss. Finally, I told the kid that he had nothing to worry about. I would see what was available and we would get him reading before he knew it. I immediately went to see the school counselor and asked about a reading program. The counselor gave me a blank look and said to me, "Why would we have a reading program? Don't students learn to read in the elementary schools?"
—(HIGH SCHOOL TEACHER, HARTFORD, CONNECTICUT, 1992)

While there is a growing sophistication in identifying the factors that contribute to students becoming at risk, most of these factors are by and large rooted in the home, the community, and the culture of poverty. Yet almost every study of the complicated problems associated with at-risk children and youth has also identified educational factors that exacerbate the problems of those who are at risk and often drive them from school (Kirst, 1993; Hodgkinson, 1993). These school-related factors cut across the entire school spectrum and are deeply imbedded in the culture of U.S. public school. A later section in this chapter will detail the problems associated with expulsion, tracking, retention, pull-out programs, and special education. But the problem is far more ominous than a particular set of school practices. The problem involves teacher attitudes toward at-risk youth, and even though most teachers would deny it, too often their belief that some children cannot learn. It involves a reluctance of schools to address the problems of certain students, whether they are pregnant, malnourished, abused, lack adequate English skills or the ability to read.

Studies have found that many classroom teachers do not work hard to teach at-risk youth; they do not question them, they do not call on them in class or demand quality work. Researchers have also documented that the public school curriculum is overwhelmingly dominated by an emphasis on college preparation, even though only 20 percent of Americans ever graduate from college. Most schools do not teach financial planning, consumer economics, or computer skills beyond simple word processing. Many schools continue to offer courses in wood and metal shop and auto mechanics that reflect a world that no longer exists. Most vocational programs lack the advanced technology and skilled instructors to teach or even introduce the student to the technical demands and requirements of today's workplace.

School counselors continue to function in a guidance role, assisting high-school students in meeting college academic requirements and selecting an appropriate college. School counselors have almost no responsibility for ensuring that public school students gain the technical, vocational, and professional skills that would enable them to find jobs after high-school graduation or after dropping out. Articulation between public schools and colleges represents a sophisticated, complex set of agreements, aptitude and achievement testing programs, and career advising related to college. The vast majority of public schools have few, if any, support programs to assist the majority of public school students to make a successful transition into the world of work.

All of these programs and practices reflect a comprehensive, institutional bias against the at-risk child that is equally as disturbing as the sociocultural factors outside the school. At-risk youth arrive at school far from ready to learn, and public school programs tend to isolate them, stigmatize them, and place them in programs that widen the academic gap between them and their better achieving fellow students. Part of the explanation for school policies and practices that intellectually and psychologically brutalize students who are already at risk is rooted in an educational mythology that has endured for decades in spite of mounting evidence to the contrary. While many of these policies and practices may grow out of overt racism and intellectual elitism, many seem to be motivated by legitimate though misguided concerns for at-risk youth. And, while research has dramatically and decisively challenged the underlying assumption of much of public education's response to at-risk youth, the policies and practices persist so widely and in such direct opposition to research evidence that many school attitudes have taken on the characteristics of mythology.

School Mythology

While comprehensive evidence regarding the negative impact of certain school policies and practices will be detailed later in this chapter, the following is a review of the major mythological assumptions that negatively impact so many children and youth and that drive them from school.

Myth #1: At-Risk Youth Need Slow Learning

The idea that at-risk children and youth need slow learning cannot be further from the truth. Over the past 20 years, research has documented again and again the disastrous effects of this slow learning myth. We now know that at-risk children and youth benefit from being academically challenged in an environment of high expectation. They need accelerated, not slow, learning if they are ever to function effectively in public education and later in adult life.

Myth #2: At-Risk Youth Should Be Retained During the Early Grades Until They Are Ready to Move Forward

While retention seems so logical and is employed out of concern over the needs of at-risk youth, recent research has documented the disastrous effects of this practice. Many agree that retention may have some positive benefits during the early grades, yet by the time the student is a teenager, early retention poses an overwhelming obstacle to graduation. Research has clearly documented that for at-risk youth, retention of one grade increases the student's likelihood of school failure, and if the child is retained twice, the chance of graduation from high school is near zero (see p. 16). Rather than repeating a grade, at-risk youth need intense, accelerated, nongraded elementary classrooms that provide for the application of mastery learning and attention to their specific needs.

Myth #3: At-Risk Youth Can Be Educated With the Same Expenditures As Other Students

While many of the effective programs that will be described in later chapters may indeed be initiated with existing resources, they require new and creative ways of allocating existing education funds. Still there are large numbers of public-school students who have such severe problems that they need immediate, long-term, intensive educational care, and this care is often very expensive. Just as the health professions provide individualized intensive care that is expensive but essential in certain situations, schools too need to address the growing problems of at-risk children and youth in a similar manner. The needs of young children often demand additional resources during preschool and the early grades to ensure that they learn to read and communicate effectively before the end of the third grade.

   The good news is that long-term cost analyses of public education show that providing early, intensive educational prevention and intervention is the most cost-effective means of confronting the massive problems at-risk children and youth face. The success of early prevention and intervention programs has a direct effect on reducing later costs of remedial reading programs, special education, and school counseling, and can provide for potentially dramatic reductions in the long-term cost of social services. While the long-term balance sheet will benefit from establishing early intervention programs, the initial start up will require additional reallocation of funds.

Myth #4: Classroom Teachers Can Adequately Address the Needs of At-Risk Youth

The problems of at-risk youth are often so complicated, so pervasive and so long-term, so rooted in the home, community, culture, and socioeconomic conditions that it is all but impossible for a classroom teacher alone to significantly address the needs of at-risk youth. The problems of at-risk students in most cases have developed and intensified over a period of years prior to entry into a particular classroom. A single teacher simply does not have the capacity to address complex problems of abuse, nutrition, home supervision and support, family disruptions, drugs, crime, gangs, violence, and other negative factors that so often impact at-risk youth. More accurate is the African saying, "it takes an entire village to raise a child." Schools must be transformed to increase student access to community services through coordinating school and social agency resources. In a very real sense a classroom teacher can only address the tip of the iceberg of their students' problems.

Myth #5: Some Students Can't Learn

In spite of the fact that almost every school in America has signs and slogans hanging in their halls, classrooms, and offices regarding the assumption that all students can learn, there is huge evidence that suggest that many teachers and school administrators not only doubt that fact but seem motivated to ensure that these "dumb kids" don't interrupt or interfere with those students who indeed can learn. Nowhere is this more evident than in the fact that elementary schools continue to fail to teach all children to read. We now know that all children can learn to read; we even know how to ensure that they do. Yet few, if any, schools can point with pride to the fact that all children read at grade level by the end of the third grade.

Myth #6: The Most Effective Way to Improve Instruction for At-Risk Youth Is to Reduce Classroom Size

The most widely held belief regarding teaching effectiveness centers on classroom size. Following teachers' salaries, it is often the second issue to be considered in teacher contract negotiations. And given the growing number of culturally different, non-English speaking, moderate and severely handicapped students crowding into the nation's classrooms, it would appear logical that reduced pupil-teacher ratio would be an essential goal. Intense lobbying has led legislatures and school boards in Tennessee, New York, Ontario, and Indiana to reduce class size by almost half. And while there is little question that reductions in class size can contribute to alleviating much of the daily stress and strain of classroom teachers, there is unfortunately little or no evidence that this practice alone provides for increased achievement of at-risk youth. A number of studies and program follow-up evaluations have found little improved student learning to occur from simply reducing pupil-teacher ratios. Preschool and early public school prevention programs and supplementary, after-school one-to-one tutoring have been evaluated to be more effective in teaching reading to at-risk youth than reducing regular classroom size.

Myth #7: Students Who Are Having Learning Difficulties Probably Need Special Education

With few other options available to teachers, there is a tendency to identify students having learning difficulties as needing special education. As special education has become more sophisticated, teachers now have a complex range of identified problems to use in diagnosing students. The largest special education designations are now learning disabled, attention deficit disorder, and hyperactivity. If a student is not learning or is misbehaving, there is a strong tendency to define the child's problem as a learning disability. For special education to serve these types of "disorders" represents a very expensive additional burden to their programs. School programs that have documented the fact that effective education in the lower elementary grades can dramatically reduce special education referrals will be described in a later chapter. School policy and practice based on myths such as these not only fail to adequately address the needs of at-risk youth, but often force these students to leave school.

Inequity in School Funding

For decades data have been collected by states, the federal government, universities, foundations, and a variety of individuals documenting the profound inequity that exists in public-school funding. Most recently, Jonathan Kozol's book *Savage Inequalities* once again vividly depicted the tragic and devastating impact of the inequitable funding of public education. While school funding in the United States is primarily based on local property taxes, there exists substantial variation between school funding levels from state to state and from school district to school district. Inevitably, the wealthy school districts support their schools unusually well while the poor districts lack the resources to support schools even at minimal levels. Tremendous variation occurs between affluent and poor communities, between teacher salaries, per-pupil expenditures, facilities, supply and equipment budgets, and virtually every other area. The property tax model for school

funding punishes and penalizes the very students who are most at risk and who
are most in need of help. In a unanimous decision the supreme court of the State
of Texas declared that the state's property-tax-based school funding system was in
violation of the state constitution. The court found many disparities in funding including one example of over $17,000 in per-pupil spending between one of the
wealthiest and one of the poorest districts. This chilling inequity originated from a
$13.9 million differential in assessed property values between two adjoining dis-
tricts. More often than not, this scenario represents today's reality in the funding
of public education (Kozol, 1991).

In spite of decades of civil rights litigation and legislation that has fought segregated schools and even concluded that "separate but equal" was not in fact
equal, property tax funding and local control of schools have combined to stratify
U.S. public education into the haves and have-nots. The state legislature in Michigan has recently begun to address the equalization of funding for public education
by abolishing the use of property tax as a funding source for public schools. Yet in
spite of a growing number of states where funding inequities have been or are
being addressed, a review of the 15,358 school districts in the United States continues to demonstrate dramatic inequities in the funding of and provision for public education (National Center for Education Statistics, 1993).

As referred to earlier, it is clearly recognized that poor children who attend
school with other poor children have an enormous challenge to overcome if they
are to succeed in school. The existence of poverty in the home and community is
too often matched by poverty in the school setting, which directly contributes to
the failure of so many at-risk youth. Too often the students who are so in need of
enriched, accelerated education are subjected to the schools with the worst financial support, the most poorly paid teachers, the most dilapidated buildings, the
worst equipment, textbooks and instructional materials, and they respond accordingly by failing, leaving, or giving up.

Programs That Isolate and Stigmatize At-Risk Children and Youth

There is a consistent record of research over the past 20 years which documents the
negative, often disastrous effects of a number of school policies and programs
specifically designed to address the needs of at-risk youth and the problems that
at-risk youth create for schools. Unfortunately, many of these school programs and
practices, including expulsion, retention, tracking, special education, and remedial
pullout programs, have in actuality proven to be harmful to at-risk youth. Recent
research has documented that a number of these school programs have led to poor
student achievement and to dropping out of school. Most unfortunate is the fact
that almost all schools use these programs and continue to use them in spite of
overwhelming negative evidence regarding their effectiveness. The following is a
summary of research findings regarding school programs that do not work or at
the very best have very limited positive results.

Expulsion

Too often, youth react to schools with inappropriate or disruptive behavior. Because of this, educators have recognized that it may be necessary to isolate or exclude some students in order to provide others with a more effective climate for learning. While much of the disruptive behavior often originates from antisocial tendencies rooted deep within the home and society, recent research indicates that often a student's negative behavior may well be precipitated by a number of school practices: inappropriate curriculum, ineffective teacher-student relations, lack of sensitivity to diversity, school failure, and insufficient support services. It is now clear that students often react to their failures in school, to teachers' negative perceptions, and to a curriculum that seems irrelevant to their needs by not attending school, or, if they come, by waging war against the teachers and schools that they perceive to be so antagonistic toward them.

Although most schools throughout the United States have developed more effective discipline policies and procedures, too many schools continue to use expulsion as a primary punitive reaction to absenteeism or to inappropriate or disruptive behavior. The effects of school expulsion, which have been carefully studied, have proven to be extremely negative. Expelled students typically fall further behind, experience increased social difficulties, and seldom return to complete school.

Jack Frymier, primary author of the nation's most comprehensive study of the factors that place youth at risk, concluded that expulsion was one of the top six factors that lead to dropping out (Frymier & Gansneder, 1989). Other studies indicate that expulsion only serves to isolate youth from school and to encourage a variety of debilitating activities such as dropping out, teenage pregnancy, drug and alcohol abuse, and crime. Nationally, 44 percent of African-American dropouts, 31 percent of Hispanic dropouts and 26 percent of Caucasian dropouts were found to have been suspended or put on probation at least once prior to leaving school (Wheelock, 1986).

Learning can seldom occur in a disruptive environment. However, schools can create orderly, safe environments by means other than suspension and expulsion. Establishing high standards for discipline and attendance and coupling these standards to clearly established and carefully followed discipline policies have proven to be successful (U.S. Department of Education, 1987b). Schools can contribute to their students' academic achievement by establishing, communicating, and enforcing fair and consistent discipline policies (U.S. Department of Education, 1987b). There is strong new evidence that expulsion can be almost totally eliminated by involving students, parents, teachers, and administrators in establishing rules and by developing a careful due process procedure that protects the individual's rights (Gathercoal, 1990). A growing number of school districts and states require that students must be provided with alternatives to expulsion or for those students who are expelled from the regular school, the opportunity to attend some type of remedial or alternative education program.

Other alternatives to expulsion include:

- Positive student-parent conferences
- Intensive counseling
- In-school time out or in-school suspension
- Alternative school programs available for students via choice (Office of Educational Research & Improvement, 1987)

Retention

The concept of retention is a simple idea and is probably as old as formal schooling. Simply put, retention is a process of requiring students who have not demonstrated minimal academic achievement to repeat a year of school. Use of retention has been encouraged by a negative reaction to the use of social promotions in public schools. Many believe that social promotion is a major contributing cause to the poor overall academic achievement of U.S. youth. Critics of public education have repeatedly cited social promotion as one of the primary reasons that many students graduate from high school unemployable and illiterate.

The practice of requiring underachieving students to repeat a grade in school is also a rather natural outgrowth of state and national assessment of learning. An increasing number of states are requiring the testing of minimal competency which prevents students from proceeding further in the curriculum until they have achieved required levels on academic achievement tests. This approach has contributed to the increase in the number of students being retained.

Public schools have long used retention as a major strategy for addressing the needs of at-risk youth. In fact, the use of formal retention policies increased significantly during the 1980s. A Phi Delta Kappa Study reported that over 26 percent of principals and 48 percent of teachers support the use of retention (Frymier & Gansneder, 1989). Another study found that many urban schools retain 15 to 20 percent of their students at each grade level, and by grade 10, up to 60 percent of the students have been retained at least once (Gottfredson, 1988).

In spite of the fact that over 700,000 U.S. youth are retained each year, research and evaluation of retention practices have shown few if any academic or social benefits (Shepard & Smith, 1989). Careful study has consistently identified this practice as one of the most significant factors in increasing the risk that students will drop out of high school before graduation (Natriello, 1988). Dropouts are five times more likely to have repeated a grade than high-school graduates. If they repeat two grades, students face close to a 100 percent probability of dropping out (Frymier & Gansneder, 1989). Few students who enter high school at age 16 or 17 will stay until 20 or 21 to graduate. Schools that continue to retain students do so despite the 20-plus years of cumulative research which does not support the practice (Glickman, 1991).

Martin Haberman and Vicky Dill eloquently summarize the practice of retention:

Hundreds of studies exist examining the effects of retention. What is so exceptional about the body of literature is not the number of studies, the scope, size, or longevity of the data, but rather the uniform conclusion: retained students are negatively affected academically, socially, and emotionally. As a strategy, retention FAILS. (1993, p. 355)

A wide variety of research suggests that a number of policies and practices offer far more promise than retention. The most effective approach appears to be a combination of programs at the early childhood, preschool, and early grade levels designed to provide students with a strong foundation for learning. These programs provide enrichment and support that allow students to catch up, both academically and socially, with their achieving peers through accelerated learning. Programs such as Head Start, Great Start, Even Start, Follow Through, Accelerated Learning, and all-day kindergarten have demonstrated strong positive successes (Holmes, 1990). Such enriched "front loading" of the educational process appears to be a sound and effective educational strategy and deserves widespread support.

Other programs have demonstrated effective alternatives to retention. They include nongraded elementary schools which permit students to proceed at their own pace through developmentally appropriate learning practices, individualized continuous progress schools at the secondary level, and schools like the K–12 St. Paul Open School which possess a long record of success using competency-based education rather than graduation requirements (McPartland & Slavin, 1990).

To effectively address the needs of at-risk youth, schools must design programs that enable students to catch up with their peers. Holding at-risk students back through retention has been clearly demonstrated as ineffective and in many cases harmful.

Tracking

In 1931, A. H. Turney summarized writings on ability grouping in the 1920s and earlier. From these writings he derived a list of advantages and disadvantages of ability grouping. They are adapted as follows:

Advantages:

1. *It permits pupils to make progress commensurate with their abilities.*
2. *It makes possible an adaptation of the technique of instruction to the needs of the group.*
3. *It reduces failures.*
4. *It helps to maintain interest and incentive, because bright students are not bored by the participation of the dull.*
5. *Slower pupils participate more when not eclipsed by those much brighter.*
6. *It makes teaching easier.*
7. *It makes possible individual instruction to small slow groups.*

Disadvantages:

1. *Slow pupils need the presence of the able students to stimulate them and encourage them.*
2. *A stigma is attached to low sections, operating to discourage the pupils in these sections.*
3. *Teachers are unable, or do not have time, to differentiate the work for different levels of ability.*

Turney's list is remarkably current. In any academic discussion or PTA meeting on ability grouping the same arguments are likely to be advanced on both sides. (Slavin, 1993, p. 13)

Tracking is used in over 95 percent of U.S. high schools and is increasingly being employed at the middle-school and elementary levels. Tracking is a highly popular school strategy for dealing with diverse student abilities and achievement. Within each grade level, schools utilize a student's previous grades, scores on standardized tests, and teacher evaluations to group students according to ability (Braddock, 1990). At the elementary level, this often occurs through ability grouping within self-contained classes, especially for instruction in reading and math. At the secondary level, there are special classes that track students into a dual curriculum approach to education. Such tracks include accelerated classes for the very able and slow learning or remedial classes for the less able. By the high-school years, these tracks are clearly established in the vast majority of schools as distinctive educational programs with differentiated curriculum and differentiated learning expectations. Today, most high schools provide distinct programs in college preparation, general education, and vocational education, with students often being segregated by ability even further into separate classes within each of these three tracks (McPartland & Slavin, 1990).

In theory, tracking is used to accommodate curriculum and instruction to the diverse needs, interests, and abilities of students found in most schools. It is believed that teachers can focus their attention on student needs and develop curricula that relate directly to student educational levels and abilities. Such homogeneous grouping is almost universally supported by teachers who believe it makes teaching and learning more efficient and more effective. However, the effect on minority students is not likely to be positive. Kuykendall in her book *From Rage To Hope* stressed:

Tracking and ability grouping are likely to send subliminal messages to Black and Hispanic youth that white and middle class students are going to have opportunities to a greater range of knowledge and, therefore, opportunities for more life-long success. (Kuykendall, 1992, p. 41)

Unfortunately, except in special comprehensive programs, research and evaluation on tracking is overwhelmingly negative (McPartland & Slavin, 1990). There is some evidence that grouped instruction in reading during the early elementary grades can be successful when used in a comprehensive school program with specially trained teachers and tutors who have high educational expectations for the students (Madden, Slavin, Karweit, Dolan, & Wasik, 1991).

Research has identified three major reasons why tracking has not been successful, at least for the students placed into the lower tracks. First, there is evidence that slower tracks receive less resources from the school. Often these classes are large, housed in inadequate facilities, and limited by antiquated methods and equipment. Second, since teachers find these classes more demanding both behaviorally and instructionally, the slower track typically does not attract the most experienced, effective teachers. An unwritten law in public education seems to be that, with experience, teachers earn the right to teach the highly sought-after advanced placement classes. Many teachers will explain that during their early years of teaching, "I did my time in the slow tracks . . . now let someone else do it." Third, and even more disturbing, teachers tend to have significantly lower expectations for student learning in the slower tracks than for the students in the faster tracks. In numerous case studies, both students and teachers feel stigmatized by being in the slower tracks and both share expectations of low achievement. The consequences of these factors for the lower-track students unfortunately include a less challenging curriculum, a slower instructional pace, test and homework assignments that are not demanding, and fewer demands for higher-order thinking skills (Oakes, 1985). Far too often, classroom instruction for lower-track students includes little beyond a parade of worksheets, day after day.

The cumulative effects of tracking during a student's educational career can be devastating. Rather than helping students to accelerate and catch up educationally, it has been demonstrated that tracking actually widens the achievement gap between the slower and more advanced students (Goodlad, 1984). Rather than alleviating the problems of students with significant educational needs, tracking often only exacerbates the problem.

Even more alarming, tracking has been shown to resegregate schools that have been racially desegregated. In racially mixed schools, often achieved through complex desegregation programs including bussing and redrawing school district boundaries, students from the poorer socioeconomic backgrounds usually are grouped together and too often are resegregated into white and non-white educational tracks within a single school (Epstein, 1985).

Students tend to be tracked more by their socioeconomic status than by their academic ability. The higher-level academic track tends to be middle-class youth from educated families and the slower track tends to be minority, poor, and from homes with limited educational backgrounds. Unfortunately, once a child is assigned to the slow track, there is little hope of ever moving up to the advanced track (Glickman, 1991). For students who are most at risk, tracking only serves to isolate, handicap, stigmatize, and actually prevent effective learning. For almost two decades, it has been known that if students were not slow learners when they were assigned to the slow track, they soon became so.

Special Education

During the past decade and a half, the number of children classified as learning disabled for placement in special education has doubled, "even though the numbers of students in special education with physical disabilities or mental retardation have not substantially changed" (McPartland & Slavin, 1990, p. 6). Too often schools have had few if any other alternatives (except tracking and retention) to address the needs of youth who are most in need of educational programs other than regular classes or special education. Most students who are typically designated by schools as learning disabled are in fact "the lowest of the low achievers in the school" (McPartland & Slavin, 1990, p. 6), but may not have any of the usual expected mental or physical handicaps associated with special education (Deshler, Schumaker, Alley, Warner, & Clark, 1982). Schools also tend to classify students they have difficulty dealing with as learning disabled, emotionally disturbed, or as having an attention or hyperactivity disorder.

Standing in marked contrast to the practices of retention, expulsion, and tracking, special education programs usually do provide enriched resources and highly trained, specialized teachers to serve their students. Yet the use of special education to serve low-achieving students with no other handicap is an extremely expensive option given the paucity of research to support the continued use of this practice. There is also the unfortunate stigmatization that seems to occur when slow learners are assigned to special education (Leinhardt & Pallas, 1982). Once students are designated for special education, they tend to maintain that status throughout the school years, which severely limits the educational and occupational opportunities that are available to these students after their school years. Thus the decision to refer low-achieving students to special education may affect these students for their entire lifetime.

A related problem has emerged as special education programs have dramatically increased the number of learning disabled students. As school districts continue to serve the special education students with special teachers, small classes, and highly individualized learning programs, resources for the rest of the school population will often decrease proportionately. Some districts, like Portland, Oregon, have developed a wide variety of alternative school programs to alleviate the pressure on special education programs and to more appropriately serve the non-special education student who is a low achiever.

Remedial Pullout Programs

Some of the most controversial school programs designed for at-risk youth are those that pull out students from regular classes for special, enriched, or remedial instruction. These federally-funded programs like Chapter 1, special education, and bilingual education have been in operation for many years, some for more than two decades. In addition to these formal, externally funded programs, many schools have established resource rooms, tutorial programs, remedial programs, and special education programs that pull students out of their regular classrooms for enriched instruction, especially in reading and math, and for bilingual students to participate in English as a Second Language programs.

Many of these federally-funded programs are controversial. Research interpretations, especially regarding Chapter 1 and bilingual education, have been highly politicized, with opponents often emphasizing only research and evaluation that support their partisan points of view. The former director of Chapter 1, Mary Jean LeTendre, states:

> *Chapter 1 has made a significant impact on American education. It has helped to equalize American educational opportunity for our neediest children at the local level and it has been a catalyst for improving instruction in basic skills, for improving the training of teachers and for increasing the involvement of parents in the education of their children. (LeTendre, 1991, p. 577)*

However, an extensive review of the literature on effective practices for students at risk concluded that "the effectiveness of most widely used supplemental/remedial programs, diagnostic prescriptive pullout programs provided under Chapter 1 or special education funding show little evidence of effectiveness" (Slavin & Madden, 1989). Yet, later, the authors of that study concluded that Chapter 1 programs did make important contributions to the education of low-achieving disadvantaged youth. Both conclusions may be correct. While Chapter 1 students do in fact learn more than the other disadvantaged children in a particular school, they do not seem to bridge the substantial gap that separates them from the more advanced students. There is also evidence that Chapter 1 programs may provide an indirect contribution in reducing the achievement gap among African American, Hispanic, and Caucasian students (Slavin, 1991a).

Although there is evidence that Chapter 1 and special education are successful in increasing student learning, research and program evaluation are beginning to lead to significant changes in these programs, causing program directors and others to reconsider the pullout option. Increasingly, educators are concerned with what students are missing from their regular classroom during the pullout enrichment. There is a trend towards inclusion-type alternatives to pullout programs, such as increased use of mainstreaming, after-school programs, or schoolwide programs. New guidelines for Chapter 1 now enable schools serving large numbers of disadvantaged students (75 percent of the school population) to use Chapter 1 dollars for schoolwide services. (A later chapter will describe programs that demonstrate how effective Chapter 1 funding can be when applied toward a comprehensive schoolwide effort.) Yet in most cases, Chapter 1 continues as a pullout program serving individual students in remedial programs.

Research indicates that schools could be more effective by employing prevention and early intervention programs rather than using pullout remediations. There is no substitute for early educational success, especially in reading. Children who are taught to read successfully the first time they are taught will rarely need remedial help. Bilingual education, possibly the most controversial federally-funded program, has received criticism that pullout programs in English as a second language are less effective than total English immersion classes or cross-cultural classes that teach bilingual youth English.

To be most effective, remediation and educational enrichment should not occur at the expense of regular classroom instruction. It should occur either before or after school or through in-classroom support to the teacher. Alternative school programs and total immersion programs have also proven to be effective in this arena.

While few schools will be willing to deprive students and teachers of the federal funds that are available for these enrichment programs, educators should work to ensure that these programs do not interfere with regular classroom learning.

Frequent Mistakes in the Development of Programs for At-Risk Youth

"Well, it was my worst nightmare come true. I had never had anything happen like this in 26 years of teaching. Talk about good intentions gone to hell! See, last year we started this program for at-risk youth. We identified 13 of the school's most difficult students and scheduled them into my classroom for two hours each day. In addition to teaching them my specialty course, Applied Mathematics, I taught them study skills, helped them with their homework, discussed their problems and worked with their other teachers to be as supportive as possible. Well, everything was great. The kids started coming to school, doing their homework, their grades went up, and they began to really try. This year we transitioned those kids back into their regular classes and then scheduled a dozen new students into my two periods. The heartbreak of this story is that nine of last year's students had already dropped out of school by November and the rest are failing most of their classes. I can't believe it. What did we do wrong?"
—*(SCHOOL ADMINISTRATOR, MADRAS, OREGON, 1987)*

In recent years, as greater attention has been focused on the problems of at-risk youth, school districts throughout the country have increasingly developed new programs to serve these students. Unfortunately, as is so often the case in public education, little attention has been given to research on program effectiveness. The results have ranged from disappointing to tragically unfortunate. Even the best of intentions have often created programs that have not only failed to help at-risk youth but have also compounded their problems. One could conclude that many of these programs have been developed not so much to provide significant assistance to at-risk youth but to get these unfortunate youth out of regular classrooms where they make teaching and learning so hard for teachers and the other, better achieving students. The following represents a number of design errors that fatally flaw the potential effectiveness of programs designed to specifically serve at-risk youth.

Intervention Rather Than Prevention

The vast majority of programs designed for at-risk youth are implemented as intervention programs at the high-school level. On a common-sense level, this is probably understandable, since teachers and principals at the secondary level are confronted by students who are dropping out or by underachieving students who are increasingly disruptive and who often wreak havoc with the school and the classrooms. Unfortunately, most intervention programs are expensive and demand longer, more intensive efforts if they are to be successful. On this issue the researchers offer clear recommendations for prevention rather than intervention. Starting as early as possible is the most cost-effective approach and holds the most promise of long-term success.

Starting Too Small

A second tendency for schools is to start at-risk programs on a very small scale. Not only are most at-risk programs initiated at the secondary level, too many start with only one or two teachers for one or two periods a day and are focused on the most severely at-risk youth in a particular school. Teachers tend to burn out quickly in programs such as these, and in turn provide little impact toward truly addressing the needs of at-risk youth. Research consistently indicates that schools need comprehensive programs to help at-risk youth and that these programs involve as much of the school day as possible.

Transition Programs

School districts will often start short-term programs for at-risk youth with a goal of quickly correcting their problems and transitioning them as soon as possible back into the regular school program. Some of these programs last only a semester; others last only a year. Research has documented that there is no quick fix for at-risk youth, whether at the kindergarten, first grade, or high-school level. At-risk students tend to have far-reaching problems. It has taken years for some of these students to develop the problems that have placed them so at risk, and it is most unusual for these problems to be corrected quickly. Even the students who find themselves suddenly at risk because of family disruptions, depression, substance abuse, or other reasons have problems that can only be addressed effectively with long-term support.

School-Only Programs

Typically, schools focus on their own environment when addressing the needs of at-risk youth and tend to create in-school programs. And while school-only programs can be designed to provide lasting benefits for at-risk youth, research indicates that any school programs can be greatly strengthened by incorporating out-of-school learning experiences, community support, and the coordination of community agencies.

Mandatory Programs

Schools often attempt to develop effective programs for at-risk youth but then err by assigning both teachers and students to the programs. This practice diminishes the effectiveness of even a good program by including the negative effects that research has documented regarding traditional tracking programs. For maximum success, at-risk programs should be developed and made available both to teachers and students who have the opportunity to choose to participate. For at-risk youth, the element of choice affords considerable power toward stimulating their desire to be in school and, once there, the willingness to learn.

Schools that move to address the needs of at-risk children and youth must be careful that their good intentions do not serve to complicate their students' difficulties. A careful review of research clearly indicates that many school attempts to help at-risk students too often backfire and become contributing factors toward forcing students out of school.

In spite of this rather depressing survey of efforts at school reform and the disappointing effects of many of the traditional approaches to the problems of at-risk youth, there remains cause for optimism. Research and practice during the last 20 years have provided a substantial and expanding foundation for confidence that schools and communities can be reformed and restructured, and that programs do exist that have a proven track record of success with at-risk youth. In the mid-1990s, we can finally speak with authority and optimism regarding the opportunity for public school educators to effectively address the needs of at-risk youth. There is indeed hope at last. The next chapters will survey the characteristics of effective programs at each age level and provide specific recommendations for schools to follow in addressing the difficult challenge of successfully teaching all children and youth.

What We Know About Effective Programs

The ninth-grade student was certainly a show stopper. Half of her head was shaved, and the other half was freaked out in a wild explosion of hair, bells, and ribbons. She had three gold studs in her nose and was wearing at least a dozen earrings that jingled like wind chimes when she moved. In her own distinctive way she was a beautiful young girl. I asked her why she had left her former high school to travel across town to a small alternative program. She thought for a moment and then explained, "At my other school everyone treated me like a geek; everybody thought I was kind of weird."

"Is it different here in the alternative school?" I asked. She cocked her head to the side and flashed a smile. "Over here I just disappeared." She wagged her head from side to side, setting her earrings chiming. "It's like, I just disappeared into this really happy family."
—(HIGH-SCHOOL STUDENT, METROPOLITAN LEARNING CENTER, PORTLAND, OREGON, 1991)

Amidst the depressing tragedy of the crisis facing so many youth, there is cause for optimism. Research and evaluation have finally begun to provide a clear, consistent set of conclusions that can be translated into recommendations for effective school programs. Even more surprising, the research and evaluation come from a number of distinctly different, independent efforts that intersect to form a nexus of common conclusions.

What We Know

Insights into effective programs for at-risk youth have emerged from research and evaluation of federal programs like Head Start, Upward Bound, Follow Through, Special Education, Job Corps, and Chapter 1. They have been strengthened by school effectiveness studies, research on school effects in small and rural schools, and evaluations of alternative public schools. Related studies regarding violence, vandalism, and school disruptions have also proven helpful. This research, coupled with further inquiry into human development, human needs, learning styles, and brain research, has finally provided a foundational knowledge for theories and effective practices.

During recent years, a new generation of educational research has provided fresh insight into the effectiveness of schools and the factors that are essential to school restructuring. More important, amidst this growing body of research, there have been several important studies that have great significance for at-risk youth. These investigations, involving both quantitative as well as qualitative methodology, provide essential insights into schools and their relationship to at-risk youth. Recent studies include a 10-year investigation of school effects that has largely rewritten the effective school research of a decade ago (Teddlie & Stringfield, 1993), a 5-year study of the Coalition of Essential Schools, one of the nation's major school reform projects (Muncey & McQuillan, 1993), an in-depth case study of 14 public schools with special at-risk programs (Wehlage, Rutter, Smith, Lesko, & Fernandez, 1989); and the combined work of Robert Slavin and his colleagues at Johns Hopkins University on effective programs at the elementary level (Slavin, et al., 1989; Slavin, 1993). Each of these studies is highly regarded within the education research community. They focus on real students, communities, and schools; represent long-term research; and have researched conclusions that are remarkably consistent with one another. The studies complement an impressive collection of more targeted research, and taken together, they dramatically redefine the educational landscape for schools and their mission for at-risk youth.

In addition, there is an impressive body of research that has been conducted during the past 25 years on alternative public schools and magnet schools. Much of this early work was completed by scholars at Indiana University and later by Mary Ann Raywid, Nolan Estes, Joe Nathan, and a large group of specialized researchers. In addition to these formal research studies, there are more than 20 years of school evaluations that have identified essential characteristics of effective school and community programs for at-risk youth.

Emerging from these efforts, essential characteristics of effective programs have been clearly identified for preschool, kindergarten, elementary school, middle school, high school, and adult education programs (Center for Research on Elementary and Middle Schools, 1987; Comer, 1988; Durian & Butler, 1987; Levin, 1993; Northwest Regional Educational Laboratory, 1990; Wehlage, et al., 1987; Wehlage, et al., 1989; Slavin, 1991b, 1993).

Together, these studies have documented that schools can be effective with at-risk youth, why they are effective, why some schools are not effective, and what are effective and dysfunctional approaches to school reform. Taken as a group, these research studies form the foundation for much of the remainder of this chapter and later chapters on school reform. Perhaps most important, there are several overriding conclusions that can no longer be ignored.

Schools Make a Difference

During the 1960s, James Coleman of the University of Chicago published his landmark research that concluded that school had little or no effect on poor children; that school could not overcome the conditions of poor homes, families, and communities. And, in spite of a barrage of criticism, conflict, and discussions, the emerging education literature, primarily the work of Christopher Jencks and his colleagues, tended to support Coleman's conclusion that school did not matter. It was not until the early 1980s that Ron Edmonds was able to offer evidence which documented that certain "effective schools" did in fact have substantial positive influences on at-risk children and youth. More recently, research by Charles Teddlie and Sam Stringfield (1993) has built on earlier effective school research and provided a new, definitive set of conclusions regarding the fact that schools do make a difference. They have also identified significant factors in schools (i.e., behaviors of principals, teachers, students, and parents) that they found to be more powerful than factors relating to socioeconomic level and racial data. Equally important, the research of Teddlie and Stringfield documented that the significant factors in effective schools could be altered and improved.

The conclusion is unavoidable and powerful. Schools make a difference to at-risk students, and schools can be improved to ensure a substantial positive impact on these kids.

All Children Can Learn

As Ron Edmonds, noted education researcher, stressed, how many effective schools would you have to see to be persuaded of the educability of all children? If your answer is more than one, then you have reasons of your own for preferring to believe that pupil performance derives from family background instead of school response to family background (Herndon, 1990). We know with absolute certainty that all children can learn. Teachers, principals, and communities can no longer take refuge in the false concept that some students are simply too dumb, too deprived, or too disadvantaged to learn. With patient and carefully prescribed instructional programs, even profoundly mentally impaired children and adults can learn. The same is equally true for at-risk youth. The question, of course, remains whether or not communities have the determination and the will to direct the resources necessary toward addressing the needs of all children and youth.

No One Best Way To Learn

We know that students learn best in very different ways and in very different educational settings. We also know that different teachers teach in very different ways. Not all students can learn effectively in a typical school classroom with 20 to 30 students involved in group learning activities and organized into 50-minute class periods. We now know that students who fail to learn in such conventional classrooms can learn effectively in other types of learning environments when different instructional approaches are used. Whenever schools have developed learning environments that have addressed the specific needs and learning characteristics of those youth, remarkably positive outcomes have occurred.

The Power of Teacher Perception

We know that our self-perceptions are based to a large degree on how others see us. Students seem to live up to or down to the expectations of their teachers. If teachers believe that all students can learn, develop realistic expectations, and plan appropriate learning experiences, all youth can and will learn. Unfortunately, the opposite is also true. It remains all but impossible for a student to overcome negative perceptions held by teachers.

The At-Risk Problem is Not Just a School Problem

It is obvious that the problems of at-risk youth start in infancy and do not end when the student leaves school at the end of each day. The problems of at-risk youth often grow from social, family, and community problems. The most effective programs currently serving at-risk youth integrate components from both inside and outside the school. All successful programs depend on school and community collaboration and partnership to coordinate their efforts toward educating at-risk youth.

Early Intervention

Research in human development and learning continues to provide an understanding of the significance of a child's early years. Increasing numbers of U.S. babies are born without adequate health, shelter, and nutrition, and at least one out of 20 of these babies enter the world with the drug addiction of their mothers. One in four can expect to be physically or sexually abused during childhood and adolescence. We now know that if an infant fails to bond with a caring adult, a lifetime of educational and social services may be unable to overcome this tragic beginning. Failure to bond is directly related to a lack of conscience, failure to develop a sensitivity to issues of right and wrong, and sociopathic behavior. It is not surprising that it has been reported that over 70 percent of the men and women in prison today were the sons and daughters of teenage parents. We also know that early intervention not only means special programs for children from early childhood through the elementary years, but also includes educating expectant teenagers and adults about prenatal health, nutrition, parenting skills, and family planning.

School Programs Can Effectively Teach At-Risk Youth

Over the past 25 years a plethora of school programs have emerged and demonstrated through rigorous evaluation and research that public education can address the needs of those who are at risk. Examples include a variety of alternative schools and programs such as dropout prevention programs, continuation schools, vocational training programs, counseling programs, drug and alcohol programs, teen parent programs, magnet schools, learning centers, and in some cases the comprehensive school when its programs effectively focus on the needs of all youth.

Schools Must Be Restructured

We know that in our current educational structure an individual teacher, whether an 11th-grade biology teacher or a 3rd-grade elementary school teacher, cannot adequately address the needs of at-risk youth. Teachers, charged with teaching academic knowledge and skills to large numbers of students, are simply not able to provide the attention necessary to counter the complex noneducational problems that affect learning. In order to adequately address the problems of at-risk youth, schools must be dramatically changed. Restructuring school curriculum, reconceiving the school calendar and daily schedule, better integrating school and community services, providing teachers with adequate planning and problem-solving time, and enhancing the climate of the school to provide for equitable inclusion and learning opportunities for every child represent the challenges our schools must address. We now know of many successful schools that have been significantly restructured around these and other issues and are succeeding in their attempts to address the problems of at-risk youth.

Shared Decision Making and Shared Vision

Over two decades of research on effective schools has dramatized the power of school-based shared decision making and consensus building to significantly improve schools and student learning. At the school level, if teachers, administrators, parents, and students can develop a shared vision regarding goals, agree to pursue those goals, and monitor their progress in achieving the goals, remarkably positive developments occur. The Northwest Regional Educational Laboratory has developed a program entitled Onward to Excellence that has been unusually successful in improving student performance at the school level by incorporating shared decision making throughout the school.

These capsulized conclusions address critical areas and issues related to learning and schooling for at-risk youth. Research, school evaluations, outcome assessments, case studies, and other forms of inquiry have conclusively identified schools that are effectively teaching at-risk youth through restructuring their schools. A review of these school and program evaluations has identified the key characteristics that make these programs so successful.

Essential Characteristics of Effective Programs for At-Risk Youth

Not only do schools make a difference, schools have been identified that are effective in helping at-risk youth perform up to the levels of their more successful peers. These schools can be found at the elementary level, middle-school level, and in special at-risk and alternative programs at the high-school level (teen parent programs, alternative schools, Job Corps, etc.). Study after study for the past 20 years has helped to identify these effective schools through in-depth, long-term, and quantitative as well as qualitative studies. This research has documented the factors that seem to be responsible for this remarkable success with at-risk youth. There is now general agreement among researchers that the following factors should be found in all schools that are effective with at-risk youth:

1. *Clear academic mission*
2. *Orderly environment*
3. *High academic engaged time on task*
4. *Frequent monitoring of student's profile*
   (Teddlie & Stringfield, 1993, p. 36).

These factors should always be found in effective schools, regardless of the socioeconomic level of the students or whether the school is urban or rural. Yet the reasons some schools are more effective in teaching at-risk youth than others are far more complex than the simple identification of four rather general characteristics. The 10-year Louisiana School Effectiveness Study helped to identify many of these complexities. This long-term study has identified a number of school characteristics that are associated with schools that are effective with students of middle and low socioeconomic status (See Table 5-1).

Even more revealing is a comparison of schools that are effective with low socioeconomic status students and those schools that are ineffective with similar students (See Tables 5-2 and 5-3).

These less affluent, successful schools had principals who motivated teachers who, in turn, motivated students. The ability to instill in students a belief that they can learn is critical in effective low socioeconomic status schools. Apparently, students in effective middle socioeconomic status schools had this belief instilled at home and reinforced at school. (Teddlie & Stringfield, 1993, p. 34)

TABLE 5-1   Characteristics Associated with Effectiveness in Middle and Low Socioeconomic Status Schools

Middle Socioeconomic Status Schools	Low Socioeconomic Status Schools
1. Promote high present and future educational expectations.	1. Promote high present educational expectations. Ensure that students believe they can perform well at their current grade level. Allow high future educational goals to develop later.
2. Hire principals with good managerial abilities. Increase teacher responsibility for and ownership of instructional leadership.	2. Hire principals who are initiators, who want to make changes in the schools. Encourage a more active role for the principal in monitoring classrooms and providing overall instructional leadership.
3. Deemphasize visible external rewards for academic achievement (such rewards should be unnecessary if an adequate orientation is found at home).	3. Increase the external reward structure for academic achievement. Make high-achieving students feel special.
4. Expand curricular offering beyond the basic skills.	4. Focus on basic skills first and foremost, with other offerings after basic skills have been mastered.
5. Increase contact with the community. Encourage parents with high educational expectations to exert pressure for school achievement.	5. Carefully evaluate the effect of the community on the school. If the community does not exert positive pressure for school achievement, create boundaries to buffer the schools from negative influences.
6. Hire more experienced teachers.	6. Hire younger, possibly more idealist teachers. Give the principal more authority in selecting staff.

(Teddlie & Stringfield, 1993, p. 37).

These characteristics are important in many ways. They help to define the types of principals and teachers who seem to be effective with at-risk youth as well as define the types of staff development that are needed for teachers and administrators in order to help schools become more effective with at-risk youth.

Other studies have likewise provided important insights into the reasons some schools are effective with at-risk youth. In in-depth case studies of 14 schools with effective at-risk youth programs, researchers at the University of Wisconsin at Madison concluded that "the key finding of our research is that effective schools provide at-risk students with a community of support" (Wehlage, Rutter, Smith, Lesko, Fernandez, 1989, p. 223).

Schools as a community of support is a broad concept in which school membership and educational engagement are central. School membership is concerned with a

TABLE 5-2   Effective Low Socioeconomic Status Schools

1. While principals and teachers had modest long-term expectations for their students' achievement, particularly in regard to higher education, they held firm present academic expectations for their students.
2. Teachers reported spending more time on reading and math and assigning more homework rather than the other two low socioeconomic status groups.
3. Students perceived teachers as pushing them academically. They also reported receiving more teacher help than did students in less successful low socioeconomic status schools.
4. Students perceived their teachers as having high present expectations for them.
5. Teachers reported that principals visited their classrooms frequently.
6. The teachers in this group [effective low socioeconomic status schools] were the youngest and least experienced of the low socioeconomic status group.
7. The teachers in this group were the most likely of all the teachers to have teacher's aides.
8. Principals in these schools were the most likely to say that they had major input in hiring teachers. Twenty-three percent of the principals in the effective low socioeconomic status schools said that they hired their teachers. No other group of schools had more than nine percent of its principals report this power.

TABLE 5-3   Ineffective Low Socioeconomic Status Schools

1. An overall negative academic climate in these schools appears to have contributed to the low student achievement. Of all the groups [studied], teachers had the lowest expectations for students and rated them the lowest academically; the teachers accepted little responsibility for and perceived having little influence on student outcomes; they also appeared less satisfied with teaching and perceived themselves as unsuccessful in helping students attain goals.
2. When compared with students in low socioeconomic status groups, students perceived their teachers as less praising, less caring, less helpful, and more critical. More than in the other groups, these students reported that their teachers did not consider learning important.
3. Principals, teachers, and pupils all perceived the lack of achievement within the schools.
4. Compared with the other groups [studied], a higher percentage (21%) of teachers in these schools would rather teach in another school. By contrast, only two percent of the teachers in the typical middle socioeconomic status schools wanted to teach elsewhere. Teachers in the low socioeconomic status, ineffective schools were absent an average of 3.51 days in the fall semester, while teachers in effective low socioeconomic status schools were absent only an average of 2.03 days (Teddlie & Stringfield, 1993, pp. 34-35.

sense of belonging and social bonding to the school and its members. Educational engagement is defined as involvement in school activities, but especially traditional classroom and academic work. (p. 223)

The conditions in a school that supported this sense of community were defined as a "professional culture among educators [who] accepted moral responsibility for educating at-risk youth, and sufficient autonomy and resources to encourage educational entrepreneurship and the development of new programs for students (p. 223).

Hank Levin of Stanford University, founder of the Accelerated Schools Network, summarized his review of research in an even more pointed conclusion: "We must do for at-risk youth what has been done for many gifted and talented students" (1989, p. 2). Levin called for accelerating at-risk student learning rather than lowering expectations.

In order to be as useful as possible, available research from the above researchers and many others has been synthesized into a set of essential characteristics of effective schools for at-risk youth. Although each component demonstrates substantial individual evidence of success with at-risk students, the combined use of these practices results in even greater effectiveness in educating at-risk youth and bringing hope to their lives. This list of component practices may also serve as evaluative criteria for the review of existing programs and as a blueprint for the design of effective new programs (see the Appendix for Self-Evaluation Checklist.

Comprehensive and Continuing Programs

While some projects and programs have demonstrated educational success by working with at-risk youth for a relatively short time each day and for a few short weeks or months, it is evident that the more comprehensive a program, the better the chance of effecting lasting, positive change. Too many school districts make the mistake of creating programs for at-risk youth that operate for a single period or two each day and sometimes only for a semester or for a year. With few exceptions, this approach often represents a fundamental mistake of many school districts' initial efforts toward addressing the needs of at-risk students. Such programs tend to offer too little, occur far too late, and cannot overcome the years of negative impact left by home, school and society. If a student has experienced 6, 12, or 16 years of negative interaction with schools and classroom environments, it is unrealistic to believe that a semester or year-long program serving students only one or two periods a day can hope to accomplish much toward adequately addressing the problems of these youth. Even the benefits gained by programs like Head Start diminish rapidly without continuing enrichment and support. Successful programs for at-risk youth must start as early as possible, be as comprehensive as possible (including academic, social, economic, and health components), and continue as long as the student is in need.

If school districts are serious about serving at-risk youth, they need to conceptualize a comprehensive program that addresses the needs of these students. The goal must not be to provide a quick fix and rapid transition back into a traditional classroom. The goal must be to help students over time to develop strong self concepts, master basic skills, and develop realistic future plans. Occasionally, students may successfully return to the conventional program, but usually they will not. Thus, a comprehensive and continuing program must serve as a bridge to employment or continuing education (Wehlage, et al., 1989; Office of Educational Research and Improvement, 1987). It is far more important to transform the entire school into a comprehensive effort to educate *all* youth.

Choice and Commitment

The power and effectiveness of alternative education programs appear to depend in good measure on the fact that students and teachers must volunteer to participate. Alternatives, by definition, must allow students to voluntarily choose to participate. This simple component seems to have unusual power. By developing schools that address the needs and interests of youth, education and learning become attractive to youth, and their choice to participate in the program elicits a commitment from the students. Choice engenders an educational investment from the student and has powerful implications for overcoming the negative effect of traditional school tracking programs. It is not surprising that 71 percent of the parents polled in a recent Gallup poll on public education wanted the right to choose the local school or program their children attended. Educational choice has also been supported by U.S. business leaders and has been heartily endorsed by a number of state and federal government leaders. The state of Minnesota recently passed new legislation enabling parents in the state to select the district, school, and educational program of their choice and to have the state funding follow the student. A growing number of other states are now considering extending educational choice to the citizens of their state. The concept of choice, to be of the greatest benefit, must involve more than permitting parents, students, and teachers to voluntarily select school programs. Choice implies diversity and demands distinctly different educational alternatives. Unfortunately, most public schools reflect a monolithic similarity which is not focused on the needs of at-risk youth. Research and evaluation of alternative schools have carefully documented the power of these programs, available by choice, to effectively address the needs of at-risk youth (Barr, 1981; Boyer, 1983; Raywid, 1983; Young & Clinchy, 1993).

Caring and Demanding Teachers

There is an abundance of research that emphasizes how important it is for teachers to care for at-risk youth, to believe that these students can learn, and then to hold high expectations for them as learners. To be successful, education programs for at-risk students must be staffed with teachers who care for and demand that these students learn. No matter how well an education program is planned, without caring and demanding teachers, program effectiveness is in jeopardy. This may well be the most powerful component in effective programs for at-risk youth (Northwest Regional Educational Laboratory, 1990; Office of Educational Research and Improvement, 1987; Parrett, 1979; Teddlie and Stringfield, 1993).

Using Needs of At-Risk Youth to Design School Programs

To be effective, education programs must be expanded to include the needs of at-risk youth. Since the lives and previous educational successes of these students often differ so dramatically from those of other students, it is not surprising that school programs that work to serve these youth are significantly different from approaches found in traditional schools.

Effective alternative or at-risk education programs have a far broader set of instructional goals than traditional schools (Raywid, 1983; Young, 1990). Since most at-risk youth suffer from low self-esteem, effective programs must add this as an essential curricular area. It is evident that when the improvement of student self-esteem becomes an instructional goal, remarkable growth can occur (Smith, Thomas, & Pugh, 1981; Young, 1990). If students lack basic skills, regardless of the students' age, this too must become one of the primary instructional goals. If students are pregnant, they need instruction in prenatal care and nutrition. If students are drug dependent, this problem must be addressed. Each of these and other special curricular components must supplement traditional curriculum and graduation requirements (Wehlage, Rutter, & Turnbaugh, 1987).

Restructuring Schools to Meet At-Risk Needs

Effective alternative education programs must tailor their school programs to the needs of at-risk youth (Raywid, 1983; Wehlage, et al., 1989; Young, 1990). Simply providing evening programs for students who work is often sufficient to keep youth in school through graduation. Some programs have developed flexible entry and exit points rather than having school terms established by calendar dates. Some programs provide opportunities for students to attend school part-time. Some alternative programs offer a menu of options to the traditional high-school diploma such as specialized area diplomas, general equivalency diplomas, or vocational educational certificates. However, while all students need basic skills and job preparation, increasingly the job market requires that students earn a standard high school diploma.

Nowhere is the need to restructure schools more evident than at the early elementary level. It is now clear that *all* children can learn to read during the first three years of school, but this cannot be accomplished without some appropriate combination of one-to-one tutoring, parent education and participation programs, and an enriched curriculum. Especially for the at-risk child, nongraded continuous progress schools seem exceptionally promising as an alternative to retention in the early grades. We know that in order to meet the needs of at-risk youth successfully, schools must be restructured in dramatic ways. Descriptions of such schools will be presented in later chapters.

Designing Instruction to Address At-Risk Learning Characteristics

Students who fail in traditional classrooms have often been found to be very successful in instructional programs that allow them to work at their own pace, focus on their own instructional needs, use incentives for learning, and use teachers as facilitators (Barr, Parrett & Colston, 1977; Wehlage, et al., 1989; Young, 1990). Such individualized, personalized learning has long been designed and available for special education students. We now recognize that it is also essential and effective for at-risk youth.

The overriding goal of a redesigned school curriculum is for the at-risk student to acquire basic skills and to begin experiencing academic success and achievement. Once this occurs, students will develop more positive attitudes towards self and school and, quite possibly, society.

Small, Supportive Environments

In a very real sense, effective at-risk programs insulate students from the negative factors of traditional schools and serve to incubate student learning and growth. Research on small schools, rural schools, and alternative education programs emphasizes the importance of small, personalized learning environments. The average enrollment of alternative schools in the United States is approximately 175 students. This means that a relatively small group of students work closely with a cadre of caring and demanding teachers. These small education environments can be viewed as communities of support or as educational intensive care units serving the critical needs of at-risk youth (Gregory, 1992; Muncey and McQuillan, 1993; Office of Educational Research and Improvement, 1987; Wehlage, et al., 1989).

Out-of-School Learning Experiences

We know that some things must be learned in school, but some things can never be learned in school. Some of the most powerful learning experiences happen outside the classroom walls (Barr & Smith, 1976; Nathan, 1989). Internships, community service programs, apprenticeships, career exploration, independent studies, and experiential or action learning programs may prove far more beneficial to students than programs that rely solely on classroom learning. Ever since the late 1960s when the Philadelphia Parkway School moved learning beyond the walls of the school—into the banks, museums, factories, businesses, farms, hospitals, and a host of other locations—out-of-school learning experiences have continued to demonstrate an effective and important pathway to learning.

Transition to Work

To be ultimately successful, education for at-risk youth must provide students with some systematic opportunity to survey career and job opportunities and to provide instruction and assistance to supplement the public school program. Few public schools provide students direct assistance in obtaining jobs during high school. Most high-school counselors invest the majority of their time and energy in ensuring that students meet graduation and college entrance requirements. Relatively little school effort is invested in helping students to select a career, obtain job information and experience, and choose a vocation. Few schools offer transition to work or follow-up support. Those schools that do provide these services have repeatedly demonstrated how important career assistance and support can be.

School and Community Partnerships

The problems confronting at-risk youth are not just school problems. For that reason, the most effective programs involve partnerships with business and industry and other social agencies. Schools must work to mobilize volunteers to work with at-risk youth, establish mentor programs, and gain essential support from local business and industry (McMullan, Garrett, Watts, & Wolf, 1992; Northwest Regional Educational Laboratory, 1990). In addition, school-community partnerships provide an invaluable service by establishing a network for transition to the workplace (Smith, 1993).

Students as Resources

There is strong evidence of the powerful positive influence school and community service can have on students, especially at-risk youth. Some agree that such service is essential to the health, growth, and development of children and youth. Effective schools for at-risk youth should offer a variety of out-of-school learning experiences and community service opportunities in child care programs, community centers, senior citizen centers, nursing homes, hospitals, as well as serving in the schools as cross-age tutors (Kohler, 1992; Kurth-Schai, 1988). These experiences not only provide dramatic benefit to at-risk students, but they also serve to support and build essential community relations and support.

Coordination of Community Services

In recent years there has been a growing realization that the most fundamental problems associated with at-risk youth are often far outside the direct influence of the school. At-risk children and youth often come from at-risk, dysfunctional families who need comprehensive, immediate assistance. Outside the school, there exists a bewildering array of community and social agencies that provide child care, health services, counseling, food stamps, welfare payments, housing, transportation, and assistance in job training and employment searches. Increasingly, effective at-risk programs have begun to help their students gain information and access to these services. To accomplish this task, many schools have established coordinators of community services or created youth service teams. Many schools, using a case management approach, work with each student to develop individualized plans to access the school and community services they so desperately need. Some schools have created community councils composed of representatives of all participating agencies and organizations. Other schools have actually housed some or all of these services in the school. To be most effective with at-risk youth, schools must help all students to obtain the community services they need and facilitate the assistance provided by the various organizations and agencies (Hobbs, 1993; Schorr, 1992).

Student Assessment, Follow-Up Evaluation, and Performance Outcomes

The most effective educational programs provide for systematic, ongoing process evaluation (Northwest Regional Educational Laboratory, 1990). It is not enough to develop programs for at-risk youth; districts must carefully evaluate the effectiveness of these new programs. Such developmental evaluation is essential in refining and improving program effectiveness for at-risk youth. Recently, interest in student assessment has expanded beyond standardized achievement testing and is beginning to focus on developing and assessing performance outcomes. This attention to course and graduation competencies is leading toward better defining the expected outcomes. Many programs are exploring the concept of requiring graduation competencies, a practice which was pioneered by the St. Paul Open School in Minnesota over two decades ago. For at-risk youth, the development of enhanced, realistic assessment models will prove indispensable to their achievement and success (Muncey & McQuillan, 1993; Spady & Marshall, 1991; Teddlie & Stringfield, 1993; Wehlage, et al., 1989).

Rural and Urban Environments

It is important to note that effective at-risk programs can work equally well in both urban and rural environments and in distinctively different community settings. In later chapters, programs will be discussed like Success For All, Accelerated Schools, Reading Recovery, and even Foxfire, which have been implemented successfully in both urban and rural settings. Also, the Louisiana School Effectiveness Study found similarities between effective programs both in rural and in urban communities. Such success leads to the conclusion that programs that utilize all or many of the essential components of effective programs may be expected to be successful regardless of setting.

A few of the essential components seem particularly suited for one type of community setting rather than another (Teddlie & Stringfield, 1993). For example, while the coordination of social services may be an essential component in urban areas, such agencies and their support are far more difficult to access in rural areas and may include very different types of service providers. Rural areas may have to depend on the U.S. Agriculture Department's Cooperative Extension Service, 4-H Clubs, Future Farmers of America programs, county social service agencies, and even local churches, while urban communities will often have a larger number of available support services. In rural areas, the Cooperative Extension Service is moving increasingly toward addressing the human needs of rural families rather than focusing only on agriculture and is currently developing prevention and intervention programs in drug and alcohol abuse, teen pregnancy, AIDS education, and other areas of concern to youth.

Other concepts, such as using youth as resources for youth, have been demonstrated with success in both rural and urban areas. Certainly, caring and demanding teachers is a program component equally effective regardless of the community setting. Rural areas will not usually be able to develop magnet schools, alternative schools, and at-risk programs that are feasible in more populous areas. However, there are examples of rural areas developing dropout prevention programs or alternative schools at the county level to serve geographically diverse school districts. Rural areas must capitalize on the small size of their schools. Nongraded schools with one and two teachers still exist in many regions of our nation, and many of these schools report strong track records of success in educating their at-risk youth. While rural and urban communities often differ dramatically, effective school programs do not. Both settings have in common the capacity to be successful with at-risk youth, if the appropriate school climate and learning opportunities exist (Teddlie & Stringfield, 1993).

For too long, schools and communities have closed their eyes to the fact that approximately one-fourth to one-third of all public school youth fail to graduate and that a growing number may graduate with few of the skills necessary to find a job and to effectively participate in contemporary society. This tragic reality can and must be changed. Not only are many schools beginning to recognize the scope of the problem and accept their essential role in addressing this challenge, but business and industry are also recognizing their responsibility regarding the educational challenges that face at-risk youth. We cannot forget that desire and commitment must be matched with adequate resources to support high-quality schools for all. This is not to suggest that the task is easy. We do, however, know how to address this problem effectively.

The effective components detailed in this chapter are absolutely essential to meeting the needs of at-risk youth. They are the building blocks of effective practices and must be used to develop programs and to maintain and evaluate them. More important, research and the evaluation of effective schools and programs have demonstrated, in the most powerful manner, that these essential components can be used with confidence to ensure that every student, even students who are profoundly at risk, can learn effectively and achieve success in public schools. In a very real sense, this is the stuff of the American dream: providing all youth with free public education that effectively prepares them for life, liberty, and the pursuit of happiness. Only time will determine whether or not communities are willing to open the door of opportunity to all youth in the United States.

The next chapters will provide a comprehensive review of how the characteristics of effective programs can be integrated into schools and school programs that work for at-risk youth.

Chapter 6

Programs That Work: Early Childhood and Elementary Schools

While visiting a small elementary school, I was walking down the halls with two teachers on our way to lunch. While passing an open classroom door, one of my friends stopped and called out to a fellow teacher, "Come and join us for lunch." The teacher left a small group of students sitting around her desk and walked over to the door and replied, "I really can't. I've got a group of kids here who are having real problems with their reading, and I've been working with them over part of their lunch period all year."

Knowing the type of students who generally attended this school I responded, "Isn't it sad how tragic so many of these poor kids' lives are?" The teacher turned and gave me a surprised look and said, "You know, I don't care who these kids are or where they're from or what their problems are. Before they leave my classroom I'm going to teach them to read. I can't do much about their home lives, but I can definitely teach them to read."
—(TEACHER, SUNRISE ELEMENTARY SCHOOL, ALBANY, OREGON, 1989)

Many schools and communities begin to develop intervention programs for at-risk students during the late middle- and high-school years when the problems confronting youth often become most visible and dramatic. However, prevention programs for very young children are the most cost-effective and have the greatest potential for lasting success. The period from conception and infancy through third grade encompasses the most critical stage in the development of children. In terms of the potential for personal development and learning, these are indeed the wonder years. For at-risk children this period is even more critical. Without early success in school, at-risk children's hope of successfully completing school diminishes with each passing year. By the end of the elementary-school years, only intensive, comprehensive, and costly intervention programs offer the potential for transforming the lives of these youth.

The period from conception through elementary school is also a time of grave danger for children and youth. Because of prenatal problems and premature births, increasing numbers of infants are being born emotionally and/or learning disabled. If children are battered or sexually abused, they will carry these emotional and psychological scars with them throughout their lives. If children do not receive adequate love and care during infancy, they may fail to bond with an adult and may live out their lives with antisocial behavior. If young children are not talked to, read to, and provided cultural and educational stimulation, their young minds will atrophy rather than grow and develop, and they will arrive at school far from ready to learn. It is these children who will be retained, be tracked into slow learning groups and slow reading groups, and often be assigned to special education. The complex problems of these children, left unattended, may never be overcome after the third or fourth grade.

The problems associated with at-risk youth often originate long before schools ever see the child. When they do arrive at school, too often they are isolated, stigmatized, and overwhelmed with the large, impersonal approach that is the norm in too many of our schools. Middle and high school becomes a time to drop out, turn to drugs, alcohol, or gangs, and enter adulthood with little or no hope of building a satisfactory life.

The opposite of all this is equally true. If children are born healthy and are cared for, supported, and stimulated, they develop security and self-esteem and their minds grow and expand. These students arrive at school with enthusiasm, equipped with an arsenal of skills and attitudes that all but ensure success at school. And if young children learn to read and experience academic success during their early elementary grades, they build a solid foundation for success in school and later life.

None of this is any longer speculation. We now know how to provide for the healthy development of all young children and how to ensure that every child learns to read during the early grades. But solutions to the problems of the nation's youth at risk remain daunting. Like the very problems they address, the solutions are interrelated, costly, long-term, and involve the home, the community, social agencies, and child-care providers as well as the school. Yet there are schools and communities throughout the country that have demonstrated and documented that they can teach all children to read, that they can help all children to learn and experience academic success, and that they can keep almost all children in school until they graduate. Many of these programs have been successful in both rural and urban areas and in wealthy and poor communities. These schools and school programs have been studied and analyzed sufficiently to provide educators with the essential components necessary for success and replication.

The previous chapter provided the theoretical framework and models that are the building blocks of successful programs for at-risk youth. This chapter will focus on a more specific, practical level. If the essential components described in the last chapters provide the beams and braces for building the internal structures of successful programs, this chapter provides the nuts and bolts, the fine line drawing that focuses on the practical, day-to-day realities of schools and communities. It deals with what to do on Monday, what to teach the parents, and how to help children learn to read. This chapter will provide descriptions of successful programs that can be replicated from early childhood through the elementary-school years. Subsequent chapters will focus on the middle and the high-school years. Taken together, these three chapters provide a blueprint for action and success for schools and communities.

In the following pages, brief descriptions are provided of a number of specific programs that have been used in public schools and communities and that have been judged through the process of research and evaluation to be effective with youth who are at risk. Yet a word of caution is necessary. While each of these programs can be successful in improving the learning of participating at-risk children and youth, no single program or practice can effectively meet the needs of such a diverse group of students. Schools must integrate a number of successful approaches into an overall, comprehensive program of intervention.

Family Planning and Health Services

Building a foundation for educational success or failure begins during infancy and possibly during pregnancy. Although there are few issues in the United States so controversial and explosive as family planning, strong evidence exists that children of unwanted pregnancies tend to be less educated, less healthy, and significantly more dependent on public assistance than other children. Unwanted pregnancies often coincide with drug and alcohol abuse, and this in turn has led to a dramatic increase in the incidence of "drug" babies, children who at birth carry the mother's drug or alcohol dependency. Some cities are reporting at least 20 percent of all births are drug babies. Long before many children come in contact with schools, substandard nutrition, sexual abuse, physical abuse, and lack of medical treatment have taken a heavy toll. Schools may never be able to reverse this negative beginning. For schools and communities to be successful with at-risk children and youth, they must provide family planning and health services to all pregnant women and infants (Schorr & Schorr, 1989).

Child Care

Because so many children are born in poverty to single parents and often to teenage parents, significant numbers of children today are reared by adults with few effective parenting skills. This is especially true for teen parents, who are often still children themselves. Research indicates that it is essential to provide child care for children in poverty and especially for teen parents. This is true for several reasons:

- In stark contrast to previous generations, the majority of women with children under five years old work away from home.
- The number of unmarried teens with babies continues to persist at alarming levels.
- There is growing consensus that young welfare mothers must have opportunities to be in educational training programs and should be employed.
- Systematic professional child care can have dramatic long-term positive benefits. (Barr & Ross, 1989; Schorr & Schorr, 1989)

It is now evident that without consistent, effective child care, many children born in poverty may not bond effectively with adults, and that, without this bonding, a life of antisocial psychopathy is predictable. Caring for children under the age of three has become the fastest-growing type of child care program. It is now generally agreed that out-of-home child care, even for very young children, is possible and effective when the staff is well trained, turnover of trained staff is low, and the child-to-staff ratio is low. However, poor-quality child care for small children can be damaging. The characteristics of effective child care have been identified as follows:

- *It must go beyond custodial care to provide intellectual stimulation—with books, the spoken word, play, the interchange of ideas, a developmental orientation, and with nurturance, hugs, approval, and responsiveness.*
- *It must include health, nutrition, and social services.*
- *It must clearly and systematically involve, collaborate with, and provide support to parents.*
- *It must be provided by competent staff, with a staff-child ratio low enough that children at each developmental state get the personal attention they need in order to thrive. (Schorr & Schorr, 1989, p. 202)*

Parent Education

Recent research has led to greater attention being focused on the early childhood years and on the role of the parent as the child's first teacher. While on a common sense level we have always recognized the importance of parents in the education of their children, research has verified such understanding and provided new insights into the influence of parenting techniques. We know that the most important factor in the education of children is not the school, the teacher, or the curriculum; it is the parent (Coleman, 1991). Long before a child arrives in school, parenting practices will have created an able young learner or will have significantly retarded the child's development. We once thought that children were born with basic intelligence, that a person's I.Q. was established at birth. This conclusion could not be further from the truth. We now know that students' mental abilities can be stimulated and expanded during the early years. The reverse is unfortunately also true. Without a fertile learning environment in the home, children will often atrophy intellectually, enter the first grade far behind their classmates, and without costly intervention never catch up. We know that the optimal time for children to learn to read is from three years of age to approximately the third grade and that the most positive force in developing strong literacy skills is the simple practice of parents reading to their children.

Recognizing the essential role of the parent as the child's first teacher, a number of states and a large number of school districts throughout the United States have developed effective parent education programs. The state of Missouri has developed a program for parent education that is often described as a model for other states. The New Parents as Teachers Project, initiated in 1981 through a Danforth grant, has grown from a four-district, 380-parent project to 53,000 families in all 543 school districts of the state. New Parents as Teachers features "education for new parents, physical and developmental screening for children ages one through four, and parent education for parents of three- and four-year olds" (National School Boards Association, 1989, p. 37).

More recently, both commercial and public television have developed programming on educating parents to be more effective teachers and parents. There is also a growing body of superb literature that has translated sophisticated research findings into easy-to-understand practices for parents to use with their children during the early childhood years. There is dramatic evidence that these rather simple practices, such as reading aloud to children and having appropriate reading materials available in the home, can be taught to parents and can have an enormous positive effect on enhancing the learning capabilities of young children (Gathercoal, 1992). Few other programs offer the promise of such lasting influence as that of improved parenting practices. Because of this, schools must recognize that parent education, combined with comprehensive preschool programs, may well be the most necessary and the most cost-effective approach to attacking the problems of at-risk youth.

There are several excellent publications and video programs that focus on a wide variety of behavior and learning outcomes that parents can influence, i.e., self-esteem, work habits, and decision making; others focus specifically on helping children learn to read. With reading problems being identified as the most common characteristic of at-risk children and youth, these publications provide a clear emphasis on these parenting practices that can help to ensure that children will learn to read.

Phi Delta Kappa and the World Book Encyclopedia company have developed a 16-minute videotape entitled *Little Things Make a Big Difference* that can be used in parent education programs. Another video entitled *Read to Me* was developed by the Idaho Literacy Project and is being distributed through the International Reading Association. The University of Illinois has developed a brief yet succinct research-based pamphlet entitled *Ten Ways to Help Your Children Become Better Readers* (Center for the Study of Reading, 1989), and the American Association of School Administrators has developed *101 Ways Parents Can Help Students Achieve* (1991).

Another superb set of brochures has been developed by the ERIC Clearinghouse on Reading and Communication Skills at Indiana University. Once again, these brochures include specific, simplified instructions for parents that are based on the best available research. The brochures include such titles as *How Can I Be Involved in My Child's Education, How Can I Improve My Child's Reading, How Important Is Homework,* and *What Do Parents Need to Know about Children's Television Viewing* (ERIC, 1993). There is also an older yet worthwhile publication developed during the Reagan administration by the Office of Education entitled *What Works,* which includes numerous activities that parents should use in helping their children learn to read and to develop learning skills (U.S. Department of Education, 1987a).

These and other publications that serve to identify effective parenting practices can have an enormous impact on small children. They are also essential to the continued success of adolescent youth. These simple practices may have a more dramatic positive effect than years of schooling. Research recommends the following approaches for all parents to make a significant, lasting, and positive impact on their children.

Parents Can Help Their Children Learn To Read

Parents can play a key role in helping their children become literate. To ensure that children will learn to read and be successful in school, parents should read aloud to young children and infants, even before they are able to comprehend the stories being read. The process of holding, cuddling, and reading to small children is critically important. Research indicates that there are few specific practices that have such positive long-lasting influence as that of reading aloud to infants and young children. Reading aloud provides both the closeness and human warmth that are essential to early bonding; it also provides an essential foundation for school success. As children grow older, parents should encourage the child to participate in the reading by identifying words and letters and talking about the story that they have read.

Parents Should Talk To Their Children, Ask Questions, and Encourage Children To Make Decisions

Talking with children about their experiences helps them to develop new words and to understand what they mean. Talking with children, asking them questions, and encouraging them to make decisions stimulates the young mind by encouraging the skills of expression, communication, and interpretation and helping students to be independent decision makers.

Parents Should Provide a Stimulating Environment for Children

Parents should try to provide a rich variety of experiences to stimulate small children. These do not need to be expensive experiences: trips to shopping malls, grocery stores, parks, zoos, and museums all provide stimulating learning opportunities for children. These excursions provide children with a forum for asking questions, talking, and experiencing real-life events that can be related to the stories that their parents read at home.

Parents Should Encourage Responsible Television Viewing

There are many wonderful, enriching television programs that help children learn about reading and language. These programs, such as Sesame Street, Reading Rainbow, and others that can be found on public television, CNN, and the Discovery Channel, are known to have a positive impact on children's learning and development. Parents should use these programs to intellectually stimulate young children and provide yet another experience about which to talk and ask questions. Careful selection of television viewing of up to ten hours per week can have a slightly positive effect on children's achievement later in school. As the number of hours increase beyond ten, television viewing becomes a negative influence. Children who watch more than 20 hours of television per week usually do poorly in school (ERIC, 1990).

Parents Should Be Interested and Involved in Their Children's School

Research indicates that the more parents are interested and involved in children's schoolwork, the better children tend to do in school. Parents should regularly visit their child's school, become acquainted with the teacher, learn how they can help their children at home, and discuss how they can encourage the child to be more effective in school.

Parents Must Provide a Safe, Loving Environment for Young Children

Overshadowing all other practices, parents must provide young children with love, care, and security in order for them to develop secure, positive self-concepts and self-esteem. While this should go without saying, we know the opposite is unfortunately true, and child abuse, sexual abuse, and poor nutrition are a way of life for many children. In this age of rampant poverty, divorce, single and teenage parents, and latchkey children, the loving, secure environment that is so essential to children's development is too often sadly lacking. Many children are so deprived of basic love and security that they fail to bond with any adult. Others spend lonely lives in front of televisions, accompanied by brothers and sisters, and arrive at school without the stimulation, support, and self-esteem that is necessary for success in school. Parents must be helped to understand how to love, care for, and discipline their children in positive ways. And in the absence of caring parents, child-care providers and school programs must attempt to provide the essential support that these children so desperately need.

Early Childhood Programs

"Success in the early childhood years is a critical prerequisite for success in later schooling and ultimately in life" (McPartland & Slavin, 1990, p. 7). The inverse is unfortunately also true. Children who begin school academically behind their peers will rarely catch up, unless provided with intensive intervention programs to address their needs.

To provide for maximum success, programs for at-risk children must begin much earlier than the school years. In fact, to be most effective, the programs should focus on the health and well-being of the child's mother before birth and continue throughout infancy and child care, preschool and kindergarten programs. There is mounting evidence that when poor preschool children and elementary school children are provided enriched early education which combines high expectations with immunizations, medical checkups, hot meals, and social services, almost all children can be successfully taught to read in the early grades and thus begin their education with a strong foundation for success (Schorr & Schorr, 1989, p. 189).

One of the most successful federal programs for providing assistance to preschool youth is Head Start. Started in 1965 as an intensive summer program during President Lyndon Johnson's "war on poverty," the federal program continues to serve over 600,000 disadvantaged preschool youth with an allocation of over $2 billion per year (Lang, 1992). A wide variety of research has documented that the Head Start program has had strong positive effects on language development and IQ scores. Lisbeth and Daniel Schorr address this issue in their classic work, *Within Our Reach:*

> *We now know that the education, health, nutrition, social services and parent support provided by these Head Start programs have prevented or ameliorated many of the educational handicaps associated with growing up in poverty. We now know that children who have attended quality early childhood programs develop social and academic competencies that are later manifested in increased school success. They enter school healthier, better fed, and with parents who are better equipped to support their educational development. . . . When three to five-year-old children are systematically helped to think, reason, and speak clearly; when they are provided hot meals, social services, health evaluations and care; when families become partners in their children's learning experiences, are*

*helped toward self-sufficiency, and greater confidence in themselves as parents
and as contributing members of the community, the results are measurable and
dramatic (Schorr & Schorr, 1989, p. 192).*

Unfortunately, research has also documented that the early positive effects of
Head Start can diminish rapidly with each subsequent year until, for the most part,
they are undetectable by the end of the second or third grade. This result has led
to a variety of follow-through programs that attempt to maintain and continue educational enrichment gains from preschool and early elementary years. There is
also evidence from longitudinal studies that Head Start children do have long-
term positive gains in high-school graduation and lack of delinquency (McPartland & Slavin, 1990). Many states have developed programs to supplement the
success of Head Start with names like Great Start, Even Start, and Strong Start.
These programs have been developed to address the needs of children unable to
participate in Head Start. These programs focus on parenting skills, literacy, and a
variety of developmental opportunities.

Kindergarten

Almost everyone has come to agree on the value of kindergarten; in most states,
kindergarten attendance is now required. Today, kindergarten enrollment is the
fastest-growing area of public education. Research focusing on full-day kindergarten compared to half-day programs and on the available curricula have found
the effects of all-day kindergarten to be similar to the effects of preschool programs: initial positive results are likely to diminish quickly without continued pro-
grammatic support. Like preschool, kindergarten is not sufficient to ensure lasting
educational success, but it is an essential foundation to later success (Schorr &
Schorr, 1989).

The debate continues regarding the most appropriate, most effective kindergarten curriculum. This debate centers around whether or not kindergartens
should be highly academic or nonacademic or how to balance these two positions.
Some feel that the first-grade curriculum should be simply moved down to the
kindergarten level while others believe that too much academic pressure on young
children is debilitating to their development. Many educators now support a developmentally appropriate curriculum (Charlesworth, 1989).

Increasingly, research has begun to identify those aspects of the kindergarten
curriculum that are most significant. And while it is important to have extended
or all-day kindergarten, how the kindergarten students spend their time appears
to be equally as important as the amount of time spent in kindergarten. Early
childhood curriculum experts believe that the kindergarten curriculum should
offer a variety and balance of activities that are provided in the context of project work which might include investigating real objects or events (Katz and
Chad, 1989). Examples of a good kindergarten curriculum include:

- *Integrated topic studies, rather than whole-group instruction in isolated skills*
- *Opportunities for children to learn by observing and experimenting with real objects*
- *A balance of child- and teacher-initiated activities*
- *Opportunities for spontaneous play and teacher-facilitated activities*
- *Group projects in which cooperation can occur naturally*
- *A range of activities requiring the use of large and small muscles*
- *Exposure to good literature and music of the children's own culture and of other cultures represented in the class*
- *Authentic assessment of each child's developmental progress*
- *Opportunities for children with diverse backgrounds and developmental levels to participate in whole-group activities*
- *Time for individuals or small groups of children to meet with the teacher for specific help in acquiring basic reading, writing, mathematical, and other skills as needed (ERIC, 1993, p. 1)*

Elementary School Programs for At-Risk Youth

As previously indicated, there is a best time to address the needs of at-risk youth. That opportune time is as early as possible. For schools, this means that the maximum opportunity to have a positive impact on children is in kindergarten and grades one through three. Increasingly, schools are establishing child-care programs, especially for their teen parents, and expanding preschool and Head Start programs.

Early intervention programs have enormous potential for at-risk students. These programs are effective because children tend to arrive at school excited and eager to learn. Unfortunately, in some urban districts, as many as 20 percent of these new students fail the first grade and are retained (Madden, Slavin, Karweit, Dolan, & Wasik, 1991). Others begin falling behind during the first grade, and each year the gap widens between their achievement and the achievement of their peers. The longer at-risk students stay in school without intervention, the farther they tend to fall behind. By the 6th grade their achievement is two years behind grade level on average, and by the 12th grade, if they are still in school, they are four years behind.

Guaranteeing That Every Child Learns to Read

The good news is that research, evaluation, and long-term student follow-up assessment have made it dramatically clear that all students, with the exception of a very small number of seriously mentally impaired, can be taught to read. Today, there are a number of programs available to schools and communities that have well-documented track records of success in teaching all children, even those seriously behind, the skills of reading.

So compelling is current research and program development in reading that it is now possible to predict success, or as a growing number of schools are doing, to guarantee parents that their children will learn to read. This remarkable development in teaching and learning represents perhaps the most important advancement in schooling since public education was made available to all children. As reported earlier, reading deficiency is the most identified problem in every study of at-risk children. Now we have the means to correct this problem (Wasik & Slavin, 1993; Slavin, Karweit, & Wasik, 1992).

Every parent should demand that local elementary schools provide assurances that their children will learn to read and seek information regarding what they can do to assist in this process. The time has come when schools must ensure that all children learn to read. This may require that certain expectations be established between the school and the home. Parents must assist their children by reading at home and monitoring homework for a specified amount of time each day. Parents must, if at all possible, keep the children in the same school for at least the first three to four years of school. With little more than these two assurances, the school should be able to teach all children to read.

Reading as an Entitlement

Because of the importance of reading and the positive developments that have occurred in reading instruction, there is a growing national consensus that learning to read is an entitlement for all children. Recently the Council of Chief State School Officers published a report that described model state statutes which would entitle every child not only to an appropriate education, but the opportunity to gain an acceptable level of achievement (1989). As Robert Slavin, one of the nation's leading scholars on the study of at-risk youth and reading instruction, has said, "If success is seen as an entitlement, educators must have methods that produce success for all non-retarded children regardless of home background, no matter how expensive these methods may be" (Wasik & Slavin, 1993, p. 180).

Recognizing the importance of learning to read early, an increasing number of elementary schools are reallocating school resources from the upper grades (fourth, fifth, and sixth) to enrich the resources of the early grades. Public education now possesses the knowledge, methodology, and access to model programs to achieve the goal of teaching every child to read. Implementing this knowledge and methodology into comprehensive, schoolwide programs represents the critical challenge public schools must confront if all children, particularly those at risk, are to succeed in school.

Schoolwide Elementary Programs

There are a number of independent instructional components that have been documented as highly successful with at-risk children during the elementary years. These components (tutoring, extended day programs, cooperative learning, and computer-assisted instruction) will be discussed later in this section. What is most promising is that when effective components are blended into a comprehensive program, truly exceptional gains can occur with at-risk children.

A number of schoolwide elementary programs and approaches have been developed which focus on at-risk youth. Evaluation data and student assessment results suggest that these schoolwide programs are extremely effective. Offering the most supportive evidence are the Success For All Programs, Accelerated Schools, Development Program Schools, Continuous Progress Schools, and Alternative Public Schools.

Success For All

> *We have been a Success For All School for three years and it has been an incredible experience. We started out providing one-to-one tutoring in reading every other day, but we failed to get the results we wanted. Now, we have trained just about every adult in the school as a tutor, moved instructional aides from the upper grades down into the lower grades and are providing daily tutoring as part of our total educational program. While we believe that we must teach children to read during the first three grades and that they will then be more successful in the upper grades with fewer instructional aides and fewer resources, we still worry about reducing resources at the upper grades. But while we are still experimenting and still learning, we have been incredibly successful. All our kids are reading up to grade level and beyond by the end of the third grade. And our students come from a relatively poor, rural area.*
> *—(A SUCCESS FOR ALL SCHOOL PRINCIPAL, CANYON ELEMENTARY SCHOOL, VALLEY VIEW, IDAHO, 1993)*

The Success For All (SFA) project, in its fourth year of operation, is coordinated by Robert Slavin and other leading scholars at Johns Hopkins University. The SFA school concept was started in seven schools in three of the most disadvantaged urban and rural school districts in the country. Today there are over 200 SFA schools throughout the United States. The SFA program prescribes a schoolwide effort that has successfully experimented with Chapter 1 funds to enrich the entire school student body, rather than to support a separate pullout program. The SFA approach is grounded in a strong foundational knowledge base and has demonstrated exceptional success in helping at-risk youth achievement (Madden, et al., 1991).

The SFA schools emphasize the importance of early intervention. As Slavin and his colleagues have stressed, "the most important goal in educational programming for students at risk is to try to make certain that we do not squander the greatest resource we have: the enthusiasm and positive self-expectations of young children themselves" (Madden, et al., 1991, p. 594). As a result of this belief, Slavin has been instrumental in developing the SFA approach, which has four major goals:

- *Ensure that every student will perform at grade level in reading, writing and mathematics by the end of the third grade.*

- *Reduce the number of students referred to special education classes.*
- *Reduce the number of children who are held back a grade.*
- *Increase attendance.*

Research has documented that the SFA program has been successful in achieving all of these goals (Education Commission of the States, 1991, p. 21).

Characteristics of the SFA schools include the following:

Reading Tutors

Chapter 1 funds are used to employ certified reading teachers who provide one-on-one reading instruction, which Slavin maintains is the "most effective form of instruction known" (Madden, et al., 1991, p. 594). The program focuses on students who are having difficulty in their reading groups and consists of 20-minute daily tutoring sessions. This tutoring is not used as a pull-out program.

Cross-Age Reading Groups

Using a method of student grouping called the Joplin Plan, first-, second-, and third-grade students are cross-age grouped for 90 minutes each day, according to reading level. This enables teachers to instruct an entire classroom of students who are functioning at the same reading level.

Family Support Teams

Family support teams are organized that encourage attendance, coordinate social services, train volunteers, work for better behavior, and help parents to ensure that their children will be successful in school.

Building Advisory Committees

SFA schools establish an advisory committee composed of the principal, facilitators, teachers, and parents to help shape policy and plan the program. A key role of this committee is to assess student reading levels at eight-week intervals. The results are then used to determine who needs tutoring. A recent evaluation of the SFA schools found that their students were far out-performing matched control groups. Students in 22 first-grade, 14 second-grade and 7 third-grade cohorts in 8 SFA schools out-performed the control groups by three months at the first-grade level, five months in the second grade and almost seven months at the end of grade three (Ascher, 1993). Although not all children in the SFA schools were reading at grade level, they were close enough to grade level that they could benefit from classroom instruction in the other subject areas (Ascher, 1993).

Perhaps most important within SFA schools, there exists a schoolwide commitment and consensus toward the belief that all children can learn. Teachers in the schools are determined that all children will learn, and classrooms exhibit high expectations and teamwork between school and community. Today, SFA schools demand that 90 percent of the teachers in a school must agree to participate in a long-range program of reform. In a continuous effort to improve, SFA schools are also using STaR, story telling and retelling, during the prekindergarten and all-day kindergarten program, and employ a variety of newly developed reading materials (Madden, et al., 1991). It is encouraging to visit SFA schools in their third or fourth year and discover that all third graders are reading at grade level.

Despite early successes, teachers and administrators working in SFA schools often worry about the effects of consolidating resources and efforts for the first three grades, even though they know that this approach is enabling students to catch up during the upper elementary grades. The SFA schools provide proof of how research-based approaches can be integrated into a schoolwide approach to effectively teach at-risk youth. No other elementary-school program has so carefully researched their program; none has reported such significant evidence of success.

Accelerated Schools

> *The school has emerged with a clearer and more unified focus, a greater capacity for understanding and overcoming its challenges, and most importantly, a deep-rooted belief in the ability of all of its children to excel if properly nurtured. (Mason Elementary School: Helping children beat the odds, 1993, p. 4)*

Growing out of a concern that the traditional elementary school model was actually inhibiting the educational progress of many youth, Levin and his associates at Stanford University developed the concept of accelerated learning and in 1986 initiated the Accelerated School Project. Levin and his colleagues are now working in over 500 schools in 30 states, all with large at-risk student populations. They are attempting to transform these schools into places of accelerated learning. The concept of accelerated schooling is based on a very simple set of principles. First, Levin believes that at-risk students need and deserve the same approach as gifted and talented students, mainly to accelerate their learning rather than slow it down. Second, the entire school must share a unity of purpose and teachers must be empowered to have control over schools. Third, everyone involved must have high expectations for student learning (Levin, 1991c).

Accelerated schools share the following characteristics:

- *Change the entire structure of the school instead of simply grafting remedial classes onto a school with a conventional agenda*
- *Empower teachers to plan the school's educational program*
- *Require substantial parental involvement (parents are expected to sign an agreement detailing their obligations to their children)*
- *Utilize the services of businesses, college students, senior citizens, and other community resources*
- *Use an extended day program with emphasis on language and problem solving*
- *Stress acceleration rather than remediation and attempt to bring all students to grade level by the end of the sixth grade (Levin, 1989, p. 3)*

These programs exceed the traditional range of practice regarding the education of at-risk students. This is done in the following manner:

- *Instead of labeling certain children as slow learners, accelerated schools have high expectations for all students.*
- *Instead of relegating students to remedial classes without setting goals for improvement, accelerated schools set deadlines for making such children academically able.*
- *Instead of slowing down the pace of instruction for at-risk students, accelerated schools combine relevant curriculum, powerful and diverse instructional techniques, and creative school organization to accelerate the progress of all students.*
- *Instead of providing instruction based on "drill and kill" worksheets, accelerated schools offer stimulating instructional programs based on problem-solving and interesting applications. (What are accelerated schools?, 1991, p. 1)*

Equally important to the success of the accelerated schools approach is the careful change strategy the Stanford team has developed. In order for a school to be associated with the accelerated school network, a school district must make an application, send a staff member for an eight-day training program at Stanford, and attain a 90 percent participation from the teaching faculty of the school or schools (typically three schools are proposed). Applicants for training are interviewed via telephone and asked to make a three-to-five-year professional commitment. The school district or the district and the university partner must commit to ongoing staff development of at least one day per week for the trainer in the school or schools, and the cost of consultants from Stanford to visit the schools several times a year. The accelerated school network staff believes that the process of change cannot be accomplished in a month, six months, or a year. A complete transformation from a traditional school to an accelerated school takes about six years (Ascher, 1993). Consistent work toward goals and the nurturing of a long-term relationship among committed, trained staff ensures a successful transition.

The accelerated school program is expanding the network of schools each year and has been funded by Chevron USA to develop satellite centers at four other universities, including Texas A&M, California State University at Los Angeles, the University of New Orleans, and San Francisco State University (What are accelerated schools? 1991). Chevron studied more than 250 projects and programs before selecting the accelerated school program as their centerpiece of educational reform. While it is too early to determine the long-term impact of accelerated schools on children at risk, progress to date of participating students is extremely encouraging (What are accelerated schools? 1991).

School Development Program

In 1968, Dr. Comer walked into the inner-city Baldwin School in New Haven for the first time. It was a school with boarded up windows and a playground strewn with glass. A school where teachers often didn't show up for work and where students ran out of control up and down the hallways. A school where, as Dr. Comer notes, you could feel the hand of hopelessness. But through the School Development Program forged by James Comer and his colleagues, the teachers, parents and community came together in new and innovative ways to turn Baldwin and several other New Haven schools around. (Edelman, 1993, p. viii)

James P. Comer, a child psychiatrist and director of the School Development Program at Yale University's Child Study Center, has developed an approach for school improvement that has experienced remarkable success with at-risk youth. Developed during several years of collaboration with the New Haven, Connecticut, public schools and later expanded to over 50 schools in Maryland, Michigan, Arkansas, Virginia, and Kansas, Comer's intervention model addresses the problems of poor minority youth who come from environments that often possess values which conflict with the mainstream American values found in public education. Students from poor minority homes often come from families who not only do not trust or support public education but often voice and act out in direct opposition to schools.

Concerned that educational reform typically focuses on instructional and curricular issues, Comer developed an approach that focuses on bridging the social and cultural gap between the home and the school. As Comer has stated:

A child from a poor, marginal family is likely to enter school without adequate preparation. The child may arrive without ever having learned such social skills as negotiation and compromise. A child who is expected to read at school may come from a home where no one reads and may never have heard a parent read bedtime stories. The child's language skills may be underdeveloped or non-standard. Expectations at home and at school may be radically at odds. For example, in some families a child who does not fight back will be punished. And yet the same behavior will get the child into trouble at school. (Comer, 1988, p. 45)

Comer's approach emphasized that the key to academic achievement was to encourage the psychological development of students, to encourage bonding between students and the school. This, he found, is best accomplished through fostering positive development between parents and school staff. In each of the Comer intervention schools, a governance and management team and a mental health team is developed. The management team includes approximately 12 individuals led by the principal and consists of elected parents, teachers, a mental health specialist, and members of the nonprofessional support staff. This group is charged with making recommendations and decisions on a broad range of issues which impact a variety of academic and social procedural changes in the school environment. Mental health teams often include a social worker, the school psychologist, counselor, nurse, speech and hearing teacher, and the principal. This group uses a case management approach to ensure that every child is progressing satisfactorily in the school. Schools where these teams work usually develop very different programs and practices. In one school, students stay with the same teacher for two years. In another, a discovery room was established for troubled children to develop positive relationships with an adult and learn through play. In another school, a crisis room was created to help students cool off and calm down in a positive atmosphere. Yet in each school, the key characteristics of the management team were having parents and teachers work together for common goals and using a case management approach to focus the attention of specialists, parents, and teachers on particular students and their problems. The management teams are guided by three simple but effective principles: no-fault assessment (the teams focus on problems rather than on affixing blame), the teams are truly collaborative, and the teams work for consensus (Ascher, 1993).

The results of this approach with the New Haven schools have been most impressive. Comer explains:

> The students had once ranked lowest in achievement among the 33 elementary schools in the city, but by 1979, without any change in the socioeconomic makeup of the schools, students in the fourth grade had caught up to their grade level. By 1984 pupils in the fourth grade in the two schools ranked third and fourth-highest on the Iowa Test of Basic Skills. By the early 1980s, attendance rates (at one of the schools) were either first or second in the city. There have been no serious behavioral problems at either of the schools in more than a decade. (Comer, 1988, p. 48)

To achieve this record of success, Comer schools each developed a collaborative school plan with specified goals, a program to monitor and assess progress toward the goals, and ongoing staff development programs designed to provide the school and community with the skills necessary to achieve their goals.

A Continuous Progress Approach to Learning and Schooling

Increasingly, successful schools have replaced the usual elementary grades with a continuous progress approach that emphasizes developmentally appropriate learning and often nongraded instruction. These schools enable the students to pursue well-defined educational goals at their own pace and ensure they are developmentally able to achieve. Instruction is provided to small groups of students, usually including children from many different age levels who have similar skill levels. Students may work in different skill levels in each of the various subject areas (McPartland & Slavin, 1990). Schools are able to avoid retaining elementary students while simultaneously focusing instruction on individual needs. Coupled with high expectations, this means that students can rapidly progress to higher achievement levels.

Overland Elementary School in Burley, Idaho, has randomly sorted second-, third-, and fourth-graders into classroom groups. Teachers in these nongraded student clusters each instruct a specific content area such as math, science, social studies, or language arts. This means that each teacher is responsible for every child in the school, and the cross-age grouping encourages peer teaching and co-operative learning. Moreover, this approach allows for a teacher to extend expertise in a given field as opposed to having to teach all content. Reading and math achievement at Overland has climbed from the 17th to the 76th percentile within the district. Most remarkable is the fact that second graders learned multiplication from the older students.

A number of schools and programs have employed the concepts of continuous progress, developmentally appropriate learning, and nongraded instruction as the building blocks of both their conventional as well as their alternative programs. The states of Oregon and Kentucky have actually mandated that all public elementary schools adopt these concepts.

Elementary Alternative Schools

Beginning in the late 1960s, public school districts throughout the United States, especially in urban areas, began to develop alternative schools. While many school districts continue to experiment and develop new and increasing numbers of alternatives, some of the most notable programs have been in operation for over 25 years. Some of these schools represent the best, most creative examples of restructured schools found in all of U.S. public education. Some of these schools are K–12, serving entire school districts, others focus on high school or middle school only, and many exist as elementary schools especially designed to meet the needs of certain groups of students. Some elementary alternative schools have been developed as small schools within schools. What makes these schools so distinctive is that parents, teachers, and students voluntarily choose to participate in a different approach from that typically available in the conventional elementary school.

Elementary alternative schools have been developed for four basic reasons:

- *The belief that children learn in different ways*
- *The belief that teachers teach in different ways*
- *The belief that students, parents, and teachers who have a particular learning style or philosophy ought to be able to choose to work together in a school setting*
- *As a component in school desegregation plans in order to enable children of different ethnic groups to attend school together (Barr, 1981)*

While some alternative elementary schools offer choices for talented, high achieving youth (science and math academies and programs focusing on language immersion, environmental studies, performing arts, and others), many of these programs were designed to address the needs of at-risk youth. Supported by a growing research base and years of practical experience regarding teaching and learning styles, these schools are flourishing.

Montessori Schools

Based on the classic work of the Italian physician Maria Montessori, the Montessori concept has been available to parents able to afford private school tuition costs for over 100 years. During the late 1970s, Cincinnati and Indianapolis became the first school districts in America to offer Montessori schools as part of public education. This growth of Montessori schools has continued for the past 15 years as more and more public schools have incorporated the highly successful Montessori approach into their educational program. Over 90 Montessori Public Schools are in operation today nationwide (Education Commission of the States, 1991). This has meant that, for the first time, many parents of at-risk children have an opportunity to enroll their children in an educational program which focuses on developmentally appropriate learning, an approach which can be critically important in the early development of these children.

School #56, one of the public Montessori options in Indianapolis, provides a K–5 program which incorporates a full-day kindergarten into its highly individualized approach to learning. Following 12 years of successful operation, School #56 clearly demonstrates the efficacy of this approach as an option within public education.

Back-to-Basics Traditional Schools

Many public schools have developed elementary alternative programs that model private schools. One of the most popular alternative programs during the 1980s was the back-to-basics school. Often requiring dress, behavior, and homework codes, these traditional schools provide an educational program based on high expectations, solid grounding in basic subjects, and relatively few special programs.

The Jefferson County public schools in Louisville, Kentucky, established several of the first back-to-basics schools in the early 1980s. Today, this district continues to offer three elementary, three middle and two high schools that focus on the traditional back-to-basics model. Greathouse Shyrock Traditional Elementary enrolls 576 students in its K–5 school which features a nongraded primary, strong parental involvement, strict dress codes, and a culturally and economically diverse student body. Despite continued success in Louisville and other cities during recent years, the nationwide popularity of the traditional back-to-basics model has begun to decline (Estes, Levin, & Waldrip, 1990).

Nongraded, Developmentally Appropriate Schools

A considerable number of elementary alternative schools have been developed throughout the United States using a nongraded, developmentally appropriate approach to learning. These schools utilize highly individualized programs that incorporate developmentally appropriate practices in a nongraded curriculum. Some of the nation's first nongraded elementary schools were established in the Minneapolis, Minnesota, public schools over 20 years ago. Today, 17 nongraded elementary schools, including open concept, continuous progress, and Montessori programs, are available by choice to parents and children in Minneapolis.

Open Schools

The K–12 St. Paul Open School in St. Paul, Minnesota, was developed in the early 1970s and provides the classic example of a U.S. open school. While the majority of open schools in the United States were modeled after the British infant school concept, the St. Paul Open School was based on the research and philosophy developed during the Eight-Year Study, which had been conducted three decades earlier to investigate the relationship between success in college and college entrance requirements. The St. Paul Open School was one of the first public schools in America to eliminate course requirements for graduation and to replace them with graduation competencies. The school serves the entire St. Paul school district and enrolls a widely diverse student body. Today each student who attends the school must validate an adequate performance in each of the school's competency areas. (See Table 7-3.)

The St. Paul Open School's elementary program incorporates the concepts of cross-age teaching and tutoring, out-of-school learning experiences, and authentic student assessment into its program of study. This school provides a proven model for restructuring public education in the U.S. today, as the St. Paul Open School may have been studied and evaluated more than any other school in the nation. When compared to students in other St. Paul schools and in follow-up studies conducted four years after graduation, the Open School students appeared to be better adjusted, possessed a better understanding of academic knowledge, and were more successful following school graduation. The St. Paul Open School has been used as a model to establish a growing number of Community Learning Centers in Minneapolis, St. Paul, and throughout the state of Minnesota. The founding principal, Wayne Jennings, and the curriculum director, Joe Nathan, of the St. Paul Open School recently have been funded by the New American Schools Corporation to expand and network these Community Learning Centers.

Magnet Schools

For over 20 years, magnet schools have been used as an effective strategy to aid in districtwide school desegregation efforts. Today, many of these schools provide rich multicultural learning opportunities for diverse urban populations. Across the nation, school districts have developed magnet schools which emphasize the visual and performing arts, environmental education, technology, foreign language study, and others. The Hawthorne Elementary School, part of the Seattle Public Schools Magnet Program, serves as an excellent example of the magnet approach. The school is characterized by a rich academic and cultural program that is focused on African-American students and their culture. The multicultural faculty, staff, parents, and students embrace the primary goal of the school, which is to ensure that all students complete the elementary years with an adequate level of student achievement. The school is organized around a number of principles, including the following:

Student Warranty:

The school emphasizes high expectations for all students; in fact, the school is one of the few in this country that provides a warranty for students and parents. The warranty assures parents that if they will keep their children in the school for five years, the school guarantees that the students will be achieving at grade level.

Each Teacher is Responsible for All Children:
Each of the teachers in the school has responsibility for all children. This means that each teacher has high expectations for all children in the school, monitors all children on the playground and in hallways, and is personally responsible for all children who are not achieving up to grade level. (Hawthorne School, 1991, pp. 1–4)

The early development of alternative schools represented the first time public schools were created specifically to attract a rich diversity of socioeconomic and ethnic backgrounds and academic abilities into a single school. Many of these alternatives accepted students who had formerly been assigned to special education yet were realizing limited success there. Each of these elementary alternative schools combined high expectations, student assessment, parental involvement, and out-of-school learning experiences to build effective programs. Research and evaluation of these schools have been extremely positive (Young, 1990).

Effective Elementary-School Practices for At-Risk Youth

The schools described above represent examples of elementary schools that have been unusually successful in addressing the needs of at-risk youth through comprehensive, schoolwide efforts. In addition to these schoolwide efforts, there are particular approaches at the elementary-school level that have been documented as highly successful with at-risk youth, even when they were not used in a schoolwide comprehensive approach. The research is quite clear that the best way to meet the needs of at-risk youth at the elementary level is through schoolwide programs that integrate the various approaches into a comprehensive effort. However, the demands placed on the schools by increasing numbers of at-risk children require that schools must begin implementing practices that are known to work.

One-to-One Tutoring

One-to-one tutoring is the most effective form of instruction known (Slavin, et al., 1992). One-to-one tutoring offers immense potential for use in the first grade to ensure that all children without serious learning disabilities can learn to read, especially when the tutor is a trained professional. Research and evaluation of one-to-one tutoring using trained professionals have demonstrated the dramatic effectiveness of this educational approach, especially with at-risk youth (Center for Research on Effective Schooling for Disadvantaged Students, 1990). First-grade success in reading has long-term positive effects on at-risk youth, either without additional intervention or with low-cost continuing intervention. "These long-term effects include achievement in later grades, less retention, fewer referrals to special education, and reduced dropouts" (Center for Research on Effective Schooling for Disadvantaged Students, 1990, p. 1).

The primary obstacle to implementing tutoring programs typically centers around cost, since the majority of the programs that have been studied use trained, certified teachers to provide the one-to-one tutoring. However, when one considers the long-term positive influences on children who learn to read versus the long-term societal costs of not learning to read and dropping out of school, implementing tutoring programs in elementary schools makes eminent sense. The Center for Research on Effective Schooling for Disadvantaged Students has identified five programs that have demonstrated considerable success. They include Reading Recovery, Success For All, Wallach Tutorial Programs, Programmed Tutorial Reading, and Prevention of Learning Disabilities. Each of these programs has been studied extensively and each provides impressive evidence documenting the effectiveness of one-to-one tutoring programs that use professional tutors (Wasik & Slavin, 1993).

The tutoring approach that has been researched most carefully over time is Reading Recovery (Pinnell, 1990; Pinnell, Lyons, DeFord, Bryk, & Seltzer, 1994; and Clay, 1991). This early early intervention approach is a unique program credited to Marie Clay, a New Zealand child psychologist. Clay designed and refined the program and conducted the early research on this intervention approach. Later, the program was expanded and studied at The Ohio State University and has emerged as a highly successful approach for teaching reading to the poorest readers in the school.

The program relies on the use of certified teachers who have been trained in the Reading Recovery approach (a training program that is approximately one year in length and requires an internship). The program is implemented in elementary schools and focuses on the lowest achieving students in the first grade. In addition to classroom reading instruction, these students are provided supplemental, intensive, one-to-one tutoring for 30 minutes each day for approximately 16 weeks. The Reading Recovery teacher tutors each child to become an independent reader. When the goal is attained, the tutoring is discontinued and the next lowest level reader takes his or her place in the program (Wasik & Slavin, 1993).

After nine years of study in New Zealand, research and evaluation of the Reading Recovery approach found that "regardless of sex, socioeconomic status, or social linguistic group, the lowest achieving children make accelerated progress in the program and continue to make satisfactory progress after release from the program" (Pinnell, 1990, p. 19). Fewer than 1 percent of the students in the program have needed further referral.

Through more recent comparative studies in Ohio, it was found that Reading Recovery children "achieved at higher levels than did children who received other compensatory treatments" (Wasik & Slavin, 1993, pp. 185–187). Reading Recovery children were found to read material three levels above comparison children. Ninety percent of the Reading Recovery children met or exceeded the average range in reading. An Ohio follow-up study of Reading Recovery graduates found that by the third grade, the Reading Recovery children could read material one grade level above comparison children, and 69 percent met or exceeded the average range of reading ability of their fellow students. The research clearly indicates that Reading Recovery has immediate as well as long-term positive results. Reading Recovery teaches low-achieving children to read and write and helps them to progress rapidly to the levels of success experienced by their classmates (Wasik & Slavin, 1993; Pinnell et al., 1994).

There are a number of other highly successful one-to-one reading tutorial programs that have accumulated solid research and evaluation data. Other successful one-to-one tutoring programs include Success For All, described earlier in this chapter, Prevention of Learning Disabilities (which uses certified teachers), Wallach Tutorial Program (paraprofessional tutors in both inner-city Chicago and rural North Carolina), and Programmed Tutorial Reading materials (once again paraprofessionals use this program in both urban and rural areas). Wasik and Slavin have conducted a detailed evaluation of the effectiveness of these one-to-one tutorial approaches and have documented each as successful. In 16 separate studies of cohorts involving the five different tutorial methods, the significant differences were substantially positive in nearly every case (Wasik & Slavin, 1993). In addition, research on these five tutorial programs led to four important conclusions:

1. *The most comprehensive models of reading, and therefore the most complete instructional interventions, have larger impacts than programs that address only a few components of the reading process. Reading Recovery and Success For All were found to be the most successful programs.*
2. *It is not enough to simply use tutors. For tutoring to be most effective, the quality of instruction must be improved. Also, better achievement occurs by increasing the amount of time, incentive value, and appropriateness to student needs.*
3. *Tutoring by certified teachers appeared to have substantially more impact than tutoring by paraprofessionals.*
4. *The initial positive effects continued into second and third grades (Wasik & Slavin, 1993, p. 196)*

Because of the cost of one-to-one tutoring, the lasting effects of this approach are of great importance. Two of the programs, Success For All and Programmed Tutorial Reading, have documented substantial reductions in student retention. Success For All reports fewer referrals to special education during the intervention and in successive years (Wasik & Slavin, 1993).

Using Volunteers and Peers for One-to-One Tutoring

Not only is this a cost-effective approach to teaching reading, there is a growing body of literature designed to help volunteers be more effective tutors. One of the best materials available is a delightful and useful collection of strategies entitled *The Volunteer Tutor's Toolbox* (Herrmann, 1994).

One-to-one tutoring can also be extremely effective using peer tutors. There is also research demonstrating the positive effects of peer tutoring on the tutor as well as the tutee. Sam Winter, noted reading scholar, describes an example of a peer tutoring program in reading:

Reading together:

1. *Read aloud with your partner, letting her set the pace and share her book.*
2. *If your partner hesitates or makes a mistake, tell her the correct word, and make her repeat it before continuing.*

Reading alone:

3. *If your partner signals that he wants to read alone, then stop reading aloud and follow the story.*
4. *If your partner hesitates or makes a mistake while reading alone, then tell him the correct word, make him repeat it, and then read aloud with him until he next signals.*
5. *Whenever your partner reads a difficult word or sentence, corrects his own mistake, or signals he can read on his own, then praise him. (Winter, 1986, p. 103)*

In a landmark peer tutoring study, "tutees were able to read faster, make fewer errors, and where a mistake was made, it was more probably self-corrected" (Winter, 1986, p. 104). This study concluded that one-to-one peer tutoring not only taught children to read, but made them more self-confident in their reading.

The use of professional, paraprofessional, and peer tutoring to help at-risk youth overcome reading deficiency in the early grades represents a practice that works and should be available in every elementary school.

Extended Day Programs

Many elementary-school programs that are especially successful with at-risk youth utilize an extended day. These programs, often referred to as latchkey programs, are often a feature of urban magnet schools which use the extended day concept to attract working parents from far distances. In Houston, Texas, the most popular magnet school is the Extended Day Program because it offers such advantages to both parents and students. For parents who leave for work before the traditional school day begins and who do not finish their work day until after school is over, these programs offer a welcome alternative to a number of undesirable options which working parents regularly encounter.

For the at-risk student, such programs provide additional time for tutoring, homework, and cultural enrichment. Extended day programs provide additional school time to help at-risk youth catch up and accelerate their learning without pulling the students out of their regular classes. Extended day programs may be staffed with teachers, aides, college or university student teachers, parents, or other volunteers. Staffing these programs with teachers can be an expensive but highly effective approach. Before and after school enrichment programs provide a wonderful means to solicit and gain community, business, and volunteer support. Many community service clubs support these programs, and many schools use these programs to mobilize school volunteers. If a college or university is nearby, before and after school programs can be largely staffed with teacher education practicum students or university volunteers. These programs can also be staffed with older students serving as cross-age tutors to help younger students.

Before and after school programs can also include supervised playtime and personal development activities, while simultaneously saving children from lonely time at home in an unsupervised situation. Many programs develop one-to-one tutoring programs for children who are having reading problems. They provide students with a supportive place to complete their homework, to get tutorial assistance from other students or from adults, and to have library and computer resources available for their work.

Research has documented the many advantages of extending the school day as well as providing a time for personalized instruction that avoids pulling students out of class. Many of these before and after school programs include free breakfast programs and health assistance. Other programs offer gymnastics, intramural sports, chess, and art and music enrichment programs in addition to academic activities. Every elementary school should seriously consider the valuable advantages of before and after school programs. Any school with a sizable at-risk student population should offer all-day kindergarten as well as extended day programs for the early elementary-school years.

Cooperative Learning

Cooperative learning is certainly no new idea, but recently it has been studied, refined, and implemented extensively throughout public education. The concept of cooperative learning encourages students to work together and helps students teach one another in highly structured small-group activities. This practice stands in rather stark contrast to the typical large-group, direct instruction model of competitive learning that traditionally characterizes most public school settings. The importance of cooperative learning has been stressed by Slavin:

> Cooperative learning has been suggested as the solution for an astonishing array of educational problems: it is often cited as a means of emphasizing thinking skills and increasing higher-order learning; as an alternative to ability grouping, remediation or special education; as a means of improving race relations and acceptance of mainstreamed students; and as a way to prepare students for an increasingly collaborative work force. (Slavin, 1991b, p. 71)

Research on cooperative learning is impressive. Through cooperative small groups, students work together to help one another master academic material. There are many quite different forms of cooperative learning, and the effectiveness of cooperative learning (particularly for achievement outcomes) depends on the particular approach used.

- *For enhancing student achievement, the most successful approaches have incorporated two key elements: group goals and individual accountability; that is, groups are rewarded based on the individual learning of all group members.*
- *When group goals and individual accountability are used, achievement effects of cooperative learning are consistently positive: 37 out of 44 experimental/control comparisons of at least four weeks' duration have found significantly positive effects, and none have favored traditional methods.*
- *Achievement effects of cooperative learning have been found to be about the same degree at all grade levels (2–12), in all major subjects, and in urban, rural, and suburban schools. Effects are equally positive for high, average, and low achievers.*
- *Positive effects of cooperative learning have been consistently found on such diverse outcomes as self-esteem, intergroup relations, acceptance of academically handicapped students, attitudes toward school, and ability to work cooperatively. (Slavin, 1991b, p. 71)*

While research on the effects of cooperative learning shows consistent improvement in student achievement as measured on standardized tests, there are two elements that must be included in cooperative learning if it is to be effective. First, groups must be rewarded as a group for doing well, and second, the group's success must depend on the individual learning of each team member.

For the at-risk student, cooperation rather than competition toward academic achievement provides for an inclusive environment. Many children arrive at school ill-equipped to learn and achieve through the traditional authoritative classroom structure. Cooperating with their peers and achieving academic success during the early years of school can help a child to overcome many barriers to success in school and life (Bauwens and Hourcade, 1994).

Counseling Programs

Over the past decade a growing number of elementary schools have added school counselors to their staffs. Unfortunately, in most cases this invaluable resource for at-risk youth is available only on a part-time basis to a limited population of students. Virtually any elementary counselor will dramatically describe the overwhelming needs of elementary youth and then lament the reality of the present-day critical underfunding of counseling interventions. Nonetheless, those elementary schools that have developed counseling programs provide at-risk youth with the critical assistance that may literally save lives.

James and JoAnne Wigtil have identified a lengthy list of issues which elementary counselors must be prepared to address, including substance and alcohol abuse, death, divorce, lack of parental bonding, depression, aggression and anger, negative body images, suicide, eating disorders, poverty, abuse, and poor school performance (Wigtil & Wigtil, 1993). When one considers that at any time 20 percent or more of the elementary school population may be confronted by one or more of these issues, the need for trained counseling personnel and programs seems imperative.

Computers and Technology

> *"When IBM moved five computers into my fifth grade classroom,*
> *I almost died. I didn't have a computer at home, didn't even know*
> *word processing; in fact, I wasn't even sure how to turn one on.*
> *But while I was terrified of the things, the kids just couldn't leave*
> *them alone. Some of the students asked to see the instruction*
> *manual and almost overnight had the machines operating. Once*
> *the class saw those shimmering blue screens, they really became*
> *excited. Well, it didn't take long before the students had me*
> *seated in front of the keyboard and patiently took me through*
> *step after tortuous step until I could call up a program and begin*
> *experimenting with some of the individualized, elementary*
> *software. Did you get this? My fifth-grade students were*
> *teaching me how to use elementary level program software*
> *and they were being patient and supportive in their teaching.*
> *I don't think I'll ever be the same!"*
> —(TEACHER, JEFFERSON ELEMENTARY SCHOOL,
> BOISE, IDAHO, 1993)

Schools have lagged far behind many other aspects of life when it comes to technology. The revolution in communications, computers, and other forms of technology networks has only recently begun to impact public schools and too often only in demonstration situations. While some entire school districts have moved energetically into technology and into connecting classes and schools with state, national, and international data systems and networks, the vast majority of schools still have only a small number of microcomputers, usually housed in a small computer laboratory with limited availability to all students.

There are several reasons for the lack of current technology in schools. First, the cost of acquiring, maintaining, and updating hardware and software is a substantial commitment. In a time of increasing taxpayer revolts, few states or communities have been willing to make the investment. An exception is the state of Texas, where schools are being provided with the equivalent of $30 per student per year for technology. Computer software has been defined as instructional materials and can be purchased with textbook funds. Second, in most school districts, the average teaching experience is approximately 15 years or more. This means that the vast majority of teachers were trained before microcomputers were a part of classroom instruction. Even if computers were available for every classroom in the school district, state, and nation, it has been estimated it would take 7 to 10 years before teachers would be able to make the adjustments to a new approach to teaching and learning and then only after extensive training. Third, even those districts that possess the resources and commitment to implement technology find the actual process is made more difficult due to the lack of direction and agreement in the field regarding method and approach. Confusion over what students should learn, when, and from whom continues to inhibit widespread adoption of technology throughout the school.

Some districts are attempting to provide computers to all classrooms at the elementary and middle-school levels. While authorities maintain that what is needed is one computer for every three children, even adding four or five computers to a classroom creates a dramatic new learning environment. To adjust to this change requires that even experienced teachers must learn to incorporate a significantly different approach to instruction. This can be a painful process for many teachers, and for some it may never be accomplished. Many districts estimated that a minimum of 20 staff development days per year may be necessary to help teachers begin to learn new skills, become comfortable with the technology, and develop new instructional materials for their classroom.

Despite the challenge of schoolwide implementation, clustering computers in elementary classrooms appears to hold great promise for at-risk youth. Since most classrooms do not possess enough computers for every child, teachers must develop learning centers and use cooperative learning techniques. The teachers can then rotate children through a number of learning experiences, including those available via the computers. Both the cooperative learning experiences and the highly individualized computer work can prove extremely effective with at-risk children. Early evaluations of schools where computers have been clustered in the classrooms report that many students often do not want to go to recess or even lunch once they participate in computer learning. Parents of at-risk youth also support using computers with elementary students.

The National Dropout Prevention Center reports considerable academic success for at-risk youth using Computer-Assisted Instruction (CAI), Integrated Learning Systems (ILS), videodisc technology, and information databases such as CD ROM (Duttweiler, 1992). However, one study of low-achieving high-school students who had been using computer-assisted instruction for four years reported that the students scored disproportionately lower on the lesson assessments than low-achieving youth in other treatment groups. The researchers concluded that using computer-assisted instruction exclusively for remediation may well have stigmatized students in the same way that ability grouping had done (Dalton, 1986).

While teachers initially rely almost exclusively on programmed software like IBM's TLC and Right to Read, once they become more secure with the technology, they tend to increase the use of the computer as a tool to develop and edit technical reports, manage classroom data, develop critical thinking assignments, and, via networks, communicate with other classes and grade levels at different schools, even schools in other countries. With regional and international networks, electronic bulletin boards, and a variety of accessible databases and services, a vast world of knowledge has become available to teachers and students (Eisenberg & Ely, 1993).

Traditional cable television and other commercial applications such as Channel 1 and a variety of satellite programming are beginning to be used extensively in public schools. And while increased programming has provided additional opportunities for student learning, the advent of fiber-optic cable will dramatically increase a school's access to specially designed educational programming. Many feel that this arena is on the verge of significant developments in terms of the instructional potential which will soon become available. For at-risk youth, who often possess highly visual and/or tactile learning styles, these developments serve to provide additional hands-on, visual, and highly personalized approaches to learning that will prove extremely effective.

Creating an Effective Model for Elementary-School Programs

Research has identified a significant number of school practices and programs that are so effective in helping at-risk youth learn and succeed in schools that they can be guaranteed. A number of experimental approaches, like the Success For All program, the Accelerated School Project, Comer Intervention Schools, and others, have demonstrated remarkable success with at-risk youth through employing a variety of nontraditional school and classroom practices. Successful intervention strategies and program components from these various approaches can be integrated to create a theoretical model for improving elementary school programs. Drawing from research and the lessons learned from programs designed to teach youth at risk, the following components, coupled with the essential characteristics for program development described in the previous chapter, create an effective model for elementary schools (see the Appendix for the Self-Evaluation Checklist).

School and Community Consensus Building

Successful elementary schools employ schoolwide consensus building among teachers, parents, and students. Some of the experimental programs require that teacher support reach the 90 percent level before starting a school reform project. Most successful programs have discovered a number of effective approaches to integrating students and parents into the planning, decision making, and governance process. For schools with culturally diverse students and parents, it is even more essential to find ways to include all participants in the school's mission.

Parent Education and Child Enrichment Programs

Effective elementary schools must create effective parent and early childhood education programs that both support parental needs and help young children learn during the critical years of transition from preschool through kindergarten and into the elementary school. Before and after school programs must then be available throughout the school years to continue this support.

Schoolwide Emphasis on Teaching All Children to Read

Successful elementary schools must focus on teaching all children to read. Schools should identify those children with reading deficiencies or problems and mobilize school and community efforts to work together to ensure that all children learn to read at grade level by the end of their third-grade year at approximately age nine.

One-to-one tutoring and an expanded reading program are essential in ensuring that every child learns to read.

Enriched Instruction During the Early Elementary Years

Recognizing that the best opportunities to positively impact children's learning begin to decline by about the end of the third grade, successful elementary schools are enriching the instructional program for preschool, kindergarten, and the first three years of elementary school. This is accomplished by using state and federally-funded programs for young children, all-day kindergarten, widespread use of volunteers, school-community partnerships, the coordination of social services, and the reallocation of school resources from the upper grades into the early grades.

High Expectations and Accelerated Learning

Successful elementary schools maintain high expectations for all students. These schools use every approach available to help at-risk children accelerate their learning so that they can catch up with their higher-acheiving peers. At the earliest possible time, high expectations and accelerated learning create an atmosphere of hope, challenge, and accomplishment which drives the school's mission of educating all students.

Continuous Progress Learning

Successful elementary schools use a highly individualized, continuous progress learning approach to help children learn at their own level without fear of failure or retention. This is often accomplished by cross-age grouping or through some type of nongraded elementary organization. A continuous progress approach is vital to providing opportunities for at-risk youth to accelerate their learning and catch up.

Counseling, Case Management, and Coordination of Social Services

For young children, the needs of health, clothing, security, and nutrition may far outweigh any educational program or service. If these needs are unmet, the likelihood of any approach to increase the achievement and hope of an at-risk child's academic success is severely diminished. The development of a schoolwide counseling program provides a crucial function needed in every elementary school. Trained counselors can help young children to persevere, to overcome, or in some cases to survive the horrors of abuse, violence, and neglect which characterize so many of their lives.

Schools should also employ a case management approach to review the comprehensive needs of each child and develop appropriate intervention strategies. This requires that schools be informed of services that are available from the many government and community social services and work closely with the providers.

Schools often need to coordinate these services with the child's education program to ensure that the needs are met. To accommodate this approach, many schools actually provide office space for a variety of human service providers so that the majority of their time can be devoted to the parents and students in the neighborhood school and its community.

Effective Practices

Successful elementary schools also employ a wide variety of specific practices that have been documented as successful or even essential with at-risk youth. These practices include one-to-one tutoring, cooperative learning, individualized learning, computer-assisted instruction, after-school enrichment or catch-up programs, and others. These practices and programs provide a wide array of instructional opportunities which, when combined, serve to stimulate the interests and meet the needs of diverse youth.

Schools that are effective with at-risk youth combine as many of these essential components as possible into their programs. If all of these factors are integrated into an elementary school program, there is a high predictability for every student to experience success. Today, a number of experimental schools are integrating most or all of these factors into a comprehensive, schoolwide approach to effectively teach all children.

Ongoing Student Assessment

A careful process-oriented review of data regarding children, growth and achievement, school effectiveness, and a variety of school-related community issues helps schools and communities to identify problems and establish goals. Continued evaluation and assessment of individual children and programs helps to document the success or failure of efforts to address problems and provides a framework for continued improvement.

The individual success of the approaches described in this chapter are compounded and enriched when combined to form a comprehensive schoolwide plan. They also become more effective when parents are involved; when parents, teachers, and administrators hold high expectations for all children; and when student performance is authentically assessed. Addressing the needs of at-risk youth during the early childhood and elementary years holds critical importance for the individual child's future as well as the opportunity for subsequent schooling to be effective.

Unfortunately, even if many of these programs, practices, and interventions are implemented in a comprehensive schoolwide effort, the student achievement gains accomplished may soon be lost as the child moves into a standard junior high or middle school. Improving early childhood and elementary schools represents an important, yet only initial, step toward guaranteeing the effective education of youth at risk.

Chapter **7**

Programs That Work: Middle Schools/Junior High Schools

"These kids keep coming and coming. It seems with every new intervention we try, new unmet needs appear. What are we going to do next? Five years ago we transformed our traditional junior high to a middle school. You know, we went to interdisciplinary teaching, collaborative teams, longer classes and breaks, more parent contact, and student rewards. We also stopped rotating kids. All of this helped. Yet we continued to lose kids. Most recently we've added Natural Helpers, peer mediation, a crisis intervention team, and started a Students Staying Straight Program and alternatives to violence. We created an Insight Program with focus groups for concerned friends, one-on-one counseling and support for problems of divorce, smoking, and drugs. We've increased nonteaching staff contact with students and initiated an intervention program for 75 of our most troubled kids. I even personally sing to each of our 742 kids on their birthday! All of this has made a dramatic difference, but we're still losing some kids. We can't do this alone. We need help!"
—(PRINCIPAL, RYAN MIDDLE SCHOOL,
FAIRBANKS, ALASKA, 1993)

Middle-level education tends to be the forgotten segment of public education. Students at this level are not only experiencing enormous biological and social changes, but advances in health, nutrition, and social conditions have quickened the adolescents' biological clock, impacting the maturation process. It is also during these middle-level years that many students turn 16 and the vast majority of dropouts leave school. If these challenges were not enough to capture the attention of any concerned educator, there are other problems as well. A fundamental weakness of most middle-level schools is that teachers are rarely adequately trained for working with this demanding age group. This lack of training is compounded by a curriculum that fails to reflect the developmental needs associated with young adolescents and tends to lack any strong theoretical foundation of learning. In a national study, John Goodlad and his colleagues discovered that teaching and learning in junior high schools tend to be removed from student needs. Teaching and learning were primarily centered around teacher lectures, preparation of assignments, and teachers monitoring student work at their desks—three activities that are teacher-centered and involve students in rather passive learning experiences. In spite of the fact that repeated studies have found that 40 percent of the students in middle-level schools have not mastered reading skills, less than 3 percent of class time is devoted to improving reading (Goodlad, 1984).

Teachers who work at this level in most cases have been trained as either elementary or high-school teachers. In a 1988 study of middle schools, 61 percent of the schools surveyed reported that less than 25 percent of their teachers had been prepared to teach at this level (Alexander & McEwin, 1989, p. 28). Teachers often report that they feel like educational retreads, trained for one or another specialty and then reprogrammed into middle-level education. As a result, there tends to be an unfortunate low status associated with teaching at the middle school/junior high level. In spite of decades of concern focused on the young adolescent years, there are few examples of middle-school programs that have been designed to meet the educational and social needs of this challenging age level. Even fewer university teacher education programs devote the time or content emphasis necessary to prepare teachers to work effectively with these youth. Unlike the elementary school level where there are a growing number of successful, schoolwide restructuring projects underway that are being carefully documented, the middle-school level has experienced little change over the past four decades.

Despite a growing interest in restructuring public education, the traditional junior high school continues to be the level with the most startling lack of experimentation and reform, particularly for at-risk youth. Even school districts with large numbers of intervention programs and alternative schools designed to serve at-risk youth tend to operate most of these efforts at the elementary and the high-school levels. Yet it is during this critical period of adolescence when the vast majority of students drop out of school. It is here that students first suffer the shock of leaving a self-contained classroom and a relatively small educational environment and stepping into a large, content-centered approach to education that requires them to work with a different adult and often different peers almost every period of the day. Studies have found that close to 50 percent of all seventh graders change class at least four times a day (Wells, 1991). Many attend seven classes per day with seven different teachers and different groups of students. Junior high or middle school tends to be a social shock for all students. For the at-risk student, it often is an overwhelming experience.

Middle or junior-high schools come in a bewildering array of grade organization. As many as 30 different grade configurations have been identified by the Center for Research on Elementary and Middle Schools (Wells, 1991). Yet the vast majority use a grade six-through-eight or seven-through-nine organization. Most middle-level schools continue to look far more like high schools than they do elementary schools and regularly employ the practices of tracking, grade retention, and expulsion—all known to exacerbate the problems of the at-risk student. Middle or junior high schools in lower-income neighborhoods also provide at-risk youth with fewer resources and fewer opportunities in curriculum and instruction than schools in more advantaged neighborhoods (MacIver & Epstein, 1990).

A recent report on adolescent development funded by the Carnegie Corporation stressed a number of recommendations for transforming middle-level education. These included the following:

- *Create small communities for learning. . . . The key elements of these communities are schools within schools or houses, with students and teachers grouped together as teams.*
- *Teach a core academic program that results in students who are literate, including in the sciences, and who know how to think critically, lead a healthy life, behave ethically, and assume the responsibilities of citizenship in a pluralistic society.*
- *Ensure success for all students through the elimination of tracking by achievement level.*
- *Staff middle-grade schools with teachers who are expert at teaching young adolescents.*
- *Improve academic performance through the fostering of health and fitness of young adolescents.*
- *Reengage families in the education of young adolescents.*
- *Connect schools with communities—which together share responsibility for each middle-grade student's success—through identifying learning opportunities in the community (Carnegie Corporation, 1993, pp. 2–3).*

This set of recommendations clearly applies research on young adolescents and effective middle-level·education to define a basic reform model for schools at this level.

Developmental Needs

In a recent phone conversation with the principal of the Barret Traditional Middle School in Louisville, Kentucky, he explained that the school was trying out a very new idea. "In the three traditional elementary school alternatives including the Barret Traditional Middle School, we are handing out laptop computers to every student and forbidding them to use any pencils or pens. How's that for catapulting kids into the new world of technology? Is this great or what? What do you think will happen when these kids go on to high school or later to college? We think this is

*simply going to transform the world. We're sure in a few years
laptops will be just like books and notebooks and every school in
America will be checking out computers to all of their students.
We are just a little ahead of our time. I think that we are the first."
—(PRINCIPAL, BARRET TRADITIONAL MIDDLE SCHOOL,
JEFFERSON COUNTY SCHOOLS, LOUISVILLE, KENTUCKY)*

Concern for at-risk youth during young adolescence has intensified as schools struggle to seek solutions for the problems confronting these youth. In response, a growing body of research into the developmental needs of this age group is emerging. Recent studies suggest that these developmental needs represent a set of characteristics and preconditions that should guide educational reform at the middle-level school, especially for at-risk youth (see Table 7-1).

TABLE 7-1   Developmental Needs of Young Adolescents

- **Structure and clear limits:** Students who are going through rapid physical and social-emotional change need security in order to learn and grow. Clear, consistent rules are appropriate, but they are more likely to be accepted and valued by students who have participated in their formulation and adoption.
- **Diversity:** In early adolescence, students' cognitive abilities are grounded largely in concrete thinking while they move toward a greater capacity for abstract thinking. This, combined with the wide range of abilities and interests of the age group, demands school routines, instruction, and curriculum which balance a variety of learning activities and materials.
- **Self-exploration and self-definition:** At the core of developmental issues for many young adolescents, the question "am I normal?" reflects students' need to define for themselves their values and their relationship to their family, friends, and school. The need for self-definition also plays into students' need for reassurance that they will be accepted as individuals in their schools.
- **Competence and achievement:** Schools play a major role in providing young adolescent students with experiences of achievement which, in turn, students incorporate into their emerging definition of themselves as competent individuals. Successful academic and social experiences are essential to building confidence and self-esteem which allow for further growth in later adolescence and young adulthood.
- **Meaningful participation in the school and community:** As young adolescent students grow into adult bodies, they also need opportunities to begin to try out adult roles. While still too inexperienced to take on total responsibility for themselves and their environment, their new roles and increasing ability to think abstractly are at the core of their need to expand their responsibilities into wider arenas, to reflect on their future, and to negotiate with responsible adults the norms and expectations for behavior in the school.
- **Positive social interaction with adults and peers:** As young adolescents begin to differentiate themselves from their own families and define their own individual identities, they need increased contact with adult role models who can represent a variety of potential choices for students. At the same time, students' preoccupation with acceptance by their peers reflects their need to develop confidence in interacting with a wide range of other students.
- **Physical activity:** The needs of young adolescents' growing bodies require frequent opportunities to release the physical energy present during early adolescence.

(Massachusetts Advocacy Center, 1988, p. 22)

These developmental needs are highly consistent with the research conclusions of other groups (Carnegie Council on Adolescent Development, 1989). Using these developmental needs as a guide, a number of middle-school programs have been developed that hold great promise for middle-level at-risk youth.

Effective Programs

Research has documented that transferring from elementary to middle school is a crucial and often negative experience for the at-risk student. For this reason, efforts to successfully transition these youth to the middle level must be developed and maintained to keep kids in school and learning effectively. And while programs that have been identified as effective for at-risk youth at the elementary and high-school levels can be used with some modification at the middle level, a number of programs have been developed that are especially effective for this age group.

Schoolwide Efforts

The following section will describe two schoolwide efforts for reforming the middle and junior high schools: the accelerated school program and alternative middle schools. Each includes descriptions of specific programs that have been evaluated as successful at the middle-school level.

Accelerated Middle Schools

As described in the previous chapter, the first accelerated schools were initiated at the elementary level. In 1989, Henry Levin and his colleagues at Stanford University extended their research effort to focus on middle schools. They were motivated by several factors. First, the teachers, administrators, and parents in the accelerated elementary schools had begun expressing concern regarding student transition to middle schools. There was fear that without systematic, continuing support at the middle-school level, the gains that had been made at the elementary level might be lost. Second, many middle schools began inquiring about the suitability of the accelerated school approach for use at the middle-school level. Third, most educators and parents agreed that the middle school was recognized as a pivotal time for all adolescents, particularly at-risk youth. Fourth, the Stanford team felt that their elementary-level projects were substantially underway and progressing quite well. Beginning in 1990, the Stanford group helped initiate the accelerated school approach at the middle-school level, and it has been expanding ever since. Today there are 21 accelerated middle schools operating in 11 different states (Development of accelerated middle schools, 1993).

In spite of the fact that accelerated middle schools differ dramatically from accelerated elementary schools in size, administration, organization, ability groupings, etc., the accelerated concept has proven to be a powerful tool for restructuring. The accelerated school program at the middle-school level has developed around five concepts:

- *Creating cadres of teachers, students, and parents working together to improve teaching and learning: accelerated middle schools are beginning to use an interdisciplinary grouping of teachers and students to address themes and lessons that include subject matter for many related areas. The incorporation of the accelerated school model led to immediate changes in the way students are organized for instruction. Many middle schools have abandoned tracking, placed all students in heterogeneous classes, and begun experimenting with interdisciplinary thematic coursework designed by teacher teams.*

- *Student involvement: Students participate in all aspects of accelerated middle schools. They participate in the accelerated school planning process that includes "taking stock" and "visioning," and later they serve in the daily governance of the school. Students not only participate in the planning and governance, but they are encouraged to be involved in what they learn and how they are learning it. Students are routinely involved in curriculum development and planning in accelerated schools.*

- *Administrative organization: accelerated middle schools create a shared decision-making model in which the principal and the assistant principals work as a management team to administer the school. The schools also create a school-community steering committee composed of teachers, students, administrators, school district administrators, and a variety of parents and community representatives selected from the PTA, bilingual advisory committee and social agencies.*

- *Parental involvement: accelerated middle schools actively encourage parents to be involved in the school site, participating in the taking stock sessions, visioning sessions, setting priorities, governance, participating in teaching/learning cadres, serving on the steering committee, and assisting in the school as a whole.*

- *Schoolwide restructuring: Even more so than in elementary schools, the accelerated middle-school model has led to rather significant schoolwide restructuring. The accelerated school process provides middle schools with a concrete model that helps parents, teachers, and students consider research, review school data, and participate in planning more effective ways of teaching, learning, and the school organization. (Development of accelerated middle schools, 1993)*

The accelerated middle-school program presents perhaps the best research, development, and restructuring effort underway in the American middle schools today. It requires a process that blends training, staff development, and communitywide participation. A growing number of communities have joined the Stanford University accelerated school group to organize and provide communities with the training and support that they need to initiate an accelerated school program. Consistent with the elementary model, over 90 percent of the teachers in the school must vote to participate in the program, which is perceived to encompass a six-to-seven-year process to fully implement the model.

Alternative Middle Level Schools

> *While evaluating the McKinley Alternative Junior High School in Fairbanks, Alaska, I conducted interviews with teachers, administrators, parents, and students. As I finished the last student group interview, one of the kids said to me, "Can I ask you a question?" "Sure," I said, "Let's hear it." "Well, we were wondering if you could help us." "Sure," I said, "If I can. What can I do for you?" The student leaned closer and said, "The teachers at this school are really screwed up." He turned to look at the three other students, who all nodded their heads. "They're driving us crazy." Now really curious, I reopened my note pad, turned on my tape recorder again and asked, "What do you mean, 'They're driving us crazy'?" Becoming impatient with me, he spoke louder and more rapidly, "It's just really screwed up. These teachers don't know that we're dumb. They're driving us crazy because they think we can learn. They just won't leave us alone. You've got to talk to them," he pleaded. "Tell them that we can't do this stuff. Go in there and tell them to get off our backs. Tell them that we're dumb."*
> —(JUNIOR HIGH STUDENT, MCKINLEY ALTERNATIVE JUNIOR HIGH SCHOOL, FAIRBANKS, ALASKA, 1988)

The vast majority of alternative public schools have been developed at the elementary and high-school levels, lending further support to the "forgotten school" notion which characterizes middle-level education. Fortunately, in recent years, this has begun to change as a number of outstanding alternative schools and schools within schools have been successfully developed at the middle level.

While alternative middle schools remain relatively rare, effective schools within schools are often found. During the 1980s, the Portland, Oregon, Public Schools conducted a careful assessment of their many alternative and magnet school programs and concluded that the middle-school level offered very few special alternative programs or choices for students. Responding to this need, the school district created funding and solicited proposals from area middle schools. Ultimately most of the new alternatives that were developed were school-within-school programs. These programs were usually located in a wing of a building or a special section of the school and provided a group of teachers and students an opportunity to work exclusively together. Some of these programs included the Whitaker Middle School Learning Lab; the Gregory Heights Middle School Alternative Program, and the Ocklea Green Middle School Green House. Consistent with the alternative school model, students and teachers chose to participate in the programs.

While a review of most large city school districts will discover a number of middle school alternative or magnet programs, the majority have been developed for the gifted and talented student. And while far fewer middle school alternative and magnet programs have been developed for at-risk youth, many good examples can be found:

- *Barret Traditional Middle School, Jefferson County Schools, Louisville, Kentucky:* As part of the National Alliance for Restructuring Education, the Barret Traditional Middle School encourages a high degree of parental involvement and functions as a site-based decision-making school. A council of three teachers, two parents and the principal share the decision-making responsibility for the school. The school is also part of the traditional, back-to-basics philosophy that characterizes three elementary schools, three middle schools, and two high schools in Jefferson County. The school is available to students on the basis of choice and has a dress code, a behavior code, required homework, and encourages high academic performance, patriotism, courtesy, respect, responsibility, and citizenship. The school also has a strong new emphasis on technology and provides every student with a laptop computer.
- *Saturn School of Tomorrow, St. Paul, Minnesota, Grades 4–8:* Reflecting the best of what is known about learning and emerging learning technology, the school serves over 280 students with a curriculum designed to prepare them to live and work successfully in the world of tomorrow. Saturn students work individually, in small groups, and in cooperative teams using advanced learning technologies such as computers and interactive videos as part of the basic curriculum. Students attend regular classes, conduct independent and group research, participate in apprenticeship and mentorship activities in state and local government offices, businesses, and art and science museums. Students explore concepts that relate to later vocational and professional opportunities and careers. Each student has a personal growth plan (PGP) developed by the student, their parents, and teachers. Students are actively involved in establishing their own learning goals and objectives and in determining their own progress.
- *Center for Visual and Communication Arts, Los Angeles Unified School District, Los Angeles, California, Grades 7–9:* One of the many LA magnet schools, the Center for Visual and Communication Arts provides interested students an opportunity to supplement and enrich the conventional middle school curriculum with special courses and internships in script writing, stage performance, dance and music, and radio and television productions.
- *Crispus Attucks Academic Academy, Indianapolis Public Schools, Indianapolis, Indiana, Grades 6–8:* Crispus Attucks is located near the city center and provides interested students with a thematic program of study that includes math, science, English, social studies, and Spanish. Themes of the academy focus on developing writing, studying, and thinking skills. The school emphasizes the use of computers, state-of-the-art instructional technologies, multicultural resources, cooperative learning strategies, study skills, and career awareness activities.

Research findings and examples of effective alternative programs that are currently operating at the elementary and high-school levels provide a wealth of quite useful information for those concerned with developing alternative programs at the middle-school level. These elementary and senior-level alternative schools are characterized by small, supportive learning environments, voluntary participation, caring and demanding teachers, and a curriculum that is tailored to the developmental needs of their constituents (Raywid, 1983). In fact, the organizational characteristics that seem to make alternative schools so successful are quite similar to the recommended components of school restructuring that research deems essential for all students at the middle level. Alternative schools indeed provide an effective model for revitalizing middle schools in America (Massachusetts Advocacy Center, 1988).

Characteristics of Effective Middle Schools

Research on effective middle schools helps to create a distinct model for restructuring schools to better serve at-risk youth. This data on effective programs also relates directly to the recommendations of the Carnegie Council on Adolescent Development described earlier. The following characteristics of effective middle schools serve as a foundation for improving educational efforts for middle-level youth.

Small Learning Communities

Many effective junior high/middle schools have developed small learning communities, teams, or schools within the larger middle-level school. Few structural accommodations seem to help young adolescents more than creating social and organizational smallness amidst the larger school. Creating this smallness enables every teacher to know every student by name and performance level and establishes a common set of rules, regulations, and expectations that provide the young adolescent with the educational stability that they need during these difficult years.

There is no better way to ensure that every teacher at this level is responsible for every student than the creation of organizational smallness. In some way, these small communities become an essential support group and often seem to serve as a surrogate family. This is done by creating interdisciplinary groups of teachers who take full responsibility or the majority of the responsibility for a cohort of students. One teacher might teach both math and science to the same students; another teaches the students language arts and social studies. Teachers are also assigned as advocates and mentors for this group of students and serve as classroom counselors. This type of program takes on the characteristics of elementary schools and alternative education programs that have proven so effective for all students, especially those who are at risk (Carnegie Council on Adolescent Development, 1989).

For the at-risk youth who feels insecure and often academically and socially incapable, the shock of arriving at the large, impersonal junior high school can be stunning. For this reason, school or program size may represent the most significant aspect of guaranteeing that at-risk youth stay in school, are provided the individual attention that they need, and have the opportunity to achieve academic success in their classes. No other level of schooling seems more in need of the benefits of smallness than does the middle school. Unfortunately, as reported earlier, more than two-thirds of the middle schools surveyed in 1988 reported that they had not created any small in-school instructional teams (Alexander & McEwin, 1989).

Interdisciplinary Core

Effective middle-level schools often organize an interdisciplinary core curriculum that includes English, fine arts, foreign language, history, literature, math, science, and social studies. The goal is to develop interrelationships between ideas through critical thinking and problem solving using a team approach (Carnegie Council on Adolescent Development, 1989). Teachers also develop curriculum by organizing themes to help integrate the diverse areas of knowledge the young adolescent is trying to learn. High-interest themes such as the Old West, dinosaurs, space exploration and travel, endangered species, and the Olympics are often found in middle-school interdisciplinary curricula.

Never before have so many contemporary curriculum resources been available to help teachers plan and deliver interdisciplinary thematic instruction. In addition, a variety of new programs and courses have been developed that integrate knowledge and skills from a number of related academic subject matter areas to teach critical thinking and problem solving. Perhaps the most useful publication for helping interdisciplinary teams was published by the Center for Research on Effective Schooling for Disadvantaged Students, entitled *Promising Practices in Major Academic Subjects in the Middle Grades* (Epstein & Salinas, 1990). This report identifies outstanding interdisciplinary course materials that are available in science and technology, survival strategies, human biology, ethnic and cultural heritage, social studies and art, politics and philosophy, and others. Many of these interdisciplinary units or courses can help teachers to combine reading, writing, thinking, and problem solving into a high-interest interdisciplinary context.

The key to interdisciplinary teaching and learning is teacher choice, cooperation, and blocks of time to plan and to work with students. Unfortunately, since most middle-level teachers graduated from teacher education programs that focus primarily on the high-school level, they often lack the preparation and experience that elementary teachers gain from teaming with other teachers to develop themes and integrated units. To be effective, middle-level teachers need a concerted staff development effort to ensure the success of interdisciplinary course planning and implementation. An example of successful instructional change is Jepson Middle School in Vacaville, California, where the school reorganized around interdisciplinary teams. The seventh grade divided into teams of approximately 160 students, each with four or five teachers representing the major subject areas. "Early results for the experiment show the test scores have improved and the school atmosphere has been changed. . . . in a positive way" (Carnegie Corporation, 1993, p. 4).

Flexible Block Scheduling
Directly related to interdisciplinary teams, schools within schools, and other groupings that allow for personalization of the curriculum, some effective middle-level schools use block scheduling. This concept allows teachers and students time for in-depth projects, field trips, and cooperative learning. It also helps to eliminate the disruption and disorganization of the 50-minute class school day (Massachusetts Advocacy Center, 1988). This might include an extended homeroom period for classroom counseling, one hour to 2 1/2 hour time periods for interdisciplinary, in-depth study, shorter 45-minute blocks of time for survey courses in career education and physical education, and a 30-to-40-minute period for high-interest mini courses (see Table 7-2).

Effective Activities, Mini Courses, and Exploration Courses
Many successful middle schools have developed a wide variety of courses and activities where students can explore, experiment, and gain new experiences. Often these courses are scheduled one period each day and provide a vast array of activities, mini courses, and survey exploration courses that focus on student interest areas. Young adolescents are extremely interested in and supportive of these courses, and the majority of middle schools offer some of these courses and activities. These courses and activities tend to break up the school day and permit students to explore a wide range of topics, skills, and activities that expand

TABLE 7-2 A Sample Day in an Effective Middle School

	Grade 6	Grade 7	Grade 8
25 min.		Homeroom Advisor-Advisee Period—1:20 ratio	
200 min.*	Academic Block 2 teachers: 60 students	Academic Block 4 teachers: 120 students 1/2 time counselor-teacher	Academic Block 4 teachers: 120 students 1/2 time teacher-counselor
45 min.		Physical Education	
45 min.	Required Exploratory Cycle (9 weeks—art, music, home economics, industrial arts)	Required Exploratory Cycle (9 or 12 weeks—foreign language, business, drama, art)	Semester Elective
35 min.	High-interest mini-courses (M-W-F) Intramural sports, schoolwide activities, clubs (T-Th)		
10 min.		Homeroom Advisor-Advisee period	

*Includes 35 minutes lunch and 20 minutes passing time. (Massachusetts Advocacy Center, 1988) their interests and abilities, permitting them to test themselves in new areas. Mini courses often include such activities as Trivial Pursuit™, sports statistics, pen pals, math games, etc. (Massachusetts Advocacy Center, 1988). Other courses and activities include:

Arrive Alive Club	Knowledge Board
Bookworms	Leather Crafts
Builders Club	Olympics of the Mind
Cheer Leaders	Outdoor Education
Chess Club	Pep Squad
Citizens in Action	Scholastic Board
Foreign Language Club	Self-Esteem Group
Future Jobs	Ski Club
History Bowl	Speech/Debate Club
Junior Great Books	Stamp/Coin Collection
"Just Say No"	Sustained Silent Reading
(Alexander & McEwin, 1989, p. 19)	

Also, intramural and interschool sports programs for both girls and boys are extremely popular. The most popular exploratory-type courses available as either a required or elective course in middle schools by order of popularity include health, computers, sex education, creative writing, and careers (Alexander & McEwin, 1989). Each of these clubs, hobbies, competitions, participation, support groups, and specialized elective courses are extremely important for the personal and social development of the young adolescent, and they often can make the school day bearable for the young at-risk adolescent.

Transition Programs

Many school districts have attempted to alleviate the transition from elementary to middle school and from middle school to high school with programs that help to bridge the different school levels. These programs provide elementary students with opportunities to visit the middle school, have orientation programs, and meet with teachers. These programs maintain contact with students to reduce the number of youth who fail to successfully transition to the middle-school level. Such programs are critical between the middle school and the high-school level, where so many students tend to drop out of school. High schools need to be extremely aggressive to ensure that all middle-school graduates enroll in high school.

Using Youth as Resources

One of the most promising concepts for middle-level education ties academic programs to school and community service projects and activities. Developing opportunities for the students through peer teaching, cross-age tutoring, and a host of public service activities enables middle-school youth to both learn from and appreciate the value of giving and sharing. Many schools use students to assist with clerical, custodial, technology, and media needs of the school. Out-of-school applications include community cleanup and improvement projects, service to child-care centers, senior citizen centers, museums, zoos, the Salvation Army, homeless shelters, and many others. Few school programs have proven so effective in enhancing self-esteem as participation in real-life community service activities (Barr & Smith, 1976; Nathan, 1989).

Cross-age tutoring is especially effective for enhancing the self-esteem of young adolescents. A study of middle-school students who had profound behavioral and attendance problems as well as deficiencies in basic skills found that when the students were trained as tutors and began working with younger children, extremely promising results occurred. The tutors learned as much as the young students they were helping, and all participants, teachers and students, voiced support for the concept (Big kids teach little kids, 1987). In another program, students from a special education emotionally disturbed class showed distinct improvements in academic achievement, attendance, and behavior when they participated in cross-age tutoring. Student attendance improved from one absence per week to approximately one per month. In study after study, year after year, dropout-prone youth who become tutors experience lower dropout rates and fewer absences and behavioral problems (Massachusetts Advocacy Center, 1988).

Another potential area for increased student participation is student governance. Over 80 percent of the schools surveyed in 1988 responded that students in every grade level (sixth, seventh, and eighth) could be involved in student council programs (Alexander & McEwin, 1989).

Health and Fitness Programs

Self-esteem and academic performance can often be improved through the creation of health and fitness programs. School-based health clinics or related health services are absolutely essential for so many young adolescents today, yet these services have been slow to develop. Often described as suffering from raging hormones, young adolescents are in urgent need of effective health and hygiene instruction as well as appropriate fitness programs. In addition to instruction, schools need to provide access to health care and counseling programs, preferably through a health coordinator, a school nurse, or through on-site health clinics that many schools are beginning to develop. While controversial, a recent Carnegie report calls for providing family planning information, sex education, and, increasingly, AIDS education to young adolescents (Carnegie Council on Adolescent Development, 1989). Today it is not uncommon to find public schools providing condoms to students at the middle-school level.

One effective approach to address the health needs of young adolescents is to coordinate school and social service agencies. In Baltimore's Canton Middle School, educators and concerned community members have organized a Primary Assessment Committee that meets weekly and focuses on individual student problems and needs through a case management approach. The committee is composed of the school nurse, the guidance counselor, a mental health therapist, a school social worker, representatives from departments of juvenile and social services, and teachers. With any particular child, the committee might assist in obtaining eyeglasses, providing dental care, arranging for counseling for emotional problems, providing medical care, family planning, or vocational training (Carnegie Corporation, 1993). Another example is from Brunswick, Maryland, where the middle school is part of the Community Agency Social Service, an agency responsible for coordinating health, mental health, nursing, and police services. This coordinated effort attempts to address the problems of alcohol, drug use, family planning, home conflict, poverty, and homelessness for middle-level students (Carnegie Corporation, 1993).

Middle schools also need strong fitness, exercise, and intramural sports programs to complement community youth programs outside the school. Intramural sports programs are particularly effective, as almost every young boy and girl in the school can be involved. While basketball, baseball, and football are always popular, soccer is proving especially good for young adolescent boys and girls. In soccer it is hard to see adolescents make mistakes, and this is the time when they are particularly sensitive to making mistakes. With the exception of the goalie, young boys and girls can run, kick, and play without being embarrassed or humiliated by mistakes. Among this age group, a regular schedule of exercise and fitness activities is essential.

Parental Involvement

As at every other school level, parental involvement is extremely important at the middle-level grades. Parents can have a powerful influence on keeping their children in school during the middle-school years by sharing a direct interest in schooling, especially for low socioeconomic status students. At-risk students whose parents reported regularly discussing future education plans with their eighth graders were less likely to drop out of school than students whose parents did not engage in such discussions (Office of Educational Research and Improvement, 1992). In addition, studies have led to the following conclusions regarding parental involvement:

- *Parental involvement increases as socioeconomic status and parents' educational attainment increase.*
- *When socioeconomic status was taken into consideration, single mothers tended to participate in their eighth grader's education at the same or in some cases higher levels than two-parent families.*
- *Most parents (79 percent) reported regularly discussing their eighth grader's current school experiences with their child.*
- *Sixty-nine percent of parents reported monitoring their eighth grader's television viewing; 62 percent limited television viewing on school nights, and 84 percent restricted early or late viewing. (Office of Educational Research and Improvement, 1992, p. 1)*

Positive parental involvement at the middle-school level is critical, as many young adolescent boys and girls spend these years striving for independence from their parents and attempting to assert themselves as mature individuals. Unfortunately, parental involvement is often not actively encouraged at the middle-school level; for these very reasons it should be emphasized.

Nancy Berla, a leading authority on parental involvement, identified examples of effective ways parents can help their children:

- *Communicate every day with your son or daughter about what happened that day at school. Be available to listen to your child's concerns and criticisms about teachers, courses, and policies without lecturing or arguing. Be ready to offer praise and extend help. Be honest—support what you feel is good about the school, but also share your concerns if you think that the school's policies and practices are harmful to your child.*
- *Encourage your child to do his or her homework every night by suggesting an acceptable time and a quiet place and being available if and when he or she needs help. If you don't know the subject or speak the language, you can be supportive and help your child by assisting him or her in identifying the steps necessary to complete the assignment.*
- *If your middle schooler consistently and continually expresses complaints about the teachers, the courses, or school policies, be prepared to take action. Call the school and make the appointment to meet with the teacher, guidance counselor, or principal at the school. Even if scheduling is a problem, contact your school before it interferes with your child's learning and success at school (Berla, 1991, p. 16).*

Effective middle schools should develop a schoolwide plan to encourage parental involvement. This should include regular communication with parents, organizing parent-to-parent discussion events, pitch-in meals with guest speakers, establishing a parent room in the school, establishing a lending library for parents, and requiring consistent and timely teacher-parent contact. Many schools build positive relationships through concerted efforts to involve parents with all forms of school government and the curriculum. Research has documented the positive impact of parent involvement at the middle-school level, and all schools should capitalize on this important aspect in helping young adolescents achieve social and academic success.

Counseling, Caring, and Self-Esteem
In the midst of transforming from child to adolescent, a student needs strong personal relationships with teachers and other adults as well as effective counseling programs. Block scheduling, an interdisciplinary core, and organizational smallness all provide improved means for teachers to relate personally to their students. These approaches often lead to teacher teaming, using intensive case management approaches to address student needs, and involving all teachers in decisions related to a particular student's program. Effective middle-level schools also use peer counseling, teacher advocates, counselors serving as consultants to teachers, counselors provided by social service agencies, and drug and alcohol counselors

(Massachusetts Advocacy Center, 1988). Effective middle schools use teachers as classroom counselors and organize the school day so that much of the one-on-one and group counseling sessions can occur in a classroom setting. Many effective middle schools use an extended homeroom period to provide for this type of counseling process.

Increasingly, at-risk youth need counseling for sexual and physical abuse, dysfunctional families, sex-related issues, and drug and alcohol problems. To address these issues, the schools also need to develop peer support groups to foster and maintain healthy life decisions. All of these programs are designed to address the problems and concerns of students and lead to better academic achievement and enhanced self-esteem. Many schools have initiated curriculum and schoolwide programs designed to enhance student self-esteem (Stern & Van Slych, 1986).

Mentors

Children entering adolescence at a significantly younger age than ever before are making crucial decisions that can alter their entire lives. Research has helped to identify the importance of adult relationships to middle-school youth since they relate directly to the developmental needs of the youth at this age. The establishment of a mentor relationship may not only be the best, but perhaps the only way for the young adolescent to develop a strong relationship with an adult.

Mentor programs have become an essential part of an effective middle school. Mentor programs can provide the organization to recruit adults and to provide at-risk middle-school students with the needed adult model to talk to and to help explore career possibilities. Effective mentor programs should

- *Recruit strong adult models;*
- *Recruit adults who have been there and made it and who can tell it like it is;*
- *Recruit adults who are ethnically and culturally attuned to the young adolescent;*
- *Provide for group discussion sessions so that students can talk about and share their mentor experiences;*
- *Develop a mentor network, i.e., use mentors who were formerly in a mentor program as a youth (Project Plus, 1990).*

Few programs can be as effective as mentoring in assisting poor, at-risk minority youth develop an ongoing relationship with an adult. A PBS documentary video entitled *One Plus One*, with host Pat Morita, star of the *Karate Kid* movies, has been exceptionally well received by young adolescents. It describes real-life examples of effective mentoring programs and provides an excellent springboard to connecting reluctant youth with the adult contact they often need (Project Plus, 1990).

Career and Vocational Education

While vocational education is almost universally viewed with hope and positive expectations, historically such programs have produced less than satisfactory results. Unfortunately, for middle-level schools, this has been even more true. In the past, vocational education at the middle level, where and if it has been available, has focused on such hands-on programs as automobile mechanics, wood and metal working, home economics, and in rural areas, agriculture. Often these courses are available in a one-year introductory-style survey course. Approximately 50 percent of the middle schools in the United States still offer home economics and industrial arts as both required and elective courses; music and art are available in 60 to 80 percent of the schools (Alexander & McEwin, 1989). One can still find home economics courses at the middle-school level where at-risk youth from dysfunctional homes are being taught how to set a formal dining table. There is little evidence that such programs keep the young adolescent in school and even less that the programs lead to job opportunities after students graduate or leave school. Even programs involving actual on-the-job work experience have proven disappointing. "Isolated work experience will not reclaim impoverished and troubled youth" (Institute for Educational Leadership, 1986, p. 59).

For successful vocational or career education programs, the developmental needs of the young adolescent must be taken into consideration and used as a basis for planning (Massachusetts Advocacy Center, 1988). Programs must consider the needs of the whole child. While older students may benefit from job skill training, for the young adolescent an effective vocational program means a concern for career education, job surveys, field trips to business and industry, and career fairs. Adult mentors can also provide role models for at-risk youth and can introduce them to the professional world and the world of work. Such educational surveys, experiential awareness programs and one-to-one mentoring programs should serve the young adolescent far better than job experience and the traditional junior-high woodshop program.

Before and After School Programs

Before and after school programs are especially valuable at the middle-school level. Non-school time becomes extremely important for young adolescents, especially during times when they are unsupervised. Studies have discovered that large numbers of young adolescents have sex and often get pregnant between 3:30 and 5:30 in the afternoon, a time when the students are out of school and their parents are not home from work (Barr & Ross, 1989). This is also a time of high incidence of violence, vandalism, shoplifting, and even burglary. In many communities there are often no adults in entire neighborhoods until after 5:30 p.m.

After-school programs for middle-school youth have proven enormously effective. In Moscow, Idaho, the junior high school attracts hundreds of students to an after-school program that has gained them state and regional recognition. Activities include intramural soccer and basketball, aerobics, gymnastics, art, music, chess, as well as computer and library access. The students enjoy these activities in a safe, supervised situation.

At Intermediate School 218, in New York's Washington Heights area, an area that has become notorious for urban unrest and drug trafficking, the school has created an all-day neighborhood school. The school is open from early morning until late at night and serves the entire community. The after-school program offers students opportunities in computers, multimedia, environmental studies, drama, dance, arts and crafts, music, photography, athletics, and academic tutoring. After 6:00 p.m. older teenagers and adults are welcomed into the school for a range of opportunities, from employment workshops to citizenship classes to health and athletics programs (Carnegie Corporation, 1993, pp. 10–11). For rural schools, transportation poses a difficult problem for before and after school programs. It is often solved by extending the school day for all students or providing additional bus service in the afternoon.

Community Youth Programs

Out-of-school community programs are vitally important throughout early adolescence. It is during young adolescence that students are experimenting and exploring social and physical limits, taking risks, learning about sexual relationships, and trying to become more independent. For these reasons, the out-of-school time becomes a crucial experience for most adolescents. It is a time of great risk as well as great opportunity. It is during the out-of-school time that youth can become involved in crime, drugs, violence, gangs, and other antisocial behavior. For any of these reasons, after-school and weekend community programs and activities are incredibly important during the middle-school years. When young adolescents were asked what they would most like during nonschool hours, they indicated "safe parks and recreation centers; exciting science museums; libraries with all the latest books, videos, and records; chances to go camping and participate in sports; long talks with trusting and trustworthy adults who know a lot about the world and who like young people; and opportunities to learn new skills" (Carnegie Council on Adolescent Development, 1992, p. 43).

The primary way young people obtain these types of services is through community youth organizations. These organizations are second only to public schools in the number of young people they reach. These organizations include both local and national groups that serve literally millions of young adolescents. Nationally, the largest of these organizations include Boys and Girls Clubs of America, Girl Scouts, Boy Scouts, Boys and Girls Campfire, 4-H, Future Farmers, Future Homemakers, YMCA, and YWCA. Together these groups reach over 30 million young people each year and provide everything from traditional programs of recreation, sports, and camping to informal education and youth development activities. They also offer teen parent programs, drug awareness programs, and some even provide foster care, protective services, remediation and treatment programs, and juvenile justice programs.

There is a growing body of literature which offers convincing evidence that young adolescents and their parents value community organizations and the many services that they provide. This seems especially true for minority and single parents. There is also substantial evidence that these youth organization programs have a strong positive effect on young adolescents. Although metropolitan areas tend to have a greater variety of youth organizations, there are many youth programs available in rural areas. The Carnegie Council on Adolescent

Development has summarized studies of the effects of these programs on both urban and rural young adolescents:

- *A 1987 survey of alumni of 4-H and other youth groups found that, on average, alumni believed that participation in the program contributed to their personal development by giving them pride in accomplishment, self-confidence, the ability to work with others, the ability to set goals and to communicate, employment and leadership skills, and encouragement of community involvement . . .*
- *Four annual evaluations of the Association of Junior Leagues' Teen Outreach Program, a school-based, life-skills management and community service program for middle and high school students, found that participants were less likely than peers who did not participate in the program to become pregnant, drop out, or be suspended from school.*
- *A multiyear evaluation of a targeted intervention developed by Girls Incorporated, called Preventing Adolescent Pregnancy, indicated that participation in all program components was associated with lower overall rates of pregnancy, and that participation in individual components led to specific pregnancy-related effects (e.g., young adolescents who took assertiveness training to learn to refuse early intercourse were only half as likely as nonparticipants to become sexually active).*
- *An evaluation of WAVE, Inc.'s drop-out prevention program found that those who participated showed improved school attendance, lower drop-out rates and improved scores on job readiness, mathematics, reading and self-esteem.*
- *An evaluation of Boys and Girls Clubs of America's SMART Moves (substance-abuse prevention) initiative showed substantial differences between housing projects that had clubs and those that did not. Residential areas with clubs experienced an overall reduction in alcohol and other drug use, drug trafficking and other drug-related crime."*
  (Carnegie Council on Adolescent Development, 1992, p. 38)

Program evaluations and related research provide a "solid rationale for strengthening and expanding the role of community-based programs in promoting healthy adolescent development" (Carnegie Council on Adolescent Development, 1992, p. 39). It is essential that schools recognize the importance of youth organizations and work to encourage youth participation and to coordinate school programs with those in the community.

School Climate

All of the program components described above contribute to creating a caring, supportive, and helping atmosphere. In addition to programs previously described, two others have proven beneficial in developing a school climate conducive to learning and support for at-risk adolescents:

Peaceful Settlement and Conflict Resolution

One of the newer approaches to combating school violence, vandalism, and disruption is peer conflict mediation. Not only has mediation led to the peaceful settlement of disputes and conflicts among students, but it has proven valuable in the adult world of divorce, child custody, and other legal and quasi-legal disputes. Such peer mediation programs can be extremely beneficial when students are carefully trained and supported by teachers and counselors. Peer conflict mediation can lower dropout and truancy rates and improve student behavior. In some schools, peer mediation has been cited as resulting in lowering the suspension rate by more than 50 percent (Dallea, 1987; Stichter, 1986). Peer conflict mediation can help students experience first-hand critical thinking and problem solving. It reduces violence and disruption problems and improves the self-esteem of the student mediators. In one study, three-quarters of students involved in disputes reported that they would have had a fight if they had not been referred for mediation (Stern & Van Slych, 1986).

Judicious Discipline

There is a solid body of evidence demonstrating the effectiveness of democratizing student discipline in schools. In comparative studies of authoritarian and democratic schools as well as in studies of student involvement in rule formulation, there is sufficient positive evidence to support such programs. One program, Judicious Discipline, has been developed to help schools apply a simple set of legal principles based on the Bill of Rights to involve students in rule formulation in schools and classrooms. Early studies of Judicious Discipline have yielded promising results as evidenced by a number of schools being able to eliminate expulsion and suspension by using this particular approach (Gathercoal, 1990).

Dramatic New Alternatives to Middle-Level Education: K–12 Schools

"Just about everyone has heard this story. When we enrolled our first-grade son at the Metropolitan Learning Center, we were of course somewhat apprehensive. Rather than walking to a neighborhood school, he was off daily across town to this really different alternative school. From the first day, our son complained that he was not able to work the combination lock on his locker. But in a few days he excitedly reported that everything was working out all right. My son explained that Mr. Jones was helping him getting his locker open and was helping him store his belongings and then making sure that the locker was locked. Later when we visited the school we wanted to express our thanks to Mr. Jones. We discovered that there was no teacher or custodian in the building named Mr. Jones. After some discussion and exploration, we discovered the delightful news that Mr. Jones was a seventh-grade student who shared a locker next to our son's."
—(PARENT OF FIRST-GRADE STUDENT, METROPOLITAN LEARNING CENTER, PORTLAND, OREGON, 1991)

The most exciting and perhaps most effective example of middle-level education in America today may not be occurring in either the traditional junior high school or the innovative middle school. A number of public schools in the United States, in both urban and rural areas, have developed K–12 public schools that seem to have an unusually positive impact on young adolescents and may in fact be superior to the traditional concept of separate middle-level schools. Unfortunately, very few of these schools are in operation today. Most of the K–12 programs exist as alternative public schools in urban areas or as small rural schools. Yet the research on K–12 schools is remarkably positive. Part of the reason for this comes from the small school size that characterizes these programs and the personalized education that such smallness encourages and accommodates. Success also originates from the continuous educational transition that these schools provide for students from preschool through high school. A review of the research and evaluation on K–12 schools, both urban alternatives as well as small rural schools, documents rather well that there is a better alternative to the concept of middle-level education. That better alternative is an educational program which provides for continuous progress from kindergarten through high school in a small, personalized educational environment with highly individualized teaching and learning.

In fact, the very characteristics that scholars recommend be employed in effective middle-level education are very similar to the characteristics of K–12 schools, except that they are not limited to a particular middle-level age group. And since K–12 schools are providing this type of education from kindergarten through graduation, the impact of these approaches seems to be magnified. This is now recognized as one of the reasons so many small, isolated rural schools are so effective at teaching all children and keeping them in school through graduation.

K–12 Alternative Schools

Over the past 25 years a number of public K–12 alternative schools have emerged and flourished throughout the United States. Several examples of this concept demonstrate the dramatic success of the approach.

Metropolitan Learning Center

One of the most widely recognized alternative public schools in the nation is the Metropolitan Learning Center, a Portland, Oregon, public school. Originating in 1968, Metropolitan Learning Center today serves approximately 450 students, makes frequent use of interage grouping, and has a schoolwide emphasis on building student responsibility at each age level. There are schoolwide goals that emphasize independence, personal decision making and responsibility, and a goal for each student to take responsibility for each other. The school works hard to encourage students to help, support, and nurture one another. Because of this, there is a remarkable caring atmosphere at the Metropolitan Learning Center. It is common to find older students working with younger students and young children dropping by high-school classes seeking information, assistance, and support.

The Metropolitan Learning Center is organized in four school teams, K–3, 4–6, 7–8, and 9–12, but simultaneously encourages cross-age grouping within and between each team. The school day is flexibly organized, including $1^1/_2$ hour instructional blocks for interdisciplinary courses like Urban Waterways and Wetlands, Graphic Metaphors, Creativity and Self, Nature Studies, and Racial Nationalism, plus a number of 45-minute classes like science and math projects, history, reading for pleasure, and integrated math.

Parents are almost militant in their support for this school. Many families come from far distances throughout the city to have their children attend the Metropolitan Learning Center. The parents participate in school governance and serve in a wide variety of volunteer instructional roles. More than 100 parents and other community volunteers are at work in the school at any given time. In spite of the fact that all types of students, including many at-risk youth, attend Metropolitan Learning Center, the student dropout rate is approximately 2 percent per year, compared with 30 percent for the entire school district. And by comparison of achievement test results, Metropolitan Learning Center students are among the best in the school district as well as the state.

Metropolitan Learning Center conducts large numbers of field trips, outings, and out-of-school study opportunities. They also have large numbers of school-wide events that bring all age groups, teachers, and parents together. Once again, for the young adolescent, the difficulties of growing up seem far less stressful in this caring, multi-age environment.

St. Paul Open School

Perhaps the best known and most widely studied school in America is the St. Paul Open School in St. Paul, Minnesota. Pursuing a set of 18 specific competencies rather than course requirements for graduation, students at this K–12 school experience learning that is structured more like that of university doctoral programs than that of the usual public school. Periodically, at each grade level, students meet with educational advisors to decide which graduation competency to pursue, determine how much time to invest in the pursuit, and continuously review progress toward achieving their learning objectives. For example, students pursuing the cultural awareness competency might develop an extended reading list, interview culturally different individuals in the community, take courses at the school or at a community college, pursue foreign language study, visit or complete a short-term stay in the home of a family of another culture, etc. Learning activities often occur in small groups and with students of different age and ability levels. Students later meet with faculty committees and demonstrate their development toward achieving the competency. Students must demonstrate competency in 18 areas (see Table 7-3).

The St. Paul Open School is organized into two academic centers: the Early Learning Center (K–6) and the Older Learning Center (7–12). All Early Learning Center and Older Learning Center students are placed in cross-age continuous progress groups. Most classes have students participating from several age levels, so that ninth graders and sixth graders might be working together at their own pace. This instructional organization has proven to have a significant positive effect on the students:

TABLE 7-3   St. Paul Open School Graduation Competencies Validation Areas

• Post High-School Plans	• Coherent Communication
• Employment Seeking Skills	• Science and Technology
• Career Investigation	• Cultural Awareness (Student's)
• Learning from the Community	• Cultural Awareness (Selected Minority)
• Service to the Community	• Cultural Awareness (Student's Choice)
• Service to the School	• Information Finding
• Current Issues	• Healthy Body
• Consumer Awareness	• Group Process
• Mathematics	• High-School Summary

(St. Paul Open School, 1993)

Open School's K–12 configuration has a number of advantages over a straight elementary or secondary school. One benefit of having primary and secondary age children in the same building is the softening effect the younger children have on the older ones. It is difficult for a 15-year-old to be a "tough" guy or keep a "hard" pose when a 7-year-old asks him for help. (Young, 1990, p. 61)

Early in the school's development, young children planned, designed, obtained external funding, and actually constructed a complex outdoor play area. Older children in the school created a consumer hotline service and provided community members with a variety of services that included tracking down and correcting situations where consumers felt they had been cheated or taken advantage of.

Over two decades of research on the St. Paul Open School has consistently shown unusually positive student achievement, attitude, and behavior results. Studies of teacher satisfaction and community support have yielded equally positive data. Any educator, parent, or individual concerned with restructuring public schools would benefit from visiting the St. Paul Open School, as this long-standing program continues to serve as a model approach for effective education.

Rural K–12 Schools

States throughout the West continue to support large numbers of small, rural schools, even many one- and two-teacher schools. There are numerous examples of small rural K–12 schools that have been successfully teaching students for over 100 years.

Meadows Valley School

Located in the mountains of West Central Idaho just north of the resort town of McCall, the K–12 Meadows Valley School serves approximately 500 students and was recently selected for the state's "Showcase of Excellence" which recognized outstanding public schools. The school exhibits a positive feeling of community, as older students regularly help younger students and serve as counselors for the fifth-grade outdoor education program. The school is able to offer small class sizes and a growing emphasis on technology. A number of innovations characterize Meadows Valley, such as a computerized "homework hotline" that permits parents and students to call the school for updates and information regarding school activities and homework assignments. Parents play an unusually important role in the governance process and the local school board serves only the Meadows Valley School.

Parents provide a daily resource throughout the school's curriculum and activities. One specific program invites parents to bring their young children to the school for preschool activities while the parents participate in intensive educational programs designed to help them better prepare their children for kindergarten and the early elementary grades. The school has a half-time counselor and a parent center that includes a parent lending library. The school has an advanced computer lab as well as a number of out-of-school learning experiences that serve all ages of children. Teachers annually take older students on a Yellowstone Park campout and, on alternate years, on study tours to Europe.

Recently the entire school and community initiated a long-term process of developing consensus regarding learning outcomes. There is growing support for a specified set of learning outcomes, and a system is being developed to assess these outcomes.

What is particularly noteworthy is the lack of upheaval for the young adolescents in this school. The close-knit community environment is an obvious factor, but this stability must also be attributed to the school-community climate and the support that all children and youth receive as they make their way through the transition to adulthood.

The conclusion that seems to be so clear from any careful review of these K–12 schools is that they have demonstrated and documented the existence of a better way of approaching education, especially for at-risk youth, than dividing schools into a three-tier approach involving an elementary, middle school, and a high school. The concept of K–12 schools simply seems to be a better idea, certainly a better idea than arbitrarily dividing and organizing schools into different age groups. Surprisingly, the K–12 organizing concept does not seem to be part of the emerging or current agenda for middle-school educational reform. Yet for the fragile learning needs of at-risk children and youth, the K–12 school may well be the best approach to organizing learning for a maximum impact, especially during the difficult years of the young adolescent.

Despite the lack of research available on effective programs at the middle-school level and the fact that fewer schoolwide reform efforts have been initiated at the middle/junior-high-school level than at other levels, there remains a compelling argument for conceptualizing middle-school programs that can better serve young, at-risk adolescents. The research and school evaluation data consistently suggest that middle-level schools should more closely resemble successful elementary school models as opposed to the current comprehensive high-school model. Middle schools should create smaller organizational units, develop cadres of interdisciplinary teams of teachers and students, and use block scheduling to provide time for thematic lessons that focus on critical thinking and problem solving. Middle-school youth need adult role models, opportunities outside of school to test themselves and explore their limits, and concerted efforts to develop healthy lifestyles and choices.

None of this is new. It reflects precisely the concepts and ideas that initiated the transition movement from the junior-high-school model to the middle-school model in the 1970s. Today, there is a growing body of evidence that urges a more complete transition and middle-school restructuring. The revitalized, reorganized middle school is desperately needed by all young adolescents, and for the at-risk youth it is indeed a matter of staying in school, career success, and perhaps even life and death.

Creating an Effective Model for Middle-School Programs

A review of the most promising approaches for at-risk youth at the middle-school level suggests a truly restructured junior-high school. And while research and evaluation is rather limited, that which is available is consistent with similar studies regarding elementary and high-school programs. Effective middle schools should include the following:

- Large junior-high school programs should be reorganized into smaller components where cohorts of students and teachers work together for most of the school day.
- The curriculum should focus on the developmental needs of the young adolescent and include interdisciplinary course subjects that foster communication, critical thinking, social development, and healthy lifestyles.
- Middle schools should use flexible scheduling to provide blocks of time for interdisciplinary study with teams of students and shorter periods of time for career exploration and specialized studies.
- Programs like cooperative learning, mentoring, computer and technical education, etc., that are described in chapters on elementary and high school programs are also especially effective for the middle-level student.
- Teachers should serve as classroom counselors and advisors.
- It is also clear that out-of-school programs in the community take on an importance that may be more crucial than in either the elementary or high-school years, for it is during early adolescence that students are placed most at risk during their time away from school.

While research and evaluation are far from abundant at the middle school level, there is sufficient evidence to conclude that all students could in fact learn effectively and succeed in schools that employ the essential components described in this chapter (see the Appendix for Self-Evaluation Checklist).

What is so disappointing is that many school districts have changed the grade level of the junior-high school, changed the name of the school from a junior high to a middle school, but have done little else to transform this school level to address the critical needs of the young adolescent.

Approximately two-thirds of middle schools surveyed in 1988 do not use an interdisciplinary curricular organization or flexible block scheduling. They continue to teach separate subjects scheduled in rigid time slots and use subject matter departmentalization in most of the upper grades (Alexander & McEwin, 1989).

There are of course a growing number of middle schools in almost every state where schools have been dramatically restructured. Furthermore, a number of states, including Delaware, Indiana, Kentucky, Maryland, New Mexico, Colorado, Vermont, and Texas, have developed guidelines and statewide policies for reforming middle-level education (Carnegie Corporation, 1993). Unfortunately, while some organizational changes seem to be occurring, the most recent survey reported that "middle school academic programs resemble those reported in 1981" (Riley, 1993, p. 6).

Chapter 8

Programs That Work: Comprehensive, Supplemental and Model High-School Programs

The student was surly and it was clear he didn't feel comfortable being in a school again. He had been expelled from school and in spite of the fact that he needed only a few credits in order to graduate, he had not been in school for over two years.

Student: *I would like to get back to school and get this over with.*

Principal: *That's good; that is exactly what our program is about.*

Student: *Do I have to wait until next January to start?*

Principal: *Why would you want to do that?*

Student: *Every school that I have ever been in started courses only in September and January.*

Principal: *No, at our school you can start any time you like do you want to start today?*

Student: *Well, I don't know, you know. I've got a part-time job, you know, and I don't want to be in school all day.*

Principal: *That's fine, you don't have to be in school all day.*

Student: *Really? Every other school that I have ever attended made you be in school all day and they checked the roll about a thousand times a day to make sure you didn't get away.*

Principal: *Well, here you can come for one course, two courses or for a full program. You can also work all day on one course and as soon as you finish it you get credit for the course.*

Student: *You mean I don't have to wait until June to get credit?*

Principal: *That's exactly right. As soon as you complete a course you get credit for it.*

Student: *Hey, what time do you open here?*

Principal: *We open at 7:30.*

Student: *How late are you open?*

Principal: *We stay open until 7:30 in the evening.*

Student: *Now let me get this right. If I came in the morning I could start at 7:30 and work as long as I could until 7:30 in the evening and continue doing that until I finish a course.*

Principal: *That's exactly right.*

Student: *Well, that's great! In a month or so I could complete these courses and then graduate! This is incredible; why don't other schools do this? I don't understand this. What kind of school is this anyway?*
—*(HIGH-SCHOOL STUDENT AND PRINCIPAL, VOCATIONAL VILLAGE, PORTLAND, OREGON, 1990)*

In a very real sense, high schools are the final battleground for the lives of at-risk youth. The students have grown up and are often angry enough to cause severe problems for teachers, principals, and communities. Many of these students are filled with rage at the humiliations schools have caused them. Imagine being unable to read and sitting in class after class, year after year, where learning centers on textbook reading. Imagine being in classes where everyone is a year or more younger because you were retained during the elementary or middle-school years. Try to imagine going to school where almost everything revolves around students who are going to college and you know that for you higher education is an impossible dream. How must it feel to have spent nine or ten years in school, being retained, tracked into slow classes with other "dumb" kids, suspended on occasion, suffering through failure after failure on test after test, and then to have high-school counselors talk down to you about graduation credit, college entrance requirements, and your poor attitude?

For the at-risk high-school student, it is obvious that most schools have compounded the problems of poverty, dysfunctional families, and low self-esteem with a decade-long barrage of humiliation, despair, and defeat. It is no wonder so many at-risk youth become pregnant during middle school and high school; why so many turn to drugs and alcohol; why so many carry guns to school and make violence, vandalism, and school disruption an everyday way of life; why too many violence-prone city youth see life as valueless and so many at-risk kids wage daily war against teachers and the school. Most remarkable is the fact that so many of these students still come to school, still hang on to the diminishing dream of high-school graduation. For many others, the decision to stay in school is not prompted by educational considerations but determined by the declining opportunities for jobs for the high-school dropout. Unlike other generations of youth who found re-markable opportunities for good jobs in the economic marketplace and in the armed forces, today's at-risk youth are held hostage to a no-win situation—trapped in schools that are not meeting their needs, with few choices or other places to go.

The high school is clearly the last chance for many of our at-risk youth. If they leave school or even graduate lacking the basic skills adequate for the workplace, there is little hope for a self-supporting, productive life. The encouraging news is that even at this late date in the development of these youth, programs are avail-able in schools that can effect dramatic, positive change. Many of these programs report truly remarkable successes. We now know that a student who has been la-beled as severely at risk and who is a dangerous troublemaker can often learn to read in a relatively short time and within a few months, can pass a high-school equivalency test. And as job opportunities continue to diminish for the unedu-cated, many dropouts are returning to public school or community colleges to complete a high-school degree or an equivalency diploma and then enroll in some type of technical program. Nearly 83 percent of 19- and 20-year-olds had com-pleted high school or its equivalent by the year 1990 (National Center for Educa-tional Statistics, 1991).

Research has documented that effective high-school programs can improve self-esteem, transform attitudes toward teachers and school, and salvage young lives from drug and alcohol addiction and abuse. Unfortunately, these tend to be stand-alone programs that address the needs of a relatively small number of high-school students. It is rare to find high-school at-risk programs serving more than ten percent of the total high-school population. Unlike elementary school, there are very few examples of schoolwide restructuring efforts at the high-school level. Public high schools continue to operate throughout the United States as college prep programs with less emphasis on general and vocational education, with ei-ther formal or informal tracking programs, and a few isolated pockets of small pro-grams for at-risk youth.

The major high-school restructuring effort underway today is the Coalition of Essential Schools, led by Ted Sizer, former dean of the Harvard Graduate School of Education. The Coalition of Essential Schools, involving more than 500 partici-pating schools, recently received a $50 million gift from the philanthropist Walter Annenburg. Unfortunately, a five-year study of the coalition reported a depress-ing lack of success in restructuring comprehensive high schools (Muncey & Mc-Quillan, 1993). In fact, it is nearly impossible to find a large comprehensive high school in the United States or Canada that has been significantly restructured.

A team from the Vancouver, Washington, public schools conducted a national search to try to find a restructured, comprehensive high school and ultimately visited a number of schools in the United States and Canada that had been recommended to them. After visiting these various schools, the team from Vancouver concluded that they could find no examples of truly restructured, comprehensive high schools.

After this study, a major planning effort was started in Vancouver that involved students, parents, teachers, administrators, school board members, and community leaders in planning and designing a totally new concept for a comprehensive high school. Teams of architects were also involved in the process that led to a preliminary design of a new type of educational facility to house a dramatically different comprehensive high school. The new school will include the following characteristics:

- Students will be involved one-third of the time in individualized study, one-third in cooperative learning activities in small groups, and one-third of the time in regular large-group classes.
- Students will have a four-day school schedule with the school being available approximately 12 hours per day. The fifth day will be available for off-campus activities and career, vocational, community service, or independent projects.
- The school will use technology in a comprehensive way, providing each student with computer access, national and international network access, and cable television.
- Graduation requirements will be reconceptualized as competencies with specific performance outcomes.
- Child care will be provided.
- An extensive vocational/technical program will serve all students.

Developments in Vancouver deserve to be carefully followed. After three years of work, one of their high schools, Fort Vancouver High School, has been reorganized from a five-period day to a four-period day, allowing approximately 90 minutes per class for in-depth and individualized, small-group study. At Columbia River High School, a Phase I and Phase II program has been developed where students obtain required skills during the 9th and 10th grades and then select career clusters to pursue during the 11th and 12th grades. The school district is also expanding their magnet school program. Descriptions of the magnet schools appear later in this chapter.

One other promising approach to restructuring high schools is occurring in New York, where schools and community leaders are developing 50 smaller, more personalized high schools. The goal of this project is to phase out two large comprehensive high schools and replace them with 12 of these smaller, more personalized schools. This coalition campus school project represents a significant effort to "humanize high school education and transform from large failing inner-city schools into successful learning environments for all students" (National Center For Restructuring Education, Schools and Teaching, 1994).

High-school restructuring, regardless of the chosen approach, must address the needs of at-risk youth. The following review presents many programs that have demonstrated an unusual effectiveness with at-risk youth at the high-school level.

Comprehensive At-Risk Programs

There are a number of programs that address the needs of high-school students in comprehensive ways that approximate an effective at-risk model. These include alternative school and magnet school programs, teen parent programs.There are also a number of other specialized programs that are especially useful for at-risk youth.

Alternative Public Schools

Alternative public schools have an established record of success at the high-school level that is based on over 25 years of effective practice. Alternative public schools may be the most important at-risk programs at the high-school level. Some see these programs as educational "intensive care" units where students who have been battered by home, community, and school are provided with immediate responsive care and support. The reasons for success are the same as they are at other school levels. An alternative high school provides the small educational atmosphere of support that seems to function as a surrogate family for at-risk youth. It provides a place to insulate and protect these fragile, often abused and angry youth. It provides a highly individualized program designed to meet the unique needs of at-risk youth, and it provides the at-risk student with strong, positive advocates to work with juvenile authorities, parents, schools, and social services. The success of alternative schools is seen in their productive longevity and an increasing recognition of their value as environments for research and development related to improving public education.

Longevity

Many alternative public schools were started during the late 1960s and have been in operation for more than 25 years. Today, it is estimated that well over 15,000 of these schools are in operation within public education. Unlike other educational innovations, these schools have endured and even led to changes in earlier research conclusions. Research studies during the 1960s conducted by the Ford Foundation concluded that once a vigorous, reform-minded principal left a school, the innovations that he or she had helped to create would quickly cease and the school would return to earlier ways of doing business (Nachtigal, 1972). During the past 20 to 25 years, almost every alternative school in America has changed principals, sometimes many times, and most have completely changed their faculty without dramatically impacting the school and the integrity of the school programs (Barr, 1981; Young, 1990). This research underscores the power of programs that address the needs of specific youth, that encourage parental involvement, and that provide teachers, parents, and students with real opportunities to participate in a relevant educational process.

Environments for Research and Development

Alternative public schools have provided the nation with the richest collection of experimental programs that has ever been developed and evaluated. Through the creation and support of alternative schools, educators have experimented with such concepts as out-of-school learning, peer tutoring, cross-age grouping, challenge education, open education, schools without walls, individualized continuous progress schools, traditional back-to-basics education, authentic assessment, nongraded learning, competency-based graduation requirements, school choice, and site-based decision making. It is startling to consider the vast numbers of concepts, approaches, and programs first developed in alternative schools that now have become widely used in traditional public schools. Nearly every major public school restructuring effort of the past 15 years is based in part on effective practices and concepts previously developed, implemented, and evaluated in alternative public schools (Barr, 1981; Raywid, 1983; Young, 1990).

Positive Research and Evaluation

Many of the nationally recognized alternative schools have been the focus of continuous study, evaluation, and research during the past 25 years. Students have been pre- and post-tested, compared to other public school students through assessments of academic performance and behavior, and evaluated through long-term follow-up studies. Most aspects of program conception, design, funding, curriculum, staffing, and community relations have been studied and evaluated (Raywid, 1983, 1993a; Smith, Barr & Burke, 1976; Young, 1990). This body of research, evaluation, and student assessment forms a foundation of confidence for public schools and represents the most positive data available for addressing the needs of at-risk youth. Research-based conclusions from alternative public school practice will continue to influence significant reform and restructure of the nation's public schools.

Characteristics of Alternative Schools

Because alternative schools have been evaluated more often and more carefully than virtually any other type of public school, their programs have constantly been refined and improved. A review of the characteristics of effective programs for at-risk youth described earlier in this book parallels closely the characteristics of alternative schools: small size, caring and demanding teachers, individualized curriculum, choice, etc. (Barr, 1981; Raywid, 1983; Wehlage, et al., 1989; Young, 1990).

Improved Self-esteem

Over time, students enrolled in alternative public schools develop more positive self-esteem and attitudes toward teachers and schools (Estes, et al., 1990; Raywid, 1983; Young, 1990). Many who have reviewed this research have concluded that the data are almost too good to be true. Yet even school dropouts, once they are away from the negative impact of traditional schools, often develop improved self-image, at least for a while. Alternative schools provide a supportive atmosphere so that these attitudes and behaviors can be enhanced.

Improved Achievement

Public school teachers and administrators are often surprised or even suspicious when their former at-risk students begin to achieve so positively, often dramatically in alternative schools (Estes, et al., 1990; Raywid, 1983; Young, 1990). This is true for both basic as well as vocational skills. Once at-risk students leave the difficult world of traditional school classes and enter the supportive, focused programs of an alternative school, truly remarkable achievement often occurs. Many alternative educators report significant improvement that is not directly related to the curriculum or the instruction (although these most certainly make a difference). It is student attitudes that seem to make the difference. Often, at-risk students who have never tried to do well in courses or on standardized tests assert themselves for the first time in alternative schools. As a result, many alternative schools report that their students learn to read almost overnight or raise their achievement scores several years in a few months. It has become an accepted belief among teachers in alternative programs that student gains in self-esteem are absolutely necessary before significant improvements in academic achievement can occur.

Improved Student Behavior

Students in alternative schools often have returned to school after brief or extended periods of complete separation from public or private education. These students tend to stay in these schools far more frequently than in their past educational experiences. Truancy and violence diminish as overall school and class attendance increase. In one study, 81 percent of those surveyed reported improved attendance and 38 percent reported a sharp rise in attendance rates (Estes, et al., 1990; Raywid, 1983; Young, 1990). School vandalism virtually disappears in alternative schools as the students, perhaps for the first time in their lives, develop school behaviors that reflect positive feelings toward teachers, peers, and learning.

Positive Teacher Attitudes

Staff morale is unusually high in alternative public schools. As many as 90 percent of alternative school teachers in one study reported they felt a real ownership of their program, and a similar number reported that they were willing to assume even greater responsibilities in order to continue working in the program (Raywid, 1983). The vast majority of effective alternative school teachers demonstrate real concern for the needs of youth at risk, which helps to create and maintain the positive environment that these youth need to succeed.

Meeting Student Needs

In one of the classic studies comparing alternative schools to other public schools, students were asked how well the school they attended met their needs, using Maslow's Hierarchy of Needs. The study discovered that students in alternative schools believe that their schools met a larger range of their needs and met them better than students in other public schools (Smith, et al., 1981). Alternative schools often have goals and curricula focused on self-esteem and study skills, and offer support groups, personal development opportunities, and subsidized breakfast and lunch programs. Students in these schools recognize the positive influence the school has on their lives.

High Quality of School Life

A number of studies over the years have identified school size, school culture, and the general quality of school life as the most important aspects of alternative education. In fact, alternative public schools reflect a similar set of conditions usually found only in highly successful elite private schools (Erickson, 1981). For many students, enrolling in an alternative school begins with a period of skeptical uncertainty, during which they evaluate the "reality" of a seemingly different type of school. After all, for many of these youth, school has never represented an environment in which they could experience success or even have fun. Over time, these students tend to develop a strong positive bonding with their schools.

Distinctive Teaching Methods

Teachers in alternative schools report that they must employ distinctive instructional approaches that relate to student needs. These include: independent study and research; peer teaching; out-of-school action learning; highly individualized self-paced instruction; tutoring; vocational training; and career exploration and computer-assisted learning. For youth at risk, a blend of diverse instructional practices that complement individual student needs, interests, and learning styles is essential.

Needs-Based Curriculum

It is not difficult to comprehend that a program planned to meet the needs of certain youth will be more successful in teaching those youth. For the first time, many youth feel responded to, respected, and connected with a school. Meeting the needs of individual students creates an environment of trust that translates into a student developing a willingness to learn in school. For many at-risk students, the basic needs of health, safety, and emotional support must first be addressed before significant learning can be expected to take place.

Choice
Ultimately, the fact that students and parents choose to participate in alternative schools carries significant power. Students and parents feel invested in the program and respond with positive efforts. Furthermore, the professionals who choose to work in alternative schools do so out of personal concern for those youth and the desire to work in a smaller, collaborative approach (Nathan, 1989; Young & Clinchy, 1993).

Alternative School Models

Public alternative schools have been providing students, parents, and communities with educational choices for the past two decades. Most were developed in response to particular community needs; many continue to operate from a similarly distinctive focus.

Schools Without Walls
Perhaps the first alternative public school to gain national attention was the Philadelphia Parkway School, which the national media described as a school without walls. Students attended classes not in a school building, but up and down the Philadelphia Parkway, their courses scheduled in banks, businesses, newspapers, museums, government agencies, hospitals, etc. Teachers in the Parkway School were joined by a variety of teachers who were noncertified professionals: bankers, artists, accountants, journalists, curators, and a host of others to teach the traditional content of the school curriculum to small groups of students who traveled beyond the walls of the school for their classes.

Almost immediately, other school districts around the country, usually in cities, began to replicate the school-without-walls concept. The Chicago Metro School, originally located in the downtown loop, holds classes at the Chicago Art Institute, the Field History Museum, the Shedd Aquarium, the mayor's office, and even Playboy, Incorporated. In a city where the dropout rate approaches 50 percent, Metro consistently graduated over 90 percent of its students. Metro students scored above the city average on reading and math tests, and follow-up studies found over 70 percent of the graduates had gone on to postsecondary education. For at-risk youth, who compose a large percentage of the student body at the Parkway and Metro schools, the programs provide cultural richness and diversity that most of these students have never experienced (Estes, et al., 1990). These schools have successfully operated for over 20 years and brought business, government, and the arts into public education in a new, dynamic, and effective manner.

Walkabout Schools
Based on the ideas of Maurice Gibbons, walkabout schools attempted to provide North American students with life challenges modeled after the Australian Aborigine walkabout experience as part of the passage through school to adulthood (Gibbons, 1976). Traditionally, it was believed that young Aborigines left their tribe and village and spent several months surviving on their own in the Outback.

If they succeeded, they would have learned and demonstrated their proficiency at skills essential for the survival of their tribe. The first walkabout school in the United States was Learning Unlimited. The school was organized as a school within a school at North Central High School, a large comprehensive school in a suburb of Indianapolis, Indiana, serving more than 4,000 students. The curriculum was focused on a number of challenge areas, as opposed to a traditional structure of required coursework. These areas include cultural diversity, academic competency, outdoor education, adventure-based learning, and other forms of out-of-school learning. Phi Delta Kappa supported this concept and for a period of time published a national walkabout newsletter.

Schools for Dropouts

For decades, dropping out of school was far more popular than staying in. In fact, only since the 1940s have more than 50 percent of the students eligible to graduate from the public schools in the U.S. done so. This phenomenon spawned a significant growth of continuation schools throughout the early 1900s. These part-time public schools for those unable to adjust helped dropouts to make the transition from adolescence to work. By the 1960s, continuation schools were rapidly being transitioned or replaced by yet another approach to help youth at risk: the alternative school (Kelly, 1993).

Some of the first alternative schools in the United States were developed to attract students who had dropped out of school or to keep those who were on the verge of dropping out from doing so. Originating in the late 1960s, schools for dropouts continue to represent the largest category of alternative public schools in operation today. A number of states have recently mandated that every public school district must offer alternative schools as a dropout prevention measure for any student who is contemplating leaving or who actually leaves public education. A few of the more recognized schools include the following:

- *Vocational Village, Portland, Oregon:* In two national studies, Vocational Village was identified as one of the best examples of a 9–12 school that met all of the requirements of an effective dropout alternative. The school has been in operation for over 20 years, has had a number of different principals, has changed locations twice, and today attracts students from throughout the Portland metropolitan area. Members of several different youth gangs attend the school together with students from all walks of life. The school is highly individualized and provides an assortment of up-to-date, technical vocational skills centers. The staff also works hard to help students make the transition to work once they have completed their schooling. They assist in job placement and maintain cooperative programs with local community colleges. The school has been recognized as one of the nation's best.
- *Westbridge Academy, Grand Rapids, Michigan:* One of the nation's oldest alternative schools, this 7–12 school pioneered the development of individualized learning, contingency contracting, and an instructional program built around positive reinforcement. Serving a challenging group of dropouts and adjudi-

cated youth, the school has succeeded by providing incentives for students to complete their homework, attend classes, and excel in academic achievement. Students earn middle-school and high-school level credit through a variety of individualized courses of study that encourage them to learn as fast as they can yet do not academically penalize them for interruptions in their schooling. Originating in 1969 as Walbridge Academy, this school continues to model the success and value of individualized instruction as one of the most effective practices known for teaching youth at risk.

- *Jefferson County High School, Louisville, Kentucky:* Opened in 1986, the Jefferson County High School serves the city of Louisville, Kentucky, and the surrounding county. The 9–12 school is for dropouts of all ages and operates 12 months a year, from 8:00 a.m. to 9:30 p.m. Approximately 85 percent of the students are between the ages of 17 and 21, about 10 percent are in their 20s and early 30s, and every class includes a few older adults. The school recently graduated a 65-year-old and often has students in their 60s and 70s attending class. During the first four years of the program, Jefferson County High School served over 5,000 students and helped 1,100 students to graduate (Gross, 1990). The school guarantees that every student who perseveres will leave the school academically competent.

  Students pursue a highly individualized program, usually focusing on one or two courses at a time. The central feature of this individualized program is computer-assisted instruction. While little homework is assigned, students must satisfactorily complete each instructional unit before they can proceed to the next. Students may attend a three-hour morning block, a three-hour afternoon block, or a three-hour evening block. Some students attend only one of the blocks, others attend a split morning/evening block to allow for child care or work, and a few attend all three.

  Most graduates of Jefferson County High School immediately go to work, but some enter college programs. Graduates believe the program prepares them well for both options. All students receive vocational guidance, job skills and aptitude assessment, and are guided toward opportunities to pursue further academic and vocational training.

Magnet Schools

Nearly every major city in the United States has developed an array of alternative schools and, in many locations, these offerings are referred to as magnet schools. While most of these programs were started initially to attract students from diverse regions and populations of a city or to provide a specific, enhanced focus, the concept quickly became the approach of choice and an integral part of court-ordered desegregation efforts. Magnet schools were evaluated during the 1970s as the most successful aspect of desegregation plans (Estes, et al., 1990; Waldrip, et al., 1993). The concept proved unusually successful as parents and students from ethnically diverse neighborhoods willingly chose to attend academically focused alternative schools and chose to do so without forced busing.

After over 20 years of success, this desegregation by choice continues to demonstrate that parents and students from different ethnic groups are willing to attend school together, even travel long distances to do so, in order to participate in quality educational experiences.

While often started by court orders, magnet schools have grown and expanded far beyond their original purpose for desegregation. Today, magnet schools have become characterized primarily by an emphasis on career, professional, and vocational programs. They have grown and thrived because of their remarkable educational success. Cities such as Houston, Dallas, Milwaukee, San Diego, Los Angeles, Boston, Louisville, St. Louis, Kansas City, Seattle, and others have developed large numbers of magnets, and many cities (like Vancouver, Washington) are currently expanding the magnet school concept. Some of the magnet programs have become significant components of public education. In Houston, for example, over 25 percent of all public school students attend one of the more than 60 magnet school programs available. With the motto "The Best Education That Money Can't Buy," the Houston public schools have attracted back to public education not only dropouts, but parents and students who had abandoned public education for private, parochial, and suburban schools (Barr, 1982).

One of the nation's most successful magnet schools is the Skyline Magnet School in Dallas. First opened in 1971, the school today serves over 800 students with a comprehensive academic program including nine foreign languages, advanced placement in the arts and sciences, and extensive preparation in communications, military science, and vocational and career training. In Houston, the Health Professional Magnet is located at the Baylor Medical Center Complex and focuses on health and medicine. Popular magnet school concepts created for at-risk youth can be found in most major U.S. cities and include the following:

- Aerospace schools
- Business or management schools
- Computer technology schools
- Environmental studies/outdoor schools
- Fundamental back-to-basics high schools
- Global studies and international focus schools
- Health careers schools
- Interdisciplinary educational parks
- Performing arts schools
- Science/math enrichment schools
- Multicultural schools

Complementing these schools are a number of more exotic magnet programs which include petrochemical engineering programs, media schools for radio and television, sports magnets, marketing and business schools, and teaching career magnets. Many of these schools and programs are available at both the middle-school and the high-school level and provide for conventional high-school graduation through intensive enrichment in their magnet emphasis.

Magnet schools enable students to select a career emphasis and pursue a major in a manner similar to students in community colleges or universities. The opportunity to focus high-school careers in an area that relates both to a student's interest and to later jobs and opportunities has had enormous success. A statewide study of 41 magnet schools in New York documented a compelling success story. The report concluded that magnet programs helped keep kids in school, helped them improve educational achievement, and when compared to public school students on standardized tests, 58 percent of the magnet school students performed better on reading and 65 percent performed better on math. Average daily attendance was also higher in 98 percent of the magnet programs (Magi Educational Services, 1985). Similar studies have been conducted with equally positive results in magnet schools in Chicago, Houston, San Diego, and St. Louis (Estes, et al., 1990).

Manhattan's District 4 in East Harlem is one of the nation's most celebrated magnet success stories. The district offers 23 magnet schools at the elementary, middle, and high-school level. In an economically devastated area where city dropout figures are reported at 78 percent for Hispanic youth and 72 percent for African-American, the District 4 Elementary Magnet could identify only two high-school dropouts in an eight-year period during the 1980s and reported that students' reading scores were raised from last in the city to over 62 percent reading at or above grade level (Estes et al., 1990).

There exist few high schools in the United States today, other than specially designed alternative schools, where comprehensive schoolwide programs have been initiated at the high-school level. One school system where such a comprehensive program is being developed and implemented is the Vancouver, Washington, public schools. During the past few years, the school district has moved to develop and implement a large number of new magnet programs, to develop schoolwide instruction programs in the high schools, and to expand the school district's alternative school for at-risk youth to sites on the other high-school campuses.

The at-risk alternative program in Vancouver is the Pan Terra High School, housed in its own building and serving approximately 250 students. Students may attend a morning, afternoon, or evening block or any combination of these sessions to pursue their learning. Each student meets with parents and teachers to develop a personalized education plan that establishes learning goals, the amount of time to be invested in the learning, a plan for achieving the goals, and an outcome assessment plan. The individualized approach has proven extremely successful over the years for Pan Terra, whose program is now being expanded to the high schools as Pan Terra Satellite Centers. Plans are being explored for similar satellites at the middle-school level.

New magnet school programs have been developed at each high school. These include Eagle's Wing, a high-school program serving approximately 250 students who pursue independent and group projects as well as individualized research, rather than participating in a course-driven curriculum. A new Performing Art-Center is being planned and developed, as well as an International High School Baccalaureate Program.

Such districtwide, comprehensive high-school magnet programs should offer great assistance for at-risk youth, providing them with the individualized, continuous progress that they need for their academic work while also assisting them in technical career and job opportunities.

While the term magnet schools became popularized during desegregation efforts and continues to be used to describe programs in many of the nation's largest cities, a number of schools have moved away from a cultural diversity theme. Today, magnet schools are often indistinguishable from other alternative public schools, and the terms magnet schools, alternative schools, optional schools, and schools of choice are often used interchangeably.

Teen Parent Programs

"Listen," she said, "these teen moms couldn't care less about school." Then holding her hand up, the director of the Teen Parent Program ticked off items one by one on each finger. "Most of these young women don't have a job, don't have child care, and most don't have a phone or a car or perhaps worse they have a car that doesn't work. They are all on food stamps or welfare, or both; many have been kicked out of their homes and have no place to live, many of them are sick, their babies are sick . . . and they have no health care. And most have been abused by their father, their boyfriend, or sometimes by both, and they all have this screaming, demanding little hellion with a dirty diaper on. You think they are interested in continuing their education? Get real! Dealing with teen parents is a monster problem. If we have any hope of helping these kids and their babies, we have to do the wildest things. We have to find a safe place for them to live, seek out all types of social services for them, go pick them up and take them home and provide health care and be very, very careful that we don't schedule anything during the afternoon soap operas or Oprah. That, my friend, is the heart and guts of a first-rate teen parent program. In this world, you get real, real quick; or you get out of the business."
—(DIRECTOR, TEEN PARENT PROGRAM,
SALEM, OREGON 1989)

The difficulties related to teen pregnancy continue to plague adolescents. While the average age of these young parents continues to drop, the actual incidence of adolescent child bearing is approximately 50% less than it was in 1955 (Scott-Jones, 1993). Today, there are 25 to 30 million teenage parents in the United States, which holds the dubious distinction of leading all nations in the Western world with a rate of 11 pregnant girls out of every 100 (*Associated Press*, 1993). Despite lowered incidence, teenage pregnancy persists at an alarming level, and as the workplace has changed, these adolescents often face a grim future in poverty.

Teen pregnancy has always been one of the major factors related to dropping out of school. Teen pregnancy is also directly related to a host of other social problems as well as to the escalating cost of health and welfare. Long-term financial savings in social services more than offset the short-term costs of operating teen parent programs and make an undeniable case for their inclusion as an essential part of high schools and middle schools (Barr & Ross, 1989).

There is probably no other type of at-risk intervention as important at the middle-school and high-school level as an effective teen parent program. The reasons for starting a teen parent program go far beyond long-term financial savings and encompass basic human concern and compassion:

- Unless there is some type of intervention, teenagers who have a child tend to have a second child. Teenage parents with two children will be on welfare for a minimum of ten years.
- Teenage parents are caught in a cycle of poverty, illiteracy, and welfare needs that are transferred from one generation to the next, causing demands for social services and welfare to escalate year after year.
- Children of teenage parents tend to be premature and small, often suffering from a variety of problems that increase health costs. Abuse is also often a problem.
- Infants of teen parents are 45 percent more likely to require neonatal intensive care. The average cost: $32,380 each.
- Each severely handicapped infant requires an average of $400,000 additional public assistance for medical conditions until age 21.
- Welfare costs for mother and child average just over $4,200 per year. Over 60 percent of those currently receiving Aid to Dependent Children are or were teen parents.
- Most teenage parents are out of school and out of work. (Barr & Ross, 1989, p. 1)

Why Would a Community Want to Start a Teenage Parent Program?

Every community has teenage parents and the number is substantial. Without intervention, a serious set of problems is being transferred from one generation to the next. Without intervention, the cost of social services and health services will continue to climb.

Teenage parent programs really work. They can help reduce unplanned second and third children by helping young mothers focus on their futures, enabling them to complete their education and find employment and thus break the cycle of poverty. And there is a direct relationship to the birth of unplanned, neglected babies (or babies who have failed to receive adequate love and care) and delinquent and criminal behavior in those children. Effective teenage parent programs are a very important factor in the long-term development of safer neighborhoods and will help to reduce the costs of welfare, health, and social services. And while it is important to develop programs for the teen parent, many argue that it is even more important to provide care and support for the teenager's baby. Research has helped to identify the essential components of an effective teen parent program (Barr & Ross, 1989).

Essential Components of a Successful Teenage Parent Program

All effective teen parent programs must offer a complex of approaches to provide for the diverse needs of adolescents. As the vast majority of these students continue to be the moms and not the dads, essential program components must be developed accordingly.

Addressing needs.   The first priority is to assess and address the most urgent needs of the teenage parent. It must be recognized that teenage parents are themselves kids. The moms often believe that a boy or a man is going to come along to take care of them, so they don't feel an urgent need for education or a job. Yet their immediate needs often include a safe place to live, food and shelter, health assistance, safety from physical abuse, child care, transportation, and may include assistance with drug and alcohol problems. Only after health, housing, and safety needs are addressed will teenage mothers be able to consider education, jobs, and other long-term goals.

Case management.   Successful teenage parent programs use a case management approach very similar to the special education individualized education plan. Each teenage parent must be evaluated, her needs identified, and a developmental plan created. It is important that this be described as a developmental plan and not a treatment plan. Each teenage parent needs a case manager who becomes a personal advocate. Case managers assess the teenage parent's cultural situation and special needs, develop personal rapport, begin to identify the most pressing problems that the teenage parent has, and work toward obtaining help. Later the teenage parent will be helped to identify goals and develop plans to pursue her goals.

Shelter.   The teenage parent and her baby must have a safe place to live. This is absolutely essential and the foremost priority. Teenage parents often go on welfare in order to gain access to public housing, but waiting lists are so long it can often take months or in some situations even years for them to obtain affordable, adequate housing. Until recently, most communities have had no shelter available for young adolescents. This is a desperate area of need in most communities.

Child care.   Most initial assumptions regarding child care tend to be wrong. Most people believe that child care centers can be staffed with part-time volunteers, and that a child care program can be created with little or no expenses. After shelter, this is the most important aspect of a teen parent's life. Teenage parents need quality child care to allow them to pursue an education. The babies of teenage parents are often premature, small, ill, and many have drug and alcohol-related problems at birth. Each of these conditions compound the care needs of infants and can reduce the availability of quality care.

Teenage parents, like all parents, must learn parenting skills. Often they do not come from stable family situations. Often they have no parent or grandparent to teach them effective parenting skills, or the adults in their family lack effective parenting skills. For this reason, high quality child care is essential. It will provide the infant with things the teenage parent may be unable to provide. It is also important for teenage parents to be involved in child care programs in order to learn parenting skills. Some feel that the effectiveness of a teenage parent program can only be measured in the cognitive and social development of teenage parents' babies.

Strong organization and staff.   A successful teen parent program must have a strong organization, including an advisory group of concerned local citizens, a strong professional staff to do the work, a network of "power people" identified in each of the related social service agencies, and a wide variety of volunteers, including all types of providers from doctors and nurses to drivers.

To succeed, teenage parent programs must have a strong, highly trained professional staff. The staff must be culturally sensitive, free of judgmental and negative values, and extremely well informed regarding agencies and social services. They need to develop networks to be able to use a case management and advocacy approach.

Multiagency model.   One of the greatest challenges of a successful teen parent program is gaining the cooperation of essential social service agencies. It takes perseverance to access and coordinate social services. There are a number of successful models for coordinating social service agencies, but none are easy. All involve some person charged with coordination and some type of social services coordinating committee (see Table 8-1).

Cultural sensitivity.   Because of the large numbers of minority teen parents, cultural sensitivity can make or break a program. Agencies need to learn how difficult and complex cultural issues can be, and they need to learn how to deal with cultural issues effectively. Only the various cultural groups themselves can help in developing sensitivity to issues regarding childbirth and child rearing in a particular ethnic group.

TABLE 8-1   Local Agencies That Can Help Teenage Parent Programs

Community Colleges	Hospitals
Children's Services Division	Welfare Offices
Juvenile Courts	United Way
Service Clubs	Public Schools
Mental Health Association Centers and County Programs	Drug and Alcohol Rehabilitation Centers
Community Services Consortia	County Health Departments
Adult and Family Services Commissions	Churches
Child Care Resource and Referral Agencies	Children and Youth Services Commissions

(Barr & Ross, 1989, p. 6)

Use of volunteers.   While successful teen parent programs cannot be staffed exclusively with volunteers, they cannot be operated without them. But the use of volunteers is in itself a complex and demanding process. Teenage parent programs must recruit, screen, train, and provide orientation to all support staff volunteers. In rural areas, volunteers are even more essential. Volunteer training should include an initial orientation and training program followed by monthly training programs. Volunteers must be coordinated, supported, and managed.

Transportation.   Transportation is always an urgent need for teenage parents. However, laws governing public school transportation of teenage parents and their babies often require split seats, seat belts, and infant seats much like special education. While pregnant, teenage parents can use public school special education transportation in many states; they do not qualify after a baby is delivered. For that reason, most successful programs use volunteers as drivers, and the drivers are trained to be counselors. The time in the car is very valuable time. Often teenage parents feel more relaxed and it is easier to talk and confide during the drive to the program. Drivers become "car-care counselors."

Mental health.   Teenage parent programs need to develop strong relationships with county mental health centers because financial assistance may require approval through these agencies. Communities may consider including mental health assistance to teen parents in their county priorities and plans.

Education.   While many teenage parent programs are started by schools and have schooling as a primary focus, the important goals of literacy and high-school graduation will simply not be achieved until the more pressing needs of the teenage parents and their children are met. To be successful, education programs need to provide the teenage parents with intensive, individualized instruction and support.

Education programs may need to be part-time and use the general equivalency diploma (GED). Also, the GED provides individualized instruction to ensure continuous, if sometimes slow, progress. Education programs should connect with community college opportunities and perhaps look beyond the high school to the community college. Often a two-year community college program is more important than a high-school diploma because it can lead directly to a job.

Job training and placement.   The ultimate goal of educational programs and successful teenage parent programs should focus on career exploration and the selection of, training for, and achievement of a job. Career education, job training, and job placement programs need to be directly linked to the educational program. The two components of a program, education and employment, should have goals that complement each other and interrelate. This kind of program design will help motivate the teen parent and show how educational and job goals work together. Cooperative work experience education programs are excellent models for incorporating career and educational goals.

TABLE 8-2 Workplace Competencies and Recommendations for the Year 2000

Workplace Competencies:

- Resources: They know how to allocate time, money, materials, space, and staff.
- Interpersonal Skills: They can work on teams, teach others, serve customers, lead, negotiate, and work well with people from culturally diverse backgrounds.
- Information: They can acquire and evaluate data, organize and maintain files, interpret and communicate, and use computers to process information.
- Systems: They understand social, organizational, and technological systems; they can monitor and correct performance; and they can design or improve systems.
- Technology: They can select equipment and tools, apply technology to specific tasks, and maintain and troubleshoot equipment.

Foundation Skills: Competent workers in the high-performance workplace need

- Basic Skills: Reading, writing, arithmetic and mathematics, speaking and listening.
- Thinking Skills: The ability to learn, to reason, to think creatively, to make decisions, and to solve problems.
- Personal Qualities: Individual responsibility, self-esteem and self-management, sociability, and integrity.

Reinventing Schools:

- Workplace know-how (the SCANS workplace competencies and foundation skills) should be taught along the entire continuum of education, from kindergarten through college.
- Every student should complete middle school (about age 14) with an introduction to workplace know-how.
- Every student should complete high school sufficiently proficient in the SCANS know-how to earn a decent living.
- All federally funded programs for youth and adults, including vocational education programs, should teach the SCANS know-how.

Fostering Work-based Learning:

- Federal, state, and local agencies should incorporate training in the SCANS workplace competencies.
- Private-sector work-based training programs should incorporate training in the SCANS workplace competencies.
- Coalitions of business, associations, government employers, and labor organizations should teach the SCANS competencies to the current workforce, including employees of small businesses.

(U.S. Dept. of Labor, Secretary's Commission on Achieving Necessary Skills, 1992, pp. xiv–xxi).

employment. High-school students should be involved in a variety of career-related experiences outside the school. These might include job shadowing, being assigned a mentor in their employment area of interest, developing networks of resource people, participating in community service, career practice in job situations,

Job training services are available through the local JTPA program. If child care, basic survival needs, and the other support services are already in place, it should be fairly easy to get job training and placement services provided by a local program at no cost. Some of the other services that are so essential, such as education, counseling, and some transportation, may also be paid for or provided by the local program.

Perhaps the most widely recognized and thoroughly studied teen parent program in the United States is the New Futures School in Albuquerque, New Mexico. Opening its doors in 1970, this school continues to be a model of community collaboration between the Albuquerque Public Schools and New Futures, Inc., a nonprofit community organization. Over the past 23 years, New Futures has helped over 4,000 adolescents to progress through the difficult experience of teen pregnancy and parenthood. The school features an academic program which leads to a regular diploma or a GED course for older students, an in-school clinic which provides for mothers' health and parental needs, counseling services, a child care facility, and a career exploration/jobs program. the National School Boards Association highlighted the success of this program:

> A five year follow-up study conducted in 1987 of students who attended the school showed that 73 percent had graduated from high school (an additional 4 percent were still in school) and more than half (54 percent) went on to postsecondary education programs. Ninty-seven percent of New Futures students in 1980–87 passed the state-mandated high school proficiency exam. Students' health and child-rearing practices also improved: they had comparatively fewer repeat pregnancies and fewer low-birth-weight babies, and more than half breastfed their babies. (National School Boards Association, 1989, p. 36)

Teen parent programs are demanding, complex, and urgently needed. They hold great promise for the education and success of young parents, the growth and development of their children, and greater stability for the entire community.

The success of the alternative school model in teaching diverse youth, particularly those at risk of leaving school, establishes this concept as the most promising of any available today. Educators and community members who are serious about improving the educational opportunities for high-school youth at risk should consider the implementation of alternative schools as an integral component of any reform or restructuring plan.

Supplemental High-School Programs

> While conducting a school evaluation of an at-risk high-school program, I was surprised to discover that nearly all of the students mentioned that the free breakfast was one of the most important aspects of the program. This intrigued me, because I wasn't aware that the program served breakfast. When I finally tracked down the breakfast program, I discovered a somewhat

embarrassed teacher who was single-handedly responsible for this
effort. He laughingly pointed to the breakfast program which
included a jar of Tang orange juice powder, a jar of instant
coffee, a jar of grape jelly, a box of day-old bread that he
purchased at a bakery outlet, and a garage sale pop-up
toaster. While the breakfast was not much in the way of
nutrition, to the students it represented a powerful message
of caring concern. As one of the high-school students said, "It
is the first time in my entire life when anyone cared enough
for me to provide me with a meal to start the day."
—*(AN ALTERNATIVE HIGH SCHOOL ON THE WEST*
COAST OF OREGON, 1990).

Today, most high schools offer a variety of supplemental programs throughout the school day and year. While many of these programs are successful in providing options and specific opportunities to diverse students, only a select few have truly impacted the achievement of at-risk youth. The following programs have been consistently evaluated as highly effective, particularly with youth at risk.

Vocational/Technical Programs

One of the greatest pressures for educational reform comes from the dramatic changes that have occurred in business and industry during the past 20 years. Clearly the world of physical work has given way to the age of the mind. Technology has ripped away the opportunity for undereducated Americans to drop out of school and find good, upwardly mobile job opportunities in the steel mills, the automotive industry, and in the forests and fields of our nation. Hammers and wrenches have been displaced by numbers and buttons. Computers, robots, automation, and high-technology machinery have all but replaced the uneducated human worker in the business affairs of the nation. Supercomputers, global communication networks, facsimile machines, and satellites connect engineers, designers, contractors, scientists, and retailers worldwide and have made daily work a transnational affair for an increasing number of people (Wirth, 1993). What's more, this global system is in a constant state of upgrade, refinement, and change. In the United States today, a new and dramatic class division is developing between those who have and those who have not, those who are educated and those who are not:

In the past 15 years the individuals who have these [new technological] skills have
prospered, those lacking them have increasingly fallen behind. By 1990, the rich-
est 20 percent received over half of the nation's income and the top 5 percent re-
ceived 26 percent—an all-time high in both cases. The poorest fifth received only
3.7 percent of total income, down from 5.5 percent in 1970. Between 1973 and
1987, the income of high school graduates declined by 12 percent; while during the
1980s the number of full-time workers falling below the poverty line rose by 43

percent. . . . By the year 2020, the top fifth may well earn more than 60 percent of
American income, while the bottom fifth may drop to 2 percent. (Wirth, 1993,
pp. 364–365)

For schools and at-risk youth, the issue is no longer simply to stay in school graduate. Demands for increasing sophistication in the worldwide marketp now require that students not only graduate from school, but that they ach high levels of educational skills and have specific technical training. We rapidly approaching the day when all workers will have to complete a two technical training program following high-school graduation.

A number of high schools have made dramatic steps to begin preparing school students for both graduation and for the training necessary for a jol gon has approved an educational reform plan that ends high school at the sion of the 10th grade, after which all students progress to two-year te training or college preparation.

In a recent report by the Secretary's Commission on Achieving N Skills (SCANS), the U.S. Department of Labor (1992) identified the essent essary for success in today's workplace. The workplace know-how iden SCANS is made up of five workplace competencies and a three-part foun skills and personal qualities that are needed for solid job performance (se 2). In order to achieve these new-age employment skills, dramatic change essary in the wood shop, metal shop, and welding classes of traditional education programs.

Many of the better-funded public school systems have completed hensive redesign of their vocational and technical programs to enhan nities for all students. The programs often start during the elemen years, when students are encouraged to explore their personal interests career awareness about the world of work. During the middle-scho dents are provided intensive career information and guidance to a concentrating their interest on two or more areas of possible employ business or communications; technical, industrial, and engineering human services; and biology, environment, and natural resources.

During the high-school years, the entire faculty is encouraged student in thinking about their future and in preparing themselves t goals. Effective high schools need to have a career center and a trai This career counselor should provide students with the same typ that college-bound students have always been provided to help stu school-to-work transition. The career center should assist each high in preparing a personalized education portfolio that includes their educational expectations, requirements needed to achieve specif sonal progress charts. By focusing student attention on large area opportunity and perceiving these areas as career paths, students understand that regardless of their educational success, they of the jobs available in their areas of interest and the education

direct work experience, and student apprenticeships. The following school-based programs address the needs for job training.

Tech Prep

One of the most promising high-school programs for at-risk youth is the Tech Prep Program. Originally proposed by Dale Parnell as president of the American Community College Association, Tech Prep recommends a K–14 public education structure. The concept attempts to transfer career education and vocational education from the failed, stigmatized programs that characterize most of public schools to advanced technology, and attractive programs that promise jobs, opportunities, profitability, and upward mobility.

During the elementary school years all students are exposed to the widest possible variety of career information regarding job opportunities and begin to consider options they will encounter during the middle- and high-school years. During middle school, students focus their studies on a number of career clusters, and during high school, their studies intensify in a specific occupational area that is integrated with a community college two-year program. These programs are developed cooperatively by high school and community college faculty along with assistance from representatives from business, labor, and government. Some students might enter the workforce after high school, while others will continue until they earn an associate degree from a community college or other postsecondary institution.

Federal funds from the Carl Perkins Vocational and Applied Technology Education Act of 1990 are currently being used throughout the country to finance Tech Prep programs. In Washington state, the Boeing Cooperation has been instrumental in assisting the development of Tech Prep public schools. Boeing has recently provided more than 50 grants of $10,000 to $30,000 to school districts throughout Washington to support this concept (Northwest Regional Educational Laboratory, 1993b).

Apprenticeships

Unlike in Germany and other developed nations, U.S. students rarely participate in apprenticeships in business, industry, or labor organizations until after high school. While U.S. youth who are at risk too often find school boring and a waste of time, European youth step out of the school classroom and into the real world classroom of the workplace via apprenticeship programs. Germany has established a dual educational system that often is confused with a rigid tracking program. Actually, the dual program involves school learning in an industrial setting and serves students bound for the job market as well as the university (Aring, 1993). German university-trained engineers often participate in an apprenticeship program prior to attending college, a career path almost unthinkable in the United States.

Three types of successful apprenticeship programs include

- Exploratory apprenticeships: *Community service work is especially appropriate for middle-grade youth who are not ready to make vocational choices. Unlike the situation with traditional apprenticeship, there is no presumption that the student will continue in this line of work. And, unlike the usual teenage jobs, service programs may give young volunteers chances to plan projects themselves and to take on higher levels of responsibility.*
- School-based apprenticeships: *In addition to the cooperative education programs and academies . . . some schools operate their own enterprises, ranging from restaurants to day care centers. School-based programs protect the young person's principle role as student and emphasize that the lessons to be learned are primarily general academic ones; job skills and occupational choice are less critical.*
- Work-based apprenticeships: *A particularly promising form of work-based apprenticeship combines schooling with apprenticeship over a period spanning two years of high school and two years of technical college. Upon completion of such a "2 + 2" program, an apprentice has earned a high-school diploma, an associate's degree, and qualification for employment as a technician, a promising occupational category with career potential (Hamilton, 1990, p. 4).*

A number of programs that resemble European apprenticeships are available in the United States today. Cooperative education programs can be found throughout the United States at both the high school and university levels. Ten percent of all U.S. vocational students are involved in some type of cooperative education program—mostly in the retail trade. In New York, Shearson Lehman Hutton has initiated an apprenticeshiplike program entitled the Academy of Finance that is now available in more than 12 cities. Through this program, students enroll in business and finance courses during the year and in summer assume jobs in the financial service industry. In California, the Peninsula Academies provide three-year, school-within-a-school programs. Each school has a particular career focus, such as health professions, in which students acquire academic skills as well as enroll in one technical class per day in their particular interest area. Block scheduling provides opportunities for field experiences and practica. Many of the magnet schools described in an earlier section likewise offer extensive apprenticeship opportunities.

Out-of-School Learning and Service Opportunitites

Research has helped to emphasize how important out-of-school learning can be for all students, especially those who are at risk. Unfortunately, schools tend to isolate the students from the rich opportunities for experience and learning that occur in business, industry, agencies, museums, and elsewhere in the community. There is a rich research body that supports experiential or action learning and a number of organizations that encourage this approach. A growing number of schools around the country provide internships and practica in courts, newspapers, television stations, social service agencies, and in business and industry, and some (schools without walls) focus their entire curriculum on community-based learning. These learning experiences can literally transform the life of a high-school student and provide great motivation toward a particular career.

Successfully learning out of school represents an expectation and an approach around which many alternative schools and programs structure their schools. One of the nation's most successful programs which for over two decades has effectively used the community as a classroom for youth at risk is Foxfire. The Foxfire program, developed in Rabun Gap, Georgia, achieved national recognition for its success with at-risk youth through documenting their study of regional community heritage with newsletters, books, and film. The Foxfire approach represents one of very few concepts in the past 20 years that has demonstrated the requisite success and sufficient national attention to qualify as a reform approach that has become a part of the curriculum of many schools.

The Foxfire Experience

Foxfire was established in a poor, rural southern area where many students traditionally dropped out of school and went to work in the region's textile mills. Beginning as an English teacher's attempt to get his students to write, over the years the Foxfire program developed into a multimillion dollar business, co-managed and operated by the students, the majority of whom were at risk of leaving school prior to joining the program. Based on the rather simple idea of collecting and publishing the folklore of their region, students traveled across the countryside interviewing parents, grandparents, and rural mountain people regarding everything from how to make homemade soap to witching for water to building log cabins. Beginning on a mimeograph machine, these collections of folklore grew into a newsletter with a national circulation, and finally to a series of best-selling volumes based on excerpts from the newsletters.

The significance of Foxfire is demonstrated in the most dramatic manner by how effective and successful disadvantaged students could be when properly motivated in a school program that addressed their needs and interests. Many of the Foxfire students have gone on to graduate from universities throughout the United States and continue to serve as shareholders in this remarkable venture. Of equal significance is the impact of the Foxfire approach on public education. Not only has the Foxfire concept been incorporated into many alternative and traditional schools throughout the United States in both urban and rural settings, it has helped to demonstrate the importance of connecting the academic work of schools to the community. This concept, while appropriate and necessary for all youth, is particularly important for at-risk youth.

Today, the Foxfire Fund serves to support the original efforts of the project and also supports the Teacher Outreach Program. This project, in its eighth year, has trained over 5,000 teachers and currently maintains 12 networks of practicing teachers throughout the United States. The Teacher Outreach Program has established 11 core practices that serve as the guiding principles for educators and others attempting to implement the Foxfire approach (see Table 8-3).

TABLE 8-3   The Foxfire Approach Core Practices

- All the work teachers and students do together must flow from student desire, student concerns.
- Therefore, the role of the teacher must be that of collaborator and team leader and guide rather than boss.
- The academic integrity of the work must be absolutely clear.
- The work is characterized by student action, rather than passive receipt of processed information.
- A constant feature of the process is its emphasis on peer teaching, small group work, and teamwork.
- Connections between the classroom work and surrounding communities and the real world outside the classroom are clear.
- There must be an audience beyond the teacher for student work.
- As the year progresses, new activities should spiral gracefully out of the old, incorporating lessons learned from past experiences, building on skills and understandings that can be amplified.
- As teachers, we must acknowledge the worth of aesthetic experience, model that attitude in our interactions with students, and resist the momentum of policies and practices that deprive students of the chance to use their imaginations.
- Reflection—some conscious, thoughtful time to stand apart from the work itself—is an essential activity that must take place at key points throughout the work.
- The work must include unstintingly honest, ongoing evaluation for skills and content, and changes in student attitude.

(Foxfire approach, 1993)

Unfortunately, the recent child abuse conviction of Eliot Wigginton, Foxfire teacher and program founder, has clouded the program's future and painfully impacted many who were closely associated with the operation's success. Despite the tragic epilogue to over 20 years of remarkable work, schools will continue to embrace and value the use of cultural journalism and heritage documentation as concepts that belong in the classrooms and work so well with youth at risk.

Entrepreneur Programs

Another type of out-of-school learning is the high-school entrepreneur program, in which students actively create and manage a small business enterprise. Other schools offer students the opportunities to conduct long-term environmental studies to monitor and document water quality of local streams and air quality, while other programs facilitate students organizing a consumer protection service for the community. High-school entrepreneur programs seem to be growing throughout the country. In North Carolina, South Carolina, and Georgia, the Rural Entrepreneurship through Action Learning project (REAL) supports a variety of programs and efforts. Students in these states have created and operated a fascinating variety of successful ventures, including a Christmas tree business, a feeder pig farm, a graphic design firm, child care centers, printing shops, boat rentals, fabric stores, shoe repair, a construction company, and a recycling business. Some of these businesses have been short-lived, others have continued for years. Some of them generated six-figure cash flows. Some have even employed adults (Rural Entrepreneurship through Action Learning, 1993).

In Alaska, students and their teachers have started a number of different businesses. In Wainwright, students operate a business to merchandize Native crafts, tapes and albums, and soda drinks. They also organize a regularly scheduled movie night, dances, raffles, and sports tournaments. The Wainwright High School Student Corporation is one of eight student corporations in the North Slope School District in Alaska. In other Alaska school districts, student corporations have developed an export enterprise with Japan and China, collected and sold Native graphic arts, produced industrial ice picks, and initiated bakeries, story knives businesses, and restaurants (Kleinfeld, McDiarmid, & Parrett, 1992).

Community Service Programs

Directly related to out-of-school learning experience is volunteer community service. A recent report of the Children's Defense Fund emphasizes the value of service activities to at-risk youth:

> *Solutions to problems such as dropping out of school, unemployment, and teen pregnancy need to incorporate a full range of strategies that improve youths' life options. Giving youths opportunities to engage in service activities plays a part in such strategies, building self-esteem and giving young people a meaningful role in their communities. With the proper guidance, encouragement, and supervision, young people respond well to new challenges and responsibilities. (Children's Defense Fund, 1989, p. 3)*

For at-risk youth, service activities may well be the first opportunity to experience the joy of a job well done. Examples abound of at-risk youth becoming excited and willing participants in these programs. They include tutoring younger children to read, helping the elderly in nursing homes, serving as a teacher aide in day care centers, helping maintain parks and rivers, serving in Big Brothers/Big Sisters programs, and a wide variety of other worthy activities. Each of these service activities help youth learn about themselves and others. Service opportunities are empowering. They can help at-risk youth prepare to accept adult responsibilities. So successful is this type of learning experience, and so worthy are the projects, that there has been growing interest in the development of a national system of required youth service (Children's Defense Fund, 1989).

To be successful, school-based programs must be carefully planned and organized. All students need organization, guidance, and motivation. Useful community projects must be identified and presented to students through positive means that will illicit an enthusiastic response. Service opportunities should also lead to the development of student academic skills, especially higher-order thinking and problem solving, and they should provide an opportunity for students to reflect on their service experiences (Children's Defense Fund, 1989).

Mentoring

> *"It was a simple program. We had our students bring sack lunches to school one day a week and spend their lunch hour*

*eating with some group in their offices and businesses nearby.
Our goals were simple. We wanted the kids to sit in lunch rooms,
loading docks, staff lounges, and listen to adults talk during their
lunch period. It struck us that most of the kids didn't know any
adult who held a job. We wanted them to hear people talk about
their car, boat, RV, their vacation and their plans for their kid's
college. I don't know how effective the program is, but the kids
seem to love it."*
*—(DIRECTOR, ALTERNATIVE SCHOOL,
MEDFORD, OREGON, 1987)*

As mentioned earlier, one of the most effective programs for at-risk students is mentoring. So many at-risk youth have never experienced a positive personal relationship with an adult. One caring adult can make a dramatic difference in a young person's life. While statistical research is relatively scarce, there is strong anecdotal, observational, and case study data to verify the positive benefits of developing a mentor program for high-school students.

Mentors can be almost anyone. They can be teachers who are willing to develop a new and different relationship with students, volunteers from business and industry, senior citizens, university students, and a host of others. The important consideration is that whoever the mentor might be, it is essential that each mentor is screened, trained, and learns to work as part of an established program. With the increasing incidence of sexual abuse, screening for past histories is awkward but extremely important. Increasingly, student-teachers, teachers, and other professionals who work with youth are being screened with background checks and fingerprinting.

Mentor programs and projects come in a variety of formats. National mentor programs include Big Brothers/Big Sisters, I Have a Dream Foundation, One Plus One, and so on. Local business programs include Project Step Up, Adopt a Student, and so on. University-based programs include Campus Contact, Linking Up, and Career Beginnings. The Adopt a Student Program in Atlanta reports great success in mentoring 11th and 12th grade students in the bottom quarter of their class. Researchers at Georgia State University report that students participating in the Adopt a Student program had a 92 percent high-school graduation rate with a 93 percent job placement or enrollment in higher education (National Dropout Prevention Center, 1990). Such success stories are common with mentor programs.

Successful mentor programs involve far more than a simple match between an adult and an at-risk youth. Considerable research has been conducted during the past decade on developing and evaluating mentor programs for a wide variety of different organizations. This research has helped to identify the essential characteristics of a successful mentor program:

- *Program compatibility: The program should be compatible with the policies
  and goals of the organization. In a program for students in a community
  group, for example, program organizers should work closely with school per-*

sonnel to ensure that the mentoring they provide complements the student's education.

- *Administrative commitment: The program must be supported from the top as well as on a grassroots level. In a school-based program, all school and district administrators, teachers, and staff must provide input and assistance. For a sponsoring business, the president or chief executive officer must view the program as important and worthy of the time and attention of the employees.*

- *Proactive: Ideally the programs should be proactive; that is, not a quick-fix reaction to a crisis. Successful mentoring programs for youth work because they are well thought out, they have specific goals and objectives, and they exist within a larger realm of programs and policies that function together.*

- *Participant oriented: The program should be based on the goals and needs of the participants. These goals will determine the program's focus, recruitment, and training. For example, if the primary aim of a mentoring program is career awareness, students should be matched with successful business people in the youth's area of interest. Activities and workshops should be job related.*

- *Pilot program: The first step should be a pilot program of 6 to 12 months, with 10 to 40 participants, in order to work out any problems before expanding to a larger audience. Trying to start out with a large-scale plan that includes more than this number can prove unwieldy and disastrous. In the words of Oregon's guide to mentorship programs, "think big but start small."*

- *Orientation: An orientation should be provided for prospective participants. It will help determine interest and enthusiasm, as well as give prospective mentors and students an idea of what to expect. In addition, it will provide them with opportunities to help design the program.*

- *Selection and matching: Mentors and their proteges should be carefully selected and matched. Questionnaires are helpful in determining needs, areas of interest, and strengths.*

- *Training: Training must be provided for all participants, including support people, throughout the program. Assuming that because a person is knowledgeable, caring, and enthusiastic he or she will make a good mentor is a mistake. Training must be geared to the specific problems experienced by at-risk youth as well as different styles of communication.*

- *Monitoring progress: The program should be periodically monitored for progress and results to resolve emerging conflicts and problems.*

- *Evaluation and revision: The program should be evaluated with respect to how well goals and objectives are achieved. This can be done using questionnaires, interviews, etc. (National Dropout Prevention Center, 1990, pp. 5–6)*

The need for mentor programs at the high-school level is clear. The fact that they are far less frequently offered than some of the more outdated vocational education programs is disturbing, since they hold great value for youth at risk.

Experience-Based Career Education

Over 20 years ago, the Northwest Regional Educational Lab helped to develop Experience-Based Career Education (CE_2). The program, first implemented in Tigard, Oregon, focused on providing community experiences in career education.

CE_2 offers a skill- and exploration-based education program that continues to prosper throughout the west and has spread to over 60 school districts nationwide. The program connects students with highly personalized career exploration, work experience, survival skill development, and academic preparation for their individual learning styles and interests. The program also develops partnerships with businesses, government, and social service agencies to provide on-site experiences. CE_2 fosters the development of seven master skills:

- *Demonstrate the use of vocabulary, speech, numerals, and other systems essential for effective communication, computation, and problem solving.*
- *Interpret the literal meanings of information presented in written, visual, and oral communication.*
- *Interpret the implied meanings of information presented in written, visual and oral communication.*
- *Evaluate content and use of written, oral, aural, and visual information.*
- *Generate, organize, express, and evaluate ideas in oral and written forms.*
- *Use reasoning skills.*
- *Manage personal habits and attitudes, time and instructional resources constructively in order to accomplish learning tasks (Northwest Regional Educational Laboratory, 1993b, p. 7).*

United States Job Corps

One of the most successful programs for older adolescents ages 17 to 20 has been the United States Job Corps. Job Corps Centers are available in every state and provide school dropouts with an expense-paid residential program focusing on education and vocational training. Most students, regardless of their background and abilities, are able to earn a general equivalency diploma (GED) in less than a year, and within 18 months to two years most have completed a job training program. The vocational programs are conducted in cooperation with trade unions and focus on entry into specific job fields. Evaluation of the Job Corps Centers is extremely positive. Most centers report that more than 90 percent of their students go on to college, join the armed services, or take a job in their area of training. Job Corps students demonstrate considerable academic and vocational ability yet were unwilling to stay in school programs that were largely unrelated to their particular needs. Public school educators would benefit from a visit to their local Job Corps Center to learn from a long-standing success in academic and vocational education.

Summer Catch-Up Programs and Evening Schools

Many communities have designed an array of programs to use the otherwise idle evenings and summer months. In cooperation with the local private industry council, the Boise, Idaho, public schools provide students who have fallen behind in credits with a summer opportunity to catch up. What is novel about this program is that students are paid to attend school. Students are able to earn four academic credits during the summer, and for each credit they may earn up to $50. Each absence or failure to complete an assignment deducts a dollar amount from their salary. If students earn the four credits and their $200, they can earn an additional $50 if they return to school the next fall and complete the semester. What is so important about this program is that large numbers of students who participate in the summer program discover for the first time that if they really apply themselves they can be successful in school. Summer programs as well as other approaches designed to fit the schedules and lifestyles of youth at risk serve the invaluable purpose of always having an educational opportunity available.

Another widely used and highly successful approach for addressing the needs of students who have dropped out of school are evening schools. Most evening schools are small, employ teachers who are interested and committed to the students, and typically enroll a very focused student body intent upon completing their degrees. Evening schools tend to serve students of all ages from teenagers to senior citizens. The reason evening programs are so successful is that they enable people to have a full or part-time job during the day and still pursue their education. In this day and age, it seems imperative that all high-school students have the opportunity to attend school either during the day or in the evening.

Equivalency Diplomas

"Aaah, man, I'm so far behind in school that I'll be 37 years old before I can ever graduate."
—10TH GRADE STUDENT, WASHINGTON, D.C., 1992)

General equivalency diplomas (GED) are absolutely essential for older students who have fallen so far behind in their credits that they have little or no hope of completing high school or for students who have already dropped out of school yet are anxious to complete their degree. The GED serves as a highly individualized fast track for graduation and must be available for students. The GED has a long history of success, but unfortunately, some employers and all but two branches of the U.S. armed services will no longer accept the GED as the equivalent of a regular high school diploma. Most community colleges and universities offer some type of GED program or high-school equivalency program, and a number of these programs are funded by the U.S. Department of Education. Despite recent concern over the value of these degrees, they continue to represent a worthy accomplishment for many dropouts and serve the important purpose of recognizing academic achievement. Most students who complete a GED use it to move on to additional education, training, or a better job.

Early College Entrance

A number of states have developed programs that not only allow but encourage students to leave high school and begin taking college courses. The state of Washington initiated a program entitled Running Start to encourage students to attend college during their high-school years. Some states allow college courses to serve as equivalents to high-school requirements so that students will eventually graduate from high school while pursuing their college degrees. Other programs simply let high-school students take a few extra courses during high school. Tech Prep and 2 + 2 programs (described earlier in this section) often provide college courses to students during the high-school years.

For at-risk youth, the opportunity to actually leave high school during the 11th or 12th grade and complete an associate degree in a vocational or technical area that leads directly to entry into the job market seems to make far more sense than attempting to complete high school with little or no vocational training. There are a number of examples of disruptive students who were not succeeding in high school and who were given the opportunity to move directly into community college programs. When a program that provides relevant, focused preparation that leads to job opportunities is available, these students have demonstrated a willingness to begin attending class, learn professional expectations and behaviors appropriate to the workplace, and achieve.

Computer Technology

While computer technology has been used primarily at the high school level for the most academically able students in math and science and for independent projects, this form of instruction holds great promise for at-risk youth. The International Association for the Evaluation of Educational Achievement, in a study of 11,284 students in grades 5, 8, and 11 from 573 schools, found that when students are provided access to computers,

- Girls use them as much as boys and almost as well.
- Poor students perform surprisingly close to affluent classmates who are more likely to have computers at home. (Henry, Dec. 15, 1993)

The hands-on, self-paced, personalized approach to learning that the computer and student-friendly software provide can equalize learning opportunities for disadvantaged youth and should be a part of every at-risk student's educational program. Computer-assisted instruction can be used to help high-school students improve basic reading, writing, and math skills while learning valuable technological lessons. Through interface networks, at-risk students at Wenatchee High School in Washington, El Paso Technical High School in Texas, Martha's Vineyard High School in Massachusetts, and the Dumholff Special Education Center in Los Angeles discuss teen pregnancy and drug prevention. Other schools develop long-term pen pals with students in other schools, cities, and states (K–12 computer networking, 1993).

The impact of technology on learning is moving beyond personal computing to dramatic advances in information networking. A poignant example of this can be found in Issaquah, Washington. When Michael Booky, one of the computer industry's most successful entrepreneurs, first visited the Issaquah public schools, he was shocked. "After 20 years working with computer networks, to enter Issaquah seemed to me like encountering an exotic tribe of primitives untouched by the modern world" (Gilder, 1993, p. 114). Having designed networks for businesses throughout the world, he believed that networks could have a revitalizing impact on public schools. As he began working with local schools, teachers tried to convince him that their "impish, mischievous, and messy students" would destroy any effort to develop a computer network. The teachers pleaded with him to keep the system restricted solely to teachers and administrators. Fortunately for Issaquah, Booky saw students as a resource rather than a problem and set out not only to develop an externally funded computerized network but to train students to take responsibility for building, maintaining, and administering the network. Many of the students who were the most successful at learning to access and work with the district's computerized network were those who had been considered at risk.

Lee Dumas was a 13-year-old student in Issaquah when the computer networking project began.

> *Dumas was a bad kid. No one at Maywood Middle School doubted that. His teachers called him "obnoxious" or even "brain-dead." He set what he believes was an all-time Maywood record by being detained after class some 60 times for insubordination. Using the approved psychobabble, he says, "I had problems with authority. I couldn't accept teachers ordering me around." After being caught breaking into the computer system, Dumas was dragged up to the principal's office. Neither the teacher nor the principal could figure out the nature of the crime or judge its seriousness. For help, they summoned Don Robertson, the administrator assigned to Issaquah's Technology Information Project (TIP). He considered the situation gravely and recommended severe punishment. Toward the end of the meeting, however, he turned to Dumas and said, "With your talent, you should become the sheriff rather than the outlaw. Why don't you come down and join TIP?" (Gilder, 1993, pp. 119–120)*

That is exactly what happened, and this at-risk, "brain-dead" troublemaker became an integral part of the student team that built and maintained the $2.7 million network and trained teachers to use it. An amazing transformation occurred in this young student. Before long he was working summers at Microsoft and was considered by the company's network development specialist as a valued employee with high promise for the future.

This vivid example underscores the importance of technology for both schools and students. It is particularly significant that many at-risk youth, not able to effectively participate and learn in teacher-dominated lecture and direct instruction, can flourish when challenged by technology. Examples like Dumas's abound in public education today and it is clear that the "children" can wisely participate in leading schools into the technological future. These kids are the "road warriors of the information highway," and they are taking teachers and schools along a journey into the future. Unfortunately, very few high schools in the United States are moving towards the type of technology and learning and networking that is occurring in Florida, Texas, and Washington.

Drug and Alcohol Programs

Drug and alcohol use among high-school students continues at an alarming level. In 1990, 44 percent of high-school students reported trying marijuana, about the same as 15 years ago. In 1975, nine percent of the same survey reported that they had tried cocaine; in 1990, the figure was over 10 percent. A number of studies suggest that these students are distributed fairly equally throughout a school, with approximately five to six in every classroom, as many as two or three starters on the football and basketball teams, and several among the school leaders. One in three high-school students also reports that they had become intoxicated from alcohol at least once over the past two weeks. Such figures offer a dramatic challenge to the concept of a drug-free school (Hawley, 1990).

With such widespread use, drugs and alcohol must be considered one of the critical problems facing high-school youth. For at-risk youth, they tend to pose even greater problems. And while "Just Say No" campaigns are impressive, the problem is so complex and so comprehensive that only widespread concentrated efforts are likely to make a significant difference. Schools today need drug and alcohol counseling and ready access to treatment programs. Schools must have support groups and even Alcoholics and Narcotics Anonymous programs. Most recently, the federal government has funded regional Drug-Free Schools programs that have provided training for teachers and administrators, for the identification of successful programs, and for a widespread public relations campaign to attack the problem.

Another approach to drug and alcohol abuse is life skills training for high-school students. In the past, these skills were often learned at home, church, through part-time work, and in the community. Today, far too many youth lack family support, strong adult role models, and a stable society, and they are often influenced by radio, television, videos, and advertisements. Role models tend to be the glamorous, drinking, rapping, often drug-using rock stars and professional athletes. Life skills training attempts to provide youth with information, role models, and mentoring, and tries to help youth consider the consequences of their actions. As Fred Heckinger in his moving book entitled *Fateful Choices* has said, "teaching young people to consider the consequences of their actions is at the heart of any effective educational approach to drug, alcohol and smoking prevention" (Heckinger, 1992, p. 109). The same could be said about sexual promiscuity and safe sex. Life skills training is for all youth, the affluent as well as the disadvantaged. It must be recognized that as youth stand on the threshold of adulthood in a wildly changing world, they will soon be making independent judgments regarding whether or not to drop out or continue schooling, whether or not to drink, smoke, try drugs, and be promiscuous. Students need information about life decisions and assistance in sorting out options and consequences, making decisions, and establishing personal goals. It is a tragic mistake to believe that at-risk youth have the ability or the home support to resist media appeal and peer pressures and make appropriate or safe decisions regarding these issues.

Life skills training is a process: "Stop and think, get information, access information, consider consequences, weigh old options or seek new ones; get feedback from persons whose judgment and integrity can be trusted" (Heckinger, 1992, p. 55). In Lowell, Massachusetts, the City Magnet School has created an entire microworld where students run a court system, representative government, and a market economy using paper currency developed by the school. Students work as lawyers, judges, reporters, editors, bankers, and business people to earn salaries and pay rent for their desktop offices. The school has subsequently experienced a significant decline in disruptive student behavior and marked improvement in academic performance (Heckinger, 1992).

There are a wide variety of prevention programs being used throughout the United States, yet little data is available at this time to evaluate their effectiveness. One issue that makes prevention programs difficult to implement is that even the experts in the field disagree over program goals. Authorities inevitably are divided between "no use" and "responsible use" programs. The result of this division of opinion is often controversy and conflict among parents and school leaders.

High-School Health Clinics

Increasingly, a number of high schools and a few middle-level and elementary schools have established school-based health centers. While almost always controversial, these clinics build on a long tradition of having a school nurse in the building and relate directly to some of the major health-related dangers to healthy teenage development: pregnancy, venereal disease, AIDS, and drug and alcohol abuse. In some schools, up to 40 percent of the student body takes advantage of health services when they are available, since many of these students have no other form of health care. There is also data to support the fact that clinics reduce the number of teenage pregnancies in the school (the role of the clinic in planning and preventing pregnancies is one of the greatest controversies). The goals of most programs are to provide for comprehensive, ongoing health care and health education as opposed to an episodic, crisis intervention approach (Northwest Regional Educational Laboratory, 1993c). Clinics are often operated by community-based social service agencies and hospitals who work together to move services closer to the needs of, and to make these services more accessible to, adolescents.

School health clinics are increasingly important because of the scarcity of health care facilities for adolescents. Unfortunately, the Center for Population Options reported in 1991 that there were only 327 such centers in 33 states and Puerto Rico (Heckinger, 1992). More than half of the users of these clinics report they have no other health care. While 51 percent of the centers serve high schools, centers serve middle schools and elementary schools as well.

While it is too early to draw any firm conclusion about the effectiveness of the centers on more positive teen behavior, several reports are very encouraging. In New York City, students who use the clinic miss fewer days of school. In Kansas City, the clinics reported a significant decline in the number of adolescents who used alcohol or drugs or smoked tobacco. Similar findings are expected as more data becomes available (Heckinger, 1992).

Building Self-Esteem

While many of the programs described in this section can lead to improved student self-esteem, students can also participate in classroom and other school-based learning experiences specifically designed to build the self-esteem of at-risk youth. When an entire school establishes improved self-esteem as a goal and develops learning experiences that focus on this crucial area, positive developments can occur.

One of the most detailed studies of a schoolwide self-esteem enhancement program was conducted in San Jose, California. In a freshman class, two groups were studied: one group was taught by teachers who adhered to three operating principles: they treated all students with unconditional positive regard, encouraged all students to be all they could be, and encouraged all students to set and achieve goals. In addition, students in this group received a 40-minute self-esteem building activity each Friday throughout their freshman year. The other control group received no special reinforcement or lessons. The results were extremely encouraging. The self-esteem group averaged only one day of absence per semester compared with 16 from the control group; 75 percent of students from the self-esteem group completed 90 percent or more of their homework compared to 25 percent in the control group; 25 percent of the self-esteem group participated in 20 or more extracurricular activities compared to only 2 percent in the control group; 75 percent of the self-esteem group served as class officers compared with none in the control group, and 83 percent of the self-esteem group graduated from high school compared to 50 percent from the control group (Canfield, 1990, pp. 48–50). One rather simple program developed by Jack Canfield provides strategies to build self-esteem (see Table 8-4).

TABLE 8-4   10 Steps to Self-Esteem

1. *Assume an attitude of 100 percent responsibility.* Students are encouraged not to blame external events or others but to take full responsibility for their own behavior.
2. *Focus on the positive.* In order to feel successful, students have to experience success. With help, students can often identify successful aspects of their life that they have not recognized before.
3. *Learn to monitor your self-talk.* It is not what others say about us, it is what we say to ourselves about ourselves. Self-esteem building programs need to help students replace negative thoughts with positive thoughts. This technique takes time and practice, but it can make a difference in a youth's life.
4. *Use support groups in the classroom.* It is possible for a student to come to school for a whole day and never once be the center of positive attention. Each day teachers might ask their students to find a partner and give them one or two minutes each of uninterrupted time to talk about a specific topic. (Topics such as who is your best friend and why, what is your favorite thing to do on the weekend, etc.) Topics such as these can be discussed in buddy groups of six kids with three sets of buddies. This exercise helps students to learn that it is a positive, healing experience to talk about their feelings and become bonded to their fellow students.
5. *Identify your strengths and resources.* An important part of expanded self-esteem is the broadening awareness of one's strengths and resources. One technique is to have students in their support groups write down and tell each other what they see as the positive qualities and strengths in others.
6. *Clarify your vision.* Without a clear vision, there is no motivation. Questions such as the following help students to clarify their vision: If you had only one year left to live, how would you spend your life? If a genie granted you three wishes, what would you wish for?
7. *Set goals and objectives.* Until our goals and life visions are broken down into specific measurable goals with timelines and deadlines, we are not likely to move toward anything very quickly. Students must be taught to set measurable goals and objectives for themselves, their families, the school and community. They should share their goals with the rest of the class and support one of those as they work toward them. The entire class should celebrate any completion of goals.
8. *Use visualization.* Some feel that the most powerful yet underutilized tool in education may be visualization. We can help students hold a clear vision of their goals as if they were already achieved. Students should spend five minutes per day visualizing each of their goals and objectives as if they were achieved. This can produce radical results very quickly.
9. *Take action.* To be successful, students must learn they have to "do the doing." Students cannot hire someone else to do their push-ups for them and expect to develop muscles.
10. *Respond to feedback and persevere.* Students need to hear stories of people like themselves who have gone on to do great things.

(Canfield, 1990 , pp. 48–50)

Outdoor Education

A successful component found in many educational programs for youth at risk is adventure-based education. Outward Bound represents one of a number of private organizations that provides outdoor education for public schools. There has been extensive research on the Outward Bound approach that has documented its effectiveness and value, particularly in the development of improved student self-esteem. Outward Bound programs integrate a number of physically challenging activities such as rock climbing, rope courses, rappelling, and others with a variety of trust-building experiences in which students discover their own limits and inner resources. Participation in these activities has proven to be of great benefit to at-risk youth who have rarely ventured outside an urban area or experienced outdoor activities in remote, wilderness areas. For many at-risk youth who may have had few successes in their community and school, these experiences have proven to be profound in building self-confidence, self-respect, and motivation.

The success of Outward Bound and other similar types of public school adventure-based education programs has led to the widespread development of ropes courses that are used for team and self-confidence building for at-risk youth. This instructional activity is often employed in drug and alcohol programs, with students who have been abused, and with other young adolescents experiencing difficulties in their lives. These programs provide students with the opportunity to work and succeed in a physically demanding outdoor environment. Schools employing adventure-based learning often describe the practice as absolutely central to their goal of inspiring, motivating, and engendering an interest in learning among youth at risk.

Creating an Effective Model for High-School Programs

> I had been invited out to speak to about 250 high-school students that the counselor and principal had identified as being in urgent danger of dropping out of school. Unfortunately, when I arrived at the auditorium where these kids were waiting, the counselor was unable to get this wild bunch quiet enough to introduce me. Her efforts were met with boos and laughter. I walked over and said, "Let me try to talk to this group." She shrugged and stepped aside. I stepped up on a front row seat and shouted to the kids, "How many of you would like a job making $30,000 a year?" This wild group of potential dropouts immediately fell silent. You could have heard a pin drop. Once we started talking about jobs and income, the group was attentive, asked intelligent questions, and a serious discussion occurred.
> —(UNIVERSITY PROFESSOR, OREGON STATE UNIVERSITY, 1990)

Effective high-school programs for at-risk youth stand in rather dramatic contrast to those at the elementary and middle-school levels. The goal at the high-school level is not so much to keep kids in school as it is to get them out of school and moving toward meaningful employment. The goal of the effective high-school at-risk program must be focused on jobs. And while this may seem a rather simplistic focus for high-school programs, it is in fact the most realistic possible goal. It is also far from an easy task. To get high-school students from where they are and ultimately to help them find meaningful employment is a staggering challenge. It is also a task that few schools can do alone. (See the Appendix for Self-Evaluation Checklist.) Successful programs at the high-school level must include the following components of an effective at-risk model.

Fast Track for Graduation or High-School Completion

Because of retention and failure, most at-risk high-school students are so far behind in academic credit that they feel high-school graduation is beyond their capacity to achieve. Even more unfortunate, the kinds of knowledge and skills that at-risk high-school students need to prepare for employment often do not relate well with traditional graduation credits. In fact, one of the most difficult problems at-risk programs face is translating interdisciplinary and applied technology courses into graduation requirements. Accelerated learning must be accompanied by an accelerated process of earning credit toward graduation. This can be accomplished with individualized computer programs, extended day classes, individualized programs that let students progress at an accelerated rate, and the availability of a high-school equivalency program. Most high-school equivalency programs can be completed in less than a year.

Basic Skill Development

Effective high-school programs must focus on developing acceptable levels of basic skills. These include the traditional basic skills as well as the new basic skills that are emerging in the contemporary workplace. Reading is the most essential, but it is also important to ensure that the high-school at-risk student is able to function adequately with communication and math. It is equally important for students to be able to function effectively with the new basic skills that are emerging in the marketplace: problem solving, decision making, and critical thinking.

Education That Permits Additional Education

What the high-school at-risk youth needs is education and skills that enable additional education. A GED should open the door to a two-year community college or Job Corps program, which should provide the foundation for additional college work. Education must be able to prepare the at-risk high-school student for the next level of education.

Technical Job Training

The most important goal for at-risk high-school students is to enter a job training program that leads directly to employment and additional education. Programs that are currently available include high school Tech Prep, two-year community college associate degrees, Job Corps training, and JTPA neighborhood programs. High schools must develop career paths that allow students to move from academic courses that they often perceive as meaningless into job training.

To enroll students in a one- to two-year job training program leading to employment is one of the most important educational accomplishments that a school can achieve. Even many outstanding alternative and magnet schools tend to focus primarily on earning academic credit and too little on job exploration and preparation. Every effective high-school program should offer a transition or bridge program that leads to community college or to job training programs.

Health and Social Support

Far more important than any academic content is the need to help at-risk youth resist or escape from drug and alcohol abuse or dependency; to provide a safe, supportive environment for abused and sexually violated teenagers; to offer child and health care for young parents; and to assist with student transportation needs to school and work. These issues often are considered beyond the scope of schools and demand that other social and community agencies provide assistance and support. Since AIDS, venereal disease, teen suicide, violence, and teen pregnancy take a huge toll on at-risk youth during the high-school years, health and mental health services are essential. The previously described case management approach has been proven particularly effective in helping high-school students cope with diverse problems. Until these essential needs are addressed, at-risk youth will not be able to successfully pursue education and job training.

Personal Choice and Planning

High-school at-risk youth must be given the opportunity to choose school and job training programs and be intimately involved in planning their future. Students at this age cannot be arbitrarily assigned into particular programs. High-school students must be involved in crucial decisions regarding their lives.

Caring and Demanding Teachers

While caring and demanding teachers are important for every educational level, they become absolutely essential at the high-school level. At-risk high-school students will usually not work with teachers whom they do not perceive to be understanding and supportive. It is the teacher who often becomes the sole point of student trust and contact within today's large and impersonal schools and their only adult friend and advocate.

Community college programs, alternative high-school programs, magnet schools, and teen parent programs currently represent the places where this at-risk model is most frequently employed for high-school-age students. There are few programs at the high-school level that are attempting to provide fundamentally effective education for all students. What is usually available are small, highly focused programs that address youth problems and needs, that keep them moving toward education and career goals and ultimately to job training and meaningful employment. Too often, even those programs focus more on academic course-work, accumulating credit, and high-school graduation. For this reason, the single best program may be to encourage these students to move out of high school and into two-year community college or federal Job Corps training programs as early as possible. And while many criticize this approach as a sinister tracking program, it is in fact the most realistic approach to provide as many high-school youth as possible with a program that leads to jobs rather than welfare, to employment rather than prison.

The most effective programs for at-risk high-school youth are consistent with those described earlier for elementary and middle-school youth. And since large comprehensive high schools have proven so difficult to change (see the next chapter for a detailed discussion), the most successful approach to addressing the needs of at-risk youth seems to be a smaller program that is associated with a high school or serves as an alternative high school. At this level, the student's entire educational program must focus on preparing for meaningful employment. That is not to say that many of these students will not go on to college. Yet it is apparent that from a motivational and economic point of view, the hope of a good job is probably the most important aspect for an at-risk high school student. If at-risk high-school students can identify a job that interests them and understand clearly what must be achieved in order to obtain the job, they can become highly motivated to complete their education. Unfortunately, research continues to identify the ultimate causes of the high-school youth being at risk as grounded in the early childhood years. The best way to serve high-school students is to address their problems during the preschool and elementary years and provide strong follow-through support during the middle-school and high-school years.

The next chapter will focus on how to transform existing public schools, expand learning alternatives, and how to develop new boundary-breaking public schools. Detailed information will be provided regarding the problems that are likely to be encountered during school reform efforts and effective strategies for addressing these problems.

Chapter 9

At Last, a Chance For Change

More than a decade after *A Nation At Risk* was published, sending shock waves throughout the United States, it is hard to capture exactly where we are today, even to determine if schools are getting better or worse, or if much of anything has actually changed at all. Experts on every side claim victory and point to defeats. The discussions surrounding school reform have become increasingly political and often reflect little more than widespread confusion. Simultaneously, there seems to be a surprising optimism that coincides with a gathering despondency; a smug confidence contrasted with utter hopelessness. Part of the problem is that almost every point of view tends to be accurate, at least for some geographic area, type of community, segment of the population, educator, or parent perspective. Public education in the United States continues to represent a cluttered mosaic of hope and pain, of technological advancement and shocking human tragedy, of violence and humility, of educational breakthroughs, and of stunning personal heartbreak. Unfortunately, it is also a snapshot of who we are, a gestalt of our national character.

From the beginning, many have argued that our schools simply could not be as bad as they had been depicted in *A Nation At Risk*. And as our improving economy coincided with recent signs that the Japanese economic machine might be faltering, it is easier to be sensitive to this point of view. From this perspective, the schools do not need to be reformed or restructured; if it ain't broke, it is often heard, don't try to fix it. That is not to say that these educators do not believe that schools need to be continually, incrementally improved; it does mean that they have resisted comprehensive overhaul. Public schools seem to resist even modest restructuring efforts. Rather than schools failing, proponents of maintaining the current system argue that it is the diverse U.S. student population who now take the SAT and those international math and science exams that have so tarnished the U.S. reputation. It is not that our schools are failing, but that they are so successful. It is that so many poor, minority and marginal students are now taking these exams, and the scores from this U.S. composite are then compared with the mono-cultural student populations of the national public school systems of Japan, Korea, and Germany. How can public schools be so bad if the United States leads the technological revolution in the world? Look at NASA, the advancements in communications and the innovations in the field of medicine, the resurgence of U.S. business, and the emerging information highways. Look at the reported declining dropout rate and the significant movement toward the America 2000 goals of the Bush Administration (Tanner, 1993). Look at American universities, where the students of the world come to complete graduate study. Look at the fall of Communism and the continued international leadership of the United States. Now really, can our schools be all that bad?

There are school districts and individual schools throughout America where public education exists in something of a 1950s time warp of changelessness; where teachers still talk 90 percent of the time and the role of the student learner is to listen, memorize, and complete work sheets; where bells still ring every 50 minutes and the primary technology means an overhead projector, a VCR, or a chalkboard. These schools and indeed a majority of public schools in America continue to employ retention and tracking, and large numbers of children still fail to learn and later drop out of school. In spite of the widespread educational experimentation and innovation that is occurring today, a number of credible surveys report that the vast majority of schools have changed little, if at all in our lifetime (Berends, 1992; Lee & Smith, 1992). To so many people, our schools are working and working well.

To others, just the opposite is true. Public education, they believe, is not only moribund and failing, but literally falling apart. They say the schools mirror the disintegration of the American family, the crumbling of U.S. social values, the hopelessness of so many urban communities, random and mindless violence, and a nation ripped apart between the haves and have-nots, between those who enjoy the good life and the growing underclass of the other America. There is hard, tangible evidence to support this view. One need only to look at the escalating cost of health and welfare, aid to families with dependent children, the judicial quagmire, and the dramatic growth in new prisons. Look at the one and a half million teen parents in the United States, the increasing birthrate of drug babies, the rise in drug and alcohol abuse by school children. Look at the 30 percent of the U.S. student population who are minority, the five million children of immigrant parents who will enter the public schools during the 1990s, bringing over 150 languages other than English into the nation's classrooms, and the 40 percent of U.S. children being reared by a single parent (Tanner, 1993). Look at the increase in the number of murders and violent crimes on our city streets. Look at state-by-state comparisons of percentage increases in the cost of crime, corrections, and health and welfare and then compare these to the stagnant budgets for K–12 and higher education. The United States today is building prisons, not schools and universities.

Add to these grim harbingers of the future the growing taxpayers' revolt—property tax limitation bills, defeated school bond elections, school closures, and the growing number of school districts that have simply declared bankruptcy and closed their doors—and a dismal picture of U.S. education begins to turn tragic. Prompted by hopelessness and despair, some urban school districts are giving up and turning over public education to outsiders. Others, in a desperate effort to salvage public education in America, are searching out a strange complex of inventive solutions (Jennings, 1993a). In Chelsea, Massachusetts, the school district has been turned over to Boston University to administer. The state of Michigan has abolished the property tax as a funding base for schools and is desperately trying to reinvent some new way to pay for public education. In Illinois, the state legislature has turned over the control of the 600 Chicago public schools to local parents. In Kentucky, the Supreme Court declared that public education was in violation of the Constitution and directed legislators to create a new system of public education. Under that new system, schools in Kentucky risk closure if they are unable to demonstrate significant student learning under the new reform efforts. In two cities, Boston and Kansas City, judges have assumed responsibility for the local school districts, and in Texas, the state legislature has required wealthy districts to begin subsidizing their less fortunate neighboring school districts.

Other school districts are hiring private companies to run their schools. Already, this has occurred in Dade County, Florida, and Baltimore, Maryland, and the Whittle Edison Channel I Project is now bidding to administer entire districts. Other school districts, like Minneapolis and San Diego, have abandoned professional educators and hired business consultants to manage their schools. More and more school districts are hiring private vendors to deliver educational services. Private school franchises, like Kindercare, Sylvan, Ombudson Ltd., and Huntington are for-profit businesses and are expanding. With all of these developments, can Kentucky Fried Learning Centers be far behind?

The Wisconsin legislature has passed a voucher plan that ensures 1,000 at-risk students in low-income neighborhoods in Milwaukee the opportunity to select from the best public and private nonsectarian schools in the area. In Minnesota, over 130,000 parents are now choosing schools and school districts, and more and more states are seeing voucher plans on their ballots. Over 500,000 children and youth in the United States have left public education for the security of home schooling. Seven states have passed charter school legislation that permits the creation of quasi-private public schools, and many states allow high-school students to leave public education and attend college with their tuition paid by the local high schools. More and more middle-class families who can afford it are abandoning public schools and entering private and parochial schools. Some see these events as the falling apart of U.S. public education; others see them as the erosion of the last great monopoly since Ma Bell and the final arrival of competition to the educational marketplace.

There is also considerable cause for optimism. The private foundations of America have been joined by corporate donors and individual philanthropists such as Walter Annenburg, who in late 1993 donated $500 million to a number of groups to help support school reform. The recipients included the Coalition for Essential Schools, the New American Schools Development Corporation, the Education Commission of the States, and nine of the nation's largest school districts.

Add to these developments the 11 new boundary-breaking schools financed by the New American Schools Development Corporation, the network of Community Learning Centers in Minnesota, and the growing number of new charter schools and a small but significant educational reform effort seems underway. There is also the Coalition of Essential Schools of Ted Sizer, the National Network for Educational Renewal directed by John Goodlad to reform both teacher education and local schools, the growing use of the International High School Baccalaureate Degree Program, and technological developments in schools in Florida and Texas. There is also the Kentucky school reform efforts. And don't forget the 500 accelerated schools that have been developed, the network using James Comer's School Development Program, the more than 200 Success For All schools, and the thousands of alternative public schools that are in operation in every state. It is evident that there is an important research, development, and experimentation effort under way in the United States. Never have so many reformed and restructured schools been in operation in this country where student learning is being so carefully assessed and programs evaluated.

On one hand, this seems to be a time of chaos and utter confusion. On the other, it is a time of rich experimentation and development; for some, it is a time of business as it has always been. What can be learned from all of these developments? What direction and insight can be discerned from the current tangle of public education? What can we learn from the contemporary educational scene? Emerging from all of this are several conclusions that cannot be ignored:

- *Social disintegration.* There are areas of social disintegration that threaten our society and our culture. These include critical changes in the family structure, crime and violence in our cities, the escalating number of children who are being born to single teenage women, and the breathtaking increases in the cost of social services for the poor and criminal. The increasing abuse of drugs and alcohol among our children and youth, growing illiteracy, and the failure of significant percentages of U.S. youth to succeed in school is pervasive and frightening.
- *International marketplace.* The international marketplace now demands a literate, educated, technologically fluent workforce. The world of work has given way to the age of the mind. There is only one way to succeed economically today, and that is through a solid, sound education and continuous lifelong learning.
- *Importance of education.* The only possible answer to any of our problems and the needs of the contemporary marketplace is better education for all, education that provides for meaningful employment. Public education must educate all children and educate them very well. The local school is the last great hope, perhaps the only hope for so many of our nation's children.
- *Large numbers of at-risk youth.* Unfortunately, a large percentage of U.S. youth arrive at school unprepared to learn, fail to succeed in school, ultimately drop out of school, and often spend their life unemployed or underemployed, many becoming wards of the state or even criminals.
- *Schools make a difference.* Based on recent educational research that has followed and assessed developments in schools for five to ten years, we now

know that schools can make a positive, significant impact on children and youth, even those from the most economically depressed and socially dysfunctional backgrounds.

- *All children can learn.* We now know how to provide high quality, effective education for all. There are thousands of schools throughout the nation that are doing just that and doing it well. There are schools that are teaching all children to read, ensuring that all children succeed in school and graduate, and documenting the fact that they are successful, even carefully identifying the reasons for their success. They are also documenting effective ways to transform public education into schools that are effective for all.
- *Failure of some schools.* If some schools and communities are providing effective education for all students in significant restructured settings, then it is a savage indictment of all of the rest. It means that large numbers of schools and communities are short-changing and failing large numbers of U.S. children and youth who could, with appropriate educational programs, succeed in school and become productive members of our society.
- *Schools can be changed and improved.* Last of all, we now understand how to restructure schools and change educational programs so that they can be effective for all. At last, there is a chance to change public education and provide high quality education for all. We know how to provide effective education; we also know how to create or re-create schools.

Now clearly is a time for action in communities throughout this country. Any less reflects a conscious intellectual separatism, no less destructive than the racial separatism of South Africa, a separatism that will continue to divide our nation between those who are educated and the growing underclass of Americans who have few skills and even less hope. It is time to end this destructive pattern of educational apartheid in the United States.

Creating Educational Reform

Since the early 1980s, there has been a proliferation of reports, monographs, books, articles, special journal issues, symposia, media and video productions, community forums, and scholarly debates on educational reform. Unfortunately, too many of the recommendations have proven to be wrong and may have actually inhibited or misdirected educational reform. Some of the reform literature has been written by the very people who support retention and tracking and continue to ignore the 30 percent dropout rate. Now these individuals presume to prescribe how public schools can be reformed and restructured.

The critical problem that continues to pervade the "how to do it" reform literature is that few of the authors have ever been involved in actually restructuring and reforming schools. Far too many of these "reformers" are not even aware of schools that have been restructured, and most seem to equate a reform "effort" with a single "success." Few report hard evaluative data including student assessment.

Check it out. In paper after paper, chapter after chapter, book after book of reform literature, look for even a name of a restructured school, let alone an address or phone number. The inverse is also true. If the reform literature has been written by someone who has been intimately involved in school restructuring, has a documented track record of success in school reform, and who can identify schools, providing names and places, then what you find might be of great value. Sadly, this informed group of educators and scholars represents a small minority of the vast array of educational reform literature available today.

The best and perhaps the only effective approach to school reform may be to identify schools that have been reformed or restructured and that have demonstrated their success at educating all children and youth. After carefully studying dozens of these schools and the accompanying long-term research and education data from their programs and after carefully reading the works of concerned scholars, including Robert Slavin, James Comer, Hank Levin, Gary Wehlage, Joe Nathan, Phil Schlechty, Barbara Wasik, Wayne Jennings, Nancy Karweit, Ted Sizer, Mary Ann Raywid, Nancy Madden, John Goodlad, Nolan Estes, Mario Fantini, and others, three distinctive approaches to school reform have emerged. These approaches should serve to inform and guide communities and public educators in transforming schools from where they are to where they need to be. The three approaches include restructuring existing schools, replicating alternative public schools, and creating new K–12 charter and contract schools (see Chapter 10). Taken together, these approaches provide schools and communities with the blueprint from which to restructure public education so that all children and youth can succeed.

Before exploring the approaches for effective school restructuring, it is important to first offer a word of caution about where to work, what to expect, and what not to do. The following eight caveats must be considered and acknowledged throughout a reform effort.

The School as the Focus for Educational Reform

Research has helped to define the limits of educational reform. The majority of effective reform efforts have focused not on teachers or individual classrooms but on the school. To date, no school district, county, borough, or state has satisfactorily restructured or reformed its schools. At this time, there is no solid evidence that we know how to systemically restructure U.S. education, the public education of a state, or even a school district, although many are trying to accomplish this task. Phil Schlechty and Bob Cole of the Center for Leadership and School Reform in Louisville, Kentucky, believe they can do it, and their work may lead to significant reform of school districts. Developments in Kentucky and other states may ultimately lead to the identification of effective statewide strategies for reform. Over time, effective strategies may well emerge which will address the larger educational system. For now, the best research evidence indicates that the best place to focus reform energies is on restructuring individual schools. We know how, and we can help others to understand the process.

School Reform Must Be Comprehensive

School reform that focuses simply on one aspect of school life is not likely to be successful. In schools that have significantly improved their effectiveness with at-risk youth, reform efforts have focused on classroom instruction as well as school climate (Teddlie & Stringfield, 1993). Such a comprehensive approach is common to successful school reform efforts. It is found in Success For All Schools, Comer schools, alternative public schools, as well as accelerated schools. Levin has maintained that successful school restructuring must focus on the total school: "Essentially, we believe that successful efforts at restructuring must address all three legs of a triangle that encompasses the schools' organization, curriculum and instruction. Efforts that address only one or two of these legs will fall flat and fail" (Levin, 1993, p. 2). Research on school reform efforts also recommends that to help at-risk youth, there must also be goals that encourage community and social services to join in efforts to improve schools.

Effective Educational Reform Cannot Be Imposed

It is essential to understand that educational reform cannot be imposed, mandated, or legislated, unless teachers, administrators, and community members agree with the reform effort. School reform cannot be accomplished by passing legislation, hiring a new superintendent or principal, establishing a new board policy, or requiring a new curriculum. The evidence is simply overwhelming. It doesn't work. As the noted architect Frank Lloyd Wright was once reported to have said, "From the ground up makes good sense for building. Beware of from the top down" (Wehlage, et al., 1989, p. vii). What state legislatures, state boards of education, and local school boards can do is to develop policies that recognize the importance of school reform and provide support and incentives to encourage school restructuring. Only time will tell whether or not efforts in Kentucky and Oregon to mandate nongraded elementary schools will be successful. Until such efforts can be documented as successful, conclusions about imposition of change will continue to stand. In the Louisiana School Effectiveness Study, the researchers were "struck by the lack of meaningful influence from the district office. In fact, the only influences we saw were negative and were of little importance to overall school effectiveness" (Teddlie & Stringfield, 1993). The researchers were surprised to find little or no relationship to exist between school district restructuring efforts and schools that were becoming more effective.

Reform is a Complex, Long-Term Process

Educational reformers have often proceeded as if they were using the H. L. Mencken quote, "For every complex question there is a simple answer." Unfortunately, they ignore Mencken's conclusion that the simple answer is invariably wrong. There is nothing simple or easy about school reform. It must be understood that educational change is a complex, personally demanding, and long-term affair.

The Accelerated Schools Project estimates that it takes at least six years to implement their program. Creating alternative public schools may be somewhat faster, but in spite of being able to initiate almost a restructured program immediately, most believe that it still takes at least three years to fully implement an effective new alternative program. Based on the Louisiana School Effectiveness Study, researchers concluded that "school improvement programs almost always take a minimum of three years to affect student achievement. Most school improvement programs should probably be conceived as a five-year process. . . . Moreover school improvement never ceases, since schools are always headed toward greater or lesser effectiveness (Teddlie & Stringfield, 1993, p. 226). Teachers, administrators, and community members need to recognize from the outset that educational reform will not happen quickly. Success will require many years of personally challenging responsibility.

Large School Size is a Fatal Flaw in School Restructuring Efforts

While there are many examples of elementary schools and some small middle schools and high schools that have been significantly restructured, it is all but impossible to identify a single, large comprehensive high school in the United States or Canada that has been successfully restructured. Large school size appears to militate against significant educational reform. Considerable evidence supports this conclusion. A recent five-year evaluation of the Coalition for Essential Schools reported little or no significant restructuring in the large, comprehensive high schools that made up this project. (Muncey & McQuillan, 1993). It is interesting to note that, in the case studies of 14 schools with special at-risk programs, the only school that was dropped from the study was a large comprehensive high school in Atlanta: "this program was found to be indistinguishable from other conventional comprehensive high schools. The special program's impact on students was minimal or even negative" (Wehlage, et al., 1989, p. 244). Recently in Fairbanks, Alaska, a high-school faculty of 80 teachers concluded two years of discussions and planning by voting down a proposal to modestly rearrange the daily schedule to create a weekly 90-minute planning and collaboration period. The school administrators and the teachers' union had agreed to implement the reform if 60 percent of the faculty voted approval. Only 58 percent supported the change, blocking the opportunity to jointly plan and collaborate toward restructuring the school.

Some Schools May Be Impossible to Improve

Research has documented that some schools stringently resist change. Teddlie and Stringfield stress that "an ineffective school did not get that way overnight—each has a unique history" (1993, p. 224). Such schools often have a long tradition of dysfunctional interpersonal relationships and an abnormal school culture. Some schools may be found in the midst of such negative community pressures that the only way to improve the school is to try to "create boundaries to buffer the school from negative influences" (Teddlie & Stringfield, 1993, p. 37).

This is not to say that all schools cannot try to face change and improve. It is to say that some will face greater challenges. Some school reform efforts may demand the assignment of a new principal or reassignment of teachers, intensive team building by an external consultant, extensive work with community members, and long-term staff development (Teddlie & Stringfield, 1993).

School Reform Requires Adequate Funding

School reform must have sufficient resources. Yet adequate finances for education continues to emerge as the most significant problem facing most communities. In the recent Gallup Poll of the public attitudes about schools, inadequate funding was clearly the "single biggest problem for local schools" (Elam, Gallup & Rose, 1993, p. 138). This was the first time in over 20 years of Gallup polling that inadequate funding was identified as the number one issue in U.S. education.

No School is an Island

What goes on inside a school cannot be separated from what occurs in the community that surrounds it. Schools tend to be a reflection of their community. No one has helped to dramatize this interrelationship so well as James Comer. He has championed the idea that it is just as important to try to rejuvenate community pride and togetherness as it is to improve the local school. His work offers a vivid tribute to the effectiveness of establishing strong, supportive ties between the neighborhood school and the neighborhoods.

Plans for school improvement, reform, or significant restructuring must be concerned with the pressures beyond the classroom which exert powerful influences, both positive and negative, on the school. This may mean increasing school security by using metal detectors to keep weapons out of the school; it may mean rigid restrictions on school clothing to keep gang colors out of the hallways; it may mean school community planning and governance teams; it may mean local alliances with government, churches, and youth groups; and it may mean the coordination of social services.

Educators and others attempting to improve schools must also remember that any significant effort to reform or restructure or even improve schools usually results in vigorous protests from some segment of the community. Opposition may come from religious fundamentalists of the radical right or the American Civil Liberties Union on the liberal left or from anyone from the Catholic Church to university historians (Molnar, 1993). Unfortunately, school improvement plans to address the most urgent needs of at-risk youth seem to bring out the most vocal reactions, for they often include controversial responses: free condoms, planned parenthood, and safe sex versus abstinence; Just Say No versus careful use; traditional values versus alternative gay lifestyles. Community groups have often focused on censoring textbooks and library books, attacking values clarification and secular humanism. More recently, parent and community groups throughout the community have generated concern regarding outcome assessments as some type of subtle, evil means of undermining U.S. youth.

The only way to ensure successful school reform is to incorporate broad-based community involvement and support from the very beginning. More than any other institution, the school is a mirror of the community. To change the school is to change the community. Yet schools cannot be timid in their work of addressing the massive problems associated with at-risk youth. When schools and communities do work together, dramatic improvements can and will occur.

A Word of Hope: There Are Allies Out There

The good news is that for school reform to be successful, schools do not have to act alone. The bad news is that to identify, mobilize, and actively involve your allies in school reform is in itself an enormous, complicated, but essential task. In school reform, as is so true with so much of life, it is always difficult at any given time to determine if circumstances are getting better or in fact getting worse; it is often hard to determine who are your friends and who is your opposition. Often in the midst of the school reform effort there will be an initial "sag of effectiveness" as the school attempts to transform itself. It is also sometimes difficult to differentiate problems from assets. Too often schools have viewed parents, community leaders, government agencies, and social service providers as problems rather than assets. That is now changing.

It is clear that educational reform must be connected with the world outside the schools: the neighborhood community, government and social service agencies, and other networks of support. Almost like an intricate web of stabilizing guy wires, strong relationships with a variety of external groups will anchor school reform to the security, support, and resources to satisfactorily address the needs of at-risk youth.

Community Support and Involvement

Community support and involvement are essential to successful school reform, especially for school reform that focuses on at-risk youth. Productive involvement includes everything from problem identification to goal setting, to management and assessment. Research has helped to identify a number of effective approaches to involving the community in school reform efforts:

Community Forums
A strategy that has proven extremely effective in many communities to elevate interest and foster increased involvement in educational reform is the community forum or town meeting. Such forums can take on any number of formats, but all begin with a public meeting or a series of meetings that bring together a cross-section of leadership throughout the community. This might include teachers;

administrators; school board members; county commissioners; the mayor; city, county, or state agency heads; police; ethnic leadership; representatives from community organizations; and newspaper, media, and religious leaders. The participants in these forums discuss their feelings about school and community problems and review data concerning community issues (school dropouts, infant mortality rates, teen parents, crime, drug use, unemployment, etc.) Through small group and directed discussions, problems and potential solutions are explored. Participants attempt to agree on a few targeted goals and plan follow-up action.

Perhaps the best available model for a community forum has been created and promoted by the Kettering Foundation. This model has been used in cities all across the country to successfully rally support to address school and community problems related to the crisis of youth at risk. The goal of the Kettering process is to get individuals and groups talking, agreeing to organize, and working together for school and community improvements. The Kettering Foundation can be contacted for advice and materials that assist communities in developing a successful forum (Kettering Foundation, 1989).

Other communities have developed a more complex process by initiating community involvement through small discussion groups, often in homes, churches, community associations, and the neighborhood school. These meetings are scheduled at a variety of times to encourage widespread participation. This provides for the broadest possible community involvement and builds toward a community-wide forum or town hall meeting. Some communities even conclude the process by televising the culminating forum.

Regardless of the approach that is used, forums or town meetings provide a vehicle to involve the school, community leaders, and interested citizens in an effort to develop agreement regarding appropriate goals for the community. A number of communities and cities in the United States, both large and small, have found the community forum a very effective approach for informing community leaders, building collaborative partnerships, and mobilizing action. Such forums can help to build trust between schools, health and family services, child care, and related human services. The forums also tend to lead to concerted action by city councils, county commissioners, school boards, and other county agencies in solving local problems.

Community Action Planning
Perhaps the most comprehensive approach to community involvement and action is a U.S. Cooperative Extension Service Program called Community Action Planning (CAP). This program has been used nationally with impressive results in both urban and rural areas. The state of Oregon has used this approach quite extensively in over 40 counties over a five-year period (State Community Children and Youth Services Commission, 1990). The Community Action Planning process combines a town forum approach with the coordination of community services to develop a more extensive long-range action plan. The Cooperative Extension Service program brings together people from the widest possible cross-section of a

community—business, government, social services, education, parents, and other community members. Students are especially encouraged to participate. These constituents work together to identify common underlying causes of problems facing children and youth in their community. As a result of this process, a plan is developed which includes a description of local needs, the causes of local problems, and a positive course of action to address identified problems.

CAP is rooted in a set of six underlying beliefs:

- *Youth problems are community problems. All members of the community have a stake in defining and solving the problems.*
- *Coordinated efforts, focused on key problems and their solutions, will maximize community resources.*
- *A dynamic balance between previous intervention and treatment must be maintained by the community.*
- *Planning strategies specific to each community are important in responding to youth problems and overcoming their causes.*
- *Every individual, group, and organization is a potential community resource. Young people are a resource, not just program recipients.*
- *Communities are invested in empowerment (State Community Children and Youth Services Commission, 1990).*

State Extension Service staff provide technical assistance and individualized consultation to aid communities in the training of volunteer leadership. Communities throughout the country can contact their local U.S. Cooperative Extension Service at one of the more than 400 offices for assistance and support. While the Extension Service has traditionally served primarily rural areas, recent years have seen a major shift from agricultural services to human services and to include urban settings as well.

Specific benefits from this cooperative program include:

- *The emergence of new leaders from the private, government and youth sectors of the community.*
- *The development of strategies specific to each community.*
- *The development of community economic plans that focus on quality future workforce strategies.*
- *A new level of commitment to youth from a cross-section of the community.*
- *The realignment of resources and programs to address youth and family problems more effectively without the addition of new money.*
- *The development of new cooperative relationships among government agencies and community organizations.*
- *The definition of new collaborative roles for traditional youth groups and organizations working with youth.*
- *The participation of youth who are a strong new resource for planning and program development (State Community Children and Youth Services Commission, 1990).*

The planning process is complex and time-consuming. Community volunteers spend an average of over 4,500 hours in a 6- to 12-month period working with Extension Service consultants in preparation for the initial CAP workshop. Planning for the workshop includes setting the vision for change, identifying committed leaders from the community, and developing a strategy for maximum community involvement with long-term solutions. Communities generally identify 90 to 125 key leaders for the first planning workshop. These leaders subsequently engage approximately 700 volunteers to carry out their solutions.

Community Action Planning is perhaps the most labor-intensive, complicated, and long-term effort that has been identified to address the needs of at-risk youth. And perhaps more than any other strategy, this process attempts to deal with the issues at the base of complex social and economic problems. The approach has proven to be very successful and represents considerable promise for communities concerned with improving the lives of their children and youth.

Community Partnerships

Another way to recruit new allies to school reform, restructuring, and school improvement is through the development of partnerships. School-community partnerships have also proven to be extremely beneficial to schools and at-risk youth. Business/Education Round Tables have been developed in cities all over the United States and have created a national network of support that is coordinated by the Business Round Table, 200 Park Avenue, New York, NY 10166 (phone 212-682-6370) or 1615 L Street NW, Washington, DC 20030 (Phone 202-872-1260). Started during the fall of 1989, the Business Round Table represents over 200 corporations who have made a 10-year commitment of personal time and company resources to improve public education (Business Round Table, 1993). Many identify Portland, Oregon, as having one of the most effective round tables in the United States. Often cities have encouraged local businesses to develop "Adopt-a-School" programs, and today almost every school district in moderate and large cities has established adopt-a-school programs. The Boise, Idaho, school district has developed an exemplary Partners In Education program that connects hundreds of businesses and university participants with public schools. Clearly, such education, business, and university partnerships can provide essential human and fiscal resources necessary for serving at-risk youth.

Integrating and Coordinating Education and Social Services

"As a county commissioner, I knew each day how many streets had been repaired, how many complaints the police received about barking dogs, how many calls went out to the fire department . . . but I had no idea how many teenagers were pregnant, on drugs, homeless, or being sexually abused. Even worse, I had no idea where to even get that type of information."
—(COUNTY COMMISSIONER, EUGENE, OREGON, 1988)

In addition to community friends and allies, there is another incredible source of services and support for school programs for at-risk youth. These are the legion of federal, state, and local government agencies and community social service organizations whose professionals can provide a comprehensive range of services and fiscal resources to support at-risk children, youth, and their families.

Integration and coordination of the many community agencies and organizations is absolutely essential for schools and for their children and youth who live in poverty or who have specific problems associated with pregnancy, drug and alcohol abuse, and parental abuse. Because children with health or family problems are unlikely to perform at their best, schools must help students achieve academically by first ensuring that various community agencies provide children and their families with health care, child services, mental health services, and even such basic needs as food, shelter, and transportation. Since the school is the one community institution that deals with every family with children, the school must take the initiative in helping stimulate and coordinate the many community agencies to assist at-risk children and their families.

In most communities, there may be a half a dozen or more agencies, youth groups, or community associations that can provide services to a particular family or a child, yet these service agencies are often uncoordinated and suffer from a significant fragmentation. Such agencies as state welfare, children services, mental health, county health departments, adult and family services, child care resources and referral, drug and alcohol rehabilitation centers, and juvenile courts all tend to work in isolation. It is almost impossible for a family or a school-age youth to be aware of the various agencies that might be available to them and even more difficult to access their services. Even educated professionals will find social services to be a bewildering array of fragmented programs that are difficult to find and sometimes impossible to access. One study concluded that if an adolescent or a teenage parent walks into any one of these agencies, the odds are that they will not get help. If an advocate working on behalf of the child makes contact, assistance is far more likely (Barr & Ross, 1989). If the services are part of a coordinated program using a case management approach to address the problems of a particular child, the services can be all but guaranteed (Hobbs, 1993).

A growing number of communities have begun an attempt to coordinate these various agencies. Usually these coordination efforts are conducted by some type of school-community council or coordinating council. Often these groups are referred to as youth service teams and invite representatives from selected agencies to attend regularly scheduled meetings to address the problems and needs of specific children and seek widespread support from a number of agencies. Such a case management approach to the needs of children and their families has enormous potential for improving the child's opportunities to learn (Hobbs, 1993).

The concept of schools and communities collaborating with local human service agencies is a recent development. As a result, the limited research that has been conducted primarily involves a number of case studies detailing efforts of community agency coordination and collaboration, national surveys, and one study of major efforts in San Diego between the schools, county, and the local community college. These studies have documented how difficult it is to break down the barriers that exist locally between various social agencies, have identified the isolation and turf issues associated with local community agencies, and have described the difficulties these agencies have in working together. The research also documents how collaboration and coordination of community service agencies can improve the delivery of services to at-risk youth and their families and can develop new kinds of services. Despite the short time that these efforts have been underway, they have been evaluated as having remarkable success in addressing the needs of at-risk youth and their families (Bruner, 1991).

A number of states including Oregon, Illinois, Florida, New Jersey, and California have developed youth services programs in every county. Each program must provide health and substance abuse services, counseling, job and employment training, information and referral services, and even recreation. Programs may also provide for child care, teen parent programs, and family planning (Children's Defense Fund, 1991). At least one national center, the Center for Community Education at Rutgers University, provides detailed descriptions of research regarding the coordination of community services, case studies of successful programs, and how-to-do-it advice with sample forms, sample letters to parents, agencies, and teenagers (Center for Comunity Education, 1991).

Unfortunately, interagency collaboration is far from easy. It demands a long-term, patient commitment to education of at-risk students. If collaboration is being considered there are seven key points to remember:

1. Collaboration is not a quick fix for many of the vexing problems society faces.
2. Collaboration is a means to an end, not an end in itself.
3. Developing interagency collaboration is extremely time-consuming and process-intensive.
4. Interagency collaboration does not guarantee the development of a client-centered service system nor the establishment of a trusting relationship between an at-risk child or family and a helping adult.
5. Collaboration occurs among people, not among institutions.
6. Creative problem-solving skills must be developed and nurtured in those who are expected to collaborate.
7. Collaboration is too important a concept to be trivialized (Bruner, 1991).

Lisbeth Schorr, coauthor of *Within Our Reach: Breaking the Cycle of Disadvantage*, has studied programs throughout the United States that have been successful in integrating education and social services. Schorr has identified six common characteristics of effective programs that work:

> 1. *Successful programs were comprehensive, intensive, flexible, and responsible. "Nobody was saying: 'This may be what you need, but it's not part of my job to help you get it.'" Successful programs took an extended role in the lives of children with extensive community networks and the ability to respond to concrete needs. Simply, they gave front-line workers the discretion to do what was necessary.*

2. *Successful programs encouraged active collaboration across professional and bureaucratic boundaries rather than separate funding and separate disciplinary approaches.*

3. *Successful programs dealt with children as part of families and families as part of the communities in which they lived. "You can't clone good programs, but you can use their experiences to set up new programs to work with your communities' special needs."*

4. *Successful programs made special efforts to nurture parents. For example, school programs gave parents the skills to help them help their children in school. However, enlisting already overwhelmed parents requires more skills and ingenuity than ever.*

5. *Successful staff members had the time, skills, and support to build relationships of trust and respect with the children and their families. For example, in a prenatal care program, the friendly staff support was the quality valued most highly by the expectant parents, not the health care services they received. Smallness of scale also seems to be crucial.*

6. *Successful programs had a long-term preventive orientation and continued to evolve over time. They were less rule-bound, more outcome-oriented, and empowered the family (Crohn, 1992, p. 4).*

Schorr warns that collaboration of service providers in schools and communities is not the solution to fragmented services, it is a means to an end. She also warns that change must be top-down as well as bottom-up. She points out that the "U.S. highway system was not a Kiwanis project" and "National Defense cannot be maintained by the local Chamber of Commerce." What is needed are state and national policies that encourage and support local collaboration (Crohn, 1992, p. 4).

Networks of Support

Too often, local schools are isolated and alone, attempting to reinvent the wheel of educational reform that has been tried, evaluated, and studied in other school districts around the country. Whether it is the faculty of an existing school or a community group determined to start a new alternative public school, one of the most important steps to successful school reform is seeking out and learning from other schools and groups attempting similar efforts. It also involves seeking out individuals and organizations who can provide consultation, technical assistance, staff development, and support. Discovering that others have attempted and been successful with similar reform efforts can be particularly encouraging to the morale of reform groups as well as vital to the process. Learning that programs really can work, learning what problems to anticipate, and even borrowing printed materials, proposals, assessment data, and curriculum materials can save months, perhaps years, of effort.

Twenty years ago, school restructuring efforts were attempted without the guidance of research, evaluation, and experience, yet today it is possible to find other schools and communities who have had documented experiences with almost every type of school reform. Not only are there other schools and communities involved in a wide variety of school reform efforts, but many have been organized into sophisticated networks of support. These include Accelerated Schools, Success For All schools, the School Development Program, the Coalition of Essential Schools, alternative public schools, and programs and approaches like Foxfire, Montessori public schools, and magnet schools. Some approaches including Montessori Education, Accelerated Schools, Reading Recovery, Success For All, and Foxfire, have affiliated with university-based teacher education programs to train teachers and administrators. The Accelerated School Project at Stanford has established satellite university centers around the country to assist local school activities. In Minnesota, a network of community learning centers has been developed that supports one another by exchanging information and ideas and sharing support. For over two decades, alternative public schools have maintained a national network of active state associations, have convened an annual international conference, and have affiliated with universities that support research and the development of alternative schools. These associations assist with a variety of school restructuring and issues, and can provide an invaluable network of support. Schools share information, schedules, curriculum, learning contracts, and funding proposals, and invite students and teachers to visit one another and maintain contact through telecommunications and computer networks. These networks also share assessment information, publish advice via newsletters, conduct workshops and conferences, and assist one another in lobbying school boards and state legislators.

Schools and communities can also obtain help and support from a number of technical assistance centers located throughout the country. In the final section of this book a detailed list is provided of regional education laboratories, technical assistance centers, research centers, and professional organizations that provide support and assistance. Taken together, these organizations can provide comprehensive, positive support and information to any restructuring effort.

Finally, there is also the local college or university that can provide a wide variety of assistance and support. Schools and colleges of education often provide public schools with consultants, research information, technical assistance, staff development, and workshops that can assist communities and schools in developing external funding proposals. Perhaps most important, teacher education programs have large numbers of undergraduate and graduate students who can provide in-school and in-classroom assistance to support school reform activities. This has proven to be a tremendous resource of human talent and energy, especially as teacher education programs have increased collaboration with local public schools to enhance professional development. These students can provide one-to-one tutoring, conduct small-group cooperative learning experiences, and even help relieve teachers for planning.

Professional Teacher Organizations

Critical allies to school improvement are the American Federation of Teachers, the National Education Association, and their state and local affiliates. No significant school restructuring project should be attempted without the active participation or support of the teacher organization and the leadership of the local or state affiliate. The teacher organization can provide considerable influence in working with the local school district administration and school board. The National Education Association has developed its own national school reform effort called the Mastery Learning Consortium that is working in six states and coordinated by the National Center for Innovation in Washington, DC. Just as it is next to impossible to change schools without community support, it is equally difficult to change schools without the support of professional teacher associations.

Student Support

Any serious school reform activity should originate and be conducted for the benefit of students, particularly those at risk of dropping out. Students' perspectives should be included in every step of the process. As indicated often in describing middle-school and high-school projects, students can serve as an influential force in education reform. Often, central office administrators, community leaders, and school board members will be far more sensitive and supportive of students than they are of principals and teachers. It is truly amazing to see students, even severely at-risk students, dress up and make a polished presentation before a board of education, a local service organization or a state legislature. Students are especially effective in reporting assessment data and gathering personal first-hand reports of the effectiveness of their school experiences. Students should provide the driving force for school reform at the middle-school and high-school levels.

Despite the encouraging developments in community support and involvement in school reform efforts, many communities face the overwhelming dilemma of pervasive school and community violence. To truly reform and improve schools, many communities must first confront the problems associated with violence and society.

Programs to Reduce School and Community Violence

Crime has become a way of life in U.S. cities, especially in areas of poverty, and increasingly a significant part of this crime is being committed by children and youth under 18 years of age. Children and teenagers are responsible for 14 percent of the nation's slayings, 26 percent of all robberies, and 44 percent of all car thefts. Murder has become such a part of our nation's cities that yearly deaths in cities like Houston, Chicago, Washington, Los Angeles, and Miami number in the thousands. Drive-by shootings, random murder, and children killing children have become a way of life in far too many communities. Murder now follows only non-gun related accidents and cancer as the leading cause of death for 5- to 14-year-olds (Manning, 1994). Juvenile arrests for murder are at the highest level in the past two decades and the number of youths arrested for carrying weapons is at a 20-year high (Crime Report, 1993). Unfortunately, many of these violent acts occur in and around schools. In 1993, Secretary of Education Richard Riley outlined the grim statistics:

- *About three million thefts and violent crimes occur on or near schools every year. That is nearly 16,000 incidents each school day.*

- *About one in five high-school students regularly carries a firearm, knife, razor, club, or other weapon; many carry them to school.*
- *About 20 percent of all public school teachers report being verbally abused, 8 percent report being physically threatened, and 2 percent report being physically attacked (Riley Outlines, 1993, p. 6).*

A 1993 poll conducted by Metropolitan Life Insurance of over 2,000 students, teachers and police found that "meaningful learning has been replaced by metal detectors." Other findings include:

- *11% of teachers and 23% of students say they have been victims of violence in or near their schools.*
- *22% of boys and 4% of girls say they've carried a weapon, such as handguns or knives, to school at some time.*
- *28% of students say they do it to impress friends, 16% say it makes them feel important, 16% are motivated by prejudice or hate, 5% by drugs.*
- *6% of boys and 1% of girls had threatened someone with a knife or gun.*
- *Those with poor grades were more likely to make the threats.*
  (Henry, Dec. 17, 1993, p. 1)

In a similar survey conducted in 1991 by the U.S. Department of Justice of over 21.6 million students ages 12 to 18, 16% reported that a student had attacked or threatened a teacher at school, 15% reported gangs at school, and 22% of the students reported taking a weapon to school (Karres, 1994).

One teacher in Chicago explained that her school children "teach us to hit the floor if we hear gunfire from the nearby housing project" and when she asked a seventh-grade class who knew somebody who had been killed or seriously injured, every hand went up (Carnegie Corporation, 1993, p. 9).

Addressing the problem of violence is a communitywide societal problem. There are no easy answers to the complex circumstances leading to everyday brutal violence. Efforts to address the problem include tightening gun control, increasing the number of local police, a national and international war on drugs, and providing unmarked rental cars for tourists. At least two states, Utah and Colorado, have become so concerned about youth violence that they are enacting specific gun-control legislation regarding teenagers. In 1993, United States Attorney General Janet Reno recommended six steps for addressing the problem:

- *Make schools a service hub, hauling in social and health workers to do the job;*
- *Ask businesses to let parents work from 8 a.m. to 3 p.m., so they can be with their children after school;*
- *Pay extra attention to children up to age three;*
- *Ask the local bar association to adopt a violence-ridden block, serve as advocates against landlords, or help youths who have no one else to stick up for them;*
- *Provide mentors for students; and*
- *Boycott the sponsors of violent television programs (Riley Outlines 2, 1993, p. 6).*

For schools, many programs that address the needs of at-risk youth are felt to be positively affected by reducing gang participation and violence. These include drug-free school programs, after-school programs, and intramural athletic programs. School efforts also include increased security in school buildings, assigning police in the hallways, removing student lockers, installing metal detectors on entrance doorways, and establishing alternative public schools and other programs for at-risk youth. In a classic study on violence, vandalism, and crime in schools conducted by a U.S. Senate subcommittee, alternative schools were identified as the most powerful positive force schools could employ in this problem area (Smith, et al., 1976).

While there is little or no recent research or even school evaluations that offer reliable insight into the problems of crime, violence, and vandalism in schools, a number of the recommendations that are being made seem appropriate:

- *Use metal detectors on school external doors.* Just like domestic and international airports, urban schools have reached the point where metal detectors are an essential way of life. Over one-fourth of all urban high schools are now using metal detectors (Pabst, 1993).
- *Conflict resolution.* As described in a previous chapter, there seems to be great promise in teaching students to mediate disputes and disagreements. In Gillmore Middle School in Racine, Wisconsin, about 75 percent of the students involved in disputes are requesting a student mediator (Pabst, 1993).
- *Peer and parent patrols.* Following the concept of the urban Guardian Angels, some schools have established peer patrols. At South Ridge Senior High School in Miami, violence, vandalism, trespassing, and other school crimes have decreased, and fights have been nearly eliminated by using former gang members to provide crowd control and monitor hallways between classes. The group is called the Spartan Patrol (Pabst, 1993). Some schools go even further by using parent patrols to screen visitors; patrol hallways, grounds, and bathrooms; and provide on-the-spot counseling and assistance to students.
- *Developing schoolwide plans of action.* All urban high schools need to develop a plan of action for dealing with crime, violence, and unusual school disruptions. As researchers Stephanie Kadel and Joseph Follman have said, "Schools that are prepared for major crises will also be able to handle more common disruptions and other crises such as the suicide or accidental deaths of students" (Pabst, 1993, p. 2).
- *Fair and consistent discipline policies.* Schools must have clear, consistent, fair disciplinary policies that students and parents are involved in developing. Many urban schools have established alternatives to suspension where students are "expelled" into an alternative education program that provides individual and group counseling.
- Combined school, community, and state efforts to combat crime and violence.
- Some schools have eliminated student lockers and require see-through backpacks and book bags.

A recent report outlined a comprehensive plan for addressing the problems of violence, vandalism, and crime in schools (see Table 9-1).

And while there is surprisingly little research on the growing problem of school violence, the 1993 Metropolitan Life Survey of school students and law enforcement officers reported over 15 widely used strategies for dealing with school violence (see Table 9-2). And while the survey provided no evidence of the effectiveness of these strategies, both students and law enforcement officers reported that the overall effect of these efforts had helped to alleviate the problems of school violence to some degree (see Table 9-3).

In another comprehensive study of youth crime, Terrance P. Thornberry completed an extensive follow-up study of over 4,000 youth in Denver, Pittsburgh, and Rochester, New York, over a five-year period (Kantrowitc, 1993, p. 46). By age 16, more than half of the students studied had admitted to some form of violent criminal behavior. The recommendations that emerged from the Thornberry study were consistent with all other research regarding at-risk youth:

- *Crime and violence is part of a long developmental process that begins in early childhood with abuse and maltreatment.*
- *Crime and violent acts have a direct relationship to poverty: parents who haven't finished high school, who are on welfare, or who were teenage parents are more likely to have delinquent children.*
- *Problems in school lead to frustrations that often lead to crime and violence. Many of the most violent youth are barely literate. Students who are illiterate and have suffered from learning disabilities are common among violent teenagers (Kantrowitc, 1993, p. 46).*

Thornberry's conclusions dramatically depict the intergenerational connection of society's most urgent problems and once again provide an urgent challenge to

TABLE 9-1   Policies, Programs, and Legislative Initiatives for Reducing School Violence

- Laws that prohibit carrying concealed weapons, that make it harder to buy and sell guns, and that increase criminal penalties for noncompliance.
- Policies that establish safe school zones with stiffer penalties for selling weapons or drugs within a 1,000 feet of the school.
- Policies that automatically transfer from juvenile to criminal court cases of minors above age 14 charged with possessing or using a weapon on school grounds.
- Laws that penalize adults when their weapons are found in a minor's possession.
- Stiffer penalties for assaults on school staff or those that occur on school grounds.
- Smaller schools or scheduling policies that reduce teacher-student ratios.
- Increased funds for programs aimed at preserving and strengthening the family unit.
- Legislation (such as California's constitutional amendment) affirming students' and staffs' right to a safe school.

(Adapted from Pabst, 1993, p. 3)

TABLE 9-2   Steps Schools Have Taken To Stop Or Reduce Violence

Question: What kinds of steps has your school taken to stop or reduce the violence in or around your school?

	Students	Law Enforcement Officers
	Percentage	
Suspended or expelled students when they were violent	81	—
Instituted a dress code or banned certain types of clothing	63	68
Started a disciplinary code	50	—
Provided counseling for students or their families	45	—
Had visitors talk to classes about crime and violence	40	99
Held meetings for your class or the entire school	37	—
Made random checks of bookbags, backpacks or lockers	31	52
Placed monitors in the hallways	29	63
Hired security guards or police in or around the school	28	70
Conducted classes on how to talk about problems, rather than fight	24	—
Started safety or anti-violence programs	14	—
Provided a hotline for students to call	13	25
Used hand held metal detectors	5	24
Made students walk through metal detectors	2	12
None of these things	2	—
Not Sure	3	—

(Reprinted by permission from The American Teacher: Violence in America's Public Schools. (1993) Metropolitan Life. New York p. 83)

TABLE 9-3   Effects Of Steps Taken

Question: Do you think these steps have helped a lot, somewhat, not much, or not at all?

	Students	Law Enforcement
		Percentage
A Lot	15	41
Some	51	40
Hardly Any	20	14
None At All	10	4
Not Sure	4	1

(Reprinted by permission from *The American Teacher:* Violence in America's Public Schools. (1993) Metropolitan Life. New York. p. 84.)

WARNING! ANYONE WHO COMMITS THE CRIME OF
CARRYING A FIREARM ON A SCHOOL CAMPUS OR SCHOOL
BUS SHALL BE IMPRISONED AT HARD LABOR FOR NOT
MORE THAN 5 YEARS.

LSA.-R.S. 14:95.2

Sign placed at outside entry doorways of all New Orleans Public
Schools.

FIGURE 9-1

(Reprinted by permission from New Orleans, LA Public Schools, 1993.)

develop teen parent programs, effective preschool and elementary programs,
and a wide variety of alternative schools and other at-risk programs.

A growing number of states are taking action to combat school related crime.
In a recent 38 state survey, 17 states reported legislation regarding violence in public schools. In nine of the 17 states, legislation was passed establishing stricter
penalties for students carrying arms into schools or committing violent acts (see
Figure 9-1); or bills permitting schools to purchase metal detectors, surveillance
systems and hiring security officers. Six states have passed legislation declaring
schools as drug-free zones (Karras, 1994).

At last there is a chance to change schools to meet the needs of at-risk children and youth. It is occurring in thousands of communities across the country
and is being carefully studied, researched, and evaluated. These restructured
schools are indeed teaching at-risk youth effectively and documenting that these
students are able to achieve at the level of their successful peers. Some schools
even guarantee to students and their parents that all will learn effectively and
succeed in school. There does exist a better understanding of the magnitude and
the complexities of school reform. We understand the problems to be confronted,
the friends and allies to be mobilized, and we have a growing arsenal of effective approaches to transform schools and communities into safe places of learning for all children and youth.

Chapter 10

Restructuring Schools for At-Risk Youth: Three Approaches That Work

To those who would dismiss the idea that the solution to the problems of high school lies in the development of very small schools because they are too expensive, I recommend the following exercise. Imagine a school district modeled not on the practices of General Motors but on those of a cottage industry. The average per-pupil expenditure in this country is about $5,260 a year. Envision a small, highly autonomous school, given that funding level. If the school has 200 kids in it, its annual operating budget is over $1,050,000. Return 20 percent of it—$210,000—to a trimmed-down central administration for its reduced services and for bus transportation. Imagine a low student/teacher ratio, say 20:1. Pay your 10 teachers well, say an average of $45,000 a year (including fringe benefits). Hire a head teacher and pay him or her $60,000. Find an appropriate building for your program in your community and rent it at $7,000 a month plus another $3,000 for utilities. Hire a secretary, a custodian, and a cleaning person at $20,000 each. Budget $1,000 a year for supplies for each of your teachers and $3,000 for the central office. Put aside $10,000 to buy books each year and $20,000 for computers and A–V equipment. If the idea of trips is appealing, lease three vans, each at $5,000 dollars a year. That's probably enough to cover maintenance of them, but include another $3,000 just to be sure. Put $12,000 into a mileage budget. Now comes the fun: figuring out what to do with the $70,000 that has yet to be spent.
(GREGORY, 1993, P. 244)

While there may be hundreds of clever strategies to improve some aspect of classroom instruction or successfully reform some portion of the entire school, there are three specific approaches to restructuring that have an impressive track record of comprehensive success. Each of these approaches has been successfully replicated, and they provide a blueprint for any school district or community concerned with improving schools to better teach all youth. The first approach, restructuring existing schools, focuses on transforming K–12 schools and represents the greatest challenge to implement. The second approach, replicating alternative public schools, focuses on expanding the use of a proven model for restructuring and diversifying public education. The third approach, creating boundary-breaking schools, focuses on the development of new charter and contract schools. While one of the approaches, that of developing alternative public schools, has been used successfully for more than 25 years, the other two have a much shorter but impressive record of success.

Each of these approaches can be unusually effective in significantly improving or restructuring schools, yet none is easy. Each of the approaches is complex, time-consuming, and fraught with pitfalls. The approaches have a number of common characteristics, including community involvement, coordinating social services, networking, and school-community consensus building, yet each has distinctive factors that set them apart. Finally, all three approaches demand years of effort to be successful. Despite the challenges, these approaches work, and each can be used to develop schools where all children and youth can learn effectively.

Restructuring Existing Schools

The most difficult, most demanding, and most time-consuming approach to school reform is to attempt to change or improve an existing school. Yet, because it focuses on improving the existing schools of the nation, it must be considered as the most important challenge. So difficult is the process that many who have attempted this approach have concluded that it was impossible to change an existing school. Discussions in Chapter 3 described the systemic and behavioral characteristics of schools that led an earlier generation of reformers to conclude that existing schools could not be changed. Because of this, these educational reformers focused their energies on creating new alternative public schools. Today the idea that existing schools cannot be changed has been challenged by a growing number of schools that have demonstrated significant progress in student achievement. Yet evidence of just how hard it is to change existing schools continues to be reported.

A recent report from the University of Wisconsin Center on Organization and Restructuring of Schools reported that three separate studies recently provided rather discouraging results regarding school reform and restructuring. In one study, 6,000 individuals throughout the nation were solicited to identify schools that had been restructured. Two hundred and sixty-eight elementary schools, middle schools, and high schools were selected for the study. Each of the schools was investigated to determine the extent to which the schools had implemented 38 school restructuring concepts (heterogeneous grouping, students participating in small group work, integrated disciplines, differentiated staffs, collaborative relationships with parents and human services, etc.). Of the 38 factors studied, less than half were frequently reported being used via telephone interviews with principals and through written questionnaires. Even more discouraging, "subsequent site visits revealed that the frequency of fulfillment was only about half that concluded from in-depth interviews, i.e., in practice, many schools fell short of their principals' descriptors of restructuring" (Center on Organization and Restructuring of Schools, 1992, p. 2.) For example, 92 percent of the principals reported that their schools used heterogeneous grouping, but only 55 percent were found to use this approach during on-site visits. And remember, these were schools that had claimed to be outstanding examples of restructuring.

In a second study that explored the use of 16 characteristics of restructured schools in 1,037 middle-grade schools, the vast majority (44.6 percent) reported using only one to five of the 16 restructuring concepts. An additional 34.7 percent reported using only six to eight concepts (Center on Organization and Restructuring of Schools, 1992). The conclusion of these two studies, plus one other which reviewed over 100 proposals randomly selected from 16,000 proposals submitted to R. J. R. Nabisco Foundation for school reform projects, was that "the elements of school restructuring are not being widely accepted. . . . It is difficult to find schools in the nation that have been comprehensively restructured" (Center on Organization and Restructuring of Schools, 1992, p. 4). In fact, there seems to be a vast number of educators who are unable to conceptualize a restructured school. One explanation for the small number of schools funded by the New American Schools Development Corporation was the lack of creative proposals (Mecklenburger, 1992).

The most recent study, based on a survey of 3,380 high school principals, reported that school reform efforts were "spotty", with "few schools . . . attempting systemic reform" (Viadero, 1994, p. 1). Only 32 percent of the schools were involved in or planning comprehensive professional development programs to assist teachers in implementing curricular changes. Only seven of the 3,380 school principals surveyed reported comprehensive reform efforts were being used.

These findings are similar to the conclusions reported in the five-year study of one of the nation's premiere restructuring efforts, the Coalition of Essential Schools. The conclusion of the Essential Schools research was devastating: "although our research spent nearly five years, the structure, dominant pedagogy, and disciplinary divisions of American secondary schools have remained relatively unchanged for nearly a hundred years" (Muncey & McQuillan, 1993, p. 489).

A large number of schools, especially at the elementary level, have been able to document significant improvements in learning, but the actual number of schools that have been significantly restructured is relatively small. At the middle and high school levels, restructured schools are even more difficult to find.

Problems to be Overcome in Restructuring Existing Schools

While success can be demonstrated in improving schools and to a lesser extent in restructuring existing schools, there are a number of factors that must first be recognized, understood, and overcome if the approach is to be successful. These factors relate directly to school size and the fact that most school faculties in existing schools have been assembled over the years with little regard to personal beliefs, commitment to educational philosophy, or preference for particular instructional approaches. The mix of different and often conflicting beliefs coupled with large school size and entrenched teaching staffs tends to paralyze and inhibit significant school reform.

Conflicting Beliefs Regarding School Reform

Many of the teachers in any existing school will not believe that school restructuring is necessary. Most teachers and administrators believe that they are being effective and that they enjoy a reputation for having a quality school. When studying the Coalition of Essential Schools, the researchers were surprised to discover that "even in schools that are characterized by poor attendance, low scores on standardized tests, and high drop-out and failure rates—schools in which outsiders might assume that there would be consensus about the need for change, there was none." (Muncey & McQuillan, 1993, p. 489). Inevitably, the faculty of schools such as these blame conditions in society; the increasing numbers of special education, at-risk, and minority students in their classes; and insufficient resources for the school's shortcomings. Often, when school restructuring projects get under way, the efforts are supported by only a few teachers and administrators. Even under the best of circumstances, there are always teachers who adamantly oppose restructuring efforts and who are offended by the implication that they are not doing an effective job. In almost every restructuring effort, one can hear teachers and administrators complain, "if only we could get rid of a few teachers, then we could be successful."

To address this problem, schools must be involved in long-term consensus building, and even then all of the teachers will most likely not be in complete agreement. School districts need to provide some type of nonpunitive, incentive-based transfer procedure that allows teachers to move to other school locations where their beliefs and practices are more congruent and compatible.

Conflicting Educational Beliefs

Faculty of any existing school will have different philosophical and methodological beliefs about teaching and learning. Until a school initiates a restructuring or improvement effort, teachers and principals rarely discuss different teaching and learning styles, instructional approaches, or educational philosophies. So often these issues are only discussed in university teacher education courses and too often are felt to represent little more than idealistic theory that has little to do with the day-to-day demands of the real world of schools and classrooms. When serious efforts at school improvement or restructuring get underway, significant and often diametrically opposed beliefs begin to emerge. As long as teaching is isolated, with individual teachers doing their own thing behind their classroom doors, a school can function with dramatically diverse types of teachers. It is only when schoolwide goals and processes are discussed that fundamental disagreements often appear. The disagreements can often develop into serious divisions within a faculty. These conflicts are often exacerbated when those representing the emerging reform philosophy are felt to have more administrative support, added resources, and more recognition. Deep personal resentments can emerge (Muncey & McQuillan, 1993).

Once again, long-term consensus building coupled with intensive staff development is essential, but even then, incentive-based transfer policies may be necessary to assist schools and communities develop schoolwide plans for restructuring.

School Size

School size has been identified as one of the most significant factors in school effectiveness and school reform. Given the lack of success public education has experienced in attempting to restructure large schools, the focus of school reform of comprehensive middle schools and high schools must be on creating some smaller unit of size (i.e., develop schools within schools, alternative public schools, or satellite programs). Large schools must be divided into small enough units so that teacher consensus can be built (Brandt, 1993b).

Experienced Teachers

Most existing school staffs are composed of a majority of mature, experienced teachers. In most schools in the United States, the average teaching experience is approximately 15 years, which means that a school faculty is composed of significant numbers of teachers who are well established in their own particular instructional approach. Many have not participated in a university training program, other than for short workshops or conferences, or a course here and there, for more than a decade and certainly long before the revolution in technology. As described in earlier chapters, the process of retraining these teachers to participate in distinctive new ways of teaching and learning is similar to that of deprogramming and can only occur through careful, long-term staff development and training.

Essential Strategies for Restructuring Existing Schools

In spite of the difficult problems facing school restructuring and improvement, there is sufficient research data available today to conclude without question that existing public schools can be changed and significantly improved. This conclusion is consistent with the major educational research that have been completed during the last decade. Studies have documented that the factors that make a difference between effective and ineffective schools are constant regardless of the type of student population they are serving or the socioeconomic and geographic setting of the school (Teddlie & Stringfield, 1993).

There are a number of successful efforts at restructuring existing schools that are being used today, and most of these efforts employ a similar set of strategies. A careful look at the process that is used in the Accelerated School Project, the Success For All Program, the School Development Program in small middle and K–12 schools, and schools that have been independently restructured offer a number of specific strategies that should prove useful. These strategies can be effective in elementary schools and in small schools at other levels. They may not be effective for large comprehensive high schools. The most effective approaches for restructuring high schools are described in the section Replicating Alternative Schools.

Most of the effective approaches for restructuring existing schools have similarities with the principles of Total Quality Management (TQM), the process that has been used so successfully in business and industry. Successful school restructuring efforts and TQM both focus on internal processes, use collaborative planning, and both have concerns for the customer or the student. Both processes rely on frequent assessment to monitor the effectiveness of efforts. Other groups, like the Northwest Regional Educational Laboratory and the Maine Academy for School Leaders, uses a similar process that involves facing criticism, welcoming self-evaluation, setting goals, nurturing new efforts, and monitoring results (Donaldson, 1993). While all successful restructuring efforts in existing schools use some approximation of the TQM model, those that seem to be most successful include additional components: partnerships with universities, intensive long-term staff development and training, and networking with other schools. And while these strategies for effectively restructuring existing schools will be presented in a logical order, each school effort approaches the process quite differently and may omit some of the specific strategies and still realize success.

Focus on Schools That are Already Improving
A review of the problems that are faced in reforming or restructuring existing schools helps to dramatize the fact that it is nearly impossible to change a school unless a sufficient percentage of the stakeholders in the school are interested and willing to participate actively. For that reason, it is obvious that some schools will be more difficult to change than others, and some schools might be impossible to change. Research has helped to verify that most schools are in a process of constant change. They are either getting better or getting worse. In the 10 years of the Louisiana School Effectiveness Study, researchers were able to document that some schools were effective, remained effective for 8 to 10 years, and seemed to be constantly improving. Other ineffective schools remained ineffective and even seemed to decline over the same period (Teddlie & Stringfield, 1993).

To ensure maximum success in school reform or restructuring efforts, schools should be carefully reviewed (data regarding achievement, attendance, retention, reading scores, etc.). Efforts should be made to identify schools with naturally occurring improvements; that is, schools that are attempting to improve their effectiveness on their own and are ready for additional restructuring efforts. In addition, communities' interest, responsiveness, and support should be given careful attention. Just as there are community forces that stimulate one school to improve, other settings may inhibit school effectiveness.

School improvement, reform, or restructuring efforts will be much more successful in schools where evidence of school improvement is already emerging. School reform should focus first on those who are trying to help themselves.

School and Community Involvement and Coordination

Every successful school restructuring effort involves parents, and most include community leaders, agencies, institutions, and students. It is interesting to note that every reform project connects with the community in its own unique way. The Accelerated School Project convenes a group of parents, teachers, and students in a process that is called "visioning." Visioning is designed to establish a unity of purpose. It leads to a discussion of commonly held values and beliefs and provides the foundation for all that follows in the restructuring project. The Accelerated School Project attempts to include parents in every aspect of the school.

Comer's School Development Program attempts to reestablish and strengthen ties between the home and the school and is equally interested in strengthening the African-American community as it is in restructuring its neighborhood schools. Parental involvement is a central focus of the program. Parents are encouraged to serve as teacher-aides, participate in the school planning and management team, and are expected to sponsor a wide variety of events (potluck suppers, fashion shows, book fairs, etc.) that bring the school and community together. Comer believes that "children's relationships with their teachers cannot be improved without drawing parents into the circle" (Ascher, 1993, p. 7). A planning and management team to involve parents and the community is also vital to the Comer School Development Program. The team consists of 12 to 15 parents, teachers, school staff members, and one or more mental health specialists and is coordinated by the principal. Another group that is organized is called a mental health team. Membership on this team varies from school to school but usually includes a social worker, a school psychologist, a counselor, a school nurse, a speech and hearing teacher, and the principal.

The Success For All Program, likewise, involves parents in a variety of ways. The program includes a family support team that helps parents understand how they can ensure their children will succeed in school, promotes good attendance, trains parent volunteers, and assists with student behavior. The family support team also coordinates services from social service agencies. Parents are encouraged to read to their children 20 minutes each evening at home, participate as volunteers in the school, and serve on the building advisory committee.

Successful restructuring projects must incorporate a significant program of community involvement that includes parents in school planning and governance and provides for parent education, volunteers, and the coordination of social services. In minority neighborhoods, the school may also need to offer ESL classes or English lessons to parents, assist families with social and legal problems, and generally serve as parent and community advocates. Each of these efforts to involve the community and to coordinate social services relates directly to the essential characteristics of effective schools for at-risk youth defined in Chapter 5.

School-Based Empowerment and Accountability

It is not enough to involve parents, teachers, school administrators, students, and social service representatives in collaboration and planning. Success in restructuring efforts demands that these groups be delegated authority for school-based decision making (Teddlie & Stringfield, 1993; Wehlage, et al., 1989). The school collaboration groups must be empowered with authority to plan, make decisions, and implement their program. Schools that are successful in restructuring efforts are always empowered to change the curriculum, the school organization, and the instructional practices in their school. This means that school boards and central administrators must be actively involved in decentralizing and delegating power and authority. Each school and its community must be authorized to govern their school and be held accountable for achieving their school district instructional goals and abiding by state and local rules and regulations. Empowerment, of course, must be coupled with responsibility, and this means holding schools accountable for student achievement.

Consensus Building

Another essential ingredient in the formula for success in school restructuring is school and community consensus building. Because of issues described earlier in this chapter regarding the conflicting beliefs of teachers and the different perceptions regarding school reform, consensus building is absolutely essential to any successful restructuring plan. Involving parents, community leaders, and social service representatives in the process also seems to have a powerful effect on helping teachers come to agreement. While there are differences in every school setting, consensus building tends to include the following steps:

- *Review school and community data.* The first step in the consensus building process is to collect, summarize, and present data about the school and community to a collaboration team. This might include reading scores; achievement test scores; absentee rates; drop-out rates; incidence of crime, violence, vandalism, and school disruption; incidence of teen pregnancies; incidence of drug and alcohol abuse; unemployment rates; child abuse rates; etc. Collaboration groups are encouraged to discuss the data, talk about how they feel about these data and express their ideas and concerns.
- *Identify problems and establish schoolwide goals.* From the review and discussion of the school and community data, the collaboration team attempts to identify and prioritize problems and then work toward agreement on a number of areas of needed action. These goals are then circulated within the school and community, among students, teachers, parents, community leaders, and social service agencies. The goal is to gain widespread consensus regarding

specific goals for the school restructuring effort. It is important for schools and communities to understand that school restructuring must focus on every aspect of the school. It must consider the community settings, parents, and social services, as well as instruction, curriculum, school organization and governance. School goals must reflect a comprehensive effort at restructuring. To focus on any one area is not likely to result in success (Levin, 1993; Teddlie & Stringfield, 1993; Wehlage, et al., 1989). Often it is far easier to gain consensus regarding the problems to be addressed and the goals of the school than it is to gain agreement on a particular plan of action.

- *Develop a plan of action.* The collaboration team then works to establish a plan of action to achieve their goals, and each plan will be unique to the local school (Teddlie & Stringfield, 1993). The great advantage of being associated with a well-established program like Accelerated Schools, School Development, or Success For All is that these programs provide a solid framework of tested approaches that can be highly predictable of success. While none of these programs provides a cookie cutter approach to school reform, each provides a process or framework for improving or restructuring. Yet schools do not need to be part of an external reform project to be successful at improving their effectiveness. Research has identified schools where naturally occurring improvements have been organized locally with little or no external restructuring stimulation.

  Often these naturally occurring improvements have been more significant than those in schools that have been part of a school district restructuring plan (Teddlie & Stringfield, 1993). If a school is not part of an established restructuring program, school representatives may need to attend conferences or workshops; develop a reading and discussion program; use consultants; work with university professors, technical assistance centers, and educational laboratories; and visit other restructured schools. The small school in Burley, Idaho, described in Chapter 6 completed a major restructuring effort virtually on its own, although the people did attend accelerated school workshops and obtained information from many different sources. Their approach, to use nongraded classes for grades 2, 3, and 4, with each teacher teaching a particular subject to every child in the school and using school specialists as regular classroom teachers to reduce per-pupil ratios, proved to be unusually inventive and highly effective. Perhaps most significant, the school accomplished the changes all on its own.

- *Ensuring schoolwide participation and support.* It is important for collaborative teams to devise an approach to keep the entire school and community informed, involved, and supportive. The Accelerated School Project does this by establishing a number of small cadres to address the specific issues of curriculum, instruction, and organization. These cadres report their recommendations to a school-community steering committee that reviews and discusses the recommendations and then in turn seeks schoolwide discussion, input and approval. This process continues as a circular involvement between the cadre, the steering committee, and the school and community as a whole.

As described earlier, it is important that the collaborative team and the rest of the school not fall into "us-them" divisions. In the five-year study of the Coalition of Essential Schools, it was reported that the recognition and support given to the coalition planning teams caused deep resentment among other teachers. The research also found that the coalition planning teams naively believed that the rest of the school would agree with whatever plans they developed and were surprised when this did not occur. Apparently, some planning teams did not invest sufficient time in convincing their colleagues of the importance and the effectiveness of their proposal and controversy and contentiousness developed (Muncey & McQuillan, 1993). Another area of concern related to participation was identified by the Coalition of Essential Schools researchers. Some coalition schools felt that, after a school faculty voted to participate in a reform, there was little need for further schoolwide training or discussion. In some schools, there seemed to be little discussion in the school as a whole after the initial vote, and in time the reform program became a source of divisiveness throughout the school (Muncey & McQuillan, 1993). Both the Accelerated School Project and the Success For All Program require a 90 percent approval through a faculty vote before inviting a school to join their programs, and each approach requires extensive, long-term planning and involvement in training. These factors appear to be critical to enable a school to maintain school and communitywide support.

School Reform Demands Staff Development

Few aspects of the educational establishment have such negative connotations and evoke such bad memories as that of professional staff development. Typically, this effort is held in school cafeterias at the end of the day or on release days and is referred to as teacher in-service. Research has repeatedly documented the futility of such efforts. Significant school reform demands long-term effective staff development which provides for the development of new personal skills and time for the slow and often difficult process of consensus building.

Staff development and training are absolutely essential to the success of any school restructuring effort, especially with the faculty of an existing school. The Accelerated School Project requires participation in a weeklong training program at Stanford University for each leadership team. This program includes representatives from the school, the school district, and often a local university professor. This training is followed by weeklong staff development and collaboration efforts at the school prior to the beginning of the school year and regular meetings convened throughout the year by the local accelerated team. Accelerated School Project personnel provide periodic onsite assistance and support. The cost for implementing the Accelerated School program is approximately $30 per child per year in addition to the standard per pupil district-level support. The Success For All Program costs, including staff training, reading tutors, and curriculum materials, is approximately $800 per child per year. The Comer School Development Program uses only existing personnel and involves only minimal initial training, and as a result the costs are low.

For schools not affiliated with an established network, effective staff development becomes even more essential to success. In the Louisiana School Effectiveness Study, the researchers stressed the importance for each local school to carefully assess the needs of teachers and administrators and to develop and implement a carefully designed staff development program. Based on their study, the Louisiana researchers concluded that staff development programs needed to be highly individualized because different teachers have very different needs. The study further emphasized the importance of allowing teachers to move to different grade levels until they found their most effective niche. The same was true for principals. For those unwilling to participate, involuntary re-assignment of principals and some teachers may be necessary (Teddlie & Stringfield, 1993).

Finally, the use of technology is critical to improving schools, and the effective use of technology in the classroom demands extensive retraining. Efforts to retrain regular classroom teachers to use clusters of four to five computers in their classroom often include a 20-day staff development program during the first year, repeated again during the second year. Additional staff development and training is likely to continue for a period of five to seven years before a successful transition to the use of technology in teaching is accomplished.

Time for Collaboration

To improve a school, dedicated planning time is essential. Unlike business and industry, which are able to close down to retool, schools usually attempt to retrofit themselves while continuing the day-to-day stress-filled demands of educating children and youth. Some have used the analogy of changing a flat tire while the car is moving to characterize the challenges of school improvement. Teachers contend with a daily schedule that typically permits only one preparation period, a required supervision assignment on playground, hallway, or bus stop, and the remaining 80 to 90 percent of the day leading classroom instruction. Elementary teachers are also often required to be with their students during the lunch time. There is simply no time for schoolwide or even departmentwide collaborative planning in the typical school. Successful schools work hard to provide teachers with time to discuss students, compare instructional approaches, design materials, conduct team planning, and critique one another. Inevitably this is one of the most challenging aspects of school reform, since teacher contracts usually limit the time that teachers can be away from the direct supervision of students. There are, however, a number of innovative approaches which schools can employ to create the critical time necessary for collaboration. Most of these approaches are relatively inexpensive and each of them has been used with success by creative local schools:

- *In order for teachers to have planning days together many schools develop partnerships with colleges or universities so that professors may serve as "teachers for a day."*
- *Some schools . . . have student volunteer service programs where students do volunteer work in their community for one afternoon each week. This*

provides a rich learning experience for the students while simultaneously providing time for teacher collaboration.

- *In some large schools and school districts, contracts have been negotiated that increase class size by one or two students. This can yield funds for additional substitute teachers to free up faculty for collaboration.*
- *In some elementary schools, groups of teachers are provided with the same lunch period and a following planning period so that they can work together.*
- *Some school districts permit schools to use professional leave in one- and two-hour blocks rather than using them as entire days. Even three to five professional leave days per year can be scheduled over many weeks in short one- to two-hour blocks of time.*
- *Some schools have lengthened the school day by 20 minutes four days a week in order to dismiss students at noon on Friday and allow teachers to work together for half a day each week.*
- *Some schools schedule hobby days or activity days one day or one half day a week or on alternate weeks and use community volunteers to work with students in their interest areas. (Raywid, 1993b, pp. 31–33)*

One of the most useful ways for school boards or state legislators to help encourage school reform is by funding additional substitute teachers to free up teachers for planning and collaboration.

Ongoing Student Assessment and Program Evaluation

Any school involved in a major improvement or restructuring effort must conduct an ongoing assessment of student learning and program effectiveness. It is essential that the school and the community be able to determine as accurately as possible the effects of a school reform activity on the students. This is a significant departure from school reform efforts of past years. Until recently, school reform was measured by the use of new curriculum materials, technology, new instructional approaches, the implementation and use of new organizational structures or even the number of staff development days. Only recently have school reform efforts been measured by the assessment of student learning, student attitudes, student self-esteem, and behavioral issues.

This change represents a significant and essential development and provides further support for restructuring. A number of schools have found that if they can reach consensus and implement schoolwide goals and regularly monitor progress in achieving those goals that the goals are almost self-fulfilling.

The teachers, principal, and parents of Denali Elementary School in Fairbanks, Alaska, decided to restructure their traditional school to become a science magnet school. After the initial year of operation, the school's standardized test scores had demonstrated the highest growth in achievement in science and every other area among the district's 18 elementary schools. Only the science curriculum had been significantly changed.

It is imperative for any school restructuring project to carefully evaluate the impact of the program on students, teachers, the school and the community. And because measuring school effectiveness is extremely complex, it is important that assessment and evaluation focus on more than achievement test results. Thorough assessments should include evidence on attitudes and behavior as well as cognitive indicators (Teddlie & Stringfield, 1993). It is not only important to measure and evaluate the impact of a program, it is essential that this information be widely shared and communicated. Parents, teachers, and administrators, as well as central administrators, school board members, and even state legislators need to be informed regarding hard, accurate evidence that school changes are providing desired results. This type of evidence might include:

- *Improvement in test scores*
- *Statistics about behavioral changes such as dropout rates, attendance rates, disciplinary actions, and so on*
- *Information about increased parental, business, and community involvement*
- *Anecdotal information for teachers, students, administrators, and parents*
- *Information about interagency agreements and projects (social agencies, libraries, recreational districts, higher education institutions)*
- *Survey results*
- *Reallocation of resources (Ledell & Arnsparger, 1993, p. 21).*

Schools can also assess student attitudes toward schools, self-esteem, and even parent attitudes. They also need to investigate various aspects of their program to discover what is working or what is not working and why. In Success For All schools, regular assessment alerts teachers when students are not responding effectively to instruction, and the school then increases the amount of time and the frequency of one-to-one tutoring.

There is no more important means of validating a school restructuring effort than to demonstrate and document the positive impact on student learning. With the data at hand, teachers, communities, and schools can no longer blame poor student learning on external social conditions. Schools and their teachers must teach all children, assess their learning, and be held strictly responsible for their effectiveness or lack of effectiveness.

Beyond the restructuring of existing schools, two approaches have demonstrated welcomed success in reforming public education. Both require the development of new models of public schools. The approaches overlap considerably yet demonstrate significant differences in the design and implementation of new schools. Replicating alternative public schools will be described first, followed by a second approach, creating boundary-breaking charter or contract schools.

These strategies do not attempt to change existing schools. Rather, they attempt to attract students, teachers, administrators, and parents who have shared beliefs about education to work together to create new public schools. All of the various stakeholders in these two approaches to restructuring voluntarily choose to participate, and as a result, these schools begin with a spirit of consensus and collaboration. Because of this, planning time can be drastically reduced, at least in terms of disagreements that require conflict resolution. Collaboration time can thus focus on the actual design of the task of improving the school. In study after study over the past 20 years, the concept of choice has been identified as paramount to successful school restructuring efforts. The success of these approaches in effectively educating all students, particularly those at risk, warrants immediate attention from any group or organization concerned with improving schools.

Replicating Alternative Schools

The most effective approach to school restructuring that has ever been developed is alternative public schools. Unfortunately, in too many school districts, despite decades of documented success, alternative schools are often viewed with suspicion by both professional educators as well as the general public (Wehlage, et al., 1989). Yet the record of alternative school success is impressive.

Starting in the mid to late 1960s, a number of schools and communities in various parts of the country began to design new approaches to education, make them available by choice to parents and students, and implement programs such as alternative public schools within existing school districts. The first such schools tended to be dropout centers or dropout prevention schools, yet a few early alternative schools were so unique, so truly restructured, that they captured the attention of educators and the national media.

One of the first such schools was the Philadelphia Parkway School, where learning was planned to occur not in the school but in the banks, businesses, and museums up and down the Philadelphia Parkway. The school served all types of students and was described as a "school without walls." Another such creative school was the K–12 St. Paul Open School in Minnesota, which replaced course graduation requirements with learning competencies and developed a highly individualized approach to education. In Berkeley, California, a cluster of alternative schools were developed and implemented that attracted national attention. Other schools like Harlem Prep in New York, the Metropolitan Learning Center and Vocational Village in Portland, Oregon, and the Chicago Metro School were also soon in operation and attracting national attention. By the early 1970s, a wide variety of completely restructured schools were in operation in communities throughout the nation. At the time there was no state or federal program requiring, supporting, or even recognizing alternative public schools. There was not a single book on the topic. And, with the exception of a few isolated articles, these alternative schools were largely unrecognized. Isolated and alone, these first alternative public schools quickly became the models for a movement to improve schools throughout the nation.

Indiana University became the first institution of higher education to identify and study these schools. They conducted the first descriptive research on these schools; created and published a newsletter entitled *Changing Schools;* published the first national directories of alternative public schools; developed a teacher education program designed to prepare teachers and administrators for the new roles that were emerging in alternative schools; and founded a national professional association, the National Consortium for Options in Public Education. Many of the early evaluations of alternative school effectiveness were conducted by researchers at Indiana University. The professors and their graduate students then began to collect evaluative studies from alternative schools throughout the country and publish research about these schools. Within a few short years, every major journal in America had published special issues on alternative schools. Even *Good Housekeeping* and other popular magazines had focused on this startling new development in public education.

While only a dozen or so alternative schools were in operation during the mid to late 1960s, by the mid 1980s there were over 15,000 of these schools in the United States, and the number continued to grow. The early scholars of alternative schools discovered that while alternative public schools represented an incredible range of diversity, and were being developed in communities largely isolated from one another, all of the schools shared a remarkably common set of characteristics:

- They were all small public schools with less than 500 students.
- They were usually designed to address the needs of a particular group of students (dropouts, potential dropouts, talented and gifted) or to reflect a particular educational philosophy (open schools, continuous progress schools, Montessori education, community based learning, etc.).
- They were available to parents, students, teachers, and administrators on the basis of voluntary choice.
- They attempted to match teaching and learning styles.
- Because of their experimental status, these schools were evaluated not only on student achievement but on other factors, including self-esteem, attitudes towards schools, and attendance rates. (Barr, 1972)

Early studies reported that these schools were among the first in America to establish agreed upon, schoolwide goals, and routinely measure the effectiveness of programs in achieving their goals (Raywid, 1983). For schools that were started primarily on the faith and confidence of small groups of teachers, administrators, and parents, the school evaluation and student assessment data that was reported was remarkably positive (see Chapter 8).

Track Record of Success

It is not surprising that the vast majority of these early alternative schools are still in operation today and the number of these schools continue to grow. In much the same way that the Accelerated Schools, Success For All Schools, and the School Development Program have created effective models for replicating other schools, many alternative schools have likewise been models for the creation of other schools (Education Commission of the States, 1991). The Philadelphia Parkway School became the model for the Chicago Metro School and dozens of other schools without walls. Montessori alternative public schools were first tried in Cincinnati and Indianapolis in the 1970s and today can be found throughout the

United States. The walkabout concept of the Learning Unlimited School in Indianapolis led Phi Delta Kappa to create a *Walkabout Newsletter* and training program that ultimately contributed to the development of dozens of similar schools nationwide. The Foxfire program which started in Rabun Gap, Georgia, in 1966 has now spread to over a 1,000 schools in urban, suburban, and rural schools across the country.

Dropout prevention programs using behavior contracts and individualized learning were replicated throughout the country. Teen parent schools have also developed strong, supportive organizations and now exist in school districts throughout the nation. The St. Paul Open School that pioneered graduation competencies later influenced the development of Minnesota's Community Learning Centers Network and other schools throughout the country. The out-of-school learning experiences used by schools without walls, Learning Unlimited, and the St. Paul Open School likewise led directly to documenting the power and effectiveness of action learning and contributed to the expansion of the concept into the Executive High School Internship Program, volunteer service programs, youth-tutoring-youth programs, and others. The success of the School for the Performance Arts in Cincinnati quickly led to the creation of similar magnet schools in many major cities in the United States. Alternative schools, operating under the umbrella concept of magnet schools, have been the focus of national conferences and training sessions and have provided a rich body of research which has helped expand this concept throughout the nation's major cities (Estes, et al., 1990; Waldrip, et al., 1993).

Recent summaries of research continue to document the strength of the alternative public school concept as an approach to significant restructuring. Tim Young, in his recent work *Public Alternative Education: Options and Choice For Today's Schools,* has identified eight characteristics of alternative schools which should be considered in any school restructuring effort.

1. *Public schools of choice typically demonstrate a willingness to innovate and experiment. They are frequently on the cutting edge of educational issues and change.*
2. *Alternative schools are close to their clients (parents and students), attending to a variety of academic and nonacademic needs through the stated concern for the whole student.*
3. *Their smallness allows greater program autonomy and decision making than is the case in most conventional schools.*
4. *Treating students with respect, emphasizing group cooperation rather than individual competition, and extending appropriate reward structures are hallmarks of public schools of choice. Student success is not dependent on the failure of others.*
5. *The smallness of schools of choice facilitates a common set of shared values and goals among students and staff.*
6. *By not attempting to be all things to all people, schools of choice can specialize in and concentrate on what they do well. The student clientele served and*

curriculum offered are frequently limited, narrowly defining the school to focus on the most important and immediate needs of students.

7. *Most public schools of choice are small. They operate with a simple organization and lean staff.*

8. *Although they operate within the guidelines of the central school district, they are able to exercise considerable individual autonomy. Sometimes that autonomy is the result of neglect by the central administration. More often, however, it is the recognition of expertise and effectiveness. (Young, 1990, p. 51)*

Alternative Schools Today

Today alternative public schools continue to grow and expand. A number of state associations have been developed that support alternative schools, and they exert growing pressure on school boards, state departments of education, and state legislatures to support and expand the concept. Nationally, there is no single professional association responsible for representing the alternative school movement. The primary strength of alternative public schools resides today in strong state associations. There does exist a national network of alternative school educators who support one another and continue to publish the newsletter *Changing Schools*. This network also continues to provide an annual international conference hosted each year by a different state association for alternative schools.

Some of the nation's strongest state organizations are the Washington Alternative Learning Association, the Oregon Association of Alternatives in Education, the Colorado Options in Education, the Iowa Alternative Education Association, and the Minnesota Association of Alternative Programs. Other state organizations can be found in Connecticut, Illinois, Kansas, Michigan, Ohio, and Pennsylvania, each of which holds annual state conferences. Many of these states have influenced state legislation to require alternatives to suspension and dropping out. A number of states have passed enabling legislation that officially recognizes alternative schools and establishes policies to govern their development. Other states such as Oregon have required every school district to establish alternative schools for at-risk youth.

The success and growth of the alternative public schools concept can be seen in the number of school districts throughout the country that now use this concept to address the needs of at-risk youth. Almost every conceivable type of program philosophy and student can be found in the many alternative public schools that exist today. Virtually every medium to large city in the United States offers a variety of alternative public schools to students and their parents. Most have large waiting lists of parents and students who would like to participate. It has also become evident that the success of alternative public schools coupled with the large numbers of parents and students unable to participate in the alternatives has fueled the growing national interest in providing all parents with educational options.

Problems in Replicating Alternative Public Schools

While the strategy of replicating alternative public schools is a proven concept in school reform, it is not without difficulties and challenges. And while the alternative school concept alleviates many of the problems associated with changing existing schools, there are five complex issues which must be addressed:

1. *Perceptions of suspicion and illegitimacy.* In spite of the fact that alternative public schools are almost universally considered an essential part in any districtwide effort at reducing dropouts and serving at-risk youth, they are often viewed with suspicion. In a study of 14 at-risk programs, Wehlage and his colleagues concluded that "in some communities . . . alternative schools still are considered illegitimate by the profession and the public. This perception of illegitimacy can make it difficult, if not impossible, for these programs to carry out the important function of offering high quality programs to students and providing leadership and innovation" (Wehlage, et al., 1989). Part of this suspicion and lack of respect may originate from the fact that many alternative schools enroll at-risk youth and thus attract the negative connotations that so many people hold for these students. Many alternative schools have been so successful at educating at-risk youth that traditional educators sometimes assume that these schools must be watering down their instruction. Too often principals, counselors, and teachers in conventional schools have believed that no one could effectively teach these youth. And since alternatives often employ instructional methods that differ substantially from conventional schools, have different rules and student policies, and offer different daily schedules, educators from conventional schools often view the success of alternative schools to be an implicit criticism of their own work.

2. *Alternative schools tend to be highly visible and vulnerable.* Because of their innovative programs and their effectiveness, alternative schools usually attract considerable interest. Often, alternative schools attract greater interest and recognition from outside their school district than they do from within. Schools often host large numbers of visitors to their community and school and serve as a subject of news stories, research reports, and media coverage. This often creates exactly the type of "us-them" problem within a school or district that was found to hamper efforts within schools in the Coalition of Essential Schools study. This type of divisiveness can create difficulties and continuing problems for alternative schools. It can lead to conflicts over resources, demands for stricter enforcement of districtwide policies, and negative publicity that can keep students and parents from choosing to leave a conventional school to attend an alternative school. And whenever a school district faces any type of financial difficulty, there are often pressures to eliminate those "extra" programs serving special student needs. As a result, alternative educators in many school districts tend to spend an inordinate amount of time defending their programs, students, and themselves and in rallying community and district support to maintain their programs.

3. *Using alternative schools as dumping grounds.* Closely related to other problems, public school teachers, counselors, and principals often use the option of alternative public schools to try and purge their classrooms and schools of the most difficult, disruptive, and emotionally disturbed students. Some school districts may have approved the creation of quasi-alternative schools simply to serve as another, more sophisticated tracking system.

   It is for this reason that most alternative schools, even though they plan to address the needs of at-risk youth, tend to focus on approaches to learning rather than on certain types of students and work to attract a cross-section of the student population.

4. *Confusion regarding the concept.* One of the consequences of starting new alternative schools is that many of the teachers, parents, and students who choose to participate in the school may not have an adequate understanding of the school concept. Many teachers believe that they hold a particular philosophical commitment only to discover that they have difficulties operationalizing their beliefs. Teachers may often feel that they would love to teach in a continuous progress program using individualized learning contracts and outcome assessments, only to discover that they miss their role in the traditional classroom. Students may also have difficulties moving from traditional classrooms to some types of alternatives, especially those that expect students to take a major responsibility for their own learning. Some students will lack the self-discipline to work effectively in this new type of situation, and almost all students will need some form of assistance in making the transition from traditional classrooms to alternative schools. Often, it will take these students several months to make the adjustment. During this time parents tend to get very uneasy about what is occurring with their child and their learning. For these reasons, teachers who choose to teach in an alternative school must have an opportunity to transfer out if they are unhappy. Students, too, must be able to readily opt in and opt out. Because of this, most alternative public schools tend to have rather liberal transfer policies for both teachers and students.

5. *Conflicts between school district policies and alternative programs.* Inevitably, there will be difficulties in trying to accommodate highly innovative alternative schools and their nontraditional instructional approaches in curriculum with state and local policies. One of the most difficult problems is attempting to relate highly individualized, interdisciplinary learning activities to state graduation requirements and college entrance requirements. This causes frustration for alternative school students and teachers alike. And since many state education policies focus on issues involving time (i.e. number of instructional days, number of hours in courses, and even the number of minutes assigned daily to required courses at the elementary level), individualized, continuous progress, and mastery learning concepts create havoc when applied to the traditional requirements.

There are also a multitude of state and local regulations, policies, transportation schedules, health and safety requirements, building and fire codes, and other things that pose continuing problems for alternative schools. Many alternative school educators report that continually trying to accommodate the policies and prepare required reports for the state and local school district is like being "nibbled to death by a duck." Unfortunately, over time such external policies and requirements can consume a considerable amount of time, detracting from a program's effectiveness.

How to Start an Alternative Public School

Starting an alternative public school has become easier during recent years. Originally, alternative schools were started by small groups of true believer activists who organized political campaigns to force school boards to allow them to create a new school that reflected their particular interest or philosophy. As more and more alternative schools have been developed, evaluated, and researched and the concept better understood, this approach has become more acceptable and easier to implement. This is largely due to the work of the professional associations of alternative schools mentioned earlier, who have lobbied successfully with legislators, state departments of education, and local school boards to support the concept. School districts are increasingly being required by states to develop alternative schools and programs as a last ditch safety net for dropouts, and many states even provide special funding formulas to support the development and maintenance of alternative schools. Many school districts like Toronto, Canada, and Eugene, Oregon, have developed enabling policies that provide an established process for groups to propose new alternative public schools, so that over time these communities will have more different learning opportunities for parents and students.

While almost every alternative public school is started in a rather distinctive way, there are a number of steps that are almost always present in the process. Sometimes parents are the motivating force for starting a new school; other times, it has been teachers, school administrators and occasionally even students. Alternative public schools have been started by a single school district, by a consortium of several school districts, by a county school district to serve a large area, by a community college, or by other groups or individuals. Regardless of who the initiating group may be, the following steps have been identified as essential.

Consensus Building
The process of consensus building in creating an alternative school is dramatically different from the process needed to restructure an existing school. Teachers, parents, and even students who share particular beliefs or particular concerns discover or seek out one another and usually create some type of school or community organization, planning committee, or action group and attempt to create a particular kind of school. Parents can be extremely forceful in these groups, especially when they are helping to develop a school that can serve their own children. These groups will often conduct extensive readings, attend alternative schools conferences or workshops, and usually visit alternative schools in other cities and

states. Educators from existing alternative schools are often sought by local groups to assist their planning effort. Inevitably, the local planning group reflects consensus toward developing an alternative school that would serve a particular type of student or provide for a particular type of educational program.

Developing a Preliminary Proposal

Out of the consensus-building phase, a preliminary proposal should be developed that includes: a rationale, philosophy, the problem(s) to be addressed, overall school goals and objectives; a general statement regarding the teaching and learning approach; curriculum to be emphasized; the type of students to be served; a timeline; and a general budget. The task of developing the preliminary proposal is in itself part of the consensus-building process, for it requires a group to assemble their ideas and beliefs into a written statement.

Seeking Authorization and Approval

In approaching the central administration of a school district or the school board, experience has taught that a group seeking to develop an alternative public school should usually not seek board approval at their initial presentation. Rather the board should be approached on at least two or three different occasions. The first time provides a briefing and information session for the board that informs the board of the group's rationale and purpose. Next the group might present a preliminary proposal or concept paper and seek board approval for an official planning process to study the issue and make recommendations. Often at the first or second board appearance, the group may solicit educational consultants, teachers, administrators, or parents from an existing alternative school to help provide information to the board and answer questions. Only after a school board has developed a positive attitude toward the alternative school and agreed to or encouraged a study group to explore the concept should the board be presented with a full proposal and asked to approve the establishment of an alternative school.

Selecting Teachers and Administrators

It is essential that the teachers and administrators who plan and develop the alternative school are also the majority of faculty who will be teaching in the new program. For this reason, the preliminary planning team must be expanded to include other teachers and administrators from the school district. This involves informing potential teachers and administrators and encouraging those interested to learn about the alternative school concept and the development of the school. Often many teachers will be identified in the process who have had extensive training or experience in exactly the type of alternative that is being developed. Some years ago when the Indianapolis School District was planning a new Montessori Alternative Elementary School, the board worried that the time and cost of training public school teachers in the Montessori approach might be prohibitive. A districtwide survey discovered that there were over 20 elementary teachers in the Indianapolis public schools who were already certified Montessori teachers and quite excited about joining the planning group and having an opportunity to teach in the new Montessori alternative. Furthermore, it is absolutely essential that the preliminary planning group has the authority to participate in the final selection of teachers and administrators for the school.

Planning and Development

The approved planning process is extremely important to the creation of an alternative school. It is a time when the new school is conceptualized and designed. For many parents, teachers, administrators, and students this is an exciting opportunity to design the school of their dreams.

While it is important that there is adequate time for planning, there can be a danger of having too much time for planning. More than one school district has approved a study group and then required a two-year planning schedule in hopes that the group will plan the program to death. Successful alternative schools should not take over a year to plan. There is only so much that can be accomplished before the school is open, and a shorter planning and implementation schedule leads to maximum participation, enthusiasm, and commitment.

Once the school has opened its doors, continued planning should include visits to other schools, not to simply replicate what is found but for the teachers, administrators, and parents of the new school to learn from experienced veterans of alternative schools. During the following summer, the alternative school faculty should have sufficient time to revise curriculum, participate in further staff development and training, and to reevaluate the school's effectiveness.

Funding the planning and development process will require modest support to provide for summer contracts, travel to other schools, consultants for staff development, and equipping the facility.

Implementation

Once the alternative school is approved, there are a large number of decisions to be made on a variety of topics:

- *Selecting a facility.* Often alternative schools are located in small, abandoned school facilities, in an isolated corridor of an existing school, or located away from schools in leased facilities in the community. Alternative schools have been started in churches, warehouses, former bank buildings, hotels, gas stations, and almost anywhere an empty retail or office building is available. Magnet schools, which are usually housed in a facility that relates to a particular curriculum focus, can be found in hospitals, aircraft hangers, shopping malls, theaters, and even at the city zoo. For at-risk youth, who often possess negative attitudes toward school, an off-campus location has many advantages. One superb location for an at-risk alternative high school is a community college. A community college campus provides a positive adult environment for the students to attend school. Care needs to be taken in advance to ensure that any facility meets state and local building, fire, and health codes for schools.

- *Selecting students.* After the number and types of students have been determined, a careful process of information, recruitment, and selection must occur. This usually includes school district communication, newspaper articles, and media announcements. It often begins with information and orientation sessions for all building principals and counselors, open community meetings, evening meetings with students and parents, and many informal contacts. Following an application period, personal interviews are held with students and their parents. It is essential that the faculty of the alternative school have responsibility for selecting students based on the approved criteria and procedure. Often alternative schools will demand a written commitment or contract from the parent to agree to become active in some form of volunteer participation in the alternative school. While available on the basis of personal choice, alternative schools can ensure a diversified student body by establishing internal quotas. Many schools establish a lottery process due to the high number of applicants and make an effort to enroll a student population that reflects their community. Thus a school can provide for ethnic, economic, and gender balance and avoid the negative connotation of serving only at-risk students.
- *Decision making.* A component as essential to effective alternative programs as school choice is shared decision making. The school decision-making process should grow out of the planning process and include a carefully planned school management team which involves parents, students, and teachers in some significant sense. The schools developed by Comer and Levin and researched by Slavin offer models for shared decision making.

Following these steps, most successful alternative schools have accomplished their initial goal of starting their program. From that point a number of other factors are critical to their success.

Ensuring Success in an Alternative Public School

After almost 30 years of experience, a number of issues have been identified that are crucial to the success of a new alternative school.

Address a Real Need

To ensure a favorable reaction from school district officials, school boards, and communities, alternative schools should address a pressing need in the schools or the community. The need might be to reduce the dropout rate, deal more effectively with the large numbers of teen parents, or help the achieving students be more intellectually challenged. Alternative schools should focus squarely on addressing a particular problem or need. There is no better reason to start an alternative school than to initiate a program to address the growing needs of at-risk youth.

Use Existing School District Funds

To be successful, alternative schools should be funded by the local school district in the same way as all other schools. The alternative school should function within the existing per pupil cost based on the established pupil-teacher ratio in a school district. This means each alternative school will obtain teachers on the basis of the number of students they attract and admit to the school. Alternative schools funded solely by external grants often do not survive once the grant expires.

Start Small But Not Too Small

Compared to other public schools, alternative schools are always relatively small. This is clearly one of the reasons that they have been so successful. Unfortunately, decisions are often made to start an alternative school as a pilot project or in some other small way and then plan to expand later. To be successful, alternative schools should begin with a sufficient number of students to justify at least four teachers. With a careful selection of the four teachers, most of the major content areas can be addressed. With fewer teachers, the school program will place unreasonable demands on the faculty and often will force students to rely on other schools to meet graduation requirements. This in fact can reduce the alternative school to only a part-time program. For maximum success with at-risk youth, alternative schools should provide as much of a total education program as possible.

Another approach to starting an alternative school is adding a grade per year (for example, a school could start with the ninth grade and each year add the next grade) until an entire high-school program is in place.

Using Existing Teachers in the School District

To be successful, alternative schools should be a home-grown product. While it might be good to recruit a few teachers with unique experience from outside the community, the school should be planned, developed, and operated by teachers and administrators from within the district. In fact, alternative schools often recruit some of the most respected teachers in a school district for their expertise and to instantly create credibility. It is also vital that teachers who will teach in the alternative schools be involved in the team that plans the program.

Alternative Schools Should Be as Autonomous as Possible

Alternative public schools should be as independent and autonomous as possible. Administratively, this means the alternative school should have a principal or head teacher who reports in exactly the same manner as any other building principal in the school district. Educationally, this means that the alternative school should work to have as much freedom as possible from rules and regulations and be evaluated on the performance outcomes of the students. Most states have policies that permit schools to apply for a waiver to the existing administrative rules governing public education and to replace them with an alternate plan.

Alternative Schools Must Be Able to Document Their Effectiveness

Because of the innovative or experimental basis of alternative schools, they must be able to document their effectiveness. Each successful alternative public school must develop a program evaluation plan as well as a student assessment plan to monitor their effectiveness, identify problems and needs, and provide a basis for making necessary adjustments. Alternative public schools pioneered the use of performance outcomes by requiring graduation competencies rather than required courses and likewise were among the first public schools to routinely assess and report student attendance rates, student attitudes, behavioral problems, as well as achievement scores. Many alternative schools also regularly conduct long-term, follow-up evaluations of their former students.

Alternative Schools Should Seek Long-Term Commitments

Boards of education should provide a three-to-five-year commitment to any alternative school plan that is approved. As noted earlier, it takes three years to document improved achievement and as many as five to seven years to truly establish any new educational program. While alternative schools should achieve a positive impact on student achievement much sooner than existing schools who are involved in a restructuring or improvement effort, it is unreasonable for school districts or school boards to evaluate an alternative program too soon. Some evaluations have been required at the end of the first semester or the first year, which is far too early to effectively assess program success. It is essential that alternative schools have sufficient time to make an adequate impact on students.

Don't Expand Alternative Schools Too Rapidly

Often large urban school districts will establish large numbers of alternative or magnet programs. Recently, New York approved over 30 "New Vision" schools that were started almost immediately with little or no opportunity for the teachers in the new schools to have time to plan and develop together. In fact, the teachers in the new schools had little time to even meet one another. When students arrived, some of the schools were almost in chaos.

Alternative Schools as a Strategy for Reform

As a strategy for significant school reform, alternative public schools have a track record of success that is unequaled. The reason is simple. Rather than trying to force teachers, students, and parents to accept a particular approach to education, as is so often the case with restructuring existing public schools, alternative schools provide people with the opportunity to choose to participate. While choice is a rather simple, truly democratic idea, it has proven revolutionary in public education, where there has been a long tradition of assignment rather than choice. Students have almost always been assigned to a school on the basis of where they live. Teacher and principals are also usually assigned. Yet, the rapid diversification of teaching and learning, the growing acceptance of very different approaches to instruction, and the growing conviction that different teachers teach in different ways and that different students learn best in very different ways have created great strain on the public school tradition of assignment.

It is this idea of assignment that has created such problems and resistance to school reform. Any time an existing school has been restructured, it forces all of the parents and students in that particular school assignment area to attend that particular school, whether or not they support the particular approach to education that is being used or whether in fact it is the most effective approach for their child. The same is true for teachers and administrators. By attempting a forced fit of teachers to a particular educational philosophy or approach, deep personal conflicts are unavoidable and consensus building becomes a challenge. If a neighborhood elementary school becomes a year-round school, a highly individualized, continuous progress school, a Montessori school, a traditional back to basics school, or even an open school, many parents would undoubtedly be very unhappy and some students would experience difficulties adjusting to the particular approach that is being implemented. A classic example of this phenomenon today is the year-round school. Because the year-round school demands a very different kind of schedule for family vacations, child care, and transportation, some parents are absolutely, adamantly opposed to the idea; others feel it is a godsend. The difference in assigning parents to year-round schools or letting them voluntarily choose to participate in year-round schools reflects the same principle of choice that characterizes the success of alternative schools. Unlike universities and community colleges where students are provided with a wide range of choices in educational programs and approaches, public schools have maintained a rather rigid and usually arbitrary approach of assigning students, teachers, and parents to particular schools and to specific kinds of programs.

Alternative public schools solve this type of problem by providing a group of teachers, students, parents, and administrators with an opportunity to develop an educational program that they have all agreed upon and supported. This group then implements the educational program and invites others who might be interested in participating. This means that alternative public schools must be very clear about their philosophy, goals, curriculum, and educational approach and must sell their approach to the community. Parents and students then have the opportunity to choose an approach to education that they support and are comfortable with.

Research has documented repeatedly during the past 25 years that students, parents, teachers, and administrators who choose to participate in a particular program tend to be happier and more content than others in public education; they are more invested in the school and in learning. In a small way, this simple idea has revolutionized public education and has given rise to wholesale calls for choice in public education. As a reform strategy for transforming schools, alternative schools have had no equal, at least until very recently.

Creating Boundary-Breaking Schools

A truly revolutionary development in public education has begun. It holds great hope for dramatic change in public education. For at-risk youth, it offers great promise. The revolution is occurring in a small handful of schools nationwide, but the surprising political and public interest that is occurring around these schools suggests a growing acceptance of a completely new concept of public education. The revolution is occurring as states and school districts have begun to establish new policies that permit contract or charter public schools. Often referred to as boundary-breaking schools or break-the-mold schools, education outside the box, or educational unbundling, these schools represent a significant paradigm shift in U.S. public education. These charter or contract schools also represent a significant shift in public policy. Where this new policy has been established, it permits school districts or states to transfer responsibility for public education to groups of teachers and parents. With the exception of a few first amendment guarantees, contract schools and charter schools provide a process that allows for most state and local regulations that govern public education to be relaxed or waived. These schools then gain the freedom to redesign or reinvent public education. In return, the state establishes rigorous accountability standards that focus on student achievement.

All school districts have the authority to negotiate contracts for almost everything from food services to janitorial services to security services to collective bargaining agreement with teachers. Large school districts may regularly maintain as many as 150 contracts for a complete range of services. School districts also have the authority to contract for educational and instructional services. Often schools will contract for special education services, media services, even for athletic coaches; often they contract for entire alternative schools. It is not unusual for a number of small school districts to work together collectively to contract with a single school district or a county school district to support an alternative public school that would serve students from each of the member districts. Recently, some school districts have been willing to negotiate contracts that permit greater flexibility in using financial resources and waiving some rules and regulations in exchange for assessing learning outcomes.

Charter schools differ from contract schools and demand state legislation to be creative. Once a state establishes charter legislation, it provides a small group of teachers and parents the opportunity to become the legal equivalent of a mini school district. "Statutes for charter schools greatly reduce the number of regulations, policies and laws governing a school, thereby freeing participants to try innovative approaches. Charters require learning results or the charter is terminated—the ultimate accountability" (Designs For Learning, 1993, p. 4). Some new charter schools are likewise attempting to gain waivers for state rules, local policies, and even freedom from the local bargaining unit—once again in exchange for accountability for student achievement.

The first charter schools in the United States were started in Minnesota in 1991 and in California in 1992. By the end of 1993, bills had been introduced into 16 state legislatures and approved in some variation in the states of Minnesota, California, Georgia, New Mexico, Colorado, Massachusetts, and Wisconsin. Both Illinois and Michigan are continuing to explore some type of charter legislation, and Michigan seems to be seriously considering a statute that would make all public schools charter schools. Roy Romer, governor of Colorado, has described the importance of charter school legislation. It provides:

> The opportunity to completely rethink and redesign a public school—from its overall vision for students, to its educational program, to the relationship between the school and its teachers, to assessment, to administrative practices and governance. It requires that a charter school, as a public school meet public imperatives of accountability and equity, but does not require that it be all things to all people. Charter school activity has the potential to create a more vibrant and diverse range of public school programs available for parents and students who want and need alternatives to the conventional approach. (Romer, 1993, p. 1)

Gary Hart, the state senator who wrote the California charter legislation, has referred to the charter concept as "a license to dream" (Riley, 1993, p. 15). In Georgia, charter school legislation has established the following concept:

> In effect, charter schools will be self-regulated like a chartered business. The "charter" will be a binding performance contract between the charter school, its local board of education and the State Board of Education. This charter, when approved by the local board of education and the State Board of Education, will substitute for state education statutes as well as state and local rules, policies, regulations and standards as a governance structure for the charter school. With the freedom provided under the Charter Schools Act, schools will be able to rethink and redesign "from the ground up," including, but not limited to, what students learn, how it is packaged and how it is delivered; how school instructional staff are deployed, how students are placed, grouped and scheduled; how school decisions are made; how funds are allocated and used; and how the community is involved in supporting the school; as well as defining the rules, roles, and responsibilities of all involved in schooling. (Wilt, 1993, p. 10)

Why Charter or Contract Schools?

The charter or contract school movement has been a logical outgrowth of a number of developments: the widespread success of alternative public schools, the growing fear of educational vouchers, the growing demand for restructuring public education, and a number of developments in the state of Minnesota, including the creation of Community Learning Centers and the legislation that established public school choice for the citizens of the state. Many of the new charter schools were formerly existing alternative schools. Charter or contract schools have been developed for a number of reasons:

The Inertia of Large Educational Bureaucracies

Just as growing frustration and an out-of-control national budget has generated growing pressure on the federal government to reinvent itself and the shocking realization that huge, bureaucratic corporations like General Motors and IBM seemed unable to respond rapidly and decisively to the changing developments in the international marketplace, so too have public school districts come under attack for the size, inertia, escalating costs, and administrative gridlock of their bureaucracies. Trying to provide high-quality public education with scarce and diminishing dollars has led a number of large city school districts to slash their administrative costs and prompted a growing number of states to pass legislation establishing charter schools. As New Jersey Governor Jim Florio has said, "the difference between school-as-usual and charter schools is like the difference between the old G.M. assembly line and the new Saturn team assembly" (Riley, 1993, p. 17.) Public education via charter schools is like replacing a Safeway supermarket chain with mom and pop vegetable stands or independent neighborhood groceries. Charter or contract schools bring cottage industry to education in much the same way that has occurred so dramatically in the high-tech industry.

Relief from Stifling Rules, Regulations, and Policies

Almost every aspect of public education is regulated by specific administrative rules, local policies, state laws, and collective bargaining agreements. In most states, these regulations assign students and their families to a particular school, establish the number of school days in year, regulate the minutes of the school day, and prescribe the kind of building that can be used to house a school, the kinds of people who can and cannot work with children and youth, formulas for defining average daily attendance, salary schedules, and even rates of salary increases. The regulations governing public education also define what can be considered a textbook and provide an approved list of acceptable instructional materials. These regulations make school innovations difficult if not impossible. Attempts to improve instruction and restructure schools have encountered the following problems:

- Some schools have attempted to develop creative approaches to student evaluations, only to discover that the state requires letter grades.
- Some schools have attempted to use the university model of having large class instruction in certain subject areas coupled with very small classes in other areas, only to discover that the school district has an established maximum class size.
- Schools attempting to employ outstanding professionals from the arts and business community have discovered that only state certified teachers can be hired.
- Schools that have tried to develop shared decision making have discovered that local school boards are only willing to provide partial autonomy at the school or community level.
- Schools that have attempted to develop extensive use of individualized, independent learning, using learning contracts and out of school practica, have

found that average daily attendance rules prescribe seat time inside a school classroom.

- Schools that have established graduation competencies have found it virtually impossible to relate student learning to the required course graduation requirements.

It is these and many other rules, regulations, and policies that have frustrated schools, especially innovative and alternative schools, and made almost any proposed educational change either impossible or, almost as bad, possible only within a very limited set of prescribed guidelines that tend to cripple the innovation.

Flat-Line Funding for Education

Given the economic and political realities of the day, it is evident that local, state, and federal funding for public education is not likely to improve during the rest of this decade. With taxpayer revolts, an economy that is growing sluggishly, and escalating costs in health, welfare, judiciary, and prisons, many fear that school funding may not even keep up with inflation. Yet most calls for reform these days carry big-ticket price tags. The cost of adding one additional day to the school year or one hour to the school day or to reduce the per-pupil ratio by one child in a state or school district is staggering. Likewise, the cost for providing computers for every three to five children seems far beyond our means. There seems no reason to believe that this situation will change significantly in the near future, and it may get worse. There is a growing conviction that new ways of utilizing existing resources must be found. Charter or contract schools provide just the sort of flexibility for using existing resources in new and creative ways.

Support From Diverse Interests

In spite of the opposition of the educational establishment, especially teachers' unions and central administrators, the concept of charter or contract schools has gained strong support from the business community. In California, the Business Round Table loved the concept and wanted the legislature to establish 500 charter schools. The California Teachers Association wanted no charter schools (Riley, 1993). Charter legislation has been supported by school boards, businesses, and by innovative and alternative school educators who see the concept as a way of gaining freedom from stifling regulation and gaining ownership of their local school. In some states, particularly California, the growth of interest in some type of statewide voucher plan tended to consolidate support for the controversial charter legislation. Out of fear that California citizens would approve a voucher plan that would see tax dollars channeled to private schools, a strange group of professional and private bedfellows emerged to support the charter legislation. (Wilt, 1993)

The charter and contract school concept has emerged from the decades of alternative public school innovations and the movement to provide choice in public education. The roots of the charter and contract school concept can be found in Minnesota. Minneapolis-St. Paul has always been one of the country's most creative areas for public education. Minneapolis and St. Paul public schools were among the first to develop alternative public schools and some of the nation's most unique programs. The Minneapolis Southeast District pioneered the creation of clusters of elementary alternative schools, while neighboring St. Paul created its famed Open School. Minnesota also became the first state to approve voluntary choice for parents in public education, providing families with the opportunity to choose preferred programs within any public school district. Recently, a group in Minneapolis was funded by the New American Schools Development Corporation to develop the first break-the-mold Community Learning Centers Network, and, as has been mentioned, Minnesota was the first state to pass charter school legislation.

Two of the individuals in Minnesota who have been instrumental in the development of these concepts are Wayne Jennings and Joe Nathan. Jennings was the first principal of the St. Paul Open School and Nathan was the school's first curriculum director. Nathan's work with the governor of Minnesota and with the Education Commission of the States was instrumental in helping to legitimize the concept of choice in public education. Today, Nathan is the director of the Center for School Change at the University of Minnesota's Hubert Humphrey Institute for Public Affairs, and Jennings is the director of a private consulting firm, Designs for Learning, and they both continue to provide leadership for the Community Learning Centers Network. The Community Learning Centers Network has incorporated many of the tested ideas from alternative public schools and has in turn provided the organizational and financial concepts that have become the model for the development of the new generation of charter and contract schools in the United States.

Characteristics of Boundary-Breaking Schools

A review of the Minnesota Community Learning Centers Network and charter and contract schools in other states provides a number of key characteristics.

Waiver of Existing State and Local Educational Requirements

Almost every state has developed a process to waive the education requirements at the state and local levels for various types of experimental schools. Proposals to waive requirements usually provide for different though educationally sound approaches to accomplish the educational goals of the state and local school districts in exchange for solid evidence that these goals are being obtained. Given what is known about systemic pressures and school cultures, attempting to change the basic rules and regulations of schooling at the state, local, and union levels seems to hold great promise for liberating public education for experimentation and innovation. Examples of waived policies include:

- *Certified teachers not required.* Perhaps most remarkable, the new charter schools that are under way are not requiring the exclusive hiring of certified teachers. Some charter school statutes require only that certified teachers or administrators be responsible for the hiring of all other instructional personnel.

- *Maintaining public school status.* Charter schools continue to be public schools and must follow the basic legal principles of public education:

> It [the charter school] may not teach religion. It may not charge tuition. It must be open to the public: no picking and choosing "nice kids"; no elite academies. It may not discriminate. It must follow health and safety requirements. It is accountable to its public sponsor for meeting the objectives that it and its sponsor agree on. (Kolderie, 1993, p. 2)

Creative Funding and the Reallocation of Resources

State and local tax dollars are used to fund charter schools and provide the resources to support instructional services to a specified group of students. The charter schools usually include:

- *Funding by existing per-pupil cost.* Funding for a charter school is based on the existing per-pupil cost of the local school district. Most states specify some percentage of the regular per-pupil cost, some states provide 100 percent funding. In Colorado, charter schools receive 80 percent of the per-pupil cost of the local school district (Wilt, 1993, p. 10).
- *Lump sum funding.* A charter school will be funded in a lump-sum amount without line-item restrictions. This provides available funds to be used in the most flexible, creative, and useful manner. This type of funding is not a revolutionary or even a new idea; it is similar to how colleges and universities have traditionally been funded.
- *Internal reallocation of existing funds.* Rather than invest the majority of existing funds in professional staff, charter schools have the freedom to invest in fewer certified teachers and administrators, or as many charter schools are doing, hiring no administrators and using these savings to hire larger numbers of aides, paraprofessionals, and to purchase or lease educational technology.

Creative Staffing

In addition to waivers for state regulations and new ways of allocating resources, charter schools are able to use new approaches to staffing and develop new concepts for the roles of teachers and administrators.

- *New roles for teachers and administrators.* Teachers become planners, managers, and coordinators of learning. In addition to the traditional responsibilities of instruction, each professional teacher supervises and coordinates a number of instructional aides and paraprofessionals who assist in some aspect of student instruction. Techniques of shared decision making seem to reduce the need to invest in school administrators.

- *Extensive use of paraprofessionals.* Using fewer professional staff, the charter school is able to dramatically reduce the per pupil ratio by employing paraprofessionals and aides (see Figure 10-1), all under the supervision of certified teachers.
- *Extensive use of volunteers and part-time teachers.* Charter and contract schools use large numbers of volunteers and part-time teachers from business, industry, the arts, and from nearby colleges and universities to supplement the curriculum, mentor students, and provide tutorial services.
- *Extensive use of cross-age tutoring.* Older students are used to tutor and mentor younger students in reading in the academic areas (Designs for Learning, 1993).

Accountability Through Competency-Based Performance Outcomes

Rather than using required courses built around class seat-time, students will be monitored and evaluated on their performance in accomplishing specified learning goals and competencies, as well as by statewide achievement tests. For example, rather than grading a person with a letter grade for a required course and using standardized tests to exclusively determine learning, students are developing portfolios of actual work used to document and evaluate their learning. With charter and contract schools, control of public education shifts from process to performance. In order to stay open, charter and contract schools must achieve the student performance objectives that are agreed to by the sponsor and must continue to attract sufficient parents and students to maintain established enrollment levels. In California, charters for new schools must contain:

> . . . description of student outcomes which are clearly stated, that reflect student engagement in a rich and challenging curriculum, and which are measurable. All charter schools will be required to administer the new statewide assessments and to meet the performance standards which are developed in conjunction with these standards. In addition to these required assessments, charter school petitioners and local governing boards should agree on a comprehensive set of measures which will, together with the required statewide tests, give both the school and the district a clear picture of how the school and its students are doing. (Wilt, 1993, p. 11)

Teachers as Owners

For the first time, public school teachers could become the owners of their schools. While a number of possible models exist, teachers could form a cooperative or a partnership and become small-business entrepreneurs. Teachers could also choose to join the local bargaining unit, form their own bargaining unit, or as owners, decide they no longer need a bargaining unit. As Stephanie Moore, an authority on California's charter school movement, has said, "it's like becoming an employee business" (Riley, 1993, p. 15).

Local Autonomy

Each charter or contract school becomes almost completely autonomous. They are in fact a mini school district, and as such, provide for the first time in the United States the opportunity for more than one organization to offer public education in a community.

Voluntary Choice

Charter and contract schools are available to families and students on the basis of choice. Teachers and all other staff also choose to participate in a charter. Some states have even permitted public school teachers the freedom to take leaves of absence to work in a charter school with the opportunity to return to their former employer if they choose.

Model Characteristics: Minnesota Community Learning Centers

The network of Community Learning Centers that are a part of the New American School Development Corporation include five Minnesota public schools. Each of these will ultimately offer preschool through adult learning centers; four are contract schools, one is a charter school. These schools include:

- *Minneapolis Community Learning Center.* The center serves a diverse urban community. The school will utilize a learner-centered Total Quality Management approach.
- *Fond du Lac Community Learning Center.* The center serves a traditional Anishinabe Native American community and uses Ojibwa language and culture. The school is partnered with the Fond du Lac Technical College and the University of Minnesota in Duluth.
- *Rothsay Community Learning Center.* Operating in cooperation with the Global Trade Center which connects Rothsay with Scandinavian countries, students will be able to design, develop, promote and implement a foreign market for Native American artwork. The school owns a storefront business, a lumber yard, and a hardware store. The school also contains a teenage cooperative that owns and operates a grocery store.
- *St. Paul Community Learning Center.* Initially consisting of two centers, the St. Paul Expo I (an elementary school) and Expo II (a middle school), the school will operate an interdisciplinary approach and an educational delivery system based on modeling, facilitating, and teamwork. The school will utilize brain-based learning, multiple-age curriculum, and flexible use of time.
- *Toivola-Meadowlands Community Learning Center.* This school is the first K–12 charter school in the United States, using large time block scheduling with flexible Fridays, field trips, peer tutoring and mentoring, and parent involvement. The school will have no principal and will use computerized planning, curriculum development, and student data management. The school will emphasize youth service, environmental awareness, multicultural celebration, student entrepreneurship, technology, and community growth. (Five Sites, 1993)

Model Characteristics: California Charter Schools

In California, 37 schools and 3 school districts have gained charters. The Los Angeles Unified School District has 10 schools; Pacific Palisades, a large middle-class community in west Los Angeles, is moving towards restructuring its entire K–12 program around two charter schools. Most of the Los Angeles charters were previously alternative public schools. Two of the schools, one in L.A. and one in San Bernardino, were previously contract schools specifically designed to serve at-risk youth. California's largest charter school is in Los Angeles, the Vaughn Next Century Learning Center. The school is K–6 with approximately 1,000 students. It will be a year-round school, using a multitrack approach with extended classes.

Interestingly, the rest of the currently operating California charter schools, the majority of the charters, are located in small, rural communities. At least five of the charters offer home study or an independent study format.

Starting a Charter or Contract School

Starting a charter or contract school tends to involve far more legal and technical issues than other school restructuring approaches. There is also a considerable difference between charter schools and contract schools. While state legislation is a prerequisite to the creation of charter schools, any school could develop some type of contract school. And depending on the state policies governing experimental public schools, some contract schools have obtained the same type of waivers of state regulations that charter schools have achieved.

Groups who have started charter schools have described how much they have gained from research literature that has documented how to start an alternative public school (Sweeney, 1993). In addition to effective strategies for starting alternative schools, some groups that have successfully started charter schools offer the lessons they have learned from satisfactorily completing the process:

1. *Spend adequate time talking about the shared vision: every word counts.*
2. *Involve key players early on in developing the vision and reaching consensus.*
3. *Coalesce with other parents and teachers in your district or area planning schools of choice or charter schools regardless of their philosophical bent.*
4. *Solicit the expert assistance of district personnel early on in planning.*
5. *Seek district flexibility and be clear about what waivers you will be asking for.*
6. *Include union participation where appropriate and when worthwhile.*
7. *Keep the programs or schools small and cohesive.*
8. *After students and teachers choose the program, continue to offer choices within the program.*
9. *Clearly define the roles of students, parents, teachers, and community members.*
10. *Experiment with the administrative hierarchy: flatten it wherever possible.*
11. *Have a distinct, themed program.*
12. *Develop curricula that is particular to your program. Programs may not be cloned.*
13. *Commit to continually renew the program and make it better. (Sweeney, 1993, p. 9)*

At-Risk Youth and Charter or Contract Schools

The concept of charter and contract schools has the potential to liberate alternative school programs that serve dropouts and to stimulate the development of more K–12 community learning centers such as have been developed in Minnesota to serve all ages and ethnic groups and to help integrate education with jobs. However, there are also nagging concerns regarding the charters. In California, both the good and bad can be found for at-risk youth. Some at-risk alternative schools and contract schools have achieved a charter status; but, "disappointingly, very few of California's charter schools have been generated by and for low income or minority communities in . . . urban inner cities" (Riley, 1993, p. 16). Unfortunately, the majority of at-risk youth are found in the nation's largest cities, and to create charter or contract schools in these urban areas confronts formidable obstacles: big-city politics, big labor unions, and local school board rivalries. The very individuals who need improved education often live in impoverished communities which may lack the sophistication and the legal assistance to develop and manage a charter school. Equally troubling, since charter schools must demonstrate high student achievement in order to stay open, there may be a tendency for groups to propose charters primarily for communities where there is already a strong track record of student success. Only time will tell.

Guaranteeing Success: The Blueprint Completed

The three approaches that have been described in this chapter, restructuring existing schools, replicating alternative schools, and creating boundary-breaking schools, have demonstrated dramatic success in restructuring schools to ensure that at-risk children and youth learn effectively and stay in school. The descriptions of effective restructuring approaches provide the final component of a complete blueprint for guaranteeing that the needs of at-risk children and youth are effectively addressed. The blueprint has included:

- Assistance in identifying those who are the at-risk.
- Documentation of school myths and programs that are ineffective or, even worse, destructive to the at risk.
- An analysis of why schools have proven so difficult to change.
- A summary of essential components of effective at-risk programs based upon significant long-term research.
- A comprehensive review of effective school and community programs for at-risk students from infancy through the high-school years.
- A description of allies in restructuring schools as well as problems to be avoided.
- And finally three detailed descriptions of successful approaches to restructuring schools to meet the needs of at-risk youth.

There has also been an effort to identify real schools and programs that continue to be effective in improving the learning of at-risk youth so that they achieve up to the levels of other students. These schools include conventional public schools in rural and urban communities and schools in a variety of poverty settings. They include the special program schools like Accelerated Schools, Success For All schools, school development programs and a wide variety of alternative public schools and magnet schools. They also include community learning centers, contract schools, and the new concept—charter schools.

These schools are transforming the lives of children and youth and are providing the last best hope for our nation's social and economic future. This book stands as a stinging challenge to communities throughout the nation to step forward and take action to do what must be done, to follow the blueprint that research has provided, to fulfill the American promise of equal education for all. At last there is hope for students at risk.

Chapter 11

Help Is Available

The sheer volume of research conducted and reported over the past 15 years relating to the education of youth at risk represents perhaps the most significant development within the field of education. This focus is particularly noteworthy given the conservative political environment that prevailed in the United States from 1980 to 1992. During this era, the administrations of two presidents significantly reduced funding for research and development in most arenas of K–12 education. Despite this reduction in federal support for research and developmental support, concerned scholars have continued to vigorously study and seek solutions to the crisis created by the growing number of youth who either drop out or graduate from high school with deficient skills. Research to date has dramatically expanded the knowledge base and identified an impressive collection of strategies and interventions which are working to save and enrich lives.

The recent proliferation of interest in improving the educational outcomes of youth at risk unfortunately includes flawed research and misleading information as well as definitive solutions to many of the perplexing problems facing schools and communities. The purpose of this section is to provide carefully screened bibliographic resource information which represents the most important works that have recently emerged. While a number of these works have been cited and discussed in the previous chapters, many, due to space limitations, have not.

This chapter presents a comprehensive review of research on youth at risk, effective practices, and resources dedicated to improving schools and the lives of youth at risk. Specific topics include:

> Where to Find Help
> > Organizations, Institutes, and Centers
> > Resource Directories
> > Newsletters and Journals
> > Media
> > Sources for Funding

Research on Critical Issues
    The Growing Crisis
    Demographics
    Dropping Out
    Drugs/Substance Abuse
    Ethnicity
    Family Involvement
    Health/AIDS
    Poverty
    School Choice
    Suicide
    Teenage Pregnancy and Parenthood
    Urban Education
Schoolwide Approaches and Interventions
    Collaboration (Schools/Communities/Social Services)
    Early Childhood
    Elementary Schools
    Middle Schools
    High Schools
    School-to-Work Transition
    Restructuring
    Rural Education
Classroom Strategies
    Cooperative Learning
    Discipline and Behavior Management
    Mentoring
    Peer Tutoring
    Ineffective Practices: Tracking and Retention

As the crisis of educating all youth continues to focus the nation's attention on improving schools and expanding community interventions, resources such as these can assist individuals and organizations with their critical efforts toward seeking solutions to this continuing peril.

Where To Find Help

Organizations, Institutes, and Centers

American Council on Rural Special Education, Miller Hall 359, Western Washington University, Bellingham, WA 98225

Center for Community Education, State University of New Jersey-Rutgers, School of Social Work, 73 Easton Avenue, New Brunswick, NJ 08903

Center for Dropout Prevention, University of Miami, School of Education, Box 248065, Coral Gables, FL 33124

Center for Early Adolescence, University of North Carolina at Chapel Hill, Suite 211, Carr Mill Mall, Carrboro, NC 27510

Center for Research on Effective Schooling for Disadvantaged Students, Johns Hopkins University, 3505 North Charles Street, Baltimore, MD 21218

Center for Research on Elementary and Middle Schools (formerly Center for Social Organization of Schools, Johns Hopkins University, 3505 North Charles Street, Baltimore, MD 21218

Center for the Study and Teaching of At-Risk Students, Institute for the Study of Educational Policy, University of Washington, Miller Hall, Seattle, WA 98195

Children's Defense Fund, 122 C Street, NW, Washington, DC 20001

Cities in Schools, Inc., 1023 15th Street, NW, Suite 600, Washington, DC 20005

Education Commission of the States, 1860 Lincoln Street, Suite 300, Denver, CO 80295

Family Resource Coalition, 230 N. Michigan Avenue, Room 1625, Chicago, IL 60601

Independent Sector, 1828 L Street Northwest, Washington, DC 20036

Institute for At-Risk Infants, Children and Youth and Their Families, University of South Florida, 4202 Fowler Avenue, Tampa, FL 33620

Institute for Children At Risk, Continuing Professional Education, Lewis and Clark College, Campus Box 85, Portland, OR 97219.

Institute for Responsive Education, 605 Commonwealth Avenue, Boston, MA 02215

Institute for the Study of At-Risk Students, College of Education, 306 Shibles Hall, University of Maine, Orono, ME 04469

National Association of Partners in Education, Inc., 601 Wythe Street, Suite 200, Alexandria, VA 22314

National Association of State Boards of Eduation, 1012 Cameron Street, Alexandria, VA 22314

National Center on Effective Secondary Schools, School of Education, University of Wisconsin-Madison, 1025 West Johnson Street, Madison, WI 53706

National Center for Parents in Dropout Prevention, National Committee for Citizens in Education, Suite 301, 10840 Little Patuxent Parkway, Columbia, MD 21044

National Committee for Citizens in Education, 10840 Little Patuxent Parkway, Suite 301, Columbia, MD 21044.

National Community Education Association, 119 North Payne Street, Alexandria, VA 22314

National Crime Prevention Council, 733 15th Street North West, Suite 540, Washington, DC 20005

National Dropout Prevention Center, Clemson University, 393 College Avenue, Clemson, SC 29634

National Dropout Prevention Network, P.O. Box 4067, Napa, CA 94558

National Dropout Prevention Network, Ohio State University, 1960 Kenny Road, Columbus, OH 43210.

National Dropout Prevention Network, 1517 L Street, Sacramento, CA, 95814.

National Resource Center for Children in Poverty, School of Public Health, Columbia University, New York, NY 10032

National Rural and Small Schools Consortium, Miller Hall 359, Western Washington University, Bellingham, WA 98225

National School Conference Institute, P.O. Box 941, Rimrock, AZ 86335

Stanford Accelerated School Project, c/o Henry M. Levin, CERAS 402, Stanford University, Stanford, CA 94305.

Vocational Studies Center, University of Wisconsin-Madison, School of Education, 964 Educational Sciences Bldg., 1025 West Johnson Street, Madison, WI 53706

Youth Service America, 1319 F Street North West, Suite 900, Washington, DC 20004

Resource Directories

Center on Organization and Restructuring of Schools. (1993). *1993 bibliography on school restructuring*. Madison, WI: Author. 35 pp.

Directory of public magnet, and theme-based schools. 1992–1993. College of Education, University of Houston, Houston, TX.

Far West Laboratory for Educational Research and Improvement. (1989). *Papers, programs, and technical assistance services for educators of at-risk students*. San Francisco: Author. 102 pp.

International Consulting Associates. (1990). *Quick reference guide to school dropouts*. Stockton, CA: Author. 52 pp.

Mastny, A. Y. (1989). *Linking schools and community services: Resource directory*. New Brunswick, NJ: Center for Community Education, School of Social Work, Rutgers, State University of New Jersey. 80 pp.

Oregon Department of Education. (1989). *Oregon's innovative approaches for students who are seriously emotionally disturbed or otherwise at risk*. Salem, OR: Author. 101 pp.

Simons, J. (1989). *Where to find data about adolescents and young adults: A guide to sources*. Washington, DC: Children's Defense Fund. 31 pp.

Trent, S. C. (1992). School choice for African-American children who live in poverty: A commitment to equity or more of the same? *Urban Education, 27*(3), 291–307.

Newsletters and Journals

Two newsletters of particular relevance are *Educating At-Risk Youth* and *National Dropout Prevention Newsletter*. Both cover a broad range of topics affecting at-risk youth and those who work with at-risk youth. These newsletters also list upcoming conferences, grants, organizations, current research, publications and resource materials, new programs, and summaries of reports and surveys—all relating to at-risk youth.

Accelerated Schools. A quarterly publication and official newsletter of the Accelerated Schools Project, Center for Educational Research at Stanford School of Education, Stanford University, Stanford, CA 94305-3084. Telephone: (415) 725-1676. Free.

CDS: The Johns Hopkins University. Published by the Center For Research on Effective Schooling for Disadvantaged Students, 3505 N. Charles St., Baltimore, MD 21218. (301) 338-7570.

Changing Schools. The Journal of Alternative Education. Published three times a year. Colorado Options in Education, 98 N. Wadsworth Blvd., #127, Box 191, Lakewood, CO 80226. $15 a year.

Community Learning Centers. Published monthly by Public School Incentives, 2550 University Ave., W., Suite 347N, St. Paul, MN 55114-1052. Telephone: (612) 645-0200. Free.

Educating At-Risk Youth. A publication of the National Professional Resources, Inc., P.O. Box 1479, Port Chester, NY 10573. Telephone: (914) 937-8879; Fax: (914) 937-9327. Published September-June (10 issues), $68 a year.

Fine Print. A periodic publication of the Center for School Change. Hubert H. Humphrey Institute of Public Affairs, 301 19th Avenue South, University of Minnesota, Minneapolis, Minnesota 55455. $5 a year.

Horace. Published five times a year at Brown University. Coalition of Essential Schools, Box 1969, Brown University, Providence, RI 02912. $11 per copy.

Educational Directions: Reaching Excellence With Alternatives. Annual publication of the Florida Association of Alternative School Educators, Inc., 7608 Royal Palm Way, Boca Raton, FL 33432. (407) 395-3063. Individual copies cost $2.00.

The Harvard Education Letter. Bi-monthly publication of the Harvard Graduate School of Education, Longfellow Hall, Apian Way, Cambridge, MA. 02138-3752. Subscription is $24.00 per year.

Issues in Restructuring Schools. Published quarterly by Center on Organization and Restructuring of Schools, School of Education, University of Wisconsin-Madison, 1025 W. Johnson Street, Madison, WI 53706. Telephone: (608) 263-7575. Free.

National Dropout Prevention Newsletter. A quarterly publication of the National Dropout Prevention Network and the National Dropout Prevention Center, Clemson University, Clemson, SC 29634-5111. (803) 656-2599. $25 a year.

Media

America's schools: Who gives a damn? (1991). New York: Columbia University, School of Journalism; Public Broadcasting System. 120 minutes.

Breaking out: Career choices for teenage parents. (1987). Madison, WI: Vocational Studies Center, University of Wisconsin-Madison. 18 minutes.

Breaking the cycle: Parent and early childhood education: The Kenan model. (1990). Louisville, KY: National Center for Family Literacy. 15 minutes.

Children in need. (1989). New York: Committee for Economic Development. 29 minutes.

Crisis: Urban education. (1989). New York: WNET-TV. 112 minutes.

Diversities in mentoring: Profiles from programs serving minority and at-risk youth. (1990). Pittsburgh, PA: Project Literacy. 56 minutes.

Effective schools for children at risk. (1991). Alexandria, VA: Association for School and Curriculum Development. 8 minutes.

A future for all children. (1988). Denver, CO: Education Commission of the States. 10 minutes.

"Every child can succeed." (1992). Bloomington, IN: Agency for Instructional Technology. (900) 451-4509. "Every child can succeed" is an educational package containing print material and 17 twenty-to-thirty minute video programs profiling elementary schools that have succeeded in effectively teaching children at risk of school failure. The material, developed as part of a systematic effort to study and document school succees, can be used separately or as a series to provide a complete professional development program for parents, teachers, and administrators.

Futures at risk. (1986). Denver, CO: Education Commission of the States. 8 minutes.

Getting back on track: Video solutions to reaching America's at-risk youth. South Carolina Educational Television, P.O. Box 11000, Columbia, SC 29211. Telephone: (800) 553-7752.

Growing up at risk. (1988). Dayton, OH: Kettering Foundation. 12 minutes.

Has anyone seen Phil? (1989). Dallas, TX: Plays for Living Production in association with J.C. Penney Company, Inc. 45 minutes.

Learning to change: Schools of excellence for at-risk students. (1990). Atlanta, GA: Southern Regional Council, Inc. 29 minutes.

Masters of disaster. (1985). Bloomington, IN: Indiana University. 29 minutes.

Milestones in mentoring. (1990). Pittsburgh, PA: Project Literacy. 120 minutes.

Not me! (1988). New York: Plays for Living, in association with J. C. Penney Co., Inc. 40 minutes.

One plus one. (1989). Pittsburgh, PA: Plus Project Literacy. 60 minutes.

Partners for success. (1990). Portland, OR: Westcom Productions, Inc. 31 minutes.

Partners in education. (1989). Northbrook, IL: Mindscape, Inc. 17 minutes.

Project second chance: Dropouts in America. (n.d.) Arkansas Educational Television Network Foundation. 60 minutes.

Restructuring America's schools: Special preview. (1991). Alexandria, VA: Association for School and Curriculum Development. 6 minutes.

Schools that work: Learning in America. (1990). Arlington, VA: MacNeil/Lehrer and WETA-TV. 120 minutes.

Why do these kids love school? (1990). Menlo Park, CA: Concentric Media. 60 minutes.

Sources For Funding

The following private and public agencies, corporations, and foundations have identified improving the lives of at-risk youth as a funding priority. For up-to-date information, funding guidelines, and applications, please contact the foundation or agency directly, as funding priorities are subject to change on a yearly basis.

Each of the following sources have, in the past, funded at-risk projects. The majority of them accept proposals on an open cycle basis without yearly deadlines. Most of these funding agencies have yearly grant amounts which are based on their own investment earnings; thus, amounts available for funding vary. This list represents a limited selection of funding sources.

When contacting a funding source, it is recommended that a careful review of guidelines and application procedures be completed prior to proposal development and submission. Those listings without telephone numbers prefer to be contacted by mail. These resources serve as an appropriate initial step toward the determination and location of appropriate external funding agencies which individuals, agencies, schools, and programs may consider for projects related to at-risk youth.

Another recommended resource, in addition to the list below, is the *National Guide to Funding for Elementary and Secondary Education*. Each of the 1,400 entries provides a portrait of the foundation and lists the kinds of projects that currently receive funding. (Available from The Foundation Center, 79 Fifth Avenue, Dept. TY, New York, NY 10003-3050; also available in major libraries.)

Aetna Life and Casualty Foundation, National Grants Program, Youth Employment, 151 Farmington Avenue, Hartford, CT 06156, (203) 273-3340

Alcoa Foundation Grants—Education, Alcoa Foundation, 1501 Alcoa Building, Pittsburgh, PA 15219, (412) 553-4696

Allstate Foundation Grants, Allstate Foundation, Allstate Plaza, F-3, Northbrook, IL 60062

American Express Foundation Grants, American Express Foundation, American Express Plaza, 19th, New York, NY 10004

AMR Corporation Grants Program, AMR Corporation, P.O. Box 61616, Dallas/Fort Worth Airport, TX 75361

Apple Computer Corporation, 4000 Kruse Way Place, Building 1 Suite 100, Lake Oswego, OR 97035, (503) 635-7711

Apple Corporate Grants, Apple Computer Corporation, 20525 Mariana Avenue, Cupertino, CA 95014, (408) 996-1010

Arco Foundation Education Grants, Arco Foundation, 515 S. Flower Street, Los Angeles, CA 90071, (213) 486-3334

Boeing Company Charitable Trust Grants, Boeing Company Charitable Trusts, 7755 E. Marginal Way S., Seattle, WA 98124, (206) 655-1131

Carnegie Corporation of New York, 437 Madison Avenue, New York, NY 10022, (212) 371-3200

Chevron Contributions Program, Chevron Corporation, P.O. Box 7753, San Francisco, CA, 94120-7753, (415) 894-5464

Coca-Cola Foundation, P.O. Drawer 1734, Atlanta, GA 30301, (404) 676-2121

Danforth Foundation, Gene Schwilck, 231 S. Bemiston Avenue, St. Louis, MO 63105, (314) 862-6200

Davis (Edwin W. & Catherine M.) Foundation, 2100 First National Bank Building, St. Paul, MN 55101, (612) 228-0935

Dayton Hudson Corporation Foundation Grants, 77 Nicollet Mall, Minneapolis, MN 55402, (612) 370-6948

Dresser Foundation Grants, Dresser Foundation, P.O. Box 718, Dallas, TX 75221

Exxon Education Foundation Grants,Exxon Education Foundation, P.O. Box 101, Florham Park, NJ 07932, (214) 444-1104

FMC Foundation Grants, 200 East Randolph Drive, Chicago, IL 60601, (312) 861-6135

Ford Foundation, 320 East 43rd Street, New York, NY 10017, (212) 573-5000

General Mills Foundation Grants, General Mills Foundation, P.O. Box 1113, Minneapolis, MN 55440, (612) 540-3338

Grant (William T.) Foundation, Faculty Scholars Program, 515 Madison Avenue, New York, NY 10022-5403, (212) 752-0071

Green (Allen P. & Josephine B.) Foundation, Box 523, Mexico, MO 65265

Hazen (Edward W.) Foundation, 505 Eighth Avenue, 23rd Floor, New York, NY 10018, (212) 967-5920

Hearst Foundation, 888 Seventh Avenue, 27th floor, New York, NY 10106, (415) 543-0400

IBM Corporation, IBM Education Systems, 4111 Northside Parkway, Atlanta, GA 30327, (404) 238-3981

Johnson (Robert Wood) Foundation, College Road, P.O. Box 2316, Princeton, NJ 08543-2316, (609) 452-8701

Joyce Foundation, Discretionary Fund, 135 South LaSalle Street, Suite 4010, Chicago, IL 60603-4886, (312) 782-2464

Kellogg (W.K.) Foundation, Executive Assistant-Programming, 400 North Avenue, Battle Creek, MI 49017-3398, (616) 968-1611

MacArthur (John D. & Catherine J.) Foundation, Education Programs, 140 South Dearborn Street, Chicago, IL 60603, (312) 726-8000

Meyer (Fred) Charitable Trust, 1515 Southwest Fifth Avenue, Suite 500, Portland, OR 97201 (503) 228-5512

Moody Foundation Grants, 704 Moody National Bank Building, Galveston, TX 77550

Mott (Charles Stewart) Foundation, 1200 Mott Foundation Bldg., Flint, MI 48502-1851, (313) 238-5651

Oregon Community Foundation, 1110 Yeon Building, 522 Southwest Fifth Avenue, Portland, OR 97204, (503) 227-6846

Pew Charitable Trust, Health and Human Services, Three Parkway, Suite 501, Philadelphia, PA 19102-1305, (215) 587-4054

Phillips Petroleum Foundation Grants, 16th Floor, Phillips Building, Bartlesville, OK 74004, (918) 661-9072

Polaroid Foundation, 750 Main Street, Cambridge, MA 02139, (617) 577-4035

Prudential Foundation Grants, Prudential Plaza, Newark, NJ 07101, (201) 802-7354

Richardson (Smith) Foundation, Children and Families At Risk Program, 266 Post Road East, Westport, CT 06880, (212) 861-8181

RJR Nabisco Foundation, RJR Nabisco, Inc., Roger Semerad, 1456 Pennsylvania Ave., NW, Suite 525, Washington, DC 20004, (202) 626-7200

Rockefeller Foundation Grant Program, Hugh B. Price, 1133 Avenue of the Americas, New York, NY 10036, (212) 869-8500

Scripps Howard Foundation, Albert J. Schottelkotte, P.O. Box 5380, Cincinatti, OH 45201, (513) 977-3825

Spencer Foundation, 900 North Michigan Avenue, Suite 2800, Chicago, IL 60611, (312) 337-7000

Templeton (Herbert A.) Foundation, 1717 S.W. Park Avenue, Portland, OR 97201, (503) 223-0036

Toyota USA Foundation, 19001 South Western Avenue, Torrance, CA 90509, (213) 618-6766

Tucker (Rose E.) Charitable Trust, 900 Southwest Fifth Avenue, 24th Floor, Portland, OR 97204 , (503) 224-3380

UPS Foundation Grants, UPS Foundation, 51 Weaver Street, Greenwich Office Park 5, Greenwich, CT 06836-3160, (203) 862-6287

Xerox Corporation Educational and Career Opportunities for Young People, Xerox Corporation, P.O. Box 1600, Stamford, CT 06904, (203) 968-3306

Research On Critical Issues

The Growing Crisis

Alderman, M. K. (1990). Motivation for at-risk students. *Educational Leadership, 48*(1), 27–30.

American Association of University Women Educational Foundation. (1993). *Hostile hallways: The AAUW survey on sexual harassment in America's schools.* 25 pp.

Baas, A. (1991). *Promising strategies for at-risk youth.* ERIC Digest. No. 59. Eugene, OR: ERIC Clearinghouse on Educational Management. 3pp.

Beane, J. A. (1991). Sorting out the self-esteem controversy. *Educational Leadership, 49*(1), 25–30.

Boyd, W. L., & Wahlberg, H. J. (Eds.). (1990). *Choice in education: Potential and problems.* Berkeley, CA: McCutchan Publishing.

Brendtro, L. K., Brokenleg, M., & Bockern, S. Van. (1990). *Reclaiming youth at-risk: Our hope for the future.* Bloomington, IN: National Educational Service.

Brodinsky, Ben & Keough, Katherine. (1989). *Students At Risk: Problems and Solutions.* Arlington, VA: American Association of School Administrators. 112 pp.

Brown, C. G. (1987). *Children at risk: The work of the states.* Washington, DC: Council of Chief State School Officers. 11 pp.

Canfield, J. (1990). Improving students' self-esteem. *Educational Leadership, 48*(1), 48–50.

Carnegie Council on Adolescent Development. (1990). *Abridged version: Turning points—preparing American youth for the 21st century.* Washington D.C.: Author. 35 pp.

Center on Evaluation, Development, Research. (1991). *The alternative school choice. Hot topics series.* Bloomington, IN: Phi Delta Kappa. 296 pp.

Center for Research on Effective Schooling for Disadvantaged Students. (1992, July). *Resilient children defy stereotypes, succeed against the odds.* The Johns Hopkins University. 16 pp.

Children's Defense Fund. (1991). *The state of America's children.* Washington, DC: Author.

Committee for Economic Development, Research and Policy Committee. (1989). *Children in need: Investment strategies for the educationally disadvantaged.* New York, NY: Author. 86 pp.

Conrath, J. (1992). Effective schools for discouraged and disadvantaged students: Rethinking some sacred cows of research. *Contemporary Education, 63*(2), 137–141.

Consortium on Educational Policy Studies. (1989). *Accelerated schools: A new strategy for at-risk students.* Policy Bulletin No. 6, May. Bloomington, IN: Indiana University.

Cuellar, A., & Cuellar, M. F. (1990). *From dropout to high achiever: An understanding of academic excellence through an analysis of dropouts and students-at-risk.* San Francisco: San Diego State Univ.; S. H. Cowell Foundation. (ERIC Document Reproduction Service No. ED 322 252) 34 pp.

Davis, W. E., & McCaul, E. J. (1990). *At-risk children and youth: A crisis in our schools and society.* Orono, ME: University of Maine, Institute for the Study of At-Risk Students, College of Education.

Donnelly, M. (1987). *At-risk students.* Eugene, OR: ERIC Clearinghouse on Educational Management. (ERIC Document Reproduction Service No. ED 292 172).

Dryfoos, J. G. (1990). *Adolescents at risk: Prevalence and prevention.* New York: Oxford University Press.

Far West Laboratory for Educational Research and Improvement. (1989). *Strategies for dropout prevention.* San Francisco: Author. (ERIC Document Reproduction Service No. ED 318 833). 41 pp.

Finn, J. D. (1993). *School engagement & students at risk.* Washington, DC: National Center for Education Statistics. 103 pp.

Frymier, J. (1989). *A study of students at risk: Collaborating to do research.* Bloomington, IN: Phi Delta Kappa Educational Foundation. 81 pp.

Frymier, J., Barber, L., Carriedo, R., Denton, W., Gansneder, B., Johnson-Lewis, S., & Robertson, N. (1992). *Growing up is risky business, and schools are not to blame.* Bloomington, IN: Phi Delta Kappa. 246 pp.

Frymier, J., & Gansneder, B. (1989). The Phi Delta Kappa study of students at risk. *Phi Delta Kappan, 17*(2), 142–146.

Gold, M., & Mann, D. W. (1984). *Expelled to a friendlier place: A study of effective alternative schools.* Ann Arbor: University of Michigan Press.

Goslin, J. C. (1989). Underachievers: A curriculum design. *Preventing School Failure, 34*(1), 22–28.

Gray, B. A. (1991). Using instructional technology with at-risk youth: A primer. *TechTrends, 36*(5), 61–63.

Hergert, L. G. (1991). School resources for at-risk youth. *Equity and Excellence, 25*(1), 10–14.

Hewlett, S. A. (1991). *When the bough breaks: The cost of neglecting our children.* Basic Books.

Hilliard, A. G., II. (1991). Do we have the will to educate all children? *Educational Leadership, 49*(1), 31–36.

Hilliard, A. G., II. (1989). *Public support for successful instructional practices for at-risk-students.* Position Paper. (ERIC Document Reproduction Service No. ED 313 464). 15 pp.

Hollins, E. R. (1990). *Professional development for teachers of "at-risk" students: A comprehensive plan.* Kansas City, MO: Presented at the Interstate New Teacher Assessment and Support Consortium Seminar. (ERIC Document Reproduction Service No. ED 325 475). 23 pp.

Kelly, D.M. (1993). *Last chance high: How girls and boys drop in and out of alternative schools.* Binghamton, NY: Yale University Press. 276 pp.

Kershner, K., & Connolly, J. (1991). *At-risk students and school restructuring.* Philadelphia, PA: Research Better. 133 pp.

Knapp, M. S. & Shields, P. M. (Eds.). (1990). *Better schooling for the children of poverty: Alternatives to conventional wisdom. Study of academic instruction for disadvantaged students. Volume II: Commissioned papers and literature review.* Washington, D.C.: Policy Studies Associates, Inc.: Menlo Park, CA: SRI International. 256 pp.

Kohl, H. (1991). *I won't learn from you: The role of assent in learning.* Minneapolis, MN: Milkweed Editions.

Leonard, M. (1992). The response of the private sector: foundations and entrepreneurs. *Teachers College Record, 93*(3), 376–381.

McPartland, J. M., & Slavin, R. E. (1990). *Policy perspectives: Increasing achievement of at-risk students at each grade.* Washington, DC: U.S. Department of Education. 36 pp.

McWhirter, J. Jeffries, McWhirter, Benedict T., McWhirter, Anna M., & McWhirter, Ellen Hawley. (1993). *At-risk youth: A comprehensive response.* Pacific Grove, CA: Brooks/Cole Publishing Company. 353 pp.

Means, B., Chelemer, C. & Knapp, M. S. (Eds). (1991). *Teaching advanced skills to at-risk students: Views from research and practice.* San Francisco, CA: Jossey-Bass Publishers. 287 pp.

Molnar, A. (1992). Too many kids are getting killed. *Educational Leadership, 50*(1), 4–5.

Nardini, M. L. & Antes, R.L. (1991). What strategies are effective with at-risk students? *NASSP Bulletin, 75*(538), 67–72.

Nash, M. A. (1990) *Improving their chances: A handbook for designing and implementing programs for at-risk youth.* Madison, WI: Vocational Studies Center, Univ. of WI, School of Education.

National Forum for Youth at Risk. (1988). *Securing our future: A report of the National Forum for Youth at Risk* (December 10-12, 1987). Denver, CO: Education Commission of the States. (ERIC Document Reproduction Service No. ED 305 207). 57 pp.

National School Boards Association. (1989). *An equal chance: Educating at-risk children to succeed: Recommendations for school board action.* Alexandria, VA: Author. 19 pp.

Natriello, G. (Ed.). (1986). *School dropouts: Patterns and policies.* New York: Teachers College Press.

Natriello, G., et al. (1990). *Schooling disadvantaged children: Racing against catastrophe.* New York, NY: Teachers College Press. 264. pp.

Natriello, G., et al. (1991). *Creating more responsive student evaluation systems for disadvantaged students. Report no. 15.* Baltimore, MD: Center for Research on Effective Schooling for Disadvantaged Students. 18 pp.

Ogden, E. H. & Germinario, V. (1988). *The at-risk student: Answers for educators.* Lancaster, PA: Technomic Pub. Co. 173 pp.

Oregon Department of Education. (1991). *Alternative education: A technical assistance manual.* Salem, OR: Author.

Robias, R. (1992). *Nurturing at-risk youth in math and science: A curriculum and teaching considerations.* Bloomington, IN: National Education Service. 147 pp.

Sagor, Richard. (1993). *At-risk students: Reading and teaching.* Swampscott, MA: Waterson.

Schlosser, L. K. (1992). Teacher distance and student disengagement: School lives on the margin. *Journal of Teacher Education, 43*(2), 128–140.

Schorr, L. B. (1989) *Within our reach: Breaking the cycle of disadvantage.* New York: Doubleday.

Simons, J. (1991). *The adolescent & young adult fact book.* Washington, DC: Children's Defense Fund. 150 pp.

Sinclair, R. L., & Ghory, W. J. (1987) *Reaching marginal students: A primary concern for school renewal.* Berkeley, CA: McCutchan Publishing Corp.

Slavin, R. E., Karweit, N. L., & Madden, N. A. (Eds.). (1989). *Effective programs for students at risk.* Needham Heights, MA: Allyn and Bacon.

Smith, Gregory. (1993). *Public schools that work.* New York: Routledge.

Smith, R. C., Lincoln, C. A., & Clark, K. B. (1988). *America's shame, America's hope: Twelve million youth at risk.* Chapel Hill, NC: MDC, Inc. 65 pp.

Sowell, T. (1991, October 14). Excuses, excuses: Society has not failed our children. The public schools have failed the children. *Forbes,* p. 43.

Taff, T. G. (1990). Success for the unsuccessful. *Educational Leadership, 48*(1), 71–72.

Taylor, W. L., & Piche, D. M. (1990). *A Report on shortchanging children: The impact of fiscal inequity on the education of students at risk.* Washington, DC: Prepared for the Committee on Education and Labor. (ERIC Document Reproduction Service No. ED 328 654). 81 pp.

Thornburg, K. R., et al. (1991). Youth at risk; society at risk. *Elementary School Journal, 91*(3), 199–208.

Uroff, S. & Greene, B. (1991). A low-risk approach to high-risk students. *NASSP Bulletin, 75*(538), 50–58.

U. S. Department of Health and Human Services. (1986). *Count me in: Youth 2000: A national campaign in support of America's youth from now to the year 2000.* Washington, DC: Author. 24 pp.

Vandergrift, J. A., et al. (1991). *Powerful stories, positive results: Arizona at-risk policy report, FY 1990–91 (Executive summary).* Tempe; Arizona State University. Morrison Inst. for Public Policy. 39 pp.

Wehlage, G. G., Rutter, R. A., Smith, G. A., Lesko, N., & Fernandez, R. R. (1989). *Reducing the risk: Schools as communities of support.* Philadelphia, PA: The Falmer Press, Taylor & Francis.

Weis, L., Farrar, E., & Petri, H. G. (Eds.). (1989). *Dropouts from school: Issues, dilemmas and solutions.* Albany, NY: State University of New York Press.

Wells, S. E. (1990). *At-risk youth: Identification, programs, and recommendations.* Englewood, CO: Teacher Ideas Press. 158 pp.

Werner, E. E. (1989, April) Children of the garden island. *Scientific American*, pp. 106–111.

Willis, H. D. (1989). *Students at risk: A review of conditions, circumstances, indicators, and educational implications.* Elmhurst, IL: (ERIC Document Reproduction Service No. ED 314 514). 38 pp.

Wyoming Department of Education. (1987). *Children at risk: Roadblocks to achieving potential: Eliminating the barriers.* Cheyenne, WY: Author. (ERIC Document Reproduction Service No. ED 286 981). 26 pp.

Demographics

Bloch, D. P. (1991). Missing measures of the who and why of school dropouts: Implications for policy and research. *Career Development Quarterly, 40*(1), 36–47.

Dougherty, V. (1987). *The first step: Understanding the data.* Denver, CO: Education Commission of the States. 27 pp.

Hodgkinson, H. L. (1985). *All one system: Demographics of education, kindergarten through graduate school.* Washington, DC: Institute for Educational Leadership. 18 pp.

Hodgkinson, H. L. (1989). *The same client: The demographics of education and service delivery systems.* Washington, DC: Institute for Educational Leadership. 28 pp.

Hodgkinson, H. L. (1990). *Colorado: The state and its educational system.* Washington, DC: Institute for Educational Leadership. 14 pp.

Hodgkinson, H. L. (1990). *The demographics of American Indians: One percent of the people; fifty percent of the diversity.* Washington, DC: Institute for Educational Leadership. 36 pp.

Horn, M. (1987, May 18). The burgeoning educational under-class. *U. S. News & World Report*, pp. 66–67.

Johnson, L. (1981). *High school dropouts: How communities can gather useful information.* Portland, OR: Greater Portland Work Education Council. 50 pp.

Koretz, D. M. (1987). *Educational achievement: Explanations and implications of recent trends.* Washington, DC: The Congress of the U.S., Congressional Budget Office. 102 pp.

McIntyre, K., et al. (1990). *Resilience among high risk youth.* Madison, Wisconsin: Wisconsin Clearinghouse. 53 pp.

Pallas, A. M., Natriello, G., & McGill, E. L. (1989). *The changing nature of the disadvantaged population: Current dimensions and future trends.* Baltimore, MD: Johns Hopkins University, Center for Research on Elementary & Middle Schools. 29 pp.

Dropping Out

Ascher, C., & Schwartz, W. (1987). *Keeping track of at-risk students.* New York: ERIC Clearinghouse on Urban Education. (ERIC Document Reproduction Service No. ED 285 961). 5 pp.

Auspos, P., et al. (1989). *Implementing JOBSTART: A demonstration for school dropouts in the JTPA system.* New York: Manpower Demonstration Research Corporation. 221 pp.

Baldwin, B., et al. (1992). The high school dropout: Antecedents and alternatives. *Journal of School Leadership, 2*(3), 355–362.

Bryk, A. S., & Thum, Y. M. (1989). *The effects of high school organization on dropping out: An exploratory investigation* (CPRE Research report series RR-012). New Brunswick, NJ: Center for Policy Research in Education. 34 pp.

Carnes, E. B. (1988). *Programs and activities to reduce school dropouts.* Columbia, SC: State Dept. of Education. 50 pp.

Conrath, J. (1984). Snatching victory from the jaws of learning defeat: How one school fought the dropout blitz. *Contemporary Education, 56*(1), 36–38.

Conrath, J. (1986). Effective schools must focus on potential dropouts. *NASSP Bulletin, 70*(487), 46–50.

Conrath, J. (1986). Ten rules for reducing your dropout rate. *Executive Educator, 8*(7), 24–25.

Conrath, J. (1988). Dropout prevention: Find out if your program passes or fails. *Executive Educator, 10*(8), 15–16.

Denton, W. T. (1987). *Dropouts, pushouts, and other casualties.* Bloomington, IN: Phi Delta Kappa, Center on Evaluation, Development and Research. 239 pp.

Duckenfield, M., Hamby, J. V., & Smink, J. (1990). *Effective strategies for dropout prevention: Twelve successful strategies to consider in a comprehensive prevention program.* Clemson, SC: National Dropout Prevention Center. (ERIC Document Reproduction Service No. ED 322 461) 27 pp.

Earle, J., Roach, V., & Fraser, K. (1987). *Female dropouts: A new perspective.* Alexandria, VI: Youth Services Program, National Association of State Boards of Education. 23 pp.

Fine, M. (1991). *Framing dropouts: Notes on the politics of an urban public high school.* Albany, NY: State University of New York Press. 299 pp.

Gage, N. L. (1990). Dealing with the dropout problem. *Phi Delta Kappan*, 72(4), 280–285.

Grossnickle, D. R. (1986). *High school dropouts: Causes, consequences, and cure*. (Fastback No. 242). Bloomington, IN: Phi Delta Kappa Educational Foundation. (ERIC Document Reproduction Service No. ED 275 943) 26 pp.

Guthrie, L. F., Long, C., & Guthrie, G. P. (1989). *Strategies for dropout prevention*. San Francisco: Far West Laboratory for Educational Research and Development. (ERIC Document Reproduction Service No. ED 318 833) 41 pp.

Hahn, A., Danzberger, J., & Lefkowitz, B. (1987). *Dropouts in America: Enough is known for action*. Washington, DC: Institute for Educational Leadership. 69 pp.

Massachusetts Advocacy Center and the Center for Early Adolescence. (1988). *Before it's too late: Dropout prevention in the middle grades*. Carrboro, NC: University of North Carolina at Chapel Hill. 87 pp.

McCaul, E. J. & et al. (1992). Consequences of dropping out of school: Findings from high school and beyond. *Journal of Educational Research, 85*(4), 198–207.

McKinlay, B., & Bloch, D. P. (1989). *Career information motivates at-risk youth*. Eugene, OR: Oregon School Study Council. 46 pp.

Myll, N. C. (1988). *The dropout prevention handbook: A guide for administrators, counselors and teachers*. Carlsbad, CA: Parker Pub. Co. 208 pp.

National Committee for Citizens in Education. (1987). *Dropout prevention: A book of sources*. Columbia, MD: National Committee for Citizens in Education. Looseleaf.

National Foundation for the Improvement of Education. (1987). *Blueprint for success: Community mobilization for dropout prevention*. Washington, DC: Author. 32 pp.

National Foundation for the Improvement of Education. (1987). *Blueprint for success: Operation Rescue*. Washington, DC: Author. 44 pp.

Natriello, G. (Ed.). (1987). *School dropouts: Patterns and policies*. New York: Teachers College Press. 185 pp.

O'Connor, P. (1985). *Dropout prevention programs that work*. Eugene, OR: Oregon School Study Council. 30 pp.

OERI Urban Superintendents Network. (1987). *Dealing with drop-outs: The urban superintendents' call to action*. Washington, DC: U. S. Government Printing Office. 75 pp.

Oregon Department of Education. (1980). *Oregon early school leavers*. Salem, OR: Author. 39 pp.

Oregon Department of Education. (1988). *Those who leave early: A study of young people leaving Oregon schools prior to graduation*. Salem, OR: Author. 15 pp.

Oregon Department of Education. (1990). *Dropout rates in Oregon high schools: The first year of the student accounting system: State summary report*. Salem, OR: Author.

Orr, M. T. (1987). *What to do about youth dropouts?* Washington, DC: Structured Employment/Economic Development Corporation. 31 pp.

Quick reference guide to school dropouts. (1990). Stockton, CA: International Consulting Associates. 52 pp.

Ranbom, S. (1986). *School dropouts: Everybody's problem.* Washington, DC: Institute for Educational Leadership. 58 pp.

Rumberger, R. W. (1983). Dropping out of high school: The influence of race, sex, and family background. *American Educational Research Journal, 20*(2), 199–220.

Rumberger, R. W. (1986). *High school dropouts: A problem for research, policy, and practice.* Stanford, CA: Stanford School of Education. 36 pp.

Rumberger, R. W. (1987). High school dropouts: A review of issues and evidence. *Review of Educational Research, 57*(2), 101–122.

Sherman, J. D. (1987). *Strategies for financing state dropout programs.* Prepared for Consortium on Education and Employment Initiatives for Dropout-Prone Youth (No. AR-87-1). Denver, CO: Education Commission of the States. 31 pp.

Staying power: Leaving school too soon. (1987). Augusta, ME: Department of Educational and Cultural Services. 23 pp.

Task Force on the New York State Dropout Problem. (1986). *Dropping out of school in New York State: The invisible people of color.* New York: New York State African American Institute of the State University of New York. 45 pp.

Texas Education Agency. (1989). *Effective schools research and dropout reduction.* Austin, TX: Texas Dropout Information Clearinghouse. 15 pp.

Weis, L., Farrar, E., & Petrie, H. G. (1989). *Dropouts from school: Issues, dilemmas, and solutions.* Albany, NY: State University of New York. 238 pp.

Zane, N. (1988). *In their own voices: Young women talk about dropping out.* Washington, DC: Project on Equal Education Rights of the NOW Defense and Education Fund. 22 pp.

Drugs/Substance Abuse

Amuleru-Marshall, O. (1990). Substance abuse among America's urban youth. *Urban League Review, 13*(1–2), 93–98.

Anderson, P. S. (1990). *Directory of course work in drugs and alcohol education: Western edition.* Portland, OR: Northwest Regional Educational Laboratory. 143 pp.

Arkin, E. B., & Funkhauser, J. E. (Eds.). (1990). *Communicating about alcohol and other drugs: Strategies for reaching populations at risk.* Rockville, MD: OSAP Prevention Monograph-5. (ERIC Document Reproduction Service No. ED 334 291). 418 pp.

Bempchat, J., et al. (1989). *Teenage pregnancy and drug abuse: Sources of problem behaviours.* Washington, DC: Office of Educational Research and Improvement. (ERIC Document Reproduction Service No. ED 316 615) 4 pp.

Cahalan, D. (1991). *An ounce of prevention: Strategies for solving tobacco, alcohol and drug problems.* San Francisco, CA: Jossey-Bass. 290 pp.

Connecticut State Dept. of Education. (1988). *Substance abuse prevention education.* Special Topics Curriculum Resources Packet. Hartford, CT: Author. (ERIC Document Reproduction Service No. ED 298 395). 89 pp.

DuPont, R. L. (Ed.). (1989). *Stopping alcohol and other drug use before it starts: The future of prevention,* Rockville, MD: Alcohol, Drug Use and Mental Health Administration. (ERIC Document Reproduction Service No. ED 332 104). 118 pp.

Gittins, N. E. (Ed.). (1988). *Fighting drugs in the schools: A legal manual.* Alexandria, VA: National School Boards Assn. (ERIC Document Reproduction Service No. ED 302 916). 143 pp.

Green, M. (1987). *Intervention strategies with adolescents: The Newton model.* Lincoln, NE: Presented at the Annual National Symposium on Building Family Strengths. (ERIC Document Reproduction Service No. ED 284 142). 17 pp.

Hansen, K. H. (1986). *Substance abuse in schools: Statewide educational policy issues.* Program Report. Portland, OR: Northwest Regional Education Lab. (ERIC Document Reproduction Service No. ED 278 118). 9 pp.

Hicks, B. H. & Wilson, G. A. (Eds.). *Kids, crack and the community: Reclaiming drug-exposed infants and children.* Bloomington, IN: National Educational Service. 163 pp.

Horan, J. J., et al. (1990). *A world of drug use.* Alexandria, VA: American School Counselor Association. (ERIC Document Reproduction Service No. ED 315 687). 51 pp.

Horton, L. (1985). *Adolescent alcohol abuse.* (Fastback No. 217). Bloomington, IN: Phi Delta Kappa Educational Foundation.

Johnson, J. L. (1988). The challenge of substance abuse. *Teaching Exceptional Children, 20*(4), 29–31.

Johnson, T. M., et al. (1987). *REACH Program.* Presented at the annual meeting of the Northwest Regional Educational Laboratory, Portland OR. (ERIC Document Reproduction Service No. ED 282 159). 9 pp.

Lachance, L. L. (1989). *Alcohol, drugs and adolescents.* First Edition. Ann Arbor, MI. ERIC Clearinghouse on Counseling and Personnel Services. (ERIC Document Reproduction Service No. ED 307 526). 116 pp.

Learning to live drug free: A curriculum model for prevention. (1990). Rockville, MD: National Clearinghouse for Alcohol and Drug Information.

Leatt, D. J. (1987). *Schools against drugs: The impact program at Newberg School District.* Eugene, OR: Oregon School Study Council. (ERIC Document Reproduction Service No. ED 278 109). 31 pp.

Melville, K. (Ed.). (1989). *The drug crisis: Public strategies for breaking the habit.* Dubuque, IA: Kettering Foundation. 28 pp.

Moore, D. (1987). *Handicapped adolescent alcohol and drug use/abuse: Some causes for concern.* Presented at the Annual Smith Research Conference, Bloomington, IN: (ERIC Document Reproduction Service No. ED 293 249). 20 pp.

Naginey, J. L., & Swisher, J. D. (1990). To whom should adolescents turn with drug problems? Implications for school professionals. *High School Journal, 73*(2), 80–85.

National Association of State Boards of Education. (1987). *Helping youth say no: A parent's guide to helping teenagers cope with peer pressure.* Alexandria, VA: Author. 20 pp.

Onestak, D. M., et al. (1989). *Family variables and alcohol use in high risk adolescents.* Rockville, MD: National Institute on Drug Abuse. (ERIC Document Reproduction Service No. ED 313 624). 22 pp.

Pearish, P. L. (1988). *An annotated bibliography of literature analyzing factors of adolescent drug use/abuse and the effectiveness of various drug abuse prevention programs.* South Bend, IN: Indiana University, Exit Project. 37 pp.

Reddick, T. L., & Peach, L. E. (1990). *A study of characteristics profiling at-risk students and influences impacting their rural environment.* presented at the Annual Conference of the National Social Science Association, Houston, TX. 15 pp.

Rist, M. C. (1990). The shadow children. *American School Board Journal, 177*(1), 18–24.

Silverman, W. H. (1987). *Guidelines for competence and skills development for substance abuse prevention.* Presented at the annual meeting of the Southeastern Psychological Association, Atlanta, GA. 17 pp.

Sparks, S. N. (1992). *Children of prenatal substance abuse.* Canton, CT: Singular Pub. Group. 192 pp.

U. S. Department of Education. (1986). *Schools without drugs: The challenge.* Washington, DC: Author.

U. S. Department of Education. (1987). *What works: Schools without drugs.* Washington, DC: Author. 78 pp.

U. S. Department of Education. (1989). *Growing up drug free: A parents' guide to prevention.* Washington, DC: Author. 52 pp.

U. S. Department of Justice. (1988). *An invitation to Project DARE: Drug abuse resistance education.* Washington, DC: U. S. Bureau of Justice Assistance. 10 pp.

Ungerleider, S., & Caudill, B. D. (1988). *IMPACT: An early intervention project.* Eugene, OR: Intergrated Research Services. 21 pp.

University of Oregon. (1991). *At-risk youth in crisis: A handbook for collaboration between schools and social services. Volume 4: Substance abuse.* Eugene, OR: Author. 64 pp.

Waller, M. B. (1993). Helping crack-affected children succeed. *Educational Leadership, 50*(4), 57–60.

Wright, L. S. (1985). High school polydrug users and abusers. *Adolescence, 20*(80), 853–861.

Ethnicity

Abi-Nader, J. (1990). *Helping minority high school students redefine their self-image through culturally sensitive instruction.* American Educational Research Association. (ERIC Document Reproduction Service No. ED 319 831). 18 pp.

Anderson, B. J. (1990). Minorities and mathematics: The new frontier and challenges of the nineties. *Journal of Negro Education, 59*(3), 260–272.

Anderson, S. E. (1990). Worldmath curriculum: Fighting ethnocentricism in mathematics. *Journal of Negro Education, 59*(3), 348–359.

Ayim, M. (1979). What price socialization? From the ledgers of the oppressed. *Interchange on Educational Policy, 10*(2), 78–94.

Bailey, R. (1990). Mathematics for millions, science for the people: Comments on black students and the mathematics, science and technology pipeline. *Journal of Negro Education, 59*(3), 239–245.

Banks, J. A. (1977). *Multiethnic education: Practices and promises.* (Fastback No. 87). Bloomington, IN: Phi Delta Kappa Educational Foundation. 34 pp.

Baruth, L. G. & Manning, M. L. (1992). Understanding and counseling Hispanic American children. *Elementary School Guidance and Counseling, 27*(2), 113–122.

Benjamin, M. P., & Morgan, P. C. (1989). *Refugee children traumatized by war and violence: The challenge offered to the service delivery system.* Washington, DC: Georgetown Univ. Child Development Center. (ERIC Document Reproduction Service No. ED 326 598). 61 pp.

Bowker, A. (1992). The American Indian female dropout. *Journal of American Indian Education, 31*(3), 3–20.

Cahape, P. & Howley, C. B. (1992). *Indian nations at risk: Listening to the people.* Charleston, WV: ERIC Clearinghouse on Rural Education and Small Schools. 116 pp.

Cardenas, J. A., et al. (1988). *The Undereducation of American youth.* San Antonio, TX: Intercultural Development Research Association. (ERIC Document Reproduction Service No. ED 309 201). 33 pp.

Chavers, D. (1991). Indian education: Dealing with a disaster. *Principal, 70*(3), 28–29.

Chavkin, N. F. (1990). Joining Forces: Education for a changing population. *Educational Horizons, 68*(4), 190–196.

Children's Defense Fund. (1990). *Latino youths at a crossroads.* Washington, DC: Author. 32 pp.

Clayton, C. (1989). Children of value: We 'can' educate all our children. *The Nation, 249*(4), 132–135.

Cordeiro, P. A. (1991). *An ethnography of high achieving at-risk Hispanic youths at two urban high schools: Implications for administrators.* Annual meeting of the American Educational Research Association, Chicago, IL. (ERIC Document Reproduction Service No. ED 330 088). 43 pp.

Dawson, M. (1987). *Minority student performance: Is the Montessori magnet school effective?* TX. (ERIC Document Reproduction Service No. ED 309 881). 24 pp.

Denbo, S. (Comp.). (1990). *Effective schools for culturally diverse students: An annotated bibliography.* Washington, DC: American Univ., Mid-Atlantic Equity Center. (ERIC Document Reproduction Service No. ED 324 391). 67 pp.

Duany, L., & Pittman, K. (1990). *Latino youths at a crossroads.* Washington, DC: Children's Defense Fund. 32 pp.

Escalante, J., & Dirmann, J. (1990). The Jaime Escalante Program. *Journal of Negro Education, 59*(3), 407–423.

Eubanks, E. E., & Parish, R. I. (1990). Why does the status quo persist? *Phi Delta Kappan, 72*(3), 196–197.

Foody, M., et al. (1990). *Developing a plan for multi-cultural education.* Syracuse, NY: Syracuse City School District. (ERIC Document Reproduction Service No. ED 327 605). 21 pp.

Frankenstein, M. (1990). Incorporating race, gender, and class issues into a critical mathematical literacy curriculum. *Journal of Negro Education, 59*(3), 336–347.

Gandara, P. (1989). Those children are ours: Moving toward community. *Equity and Choice, 5*(2), 5–12.

Garcia, E. E. (1990). *An analysis of literacy enhancement for middle school Hispanic students through curriculum integration.* Annual meeting of the National Reading Conference, Miami, FL. (ERIC Document Reproduction Service No. ED 331–008). 25 pp.

Glenn, C. L. (1989). Just schools for minority children. *Phi Delta Kappan, 70*(10), 777–779.

Goodstein, C. (1989). Educating the children about race relations: The role of teachers and parents. *Crisis, 96*(9), 23–25.

Harris, J. J., III, & Ford, D. V. (1991). Identifying and nurturing the promise of gifted black American children. *Journal of Negro Education, 60*(1), 3–18.

Haycock, K., & Duany, L. (1991). Developing the potential of Latino students. *Principal, 70*(3), 25–27.

Holzman, L., & Strickland, G. (1988). *Braking the abuser abused paradigm in the classroom.* American Psychological Association Convention, Atlanta, GA. (ERIC Document Reproduction Service No. ED 301 630). 7 pp.

Hopkins, D. (1987). *The first Americans: A review of the births and deaths of American Indians in Oregon.* Portland, OR: Oregon Department of Human Resources. 45 pp.

Houston, R. L. (1988). *The education of minority students in non-urban schools.* Philadelphia, PA: Research for Better Schools. (ERIC Document Reproduction Service No. ED 328 634). 29 pp.

Hunter, R. C. (1988). *Children at risk.* MD: Southern Education Foundation. (ERIC Document Reproduction Service No. ED 314 532). 18 pp.

King-Stoops, J. (1980). *Migrant education: Teaching the wandering ones.* (Fastback No. 145). Bloomington, IN: Phi Delta Kappa Educational Foundation. 44 pp.

Lake, R. (Medicine Grizzlybear). (1990). An Indian father's plea. *Teacher Magazine, 2*(1), 48–53. September.

Lincoln, C. A., & Higgins, N. M. (1991). Making schools that work for all children. *Principal, 70*(3), 6–8.

Majka, L. (1990). Vietnamese Amerasians in the United States. *Migration World Magazine, 18*(1), 4–7.

Maker, C. J., & Schiever, S. W. (Eds.). (1989). *Defensible programs for cultural and ethnic minorities. Critical issues in gifted education,* Vol. II. Austin, TX: Pro-Ed. (ERIC Document Reproduction Service No. ED 329 634). 376 pp.

Martin, R. (1990). *Making the computer laboratory accessible to minorities.* Annual meeting of the Association of Teacher Educators, Last Vegas, NV. (ERIC Document Reproduction Service No ED 322 896). 16 pp.

Massachusetts Institute of Technology, Quality Education for Minorities Project. (1990). *Education that works: An action plan for the education of minorities.* Cambridge, MA: Author. (ERIC Document Reproduction Service no. ED 316 627). 24 pp.

McDowell, C. L. (1990). The unseen world: Race, class and gender analysis in science education research. *Journal of Negro Education, 59*(3), 273–291.

Melville, K. (Ed.). (1990). *Remedies for racial inequality: Why progress has stalled, what should be done.* Dubuque, IA: Kendall/Hunt. 39 pp.

Mock, K. R. (1988). *Multicultural and anti-racist education: The developmental rationale and practical implications.* Ontario, Canada. (ERIC Document Reproduction Service No. ED 304 243). 19 pp.

Morrow, R. D. (1991). The challenge of Southeast Asian parental involvement. *Principal, 70*(3), 20–22.

Murray, C. B., & Clark, R. M. (1990). Targets of racism. *American School Board Journal, 177*(6), 22–24.

National Education Association. (1987). *American Indian/Alaska Native Concerns.* Washington, DC: Author. (ERIC Document Reproduction Service No. ED 310 185). 31 pp.

National Education Association. (1987). *And justice for all.* Washington, DC: Author. (ERIC Document Reproduction Service No. ED 310 184). 113 pp.

National Education Association. (1987). *Hispanic concerns.* Washington, DC: Author. (ERIC Document Reproduction Service No. ED 310 188). 23 pp.

North Carolina State Department of Public Instruction. (1989). *Bright ideas that work: A booklet of school programs that impact minority and equity issues.* Raleigh, NC: Author. (ERIC Document Reproduction Service No. ED 310 196). 42 pp.

Northwest Regional Educational Lab. (1989). *Resegregation of public schools: The third generation.* A Report on the condition of desegregation in America's public schools by the Network of Regional Desegregation Assistance Centers. Portland, OR: Author. (ERIC Document Reproduction Service No. ED 331 895). 54 pp.

Pevonka, D., et al. (1988). Positive role models combat race and sex stereotypes. *Executive Educator, 10*(11), 26, 28.

Pulido, A. (1991). One big family. *Thrust for Educational Leadership, 20*(4), 12–14.

Ready, T. (1989). *Washington Latinos at the crossroads: Passages of at-risk youths from adolescence to adulthood.* Washington, DC: Catholic Univ. of America., Dept. of Anthropology. (ERIC Document Reproduction Service No. ED 329 614). 177 pp.

Reyes, P., & Capper, C. (1990). *Urban principals: A critical perspective on the context of minority student outcomes.* Wisconsin. (ERIC Document Reproduction Service No. ED 320 995). 50 pp.

Reyhner, J. (1992). American Indians out of school: A review of school-based causes and solutions. *Journal of American Indian Education, 31*(3), 21–36.

Rong, X. L., & Grant, L. (1990). *Ethnicity, immigrant generation status, and school attainment of Asians, Hispanics and non-Hispanic Whites.* Annual meeting of the American Educational Research Association, Boston. (ERIC Document Reproduction Service No. ED 319 828). 52 pp.

Rong, X. L., & Preissle-Goetz, J. (1990). *High school dropouts among foreign-born Whites, Hispanics and Asians.* Annual meeting of the American Educational Research Association, Boston. (ERIC Document Reproduction Service No. ED 319 827). 37 pp.

Samuda, R. J., et al. (1989). *Assessment and placement of minority students.* Toronto, Ont: (ERIC Document Reproduction Service No. ED 318 822). 243 pp.

Sanchez, J. & et al. (1992). Dropping out: Hispanic students, attrition, and the family. *College and University, 67*(2), 145–150.

Schwartz, W. (1988). *Recent literature on urban and minority education.* New York: ERIC Clearinghouse on Urban Education. (ERIC Document Reproduction Service No. ED 311 136). 4 pp.

Spencer, M. B. (1990). Development of minority children: An introduction. *Child Development, 61*(2), 267–269.

Spencer, M. B., & Markstrom-Adams, C. (1990). Identity processing among racial and ethnic minority children in America. *Child Development, 61*(2), 290–309.

Swisher, K. & Hoisch, M. (1992). Dropping out among American Indians and Alaska natives: A review of studies. *Journal of American Indian Education, 31*(2), 3–23.

Thompson, H. G. (1987). *Oregon women: A report on their education, employment, and economic status.* Salem, OR: Oregon Department of Education. 44 pp.

Tyler, R. H. (1989). Educating children from minority families. *Educational Horizons, 67*(4), 114–118.

Washington Office of the State Superintendent of Public Instruction. *(1989). Perspectives on equal educational opportunities. Something for thought: What is the answer?* Olympia, WA: Author. (ERIC Document Reproduction Service No. ED 309 223). 20 pp.

Zanger, V. V., et al. (1990). *Drawing on diversity: A handbook for and by Boston teachers in multicultural, multiracial classrooms.* Boston: Boston Public Schools. (ERIC Document Reproduction Service No. ED 323 281). 48 pp.

Family Involvement

Comer, J. P., et al. (1986, August). *Academic and affective gains from the School Development Program: A model for school improvement.* Paper presented at the annual meeting of the American Psychological Association, Washington, DC. (ERIC Document Reproduction Service No. ED 274 750). 56 pp.

Comer, J. P. (1986). Parent participation in the schools. *Phi Delta Kappan, 67*(6), 442–446.

Comer, J. P. (1985). *Psychosocial and academic effects of an intervention program among minority school children.* New Haven, CT: Yale University, Child Study Center. (ERIC Document Reproduction No. ED 286 946). 20 pp.

Comer, J. P. (1986). *Yale Child Study Center School Development Program: Development history and long-term effects.* New Haven, CT: Yale University, Child Study Center. (ERIC Document Reproduction No. ED 283 910). 25 pp.

Duquette, D. M., & Boo, K. (1986). *Helping youth decide: A workshop guide.* Alexandria, VA: National Association of State Boards of Education. 41 pp.

Education Commission of the States. (1988). *Drawing in the family: Family involvement in the schools.* Denver, CO: Author. 32 pp.

Education Writers Association. (1988). *Myth #6: Schools know how to work with parents*. Washington, DC: Author. (ERIC Document Reproduction Service No. ED 317 869). 7 pp.

Henderson, A. T., & Marburger, C. L. (1990). *A workbook on parent involvement for district leaders*. Columbia, MD: National Committee for Citizens in Education. 160 pp.

Henderson, A. T., Marburger, C. L., & Ooms, T. (1986). *Beyond the bake sale: An educator's guide to working with parents*. Columbia, MD: National Committee for Citizens in Education. 139 pp.

Lareau, A. (1989). *Home advantage*. Philadelphia: Falmer. 252 pp.

Lindner, B. (1987). *Family diversity and school policy*. Denver, CO: Education Commission of the States. 21 pp.

Melaville, A., Blank, M., Asayesh, G. (1993). *Together we can: A guide for crafting a pro-family system of education and human services*. Washington, DC: U.S. Department of Education.

Peterson, D. (1989). *Parent involvement in the educational process*. (ERIC Digest Series No. EA 43). (ERIC Document Reproduction Service No. ED 312 776). 4 pp.

Swap, S. M. (1990). *Parent involvement and success for all children: What we know now*. Boston: Institute for Responsive Education. 82 pp.

Wikelund, K. R. (1990). *Schools and communities together: A guide to parent involvement*. Portland, OR: Northwest Regional Educational Laboratory. 93 pp.

Health/AIDS

AIDS, suicide, drugs. The best of ERIC on educational management No. 95. (1988). Eugene, OR: ERIC Clearinghouse on Educational Management. (ERIC Document Reproduction No. ED 311 604). 5 pp.

AIDS and teenagers: Emerging issues. (1988). Hearing before the Select Committee on Children, Youth and Families. House of Rep., 100th Congress, 1st Session. Washington, DC. (ERIC Document Reproduction Service No. ED 293 070). 244 pp.

Calamidas, E. G. (1991). Teaching youth about AIDS: Challenges confronting health educators. *Health Values: Health Behavior, Education and Promotion, 15*(6), 55–61.

Canadian Association of Principals. (1991). *AIDS: preparing your school and community*. Ottawa, Canada: Author. 73 pp.

Center for Population Options. (1990). *AIDS facts pack*. Washington, D.C: Author. (ERIC Document Reproduction Service No. ED 328 868). 8 pp.

Center for Population Options. (1990). *Reaching high-risk youth through model AIDS education programs: A case by case study*. Washington, DC: Author. (ERIC Document Reproduction Service No. ED 331 910). 21 pp.

Claymore, B. J., & Taylor, M. A. (1989). AIDS—tribal nations face the newest communicable disease: An Aberdeen Area perspective. *American Indian Culture and Research Journal, 13*(3–4), 21–31.

Dryfoos, J. G. (1991). School-based social and health services for at-risk students. *Urban Education, 26*(1), 118–137.

DuRant, R. H. & et al. (1992). High school students' knowledge of HIV/AIDS and perceived risk of currently having AIDS. *Journal of School Health, 62*(2), 59–63.

Gardner, W., et al. (1990). Adolescents' AIDS risk taking: A rational choice perspective. *New Directions for Child Development, 50,* 17–34.

Grossman, A. H. (1991). HIV and at-risk youth: The myth of invulnerability. *Parks and Recreation, 26*(11), 52–55.

Haffner, D. W. (1987). *AIDS and adolescents: The time for prevention is now.* Washington, DC: Center for Population Options. 31 pp.

House, R. M. & Walker, C. M. (1993). Preventing AIDS via education. *Journal of Counseling and Development, 71*(3), 282–289.

Johnson, K. A. (1986). *Building health programs for teenagers.* Washington, DC: Children's Defense Fund. 19 pp.

Johnson, K. A. (1988). *Teens and AIDS: Opportunities for prevention.* Washington, DC: Children's Defense Fund. 30 pp.

Johnson, K. A. (1990). *Improving health programs for low-income youths.* Washington, DC: Children's Defense Fund. 17 pp.

Krueger, M. (1993). Everyone is an exception: Assumptions to avoid in the sex education classroom. *Phi Delta Kappan, 74*(7), 569–572.

Levy, S. (1987). Investing in the health of at-risk youth: School based health clinics in the south. Model Programs for Southern Economic Development. *Foresight* 4(3). (ERIC Document Reproduction Service No. ED 290 826). 24 pp.

Liontos, L. B. (1991). *Involving the families of at-risk youth in the educational process.* Trends and Issues Series, No. 5. Washington, DC: Office of Educational Research and Improvement. (ERIC Document Reproduction Service No. ED 328 946). 39 pp.

Lumsden, L. S. (1990). HIV/AIDS education: The challenge of reducing high-risk behaviours. Eugene, OR: *Oregon School Study Council Bulletin,* 34(3). (ERIC Document Reproduction Service No. ED 326 950). 48 pp.

Luna, G. C. (1989). *AIDS and Native youth.* Vancouver, BC: Paper presented at the Canadian Conference on AIDS and Related Issues in the Native Community. (ERIC Document Reproduction Service No. ED 324 186). 7 pp.

Melville, K. (1988). *Coping with AIDS: The public response to the epidemic.* Dayton, OH: Kendall/Hunt. 44 pp.

Miller, L. & Becker-Dunn, E. (1993). HIV at school. *American School Board Journal, 180*(2), 42–45.

Nadel, M. V. (1990). *AIDS education: Gaps in coverage still exist.* Washington, DC: General Accounting Office. (ERIC Document Reproduction Service No. ED 318 978). 14 pp.

Natale, J. A. (1993). Bad timing in education's battle against AIDS. *American School Board Journal, 180*(2), 40–41.

National School Boards Association. (1989). *Reducing the risk: A school leader's guide to AIDS education.* Alexandria, VA: (ERIC Document Reproduction Service No. ED3 20 272). 49 pp.

National School Boards Association. (1990). *HIV prevention education in the nation's public schools.* Alexandria, VA: Author. (ERIC Document Reproduction Service No. ED 320 308). 32 pp.

Perez, R., & Johnson, K. A. (1989). *Lack of health insurance makes a difference.* Washington, DC: Children's Defense Fund.

Quackenbush, M., & Sargent, P. (1986). *Teaching AIDS: A resource guide on acquired immune deficiency syndrome.* Santa Cruz, CA: Network Publications. (ERIC Document Reproduction Service No. ED 277 936). 116 pp.

Sheckler, P. (1993). When a student is HIV positive. *Educational Leadership, 50*(4), 55–56.

Summerfield, L. (1990). *Adolescents and AIDS.* Washington, DC: ERIC Clearinghouse on Teacher Education. (ERIC Document Reproduction Service No. ED 319 742). 4 pp.

Tonks, D. (1993). Can you save your students' lives? Educating to prevent AIDS. *Educational Leadership, 50*(4), 48–51.

Weed, D. S. (1990). *Providing consultation to primary prevention programs: Applying the technology of community psychology.* Paper presented at the Annual Convention of the American Psychological Association, Boston. (ERIC Document Reproduction Service No. ED 326 773). 17 pp.

Wilcox, B. L., et al. (1990). Protecting adolescents from AIDS. *New Directions for Child Development, 50,* 71–75.

Woodruff, J. O., et al. (1989). *Troubled adolescents and HIV infection.* Washington, DC: Georgetown Univ. Child Development Center. (ERIC Document Reproduction Service No. ED 325 776). 152 pp.

Poverty

Baas, A. (1991). *Promising strategies for at-risk youth.* ERIC Digest. No. 59. Eugene, OR: ERIC Clearinghouse on Educational Management. (ERIC Document Reproduction Service No. ED 328 958). 3 pp.

Children's Defense Fund. (1990). *Children 1990: A report card, briefing book and action primer.* Washington, DC: Author. (ERIC Document Reproduction Service No. ED 315 188). 111 pp.

Children's Defense Fund. (1991). *Child poverty in America.* Washington, DC: Author. 39 pp.

Council of Chief State School Officers. (1989). *Family support: Education and involvement. A guide for state action.* Washington, DC: Author. (ERIC Document Reproduction Service No. ED 319 112). 71 pp.

Farkas, G. (1990). Cultural resources and school success: Gender, ethnicity and poverty groups within an urban school district. *American Sociological Review, 55*(1), 127–142.

Golden, O. (1992). *Poor children and welfare reform.* New York: Foundation for Child Development. 205 pp.

Hill, D. (1990). A theory of success and failure. *Teacher Magazine, 1*(9), 40–45.

Hogue, C. J. R., & Hargraves, M. A. (1993). Class, race, and infant mortality in the United States. *American Journal of Public Health, 83*(1), 9–12.

Kennedy, M. M., et al. (1986). *Poverty, achievement and the distribution of compensatory education services.* (1986). Designs for Contemporary Education: Conference proceedings and papers, Washington, DC. (ERIC Document Reproduction Service No. ED 292 902). 13 pp.

KleeMihaly, L. (1991). *Homeless families: Failed policies and young victims.* Washington, DC: Children's Defense Fund. 25 pp.

Knapp, M. S., & Shields, P. M. (Eds.). (1991). *Better schooling for the children of poverty: Attitudes to conventional wisdom.* Berkeley, CA: McCutchan Publishing Corp.

Knapp, M. S., Turnbull, B. J., & Shields, P. M. (1990). New directions for educating the children of poverty. *Educational Leadership, 48*(1), 4–8.

Liontos, L. B. (1990). *Collaboration between schools and social services.* ERIC Digest Series, No. EA 48. ERIC Clearinghouse on Educational Management, Eugene, OR. (ERIC Document Reproduction Service No. ED 320 197). 4 pp.

Liontos, L. B. (1991). Involving the families of at-risk youth in the educational process. Trends and Issues series, No. 5. Eugene, OR: ERIC Clearinghouse on Educational Management. (ERIC Document Reproduction Service No. ED 328 946). 39 pp.

Nathan, J. (1991). Towards educational change and economic justice: An interview with Herbert Kohl. *Phi Delta Kappan, 72*(9), 678–681.

National Association of State Boards of Education. (1989). *Joining forces: Linking the education and social welfare systems to help at-risk children and youth.* Alexandria, VA: Author. (ERIC Document Reproduction Service No. ED 302 917). 7 pp.

National Center for Children in Poverty. (1990). *Five million children: A statistical profile of our poorest young citizens.* New York: Columbia Univ. (ERIC Document Reproduction Service No. ED 330 740). 17 pp.

Ramey, C. T., & Ramey, S. L. (1990). Intensive educational intervention for children of poverty. *Intelligence, 14*(1), 1–9.

Urban Strategies Council. (1988). *A chance for every child: Oakland's infants, children and youth at risk for persistent poverty.* Oakland, CA: Author. (ERIC Document Reproduction Service No. ED 330 729). 74 pp.

School Choice

Archbald, D. A. (1991). School choice and changing authority: An analysis of the controversy over the Minnesota Postsecondary Enrollment Options Law. *Journal of Education Policy, 6*(1), 1–16.

Ascher, C. (1993). *Changing schools for urban students: the school development program, accelerated schools, and success for all.* New York: ERIC Clearinghouse on Urban Education, Columbia University. 41 pp.

Association for Supervision and Curriculum Development. (1990). *Public schools of choice.* Alexandria, VA: Author. (ERIC Document Reproduction Service No. ED 322 596). 53 pp.

Barr, R. D. (1982). Magnet schools: An attractive alternative. *Principal, 61*(3), 37–40.

Boyd, W. L., & Walberg, H. J. (1990). *Choice in education: Potential and problems.* Berkeley, CA: McCutchan. 287 pp.

Carver, R. L., & Salganik, L. H. (1991). You can't have choice without information: Strategies for reaching families. *Equity and Choice, 7*(2–3), 71–75.

Clinchy, E. (1989). Public school choice: Absolutely necessary, but not wholly sufficient. *Phi Delta Kappan, 71*(4), 289–294.

Cookson, P. W., Jr. (1991). Private schooling and equity: Dilemmas of choice. *Education and Urban Society, 23*(2), 185–199.

Elmore, R. F. (1990). *Working models of choice in public education.* CPRE Report Series RR-018. Center for Policy Research in Education. (ERIC Document Reproduction Service No. ED 332 350). 30 pp.

Farrell, Walter C., Jr., & Mathews, Jackolyn E. (1990). School choice and the educational opportunities of African American children. *Journal of Negro Education, 59*(4), 526–537.

Glenn, C. L. (1989). Putting school choice in place. *Phi Delta Kappan, 71*(4), 295–300.

Harris, J. J., III, et al. (1991). What should our public choose? The debate over School Choice Policy. *Education and Urban Society, 23*(2), 159–174.

Hopfenberg, W. S., Levin, H. M., et al. (1993). *The accelerated schools: Resource guide.* San Francisco, CA: Jossey-Bass Inc. 369 pp.

Kroeger, M., et al. (1989). *Choice: Implementation issues. A national perspective.* Policy Briefs No. 3. Elmhurst, IL: North Central Regional Educational Lab. (ERIC Document Reproduction Service No. ED 330 092). 8 pp.

Levin, H. M. (1991). The economics of educational choice. *Economics of Education Review, 10*(2), 137–158.

McCurdy, J. (1985). *Choices in schools: What's ahead and what to do.* Arlington, VA: National School Public Relations Assoc. (ERIC Document Reproduction Service No. ED 264 649). 62 pp.

McDowelle, J. O., & Wilson, H. E. (1991). *Clarifying issues of educational choice for the parent.* Presented at the annual meeting of the American Association of School Administrators, New Orleans, LA. (ERIC Document Reproduction Service No. ED 330 120). 18 pp.

Moore, D. R., & Davenport, S. (1989). *The new improved sorting machine: Concerning school choice.* Chicago: Designs for Change. 120 pp.

Nathan, J. (1989). Helping all children, empowering all educators: Another view of school choice. *Phi Delta Kappan, 71*(4), 304–307.

Oakland University School of Human and Educational Services. (1988). *Schools of choice: An annotated catalog of key choice elements: Open enrollment, diversity and empowerment.* Rochester, MI: Author. (ERIC Document Reproduction Service No. ED 329 600). 69 pp.

Paulu, N. (1989). *Improving schools and empowering parents: Choice in American education.* Washington, DC: U.S. Department of Education, Office of Educational Research and Improvement. 48 pp.

Pearson, J. (1989). Response to Joe Nathan. *Phi Delta Kappan, 71*(4), 308–310.

Raywid, M. A. (1989). *The case for public schools of choice.* (Fastback No. 283). Bloomington, IN: Phi Delta Kappa Educational Foundation. 45 pp.

Scovic, S. P. (1991). Let's stop thinking educational choice is the answer to restructured schools. *School Administrator, 48*(1), 16–17, 19, 21.

Seeley, D. S. (1991). The major new case for choice is only half right. *Equity and Choice, 7*(1), 28–33.

Uchitelle, S. (1989). What it really takes to make school choice work. *Phi Delta Kappan, 71*(4), 301–303.

Whealey, L. D. (1991). Choice or elitism? *American School Board Journal, 178*(4), 33, 44.

Willie, C. V. (1991). Controlled choice: An alternative desegregation plan for minorities who feel betrayed. *Education and Urban Society, 23*(2), 200–207.

Willie, C. V. (1991). Controlled choice avoids the pitfalls of choice plans: Response to John Chubb and Terry Moe. *Educational Leadership, 48*(4), 62–64.

Yap, K. O. (1991). *Educational empowerment: A formative look at choice and equity.* Presented at the annual meeting of the American Educational Research Association, Chicago, IL.

Young, T. W. (1990). *Public alternative education: Options and choice for today's schools.* New York: Teachers College Press. 144 pp.

Suicide

Andrews, J. A., & Lewisohn, P. M. (1990). *The prevalence, lethality and intent of suicide attempts among adolescents.* Boston: Annual Convention of the American Psychological Association. (ERIC Document Reproduction Service No. ED 327 800). 10 pp.

Bar-Joseph, H., & Tzuriel, D. (1990). Suicidal tendencies and ego identity in adolescents. *Adolescence, 25*(97), 215–223.

Barrett, T. C. (1987). *Youth in crisis: Seeking solutions to self-destructive behavior.* Longmont, CO: Sopris West. Looseleaf, 217 pp.

Capuzzi, D., & Gross, D. R. (Eds.). (1989). *Youth at risk: A resource for counselors, teachers and parents.* Alexandria, VA: American Association for Counseling and Development. (ERIC Document Reproduction Service No. ED 323 454). 401 pp.

Charles, G., & Coleman, H. (1990). Child and adolescent suicide. *Canadian Home Economics Journal, 40*(2), 72–75.

Charles, G., & Matheson, J. (1991). Suicide prevention and intervention with young people in foster care in Canada. *Child Welfare, 70*(2), 185–191.

Cochran, K. S., & Turner, A. L. (1986). *Adolescent suicide and the role of the school as seen by secondary school principals. Research monograph.* Commerce, Texas: East Texas School Study Council. (ERIC Document Reproduction Service No. ED 297 474). 56 pp.

Cole, R. W., Jr. (Ed). (1988). *Adolescent suicide.* (Hot Topics Series). Bloomington, IN: Phi Delta Kappa Educational Foundation. 251 pp.

Davis, J. M. & Sandoval, J. (1991). *Suicidal youth: School-based intervention and prevention.* San Francisco, CA: Jossey-Bass. 269 pp.

Delisle, J. R. (1990). The gifted adolescent at risk: Strategies and resources for suicide prevention among gifted youth. *Journal for the Education of the Gifted, 13*(3), 212–228.

Dempsey, R. A. (1986). *Adolescent suicide. The trauma of adolescent suicide. A time for special leadership by principals.* Reston, VA: National Association of Secondary School Principals. (ERIC Document Reproduction Service No. ED 276 916). 25 pp.

Frymier, J. (1988). Understanding and preventing teen suicide. *Phi Delta Kappan, 70*(4), 290–93.

Gebbie, K. M. (1986). *Teenage suicide in Oregon: 1983–1985.* Portland, OR: Oregon Department of Human Resources, Center for Health Statistics. 17 pp.

Gray, J. B., Jr., & Cannon, G. (1989). A model for suicide prevention and intervention for rural areas. *Rural Special Education Quarterly, 10*(1), 17–25.

Gray, L. A. (Ed.). (1990). *At-risk youth: A compilation of counseling technique papers.* Oregon. (ERIC Document Reproduction Service No. ED 323 425). 231 pp.

Hart, T. E. (1989). *Student stress and suicide: How schools are helping.* Eugene, OR: Oregon School Study Council Bulletin, 32(6), (ERIC Document Reproduction Service No. ED 303 887). 45 pp.

Hayes, M. L., & Sloat, R. S. (1989). Gifted students at risk for suicide. *Roeper Review, 12*(2), 102–107.

Hechinger, F. M. (1992). *Fateful choices: Healthy youth for the 21st century.* Washington, DC: Carnegie Council on Adolescent Development. 243 pp.

Hicks, B. B. (1990). *Youth suicide: A comprehensive manual for prevention and intervention.* Bloomington, IN: National Educational Service. 131 pp.

Lennox, C. *(1987). Guidelines for high school suicide prevention programs.* Part of a doctoral program, East Texas State University. (ERIC Document Reproduction Service No. ED 290 099). 35 pp.

Mauk, G. W. (1991). *Adolescent suicide prevention in schools: Managing grief of peer survivors.* Presented at the annual meeting of the Western Psychological Association, San Francisco. (ERIC Document Reproduction Service No. ED 332 127). 33 pp.

Oneal, Z. (1987). Books to help kids deal with difficult times II *School Library Media Quarterly, 15*(3), 165–167.

Pfeifer, J. K. (1988). *Teenage suicide: What can the schools do?* (Fastback No. 234). Bloomington, IN: Phi Delta Kappa Educational Foundation. 36 pp.

Responding to adolescent suicide. (1988). Bloomington, IN: Phi Delta Kappa Educational Task Force on Adolescent Suicide. (ERIC Document Reproduction Service No. ED 301 813). 35 pp.

Sadoff, W. L., & Crandall, A. B. (1987). *A multidisciplinary teen suicide prevention program.* Presented at the annual meeting of the National Association of School Psychologists, New Orleans, LA. (ERIC Document Reproduction Service No. ED 287 127). 13 pp.

Sapp, A. D. (1988). *Songs of despair: A case study of adolescent suicide.* Presented at the annual meeting of the Academy of Criminal Justice Sciences, San Francisco. (ERIC Document Reproduction Service No. ED 297 245). 24 pp.

Stefanowski-Harding, S. (1990). Child suicide: A review of the literature and implications for school counselors. *School Counselor, 37*(5), 328–336.

Suicide prevention and coping: A manual for teachers, counsellors and administrators. (1987). Edmonton, Alberta: Alberta Dept. of Education, Edmonton. Special

Education Services Branch. (ERIC Document Reproduction Service No. ED 289 109). 23 pp.

Suicide prevention program for California public schools. (1987) Sacramento, CA: CA State Dept. of Education. (ERIC Document Reproduction Service No. ED 290 085). 241 pp.

Taylor-Mearhoff, C. (1990). *Suicide prevention: The student assistance model.* PA. (ERIC Document Reproduction Service No. ED 322 410). 8 pp.

University of Oregon. (1991). *At-risk youth in crisis: A handbook for collaboration between schools and social services. Volume 2: suicide.* Eugene, OR: Author. 86 pp.

Van Dyke, C. A. (1988). *An annotated bibliography of the literature dealing with adolescent suicide and what educators can do to help reduce this problem.* South Bend, IN: Indiana University, Exit Project. (ERIC Document Reproduction Service No. ED 307 566). 54 pp.

Vidal, J. A. (1989). *Student suicide: A guide for intervention.* Washington, DC: National Education Association. (ERIC Document Reproduction Service No. ED 311 334). 59 pp.

White, G. L., et al. (1990). Developing a tool to assess suicide risk factors in urban adolescents. *Adolescence, 25*(99), 655–666.

Wolfle, J. A., & Siehl, P. M. (1990). *Adolescent suicide: Prevention starts in childhood.* Ohio. (ERIC Document Reproduction Service No. ED 330 940). 11 pp.

Woodruff, J. (1987). *An educator's guide to the literature dealing with teenage suicide.* South Bend, IN: Indiana University, Exit Project. (ERIC Document Reproduction Service No. ED 292 004). 43 pp.

Teenage Pregnancy and Parenthood

Allen, M. L., Miller, S. R., & Abbey, J. (1987). *Teens in foster care: Preventing pregnancy and building youth self-sufficiency.* Washington, DC: Children's Defense Fund. 27 pp.

Allen, M. L., & Pittman, K. J. (1986). *Welfare and teen pregnancy: What do we know? What do we do?* Washington, DC: Children's Defense Fund. 19 pp.

Bonjean, L. M., & Rittenmeyer, D. C. (1987). *Teenage parenthood: The school's response.* (Fastback No. 264). Bloomington, IN: Phi Delta Kappa Educational Foundation. 30 pp.

Burt, R., & Haffner, D. (1986). *Teenage childbearing: How much does it cost? A guide to determining the local costs of teenage childbearing.* Washington, DC: Center for Population Options. 87 pp.

Children's Defense Fund. (1987). *Adolescent pregnancy: An anatomy of a social problem in search of comprehensive solutions.* Washington, DC: Author. 15 pp.

Children's Defense Fund. (1987). *Child support and teen parents.* Washington, DC: Author. 19 pp.

Collins, K. (1987). *Child care: The time is now.* Washington, DC: Children's Defense Fund. 13 pp.

Dougherty, B., & Lindner, A. F. (1989). *Resources for strengthening teen pregnancy and parenting programs.* Madison, WI: School of Education, University of Wisconsin-Madison.

Drummond, R. J. & Hansford, S. G. (1992). Career aspirations of pregnant teens. *Journal of Employment Conseling, 29*(4), 166–171.

Elster, A. B., & Lamb, M. E. (1986). *Adolescent fatherhood.* Hillsdale, NJ: Erlbaum. 204 pp.

Govan, C., Savage, B., & Pittman, K. J. (1986). *Adolescent pregnancy: What the states are saying.* Washington, DC: Children's Defense Fund. 11 pp.

Harriman, L. C., Wilson, E., & Hale, D. E. (1989). Cooperative extension programs in teen parenting and pregnancy prevention. *Journal of Home Economics, 81*(4), 25–39.

Helge, D. (1989). *Preventing teenage pregnancies in rural America.* [U.S.]. National Rural Development Institute. 34 pp.

Johnson, C., & Sum, A. (1987). *Declining earnings of young men: Their relation to poverty, teen pregnancy, and family formation.* Washington, DC: Children's Defense Fund. 19 pp.

Kallembach, S. C. (1990). *Teen parents: Selected resources for vocational preparation.* Berkeley, CA: National Center for Research in Vocational Education. 52 pp.

Kolb, F. A. (1987). *Pregnant and parenting teens: Keeping them in school.* Andover, MA: Regional Laboratory for Educational Improvement of the Northeast and Islands. 13 pp.

Lerman, R. I. (1986, October). *A national profile of young unwed fathers: Who are they and how are they parenting?* Prepared for Conference on Unwed Fathers, Catholic University. 32 pp.

Lindner, A. F. (1987). *Career planning workbook: From astronaut to zoologist.* Madison, WI: School of Education, University of Wisconsin-Madison. 165 pp.

McClellan, M. C. (Ed.). (1987). *Teenage pregnancy. Hot Topics Series.* Bloomington, IN: Phi Delta Kappa, Center on Evaluation, Development, and Research. 282 pp.

McGee, E. (1985). *Training for transition: A guide for training young mothers in employability skills.* New York: Manpower Demonstration Research Corporation.

Miller, S. R., & Pittman, K. J. (1987). *Opportunities for prevention: Building after-school and summer programs for young adolescents.* Washington, DC: Children's Defense Fund. 26 pp.

Mitchell, F., & Brandis, C. (1987). Adolescent pregnancy: The responsibilities of policymakers. *Health Services Research, 22*(3), 399–437.

Philliber, S. (1989). *Evaluating your adolescent pregnancy program: How to get started.* Washington, DC: Children's Defense Fund. 19 pp.

Pittman, K. J. (1985). *Preventing children having children.* Washington, DC: Children's Defense Fund. 15 pp.

Pittman, K. J. (1986). *Preventing adolescent pregnancy: What schools can do.* Washington, DC: Children's Defense Fund. 15 pp.

Pittman, K. J. (1986). *Adolescent pregnancy: Whose problem is it?* Washington, DC: Children's Defense Fund. 11 pp.

Pittman, K. J., & Adams, G. (1988). *Teenage pregnancy: An advocates's guide to the numbers.* Washington, DC: Children's Defense Fund. 50 pp.

Pittman, K. J., & Adams, G. (1988). *What about the boys? Teenage pregnancy prevention strategies.* Washington, DC: Children's Defense Fund. 42 pp.

Pittman, K. J., Adams-Taylor, S., & O'Brien, R. (1989). *The lessons of multi-site initiatives serving high-risk youths.* Washington, DC: Children's Defense Fund. 27 pp.

Pittman, K. J., & Govan, C. (1986). *Model programs: Preventing adolescent pregnancy and building youth self-sufficiency.* Washington, DC: Children's Defense Fund. 19 pp.

Polit, D. F. (1986). *Building self-sufficiency: A guide to vocational and employment services for teenage parents.* Jefferson City, MO: Humanalysis, Inc. 129 pp.

Polit, D. F., Quint, J. C., & Riccio, J. A. (1988). *The challenge of serving teenage mothers: Lessons from redirection.* New York: Manpower Demonstration Research Corporation. 32 pp.

Prater, L. P. (1992). Early pregnancy and academic achievement of African-American youth. *Exceptional Children, 59*(2), 141–149.

Quint, J. C., & Guy, C. A. (1989). *New chance: Lessons from the pilot phase.* New York: Manpower Demonstration Research Corporation. (ERIC Document Reproduction Service No. ED 326 623). 153 pp.

Real, M. (1987). *A high price to pay: Teenage pregnancy in Ohio.* Columbus, OH: Children's Defense Fund. 172 pp.

Smollar, J., & Ooms, T. (1987). *Young unwed fathers: Research review, policy dilemmas, and options.* Austin, TX: Texas Education Agency. (ERIC Document Reproduction Service No. ED 321 206). 105 pp.

Stafford, J. (1987). Accounting for the persistence of teenage pregnancy. *Social Casework: The Journal of Contemporary Social Work, 68*(8), 471–476.

Zabin, L. S., Hirsch, M. B., Streett, R., Emerson, M. R., Smith, M., Hardy, J. B., & King, T. M. (1988). The Baltimore pregnancy prevention program for urban teenagers. *Family Planning Perspectives, 20*(4), 182–187.

Urban Education

Barriers and opportunities for America's young Black men. Hearing before the Select Committee on Children, Youth, and Families. House of Rep., 101st Congress, First Session. Washington, DC. (ERIC Document Reproduction Service No. ED 314 526). 173 pp.

Bempechat, J., & Ginsburg, H. P. (1989). *Underachievement and educational disadvantage: The home and school experience of at-risk youth.* New York: ERIC Clearinghouse on Urban Education. (ERIC Document Reproduction Service No. ED 315 485). 64 pp.

Cuban, L. (1989). The "at-risk" label and the problem of urban school reform. *Phi Delta Kappan, 70*(10), 799–801.

Eppenauer, P. A., & Smith, W. C. (1990). *Redefining a knowledge base: A proposal for reform in an urban setting.* Presented at the annual meeting of the American Association of Teacher Educators, Las Vegas, NV. (ERIC Document Reproduction Service No. ED 331 796). 22 pp.

Hunter, R. C. (1988). *Children at risk.* (ERIC Document Reproduction Service No. ED 314 532). 18 pp.

Husk, S. (1987). *Challenges to urban education: Results in the making.* Washington, DC: Council of the Great City Schools. 10 pp.

Lytle, J. H. (1990). Reforming urban education: A review of recent reports and legislation. *Urban Review, 22*(3), 199–220.

National Commission for Employment Policy. (1988). *Five case studies for youth-at-risk project.* Research Report No. 88-11. Washington, DC: (ERIC Document Reproduction Service No. ED 328 779). 209 pp.

National Education Association. (1988). *At-risk students and thinking: Perspectives from research.* Washington, DC: Author. (ERIC Document Reproduction Service No. ED 302 604). 161 pp.

Northwest Regional Educational Lab. (1989). *Takin' it to the streets. Basic skills training for street youth. A manual for volunteer tutors.* Portland, OR: Author. (ERIC Document Reproduction Service No. ED 306 333). 238 pp.

Reyes, P., & Capper, C. (1990). *Urban principals: A critical perspective on the context of minortiy student outcomes.* (ERIC Document Reproduction Service No. ED 320 995). 50 pp.

Schwartz, W. (1988). *Recent literature on urban and minority education.* ERIC/CUE Digest No. 44. New York: ERIC Clearinghouse on Urban Education. (ERIC Document Reproduction Service No. ED 311 136). 4 pp.

Strategies for success: Achieving the National Urban Education goals. (1990). Proceedings from meetings with representatives from 70 national education, business and philanthropic organizations. Council of the Great City Schools, Washington, DC. (ERIC Document Reproduction Service No. ED 333 090). 71 pp.

The time for assertive action: School strategies for promoting the education success of at-risk children. Report of the Commissioner's Task Force on the Education of Children and Youth At-Risk. Albany, NY: New York State Education Dept. (ERIC Document Reproduction Service No. ED 303 534). 35 pp.

Wilensky, R., & Kline, D. M., III. (1988). *Renewing urban schools: The community connection.* Denver, CO: Education Commission of the States. 41 pp.

Willis, H. D. (1989). *Students at risk: A review of conditions, circumstances, indicators and educational implications.* Elmhurst, IL: North Central Regional Educational Lab. (ERIC Document Reproduction Service No. ED 314 514). 38 pp.

Schoolwide Approaches and Interventions

Collaboration (Schools/Communities/Social Services)

Academy for Educational Development. (1989). *Partnerships for learning: School completion and employment preparation in the high school academies.* New York: Author.

Archer, E. & Cahill, M. (1991). *Building life options: School-community collaboratins for pregnancy prevention in the middle grades.* Washington, D. C.: Academy for educational Development, Inc. 147 pp.

At-risk youth in crisis: A handbook for collaboration between schools and social services. (1991). Eugene, OR: Linn-Benton Education Service District and ERIC Clearinghouse on Educational Management.

Behrman, R. (ed.). (1992). *The future of children: School linked services.* Vol. 2, no. 1. Los Altos, CA: Center for the Future of Children: The David and Lucille Packard Foundation.

Building a quality workforce: A joint initiative. (1988). Washington, DC: U. S. Department of Labor, U. S. Department of Education, U. S. Department of Commerce. (ERIC Document Reproduction Service No. ED 298 300). 87 pp.

Center for the Future of Children. (1992). *The future of children: School linked services.* Los Altos, CA: The David and Lucille Packard Foundation. 144 pp.

Comer, James P. (1993). *School power: Implications of an intervention project.* New York: Free Press. 317 pp.

Committee for Economic Development. (1985). *Investing in our children: Business and the public schools: A statement.* New York: Author. 107 pp.

Committee for Economic Development. (1987). *Children in need: Investment strategies for the educationally disadvantaged.* New York: Author. 86 pp.

Dougherty, V., et al. (Eds.). (1987). *Communities respond.* Denver, CO: Education Commission of the States. 56 pp.

Doyle, D. P. (1989). *Endangered species: Children of promise.* New York: McGraw-Hill. 135 pp.

Guthrie, L. F., Boothroyd, M., Baker, R. F., & Van Heusden, S. (1989). *Educational partnerships in California: A survey of the California Educational Partnership Consortium.* San Francisco: Far West Laboratory for Educational Research and Development. (ERIC Document Reproduction Service No. ED 322 610). 31 pp.

Guthrie, G. P., & Guthrie, L. F. (1990). *Streamlining interagency collaboration for youth at risk.* San Francisco: Far West Laboratory for Educational Research and Development. 14 pp.

Guthrie, G. P., & Guthrie, L. F. (1990). Streamlining interagency collaboration for youth at risk. *Educational Leadership, 49*(1), 17–22.

Hawaii Department of Education. (1989). *School/Community-Based Management.* Honolulu, HI: Author. (ERIC Document Reproduction Service No. ED 312 735). 35 pp.

Henry, M., & Kline, D. M., III. (1990). *Growing up at-risk.* Dubuque, IA: Kettering Foundation. 32 pp.

Hodgkinson, H. L., et al. (1991). *Beyond the schools: How schools and communities must collaborate to solve the problems facing America's youth.* Alexandria, VA: National School Boards Association; and Arlington, VA: American Association of School Administrators. 32 pp.

Kagan, S. L., Rivera, A. M., & Parker, F. L. (1990). *Collaborations in action: Reshaping services to young children and their families: Executive summary.* New Haven, CT: Yale Univ. Press. 240 pp.

Kellaghan, T., Sloan, K., Alvarez, B., & Bloom, B. (1993). *The home environment and school learning: Promoting parental involvement in the education of children.* San Francisco, CA: Jossey-Bass.

Kettering Foundation. (1989). *Growing up at risk.* Dayton, OH: Author.

Levin, L. (1987). *Ventures in Community Improvement (VICI): Findings from a four-site replication initiative, 1984–1987.* Philadelphia, PA: Public/Private Ventures. 5 pp.

Lewis, A. C. (1988). *Facts and faith: Status report on youth service.* Washington, DC: Youth and America's Future, The William T. Grant Foundation, Commission on Work, Family, and Citizenship. 32 pp.

Madden, N. A., et al. (1991). *Success for all.* Baltimore, MD: Center for Research on Effective Schooling for Disadvantaged Students. 21 pp.

Manning, A. C. (1987). *Adopt a school, adopt a business.* (Fastback No. 263). Bloomington, IN: Phi Delta Kappa Educational Foundation. (ERIC Document Reproduction Service No. ED 289 001). 47 pp.

Mastny, A. Y. (1989). *Linking schools and community services: Resource directory.* New Brunswick, NJ: Rutgers University, School of Social Work, Center for Community Education. 72 pp.

Nash, M. A. (1990). *Improving their chances: A handbook for designing and implementing programs for at-risk youth.* Madison, WI: University of Wisconsin, School of Education, Vocational Studies Center. 212 pp.

Peel, H. A. & Walker, B. L. (1993). Collaboration: Getting all hands on deck facilitates school change. *Journal of School Leadership, 3*(1), 30–39.

Public/Private Ventures. (1989). *Consumer's perspective: At-risk talk about programs.* Philadelphia, PA: Author. (ERIC Document Reproduction Service No. ED 311 123). 17 pp.

Rodriguez, E., McQuaid, P., & Rosauer, R. (1988). *Community of purpose: Promoting collaboration through state action.* Denver, CO: Education Commission of the States. 105 pp.

Rosen, M. (1993). Sharing power: A blueprint for collaboration. *Principal, 72*(3), 37–39.

San Diego City Schools. (1990). *New beginnings: A feasibility study of integrated services for children and families.* San Diego, CA: City of San Diego. 46 pp.

Schwartz, H. S. (Ed.). (1990). *Collaboration: Building common agendas.* Washington, DC: American Association of Colleges for Teacher Education. (ERIC Document Reproductive Service No. ED 320 890). 253 pp.

Sergiovanni, T. (1994). *Building community in schools.* San Francisco, CA: Jossey-Bass.

Smith, Gregory A. (Ed.) (1993). *Public schools that work.* NY, NY: Routledge. 254 pp.

Thornburg, K. R., et al. (1991). Youth at risk; society at risk. *Elementary School Journal, 91*(3), 199–208.

University of Oregon. (1991). *At-risk youth in crisis: A handbook for collaboration between schools and social services. Volume 1: Introduction and resources.* Eugene, OR: Author. 66 pp.

University of Oregon. (1991). *At-risk youth in crisis: A handbook for collaboration between schools and social services. Volume 2: Suicide.* Eugene, OR: Author. 86 pp.

University of Oregon. (1991). *At-risk youth in crisis: A handbook for collaboration between schools and social services. Volume 3: Child abuse.* Eugene, OR: Author. 66 pp.

University of Oregon. (1991). *At-risk youth in crisis: A handbook for collaboration between schools and social services. Volume 4: Substance abuse.* Eugene, OR: Author. 64 pp.

University of Oregon. (1991). *At-risk youth in crisis: A handbook for collaboration between schools and social services. Volume 5: Attendance services.* Eugene, OR: Author. 71 pp.

Western Regional Center for Drug-free Schools and Communities. (1991). *Fostering resiliency in kids: Protective factors in the family, school, and community.* Portland, OR: Northwest Regional Educational Laboratory. 27 pp.

Early Childhood

Balasubramaniam, M., & Turnbull, B. J. (1988). *Exemplary preschool programs for at-risk children: A review of recent literature.* Washington, DC: Policy Studies Associates. (ERIC Document Reproduction Service No. ED 315 193). 32 pp.

Brook, J. S., Whiteman, M. G., & Cohen, P. (1986). Some models and mechanisms for explaining the impact of maternal and adolescent characteristics on adolescent stage of drug use. *Developmental Psychology, 22*(4), 460–467.

Butler, O. B. (1989). Early help for kids at risk: Our nation's best investment. *NEA Today, 7*(6), 50–53.

Cahan, E. D. (1989). *Past caring: A history of U. S. preschool care and education for the poor, 1820–1965.* New York: National Center for Children in Poverty. 59 pp.

Charlesworth, R. (1989). "Behind" before they start? Deciding how to deal with the risk of kindergarten "failure." *Young Children, 44*(3), 5–13.

Center on Evaluation, Development, Research. (1991). *Child-care programs: Raising the standards. Hot topics series.* Bloomington, IN: Phi Delta Kappa. 319 pp.

Cohen, S., & Taharally, C. (1992). Getting ready for young children with prenatal drug exposure. *Childhood Education, 69*(1), 5–9.

Fink, B. B. (1990). *Increasing services to early childhood students by providing more classrooms and integrating students.* (1990). Florida. Ed.D Practicum, Nova University. (ERIC Document Reproduction Service No. ED 325 250). 43 pp.

Gray, E. (1988). *Identification and intervention strategies for preschool, kindergarten, first and second grade children at risk for reading difficulties.* California. (ERIC Document Reproduction Service No. ED 297 512). 31 pp.

Holden, C. (1990). Head start enters adulthood. *Science.* 247, 1400–1402.

Honig, A. (1984). Research in review: Risk factors in infants and young children. *Young Children, 39*(4), 60–73.

Kagan, S. L. (1990). *Policy perspectives: Excellence in early childhood education: Defining characteristics and next-decade strategies.* Washington, DC: U.S. Government Printing Office. 29 pp.

Karen, R. (1990, February). Becoming attached. *Atlantic Monthly,* pp. 35–70.

Karweit, N. L. (1987). *Effective kindergarten programs and practices for students at risk.* (Report No. 21). Baltimore, MD: Johns Hopkins University. (ERIC Document Reproduction Service No. ED 291 835). 34 pp.

Karweit, N. L. (In press). *Can preschools alone prevent early learning failure?* In *preventing early school failure: Research on effective strategies.* Edited by R. E. Slavin, N. L. Karweit, and B. A. Wasik. Boston: Allyn and Bacon.

Karweit, N. L. (In press). *Extra-year kindergarten programs and transitional first grades.* In *preventing early school failure: Research on effective strategies.* Edited by R. E. Slavin, N. L. Karweit, and B. A. Wasik. Boston: Allyn and Bacon.

Lang, Cynthia. (1992). *Head start: New challenges, new chances.* Newton, MA: Education Development Center, Inc. 35 pp.

McDonnell, A., & Hardman, M. (1988). A synthesis of "best practice" guidelines for early childhood services. *Journal of the Division for Early Childhood, 12*(4), 328–341.

National Coalition of Advocates for Students. (1985). *Barriers to excellence: Our children at risk.* Boston: Author. (ERIC Document Reproduction Service No. ED 260 148). 162 pp.

Oyemade, U. J., & Washington, V. (1989). Drug abuse prevention begins in early childhood. *Young Children, 44*(5), 6–12.

Parnell, D. (1985). *The neglected majority.* Washington D. C.: The Community College Press. 184 pp.

Ramey, C. T., & Farran, D. C. (1983). *Intervening with high-risk families via infant daycare.* Presented at the Biennial Meeting of the Society for Research in Child Development, Detroit, MI. (ERIC Document Reproduction Service No. ED 230 289). 17 pp.

Riley, R. W. (1986). Can we reduce the risk of failure? *Phi Delta Kappan, 64*(4), 214–219.

Salzer, R. (1986). Why not assume they're all gifted rather than handicapped? *Educational Leadership, 44*(3), 74–44.

Slavin, R. E., et al. (1991). *Preventing early school failure: What works? Report No, 26.* Baltimore, MD: Center for Research on Effective Schooling for disadvantaged Students. 23 pp.

Slavin, R. E., Karweit, N. L., & Wasik, B. A. (In press). *Preventing early school failure: Research on effective strategies.* Boston: Allyn and Bacon.

Smyser, S. (1990). Prekindergarten: The impossible dream. *Principal, 69*(5), 17–19.

Stowe, C. A. (1992). *At risk: Language minority preschool children.* Presented at the Annual Meeting of the American Educational Research Association, San Francisco. 11 pp.

Wisconsin State Department of Public Instruction. (1990). *Children at risk: A resource and planning guide.* Bulletin No. 91065. Madison, WI: Author. (ERIC Document Reproduction Service No. ED 324 576). 237 pp.

Elementary Schools

Cuban, L. (1989). At-risk students: What teachers and pricipals can do. *Educational Leadership, 46*(5), 29–32.

Ebert, C. C. (November, 1990). *The importance of dropout prevention and education in breaking the cycle of poverty.* Paper presented at the Conference on Appalachia, Lexington, KY. 8pp.

Gersten, R. M., & Dimino, J. (1990). *Reading instruction for at-risk students: Implications of current research.* Eugene, OR: Oregon School Study Council. 30 pp.

Germinario, V. (1992). *All children successful: Real answers for helping at-risk elementary students.* Lancaster, PA: Technomic Pub. Co. 204 pp.

Goodlad, J.I., & Anderson, R. H. (1963). *The nongraded elementary school.* Rev. Ed. New York: Harcourt, Brace, and World.

Gutierrez, & Slavin, R. E. (1992, April). *Achievement effects of the nongraded elementary school: A retrospective and prospective review.* Paper presented at the annual meeting of the American Educational Research Association, San Francisco.

Hopfenberg, W., & Levin, H. (1993). *The accelerated schools resource guide.* San Francisco, CA: Jossey-Bass.

Howe, R. W. & Kasten, M. (1992). *Students at risk in mathematics: Prevention and recovery in elementary schools.* Columbus, OH: ERIC Clearinghouse for Science, Mathematics, and Environmental Education. 61 pp.

Kennedy, M. M., B. F. Birman, & Demaline, R. E. (1986). *The effectiveness of Chapter 1 services.* Washington, D. C.: Office of Educational Research and Improvement, U.S. Department of Education.

Knapp, M. S., & Shields, P. M. (Eds.). (1990). *Better schooling for the children of poverty: Alternatives to conventional wisdom.* Washington, DC: U. S. Department of Education.

Legters, N. & Slavin, R. E. (1992). *Elementary students at risk: A status report.* Baltimore, MD: Center for Research on Effective Schooling for Disadvantaged Students. 85 pp.

Levin, H. M. (1987). Accelerated schools for disadvantaged students. *Educational Leadership, 44*(6), 19–21.

Madden, N. A., & Slavin, R. E. (1987). *Effective pull-out programs for students at risk.* Baltimore, MD: Johns Hopkins Univ. 22 pp.

Madden, N. A., et al. (1989). Restructuring the urban elementary school. *Educational Leadership, 46*(5), 14–18.

McCarthy, J. (1992, April). *The effect of the accelerated schools process on individual teachers' decision-making and instructional strategies.* Paper presented at the Annual Meeting of the American Educational Reseach Association, San Francisco, CA. 19 pp.

Mortimore, P., & Sammons, P. (1987). New evidence on effective elementary schools. *Educational Leadership, 45*(1), 4–8.

Nye, B. A., et al. (1991). *The lasting benefits study: A continuing analysis of the effect of small class size in kindergarten through third grade on student achievement test scores in subsequent grade levels.* Nashville: Tennessee State University.

Roser, N. L., Hoffman, J. V., & Farest, C. (1990). Language, literature and at-risk children. *Reading Teacher, 43*(8), 554–559.

Slavin, R. E., Karweit, N. L., & Madden, N. A. (1989). *Effective programs for students at risk.* Boston: Allyn and Bacon. 376 pp.

Slavin, R. E., & Madden, N. A. (1989). What works for students at risk: A research synthesis. *Educational Leadership, 46*(5), 4–13.

U. S. Department of Education. (1988). *James Madison Elementary School: A curriculum for American students.* Washington, DC: Author. 61 pp.

Wasik, B. A. & Slavin, R. E. (1993). Preventing early reading failure with one-to-one tutoring: A review of five programs. *Reading Research Quarterly, 28*(2), 179–200.

Wilson, B. L. (1987). *Places where children succeed: A profile of outstanding elementary schools.* Philadelphia, PA: Research for Better Schools. 63 pp.

Middle Schools

Becker, H. J. (1987). *Addressing the needs of different groups of early adolescents: Effects of varying school and classroom organizational practices on students from different social backgrounds and abilities.* Baltimore, MD: Johns Hopkins University. 35 pp.

Carnegie Council on Adolescent Development. (1989). *Turning points: Preparing American youth for the 21st century* (the report of the Task Force on Education of Young Adolescents). Waldorf, MD: Author. 106 pp.

Children's Defense Fund. (1988). *Making the middle grades work.* Washington, DC: Author. 31 pp.

Dougherty, J. W. (1990). *Effective programs for at-risk adolescents.* (Fastback No. 308). Bloomington, IN: Phi Delta Kappa Educational Foundation. 39 pp.

Gray-Shoffner, C. (1986). A rescue program for potential dropouts. *Principal, 66*(2), 53–54.

Hopfenberg, W., & Levin, H. (1993). *The accelerated schools resource guide.* San Francisco, CA: Jossey-Bass.

Hopfenberg, W. S., et al. (1990). *Toward accelerated middle schools.* Prepared for the Project to Develop Accelerated Middle Schools for At-Risk Youth. (ERIC Document Reproduction Service No. ED 326 922). 115 pp.

Kohut, S. (1988). *The middle school: A bridge between elementary and high schools (2nd ed.).* Washington, DC: National Educational Association. 32 pp.

Massachusetts Advocacy Center and the Center for Early Adolescence. (1988). *Before it's too late: Dropout prevention in the middle grades.* Boston: Author.

Phelan, W. T. (1992). Building bonds to high school graduation: Dropout intervention with seventh and eighth graders. *Middle School Journal, 24*(2), 33–35.

Swaim, J., & Needham, R. (1984). *In search of excellence: The national reports—implications for middle schools.* Columbus, OH: National Middle School Association. (ERIC Document Reproduction Service No. ED 260 516). 59 pp.

High Schools

Archer, E., & Montesano, P. (1990). High school academies: Engaging students in school and work. *Equity and Choice, 6*(2), 16–18.

Baker, J., & Sansone, J. (1988). *Interventions with students at risk for dropping out of school: A high school responds.* Presented at the annual meeting of the American Educational Research Association, New Orleans, LA. (ERIC Document Reproduction Service No. ED 310 501). 21 pp.

Barnes, S., & Stewart, J. (1991). *A study of an alternative high school: Focus, features and impact.* Presented at the annual meeting of the American Educational Research Association, Chicago, IL. (ERIC Document Reproduction Service No. ED 333 584). 49 pp.

deBettencourt, L. U., & Zigmond, N. (1990). The learning disabled secondary school dropout: What teachers should know. *Teacher Education and Special Education, 13*(1), 17–20.

Diem, Richard A., et al. (1989). *An analysis of an academic and support group program for at-risk secondary schools.* Presented at the annual meeting of the American Educational Research Association, San Francisco. (ERIC Document Reproduction Service No. ED 308 573). 15 pp.

Dougherty, V., de Lone, R., & Odden, A. (1989). *Current practice: Is it enough?* Denver, CO: Education Commission of the States. 31 pp.

Farrar, E., & Hampel, R. L. (1987). Social services in American high schools. *Phi Delta Kappan, 69*(4), 297–303.

Franks, M. E., et al. (1990). *A profile of a dropout population in a Native American high school: A local perspective.* Presented at the annual meeting of the American Education Research Association, Boston. (ERIC Document Reproduction Service No. ED 330 529). 17 pp.

Gersten, R. M., & Dimino, J. (1989). Teaching literature to at-risk students. *Educational Leadership, 46*(5), 53–57.

Gregory, Thomas. (1993). *Making high school work: Lessons from the open school.* New York: Teacher's College Press. 288 pp.

Gunderson, L. A. (1986). *Improving attendence of reservation students by an individualized alternative school which emphasizes Native American culture.* M.S. Practicum, Nova University. (ERIC Document Reproduction Service No. ED 323 070). 42 pp.

Halpern, A. S., & Benz, M. R. (1984). *Toward excellence in secondary special education: A statewide study of Oregon's high school programs for students with mild disabilities.* Eugene, OR: University of Oregon. 61 pp.

Hendrickson, J. M., & Roth, J. (1990). *Challenging the high risk student.* Presented at the annual National Dropout Prevention Conference, Nashville, TN. (ERIC Document Reproduction Service No. ED 321 207). 42 pp.

Kallembach, S. C. (1990). *Students at-risk: Selected resources for vocational preparation.* Macomb, IL: National Center for Research in Vocational Education. (ERIC Document Reproduction Service No. ED 324 416). 85 pp.

Kelly, Deirdre. (1993). *Last chance high: How boys and girls drop in and out of alternative schools.* New Haven, CT: Yale University Press.

Lee, V. E. & Burkam, D. T. (1992). Transferring high schools: An alternative to dropping out? *American Journal of Education, 100*(4), 420–253.

Moore, D. R., & Davenport, S. (1989). High school choice and students at risk. *Equity and Choice, 5*(1), 5–10.

Newmann, F. M., & Thompson, J. A. (1987). *Effects of cooperative learning on achievement in secondary schools: A summary of research.* Madison, WI: National Center on Effective Secondary Schools. 30 pp.

Newmann, Fred M. (1992). *Student engagement and achievement in American secondary schools.* New York: Teachers College Press. 231 pp.

Owens, T., & McClure, L. (1989). *New developments in improving the integration of academic and vocational education.* Portland, OR: Northwest Regional Educational Laboratory. (ERIC Document Reproduction Service No. ED 314 841). 30 pp.

Pellicer, L. O., et al. (1988–1990). *High school leaders and their schools.* Vol. 1: *A National Profile.* (ERIC Document Reproduction Service No. ED 299 711); Vol. 2: *Profiles of Effectiveness.* (ERIC Document Reproduction Service No. ED 319 139) Reston, VA: National Association of Secondary School Principals.

Reglin, G. L. (1990). A model program for educating at-risk students. *T.H.E. (Technological Horizons in Education) Journal, 17*(6), 65–67.

Roweton, W. E., & Bare, C. (1990). *Profiling high schools with high/low "holding power": A comparative study.* Presented at the Annual Convention of the American Psychological Association, Boston. (ERIC Document Reproduction Service No. ED 326 769). 8 pp.

Sizer, Theodore R. (1984). *Horace's compromise: The dilemma of the American high school.* Boston: Houghton Mifflin. 241 pp.

Sizer, Theodore R. (1992). *Horace's school: Redesigning the American high school.* Boston: Houghton Mifflin. 238 pp.

Steinberg, L., et al. (1988). *Noninstructional influences on high school student achievement: The contributions of parents, peers, extracurricular activities, and part-time work.* Madison, WI: National Center on Effective Secondary Schools. (ERIC Document Reproduction Service No. ED 307 509). 62 pp.

Weber, J. M. (1987). *Strengthening vocational education's role in decreasing the dropout rate.* Columbus, OH: National Center for Research in Vocational Education. (ERIC Document Reproduction Service No. ED 284 062). 36 pp.

Wehlage, G. G. (1983). *Effective programs for the marginal high school student.* (Fastback No. 197). Bloomington, IN: Phi Delta Kappa Educational Foundation. 43 pp.

Wehlage, G. G., Rutter, R. A., & Turnbaugh, A. (1987). A program model for at-risk high school students. *Educational Leadership, 44*(6), 70–73.

School-To-Work Transition

Barton, P. E. (1990). *From school to work: Policy information report.* Princeton, NJ: Educational Testing Service, Policy Information Center. (ERIC Document Reproduction Service No. ED 320 947). 34 pp.

Barton, P. E., & Kirsch, I. S. (1990). *Workplace competencies: The need to improve literacy and employment readiness.* Washington, DC: Government Printing Office. 35 pp.

Bossone, R. M., & Polishook, I. H. (Eds.). (1985). *School-to-work transition.* Proceedings of the Conference of the University/Urban Schools National Task Force. New York: City Univ. of New York. (ERIC Document Reproduction Service No. ED 266 200). 130 pp.

Brand, B. (1990). *Preparing students for leadership in tomorrow's work.* Presented at the American Vocational Association Convention, Washington, DC. (ERIC Document Reproduction Service No. ED 331 952). 11 pp.

Brand, B. (1990). *What's ahead for employment and training.* Presented at the American Vocational Association Convention, Washington, DC. (ERIC Document Reproduction Service No. ED 328 751). 11 pp.

Carlson, C. G. (1990). *Beyond high school: The transition to work.* Princeton, NJ: Educational Testing Service. (ERIC Document Reproduction Service No. ED 325 716). 23 pp.

Case, E. J. (1989). *Transition to the world of work.* Evaluation Report. Albuquerque, NM: Albuquerque Public Schools. (ERIC Document Reproduction Service No. ED 320 332). 26 pp.

Columbia College of Education. (1989). *Transition from school to work. Missouri LINC module.* Columbia, MO: Author. (ERIC Document Reproduction Service No. ED 321 145). 17 pp.

Committee for Economic Development. (1987). *Children in need: Investment strategies for the educationally disadvantaged.* New York: Author. (ERIC Document Reproduction Service No. ED 300 466). 113 pp.

Coyle-Williams, M. (1989). *What works in vocational education for students who are at risk.* Berkeley, CA: National Center for Research in Vocational Education. (ERIC Document Reproduction Service No. ED 313 535). 5 pp.

Duttweiler, P. C. (1992). Engaging at-risk students with technology. *Media and Methods, 29*(2), 6–8.

Education Writers Association. (1990). *Training for work: What the U. S. can learn from Europe.* Washington, DC: Author. (ERIC Document Reproduction Service No. ED 327 641). 53 pp.

Faddis, B., et al. (1988). *Student career journal.* Portland, OR: Northwest Regional Educational Laboratory. (ERIC Document Reproduction Service No. ED 318 973). 61 pp.

Feichtner, S. H. (1989). *School-to-work transition for at-risk youth.* Columbus, OH: Center on Education and Training for Employment. (ERIC Document Reproduction Service No. ED 315 666). 86 pp.

Fortune, D., & Sims, A. (1990). *The student transition and retention program (STAR) and student guidebook, 1990–1991.* Washington, DC: Office of Vocational and Adult Education. (ERIC Document Reproduction Service No. ED 330 376). 81 pp.

General Accounting Office. (1990). *Training strategies: Preparing non-college youth for employment in the U.S. and foreign countries.* Washington, DC: Author. (ERIC Document Reproduction Service No. ED 321 096). 69 pp.

Imel, S. (1991). *School-to-work transition: Its role in achieving universal literacy.* Columbus, OH: ERIC Clearinghouse on Adult, Career and Vocational Education. (ERIC Document Reproduction Service No. ED 329 806). 3 pp.

Kazis, R., & Roche, B. (1991). *The new U.S. initiatives for the transition from school to work.* Occccasional paper No. 8. Geneva, Switzerland. International Labor Office. (ERIC Document Reproduction Service No. ED 333 154). 10 pp.

National Center on Education and the Economy. (1990). *America's choice: High skills or low wages!* The report of the Commission on the Skills of the American Workforce. Rochester, NY: Author. 209 pp.

Neubert, D. A., & Leak, L. E. (1990). *Serving urban youth with special needs in vocational education: Issues and strategies for change.* Berkeley, CA: National Center for Research in Vocational Education. (ERIC Document Reproduction Service No. ED 326 695). 5 pp.

Palmateer, R. (1988). *Educare: Evaluation of a transition program for culturally disadvantaged and educationally handicapped youth. Executive Summary.* Nederland, CO: Institutional Development and Economic Affairs Service. (ERIC Document Reproduction Service No. ED 305 791). 12 pp.

Philippi, J. W. (1989). *Facilitating the flow of information between the business and education communities.* Background paper No. 12. Washington, DC: Dept. of Labor. (ERIC Document Reproduction Service No. ED 317 679). 55 pp.

Rosenbaum, J. E. (1989). *Empowering schools and teachers: A new link to jobs for the non-college bound.* Background Paper No. 4. Washington, DC: Dept. of Labor. (ERIC Document Reproduction Service No. ED 317 668). 28 pp.

Stone, J. R., III, & Hopkins, C. (1990). *Working teens: The influence of school intervention. Marketing Education Focus: Vol. 2.* Reston, VA: Marketing Education Association. (ERIC Document Reproduction Service No. ED 323 352). 36 pp.

Surich, W. L. (1990). *The development and implementation of a functional transition class work study program at the high school level.* Florida. M.S. Practicum, Nova University. (ERIC Document Reproduction Service No. ED 324 529). 59 pp.

William T. Grant Foundation on Work, Family, and Citizenship. (1988). *The forgotten half: Non-college youth in America.* Washington, DC: Author. 102 pp.

William T. Grant Foundation on Work, Family, and Citizenship. (1988). The forgotten half: Pathways to success for America's youth and young families. *Phi Delta Kappan, 70*(4), 280–289.

Wilson, R. D. (1991). Transition to life off the job. This high school course teaches students how to cope. *Vocational Education Journal, 66*(3), 28.

Restructuring

Ahearn, E. M. (1991). Real restructuring through technology., *Perspectives,* 3(1). (ERIC Document Reproduction Service No. ED 332 318). 17 pp.

Aschbacher, P. R. (1991). *Effects of restructuring on disadvantaged students: Humanitas—a case study.* Presented at the annual meeting of the American Educational Research Association, Chicago, IL. (ERIC Document Reproduction Service No. ED 335 438). 48 pp.

Chafel, J. A. (1990). Needed: A legislative agenda for children at risk. *Childhood Education, 66*(4), 241–242.

Clabaugh, G. K. (1991). *Examining the costs of the restructuring crusade.* Presented at the annual meeting of the American Educational Research Association, Chicago, IL. (ERIC Document Reproduction Service No. ED 331 165). 12 pp.

Conley, D. T. (1991). *Restructuring schools: Educators adapt to a changing world.* Trends and Issues Series, No. 6. ERIC Clearinghouse on Educational Management. (ERIC Document Reproduction Service No. ED 328 954). 57 pp.

Conley, D. T. (1993). *Roadmap to restructuring schools: Policies, practices and the emerging visions of schooling.* ERIC Clearinghouse on Educational Management. Eugene, OR: University of Oregon. 432 pp.

David, J. L. (1991). What it takes to restructure education. *Educational Leadership, 48*(8), 11–15.

Duttweiler, P. C. (1989). *Restructuring the educational system. Insights on educational policy and practice, No. 13.* Austin, TX: Southwest Educational Development Lab. (ERIC Document Reproduction Service No. ED 330 054). 6 pp.

English, F. W., & Hill, J. C. (1990). *Restructuring: The principal and curriculum change.* Reston, VA: National Association of Secondary School Principals. 24 pp.

Finn, C. E., Jr. (1991). *We must take charge: Our schools and our future.* New York: The Free Press. 365 pp.

Gandara, P., & Fish, J. (1991). *An experiment in restructuring K–6 education: The Orchard Plan.* Presented at the annual meeting of the American Educational Research Association, Chicago, IL. (ERIC Document Reproduction Service No. ED 331 169). 23 pp.

Glickman, C. D. (1990). Pushing school reform to the new edge: The seven ironies of school empowerment. *Phi Delta Kappan, 72*(1), 68–75.

Goodlad, John I. (1984). *A place called school: Prospects for the future.* New York, NY: McGraw-Hill. 396 pp.

Goodlad, John I. (1990). *Teachers for our nation's schools.* San Francisco, CA: Jossey-Bass. 427 pp.

Goodlad, John I. (1994). *Educational renewal: Better teachers, better schools.* San Francisco, CA: Jossey-Bass. 305 pp.

Goodlad, John I., Soder, Roger & Srotnik, Kenneth A. *The moral dimensions of teaching.* San Francisco, CA: Jossey-Bass. 340 pp.

Hallinger, P., et al. *Restructuring schools: Principals' perceptions of fundamental educational reform.* Nashville, TN: National Center for Educational Leadership. (ERIC Document Reproduction Service No. ED 334 681). 42 pp.

Hansen, J. B. (1991). *Accountability as a tool for educational reform: Is it an oxymoron?* Presented at the annual meeting of the American Educational Research Association, Chicago, IL. (ERIC Document Reproduction Service No. ED 333 010). 24 pp.

Hilliard, R. D. (1991). *Restructuring education: Agenda for the 1990s.* Presented at the annual meeting of the Association of Teacher Educators, New Orleans, LA. (ERIC Document Reproduction Service No. ED 329 530). 19 pp.

Hixson, J., & Tinzmann, M. B. (1990). *Reconnecting students at risk to the learning process: restructuring to promote learning in America's schools.* Elmhurst, IL: North Central Regional Educational Lab. (ERIC Document Reproduction Service No. ED 327 937). 75 pp.

Holmes Group. (1990). *Tomorrow's schools: Principles for the design of professional development schools.* East Lansing, MI: Author. (ERIC Reproduction Service No. ED 328 533). 121 pp.

Joyce, B. R., Wolf, J. & Calhoun, E. (1993). *The self-renewing school.* Alexandria, VA: Association for Supervision and Curriculum Development. 97 pp.

Keating, P. T., & Oakes, J. (1988). *Access to knowledge: Removing school barriers to learning.* Denver, CO: Education Commission of the States. 18 pp.

Kershner, K. M., & Connolly, J. A. (Eds.). (1991). *At-risk students and school restructuring.* Philadelphia, PA: Research for Better Schools, Inc. (ERIC Document Reproduction Service No. ED 335 425). 129 pp.

Lezotte, L. W., & Bancroft, B. A. (1985). Growing use of the Effective Schools Model for school improvement. *Educational Leadership, 42*(6), 23–27.

Maehr, M. L., & Midgley, C. (1991). *Restructuring the school environment to enhance student motivation and learning.* Urbana, IL: National Center for School Leadership. (ERIC Document Reproduction Service No. ED 333 534). 18 pp.

McCarthy, M. M., & Hall, G. C. (1989). *The emergence of university-based education policy centers: Trends and issues.* Eugene, OR: ERIC Clearinghouse on Educational Management. (ERIC Document Reproduction Service No. ED 303 878). 23 pp.

McGrail, J., et al. (1989). *Looking at schools: Instruments and processes for school analysis.* Philadelphia: Research for Better Schools. (ERIC Document Reproduction Service No. ED 280 885). 124 pp.

Murphy, J. & Hallinger, P. (1993). *Restructuring schooling: Learning from ongoing efforts.* Newbury Park, CA: Corwin Press, Inc. 280 pp.

Paulu, N. (1988). *Experiences in school improvement: The story of sixteen American districts.* Washington, DC: Office of Educational Research and Improvement. (ERIC Document Reproduction Service No. ED 297 480). 92 pp.

Schlecty, Phillip C. (1990). *School's for the 21st century.* San Francisco, CA: Jossey-Bass. 164 pp.

Rungeling, B., & Glover, R. W. (1991). Educational restructuring: The process for change? *Urban Education, 25*(4) 415–427.

Scott, J. J., & Smith, S. C. (1987). *From isolation to collaboration: Improving the work environment of teaching.* Eugene, OR: ERIC Clearinghouse on Educational Management. 92 pp.

Seeley, D. S. (1991). *Brother can you paradigm? Finding a banner around which to rally in restructuring schools.* Presented at the annual meeting of the American Educational Research Association, Chicago, IL. (ERIC Document Reproduction Service No. ED 333 541). 46 pp.

Sizer, Theodore R. (1984). *Horace's compromise: The dilemma of the American high school.* Boston: Houghton Mifflin, 241 pp.

Sizer, Theodore R. (1992). *Horace's school: Redesigning the American high school.* Boston: Houghton Mifflin. 238 pp.

Tayor, A. (1993). How schools are redesigning their space. *Educational Leadership, 52*(2), 36–41.

Tyack, D. (1990). "Restructuring" in historical perspective: Tinkering toward utopia. *Teachers College Record, 92*(2), 170–191.

Wirt, F. M. (1991). *Value organization linkages, educational restructuring, and historical reforms.* Chicago, IL: Presented at the annual meeting of the American Educational Research Association. (ERIC Document Reproduction Service No. ED 332 359). 30 pp.

Rural Education

Benally, E. R., et al. (1987). *Issues in American education, Mexican American education, rural education, and small schools.* (1987). Las Cruces, NM: ERIC Clearinghouse on Rural Education and Small Schools. (ERIC Document Reproduction Service No. ED 281 909). 21 pp.

Bull, K. S., & Garrett, M. (1989). At risk in rural America: Strategies for educators. *Educational Considerations, 17*(1), 44–47.

Conklin, N. F. (1988). *Toward more effective education for poor, minority students in rural areas: What research suggests.* Portland, OR: Northwest Regional Educational Laboratory. 24 pp.

Cox, J. L., & Spivey, R. (1986). *High school dropout in Appalachia: Problems and palliatives.* North Carolina. Research Triangle Institute. (ERIC Document Reproduction Service No. ED 272 343). 22 pp.

D'Alonzo, B., et al. (1990). *Dropout prevention for rural at-risk youth.* Tucson, AZ: Presented at the American Council on Rural Special Education/National Rural and Small Schools Consortium. (ERIC Document Reproduction Service No. ED 331 662). 32 pp.

Guthrie, L. F., et al. (1989). *Principles of successful Chapter 1 programs: A guidebook for rural educators.* San Francisco: Far West Laboratory for Educational Research and Development. 60 pp.

Helge, D. (1989). Rural "at-risk" students: Directions for Policy and Intervention. *Rural Education Quarterly, 10*(1), 3–16.

Helge, D. (1989). *Rural family-community partnerships: Resources, strategies, and models.* Bellingham, WA: Western Washington University, National Rural Development Institute. (ERIC Document Reproduction Service No. ED 320 736). 40 pp.

Helge, D. (1987). *Serving at-risk populations in rural America.* Bellingham, WA: American Council on Rural Special Education. 13 pp.

Helge, D. (1984). The commission on excellence: The rural perspective. *Small School Forum, 5*(3), 6–8.

McCaul, E. (1989). Rural public school dropouts: Findings from high school and beyond. *Research in Rural Education, 6*(1), 19–24.

Muse, I. (1984). *Excellence in rural education: "A Nation At Risk" revisited.* Rural Education Mini Review. Las Cruces, NM: ERIC Clearinghouse on Rural Education and Small Schools. (ERIC Document Reproduction Service No. ED 261 819). 18 pp.

Reddick, T. L., & Peach, L. E. (1990). *A study of characteristics profiling at-risk students and influences impacting their rural environment.* Presented at the Annual Conference of the National Social Science Association, Houston, TX. (ERIC Document Reproduction Service No. ED 326 355). 15 pp.

Shuler, S. (1992). Reaching at-risk students through music education. *NASSP Bulletin, 76*(544), 30–35.

U. S. Department of Education. (1989). *Rural education: A changing landscape.* Washington, DC: Author. 77 pp.

Classroom Strategies

Cooperative Learning

Brickle, W., II. (1990). *Improving the problem solving skills of at-risk high school mathematics students through cooperative work groups and computer assisted instruction.* Practicum Report, Nova University. (ERIC Document Reproduction Service No. ED 332 874). 76 pp.

Compton, J. E., & Smith, C. (Comp.). (1990). *Collaborative and cooperative learning teachniques.* Learning Package No. 6. Bloomington, IN: Indiana University, School of Education. (ERIC Document Reproduction Service No. ED 333 372). 35 pp.

Hassard, J. (1991). Cooperative learning and science education: A humanistic and ecological approach. *Cooperative Learning, 11*(3), 4–8.

Hilke, E. V. (1990). *Cooperative learning.* (Fastback No. 299). Bloomington, IN: Phi Delta Kappa Educational Foundation. 32 pp.

Johnson, D. W., Johnson, R. T., & Holubec, E. J. (1990). *Circles of learning: Cooperation in the classroom.* Edina, MN: Interaction Book Company.

Melaville, A. I. & Blank, M. J. (1993). *Together we can: A guide for crafting a profamily system of education and human services.* U.S. Department of Education & U.S. Department of Health and Human Services. 157 pp.

Slavin, R. E. (1981). Synthesis of research on cooperative learning. *Educational Leadership, 38*(8), 655–660.

Slavin, R. E. (1983). *Team-assisted individualization: A cooperative learning solution for adaptive instruction in mathematics.* Baltimore, MD: Center for Social Organization of Schools. (ERIC Document Reproduction Service No. ED 232 852). 31 pp.

Slavin, R. E. (1986). Learning together. *American Educator: The Professional Journal of the American Federation of Teachers, 10*(2), 6–11.

Slavin, R. E. (1987). Cooperative learning: Can students help students learn? *Instructor, 96*(7), 74–76, 78.

Slavin, R. E. (1987). *Cooperative learning: Student teams* (2nd ed.). Washington, DC: National Education Association. (ERIC Document Reproduction Service No. ED 282 862). 31 pp.

Slavin, R. E. (1991). Are cooperative learning and 'untracking' harmful to the gifted? Response to Allen. *Educational Leadership, 48*(6), 68–71.

Stevens, R. J. (1989). *A cooperative learning approach to studying expository text.* Baltimore, MD: Johns Hopkins Univ., Center for Research on Elementary and Secondary Schools. 16 pp.

Stevens, R. J., et al. (1987). *Cooperative integrated reading and composition: Two field experiments.* Baltimore, MD: Center for Research on Elementary and Middle Schools. 47 pp.

Wang, M. C., & Walberg, H. J. (Eds.). (1985). *Adapting instruction to individual differences.* Berkeley, CA: McCutchan. 329 pp.

Discipline and Behavior Management

Bacon, E. H. (1990). Using negative consequences effectively. *Academic Therapy, 25*(5), 599–611.

Bain, A. (1988). Issues in the suspension and exclusion of disruptive students. *Australasian Journal of Special Education, 12*(2), 19–24.

Carter, M. (1987). *A model for effective school discipline.* (Fastback No. 250). Bloomington, IN: Phi Delta Kappa Educational Foundation. 34 pp.

Gathercoal, F. (1990). *Judicious discipline* (2nd ed.). Ann Arbor, MI: Caddo Gap Press. 136 pp.

Glenn, H. S., & Nelsen, J. (1989). *Raising self-reliant children in a self-indulgent world: Seven building blocks for developing capable young people.* Toronto: Random House. 243 pp.

Gottfredson, D. G. (1989). *Reducing disorderly behavior in middle schools.* Report No. 37. Baltimore, MD: Center for Research on Elementary and Middle Schools. (ERIC Document Reproduction Service No. ED 320 654). 26 pp.

Houston, R., & Grubaugh, S. (1989). Language for preventing and defusing violence in the classroom. *Urban Education, 24*(1), 25–37.

Leatt, D. J. (1987). *Inschool suspension programs for at-risk youth.* Eugene, OR: Oregon School Study Council. 28 pp.

Lentz, F. E., Jr. (1988). On-task behavior, academic performance and classroom disruptions: Untangling the target selection problem in classroom interventions. *School Psychology Review, 17*(2), 243–257.

Nelson, J. (1987). *Positive discipline.* New York: Ballantine. 242 pp.

Rossow, L. F. (1989). *The law of student expulsions and suspensions.* NOLPE Monograph. Topeka, KS: National Organization on Legal Problems of Education. (ERIC Document Reproduction Service No. ED 320 244). 59 pp.

Stoops, E., & King-Stoops, J. (1972). *Discipline or disaster?* (Fastback No. 8). Bloomington, IN: Phi Delta Kappa Educational Foundation. 38 pp.

Sullivan, J. S. (1989). Planning, implementing and maintaining an effective inschool suspension program. *Clearing House, 62*(9), 409–410.

Swick, K. J. (1991). *Discipline: Toward positive student behavior. What research says to the teacher.* Washington, DC: National Education Association. (ERIC Document Reproduction Service No. ED 335 135). 34 pp.

Mentoring

Ascher, C. (1988). *The mentoring of disadvantaged youth.* ERIC/CUE Digest No. 47. New York: ERIC Clearinghouse on Urban Education. (ERIC Document Reproduction Service No. ED 306 326). 4 pp.

Barnes, S. (1990). *A contrastive study of mentor and nonmentor teachers in their interactions with at-risk students.* Presented at the annual meeting of the American Educational Research Association, Boston. (ERIC Document Reproduction Service No. ED 323 200). 14 pp.

Education Commission of the States. (1989). *At-risk youth and the role of college and university students.* Denver, CO: Author. (ERIC Document Reproduction Service No. ED 315 463). 8 pp.

Faddis, B., et al. (1988). *Guide for planning, implementing, and evaluating a mentoring program.* Portland, OR: Northwest Regional Educational Laboratory. (ERIC Document Reproduction Service No. ED 318 971). 114 pp.

Faddis, B., et al. (1988). *Idea book for mentors.* Portland, OR: Northwest Regional Educational Laboratory. (ERIC Document Reproduction Service No. ED 318 972). 39 pp.

Flaxman, E., et al. (1988). *Youth mentoring: Programs and practices.* Urban Diversity Series No. 97. New York: Columbia Univ. Teachers College. (ERIC Document Reproduction Service No. ED 308 257). 76 pp.

Glass, R. S. (1991). Opening windows for teenagers: How mentors can help. *American Educator: The Professional Journal of the American Federation of Teachers, 15*(1), 21–26.

Kalbfleisch, P. J., & Davies, A. B. (1991). Minorities and mentoring: Managing the multicultural institution. *Communication Education, 40*(3), 266–271.

Lowney, R. G. (1986). *Mentor teachers: The California model.* Bloomington, IN: Phi Delta Kappa Educational Foundation. (ERIC Document Reproduction Service No. ED 275 646). 32 pp.

McHale, G. (1990). *Turning point: A white paper on the course of mentoring.* Proceedings of the National Mentoring Conference, Washington, DC. (ERIC Document Reproduction Service No. ED 329 613). 49 pp.

Mosqueda, P. F., & Palaich, R. (1990). *Mentoring young people makes a difference.* Denver, CO: Education Commission of the States. (ERIC Document Reproduction Service No. ED 317 945). 24 pp.

National Education Association. (1990). *A special report on mentoring from Project PLUS and the National Urban League, Inc.* Washington, DC: Author. (ERIC Document Reproduction Service No. ED 329 611). 9 pp.

National Media Outreach Center. (1991). *The power of mentoring: An age-old strategy is helping today's youth.* Pittsburgh, PA: Author. (ERIC Document Reproduction Service No. ED 335 424). 26 pp.

Norton, C. S. (1988). *Mentoring: A representative bibliography.* New York: Columbia Univ. Teachers College. (ERIC Document Reproduction Service No. ED 308 278). 47 pp.

One to One. (1990). *Mentoring Kit.* Washington, DC: Author. (ERIC Document Reproduction Service No. ED 325 785). 53 pp.

Raughton, J. L. (1989). *The Partners Program.* Denver, CO: Colorado Community College and Occupational Educational System. (ERIC Document Reproduction Service No. ED 307 945). 20 pp.

Reisner, E. R., et al. (1989). *Review of programs involving college students as tutors or mentors in grades K–12.* Washington, DC: U. S. Department of Education. (ERIC Document Reproduction Service No. ED 318 832). 73 pp.

Smink, J. (1990). *Mentoring programs for at-risk youth: Dropout prevention reports.* Clemson, SC: National Dropout Prevention Center. (ERIC Document Reproduction Service No. ED 318 931). 38 pp.

Weinberger, S. G. (1990). *The mentor handbook.* Norwalk, CT: Educational Resources Network, Inc. 31 pp.

Peer Tutoring

Assinder, W. (1991). Peer teaching, peer learning. One model. *ELT Journal, 45*(3), 218–229.

Benard, B. (1990). *The case for peers.* Washington, DC: Dept. of Education. (ERIC Document Reproduction Service No. ED 327 755). 16 pp.

Bowers, D. (1991). *Using peer tutoring as a form of individualized instruction for the at-risk students in a regular classroom.* Miami, Florida. M.S. Practicum, Nova University. (ERIC Document Reproduction Service No. ED 331 631). 49 pp.

Britz, M. W., et al. (1989). The effects of peer tutoring on mathematics performance: A recent review. *B.C. Journal of Special Education, 13*(1), 17–33.

Fitz-Gibbon, C. T. (1988). Peer tutoring as a teaching strategy. *Educational Management and Administration, 16*(3), 217–229.

Greenwood, C. R. (1989). Longitudinal effects of classwide peer tutoring. *Journal of Educational Psychology, 81*(3), 371–383.

Greenwood, C. R., et al. (1988). The use of peer tutoring strategies in classroom management and educational instruction. *School Psychology Review, 17*(2), 258–275.

Lee, S., et al. (1989). *Keep youth in school: A community-based practice model to keep at risk youth in school. Final Report.* Washington, DC: Catholic Univ. of America. (ERIC Document Reproduction Service No. ED 314 676). 127 pp.

Okawa, G. Y. (1988). *Dimensions of diversity: Peer tutoring in a multi-cultural setting.* Presented at the annual meeting of the Conference on College Composition and Communication, St. Louis, MO. (ERIC Document Reproduction Service No. ED 295 190). 15 pp.

Perry, M. J. (1991). *The effects of a peer tutoring intervention program on the reading levels of underachieving fifth grade students.* M.S. Practicum, Nova University. (ERIC Document Reproduction Service No. ED 333 360). 59 pp.

Pickens, J., & McNaughton, S. (1988). Peer tutoring of comprehension strategies. *Educational Psychology, 8*(1–2), 67–80.

Raschke, D., et al. (1988). Cross-age tutorials and attitudes of kindergartners toward older students. *Teacher Educator, 23*(4), 10–18.

Tucker, A. (1990). *The effects of peer tutoring on writing improvement in a combined kindergarten-first grade class.* Virginia. (ERIC Document Reproduction Service No. ED 331 071). 21 pp.

Webb, M. (1987). *Peer helping relationships in urban schools.* (ERIC Digest). New York: ERIC Clearinghouse on Urban Education. (ERIC Document Reproduction Service No. ED 289 949). 4 pp.

Winter, S. (1986). Peers as paired reading tutors. *British Journal of Special Education, 13*(3), 103–106.

Zsiray, S. W., Jr., & Peterson, H. (1990). *Developing a peer tutoring program for year-round education.* Presented at the annual meeting of the National Middle School Association, Long Beach, CA. (ERIC Document Reproduction Service No. ED 332 283). 11 pp.

Ineffective Practices: Tracking and Retention

Ascher, C. (1988). *Grade retention: Making the decision.* ERIC/CUE Digest No. 46. New York: ERIC Clearinghouse on Urban Education. (ERIC Document Reproduction Service No. ED 304 498). 4 pp.

Baenen, N. R., & Hopkins, P. (1989). *Secondary retention alternative.* Austin, TX: Austin Independent School District, Office of Research and Evaluation. (ERIC Document Reproduction Service No. ED 306 227). 20 pp.

Balow, I. H., & Schwager, M. (1990). *Retention in grade: A failed procedure.* Riverside, CA: California Educational Research Cooperative. (ERIC Document Reproduction Service No. ED 315 710). 46 pp.

Braddock, J. H., II. (1990). Tracking the middle grades: National patterns of grouping for instruction. *Phi Delta Kappan, 71*(6), 445–449.

Braddock, J. H., II. (1990). *Tracking: Implications for student ethnic subgroups.* Report No. 1. Baltimore, MD: Center for Research of Effective Schooling for Disadvantaged Students. (ERIC Document Reproduction Service No. ED 325 600). 24 pp.

Bucke, J. (Ed.). (1986). Retention Strategies. *Linkages, 4*(1). (ERIC Document Reproduction Service No. ED 315 493). 186 pp.

Butler, J. M., & Handley, H. M. (1990). *Effects of retention on achievement and self-concept of kindergarten and first grade students.* Presented at the annual meeting of the Mid-South Educational Research Association, New Orleans, LA. (ERIC Document Reproduction Service No. ED 327 287). 19 pp.

Carter, E. F. (1990). *Decreasing the incidence of first grade retention through a diagnostic-prescriptive intervention program and teacher in-service.* Ed.D. Practicum, Nova Univeristy. (ERIC Document Reproduction Service No. ED 327 341). 98 pp.

Center for Policy Research in Education. (1990). *Repeating grades in school: Current practice and research evidence.* (ERIC Document Reproduction Service No. ED 323 585). 9 pp.

Chunn, E. W. (1988). Sorting black students for success and failure: The inequality of ability grouping and tracking. *Urban League Review, 11*(1–2), 93–106.

Doyle, R. P. (1989). The resistence of conventional wisdom to research evidence: The case of retention in grade. *Phi Delta Kappan, 71*(3), 215–220.

Dufour, R. P., & Schwartz, W. (1990). Addressing the tracking controversy by promoting educational opportunity. *NASSP Bulletin, 74*(530), 88–94.

Findley, W. G., & Bryan, M. M. (1975). *The pros and cons of ability grouping.* (Fastback No. 66). Bloomington, IN: Phi Delta Kappa Educational Foundation. 30 pp.

French, D., & Rothman, S. (1990). *Structuring schools for student success: A focus on ability grouping.* Quincy, MA: Mass. State Dept. of Education, Bur. of Research, Planning and Evaluation. (ERIC Document Reproduction Service No. ED 315 501). 35 pp.

Frymier, J. (1990). A tale of two crises. *Principal, 69*(3), 52–53.

Gamoran, A. (1990). *The variable effects of tracking: Inequality and productivity in American high schools.* Madison, WI: National Center on Effective Secondary Schools. (ERIC Document Reproduction Service No. ED 328 632). 40 pp.

Gamoran, A., & Berends, M. (1987). *The effects of stratification in secondary schools: Synthesis of survey and ethnographic research.* Madison, WI: National Center on Effective Secondary Schools. (ERIC Document Reproduction Service No. ED 288 855). 34 pp.

Goll, P. S., et al. (1989). *Variables associated with students being classified as "at-risk."* Chicago, IL: Presented at the annual meeting of the Mid-Western Educational Research Association. (ERIC Document Reproduction Service No. ED 312 305). 18 pp.

Greenbaum, V., et al. (1990). The other side of the tracking issues (Rebuttal). *English Journal, 79*(8), 68–73.

Gursky, D. (1990). On the wrong track? *Teacher Magazine, 1*(8), 42–51.

Haberman, M. & Dill, V. (1993). The knowledge base on retention vs. teacher ideology: Implications for teacher preparation. *Journal of Teacher Education, 44*(5), 352–360.

Hill, K. G. (1989). *Grade retention and dropping out of school*. Presented at the annual meeting of the American Educational Research Association, San Francisco. (ERIC Document Reproduction Service No. ED 309 546). 10 pp.

Jones, B. F. (Ed.). (1989). *Managing instruction for equity and excellence: Effective alternatives to tracking*. Teleconference Resource Guide. Washington, DC: Public Broadcasting Service. (ERIC Document Reproduction Service No. ED 327 956). 158 pp.

Juel, C., & Leavell, J. A. (1988). Retention and non-retention of at-risk readers in first grade and their subsequent reading achievement. *Journal of Learning Disabilities, 21*(9), 571–580.

Lake, S. (1988). *Equal access to education. Alternatives to tracking and ability grouping*. Practitioner's Monograph No. 2. Sacramento, CA: California League Middle Schools. (ERIC Document Reproduction Service No. ED 303 553). 19 pp.

Lenarduzzi, G. P., & McLaughlin, T. F. (1990). The effects of nonpromotion in junior high school on academic achievement and scholastic effort. *Reading Improvement, 27*(3), 212–217.

Marion, S. F., et al. (1989). *Grade retention and student outcomes: Data from high school and beyond*. Presented at the annual meeting of the New England Educational Research Organization, Portsmouth, NH. (ERIC Document Reproduction Service No. ED 323 255). 20 pp.

Massachusetts Advocacy Center. (1990). *Locked in/locked out: Tracking and placement practices in Boston public schools*. Boston: Author. (ERIC Document Reproduction Service No. ED 320 229). 203 pp.

Meisels, S. J., et al. (1989). *Testing, tracking and retaining young children: An analysis of research and social policy*. Washington, DC: National Center for Education Statistics. (ERIC Document Reproduction Service No. ED 326 312). 46 pp.

Meyers, H. W. (1991). *Curricular tracking in six Vermont high schools in 1989: A longitudinal discriminant analysis*. Presented at the annual meeting of the American Educational Research Association, Chicago, IL. (ERIC Document Reproduction Service No. ED 331 861). 29 pp.

National Association of State Boards of Education. (1990). *More than a vision: Real improvements in urban education*. Alexandria, VA: Author. (ERIC Document Reproduction Service No. ED 327 630). 54 pp.

National Education Association. (1990). *Academic tracking: Report of the NEA Executive committee/subcommittee on academic tracking*. Washington, DC: Author. (ERIC Document Reproduction Service No. ED 322 642). 42 pp.

Norton, M. S. (1990). Practical alternatives to student retention. *Contemporary Education, 61*(4), 204–208.

Oakes, J. (1987). Curriculum inequality and school reform. *Equity and Excellence, 23*(1–2), 8–14.

Oakes, J. (1988). Tracking: Can schools take a different route? *NEA Today, 6*(6), 41–47.

Oakes, J., & Lipton, M. (1992). Detracking schools: Early lessons from the field. *Phi Delta Kappan, 73*(6), 448–454.

Phillips, N. H. (1990). *Retention, promotion, or two-tier kindergarten: Which reaches the at-risk reader more effectively?* Presented at the annual meeting of the International Reading Association, Atlanta, GA. (ERIC Document Reproduction Service No. ED 321 230). 20 pp.

Poppish, S., et al. *(1990). Assessing student attitudes toward heterogeneous grouping: A pilot study.* (ERIC Document Reproduction Service No. ED 328 397). 33 pp.

Pottorff, D. D. (1991). Grade retention: Does it hold children back? *PTA Today, 16*(3), 22–23.

Schneider, J. M. (1989). Tracking: A national perspective. *Equity and Choice, 6*(1), 11–17.

Schwager, M., & Balow, I. H. (1990). *An analysis of retention policies and their possible effects on retention rates.* Presented at the annual meeting of the American Educational Research Association, Boston. (ERIC Document Reproduction Service No. ED 318 572). 23 pp.

Shepard, L. A., & Smith, M. L. (1989). *Flunking grades: Research and policies on retention.* New York: Falmer. 243 pp.

Shepard, L. A., & Smith, M. L. (1988). Flunking kindergarten: Escalating curriculum leaves many behind. *American Educator: The Professional Journal of the American Federation of Teachers, 12*(2), 34–38.

Shepard, L. A., & Smith, M. L. (Eds.). (1989). *Flunking grades: Research and policies on retention. Educational Policy Perspectives.* (ERIC Document Reproduction Service No. ED 307 350). 243 pp.

Shepard, L. A., & Smith, M. L. (1990). Synthesis of research on grade retention. *Educational Leadership, 47*(8), 84–88.

Swartzbaugh, P. (1988). Eliminating tracking successfully. *Educational Leadership, 45*(5), 20.

Wallach, A. (1987). A second look at "Keeping Track." *Thrust For Educational Leadership, 16*(7), 34–37.

Works Cited

A nation at risk. (1983). A report by the National Commission on Excellence in Education. Washington, DC: U. S. Department of Education.

Alexander, William M., & McEwin, D. Kenneth. (1989). *Earmarks of schools in the middle: A research report.* (ERIC Document Reproduction Service No. ED 312 312).

American Association of School Administrators. (1991). *101 ways parents can help students achieve.* Washington, DC: Author.

Aring, Monika. (1993). What the "V" word is costing America's economy. *Phi Delta Kappan, 74*(5), 396–404.

Ascher, Carol. (1993). *Changing schools for urban students: The school development program, accelerated schools, and success for all.* (Trends and Issues No. 18). New York: ERIC Clearinghouse on Urban Education, Columbia University.

Associated Press. (1993, Nov. 17). Gunshot injuries in children cost in medical bills, lives. *Fairbanks Daily News-Miner,* p. A-1.

Barr, Robert D. (1972). The age of alternatives: A developing trend in education reform. *Changing Schools, 1*(1), 1–3.

Barr, Robert D. (1973). Reflections on educational reform. *Changing Schools, 2*(2), 1–6.

Barr, Robert D. (1981). Alternatives for the eighties: A second of development. *Phi Delta Kappan, 62*(8), 570–73.

Barr, Robert D. (1982). Magnet schools: An attractive alternative. *The Elementary Principal, 28*(2), 37–40.

Barr, Robert D., Barth, James, & Shermis, S. Samuel. (1977). *Defining the social studies.* Washington, DC: National Council of the Social Studies.

Barr, Robert D., Parrett, William, & Colston, B. (1977). An analysis of six school evaluations: The effectiveness of alternative public schools. *Viewpoints, 53*(4), 1–30.

Barr, Robert D., & Ross, Barbara. (1989). *Teenage parent programs: The problems and possibilities.* Corvallis, OR: Oregon State University.

Barr, Robert D., & Smith, Vernon H. (1976). Where should learning take place? In William Van Til (Ed.), *Issues in secondary education: The seventy-fifth yearbook of the National Society for the Study of Education* (pp. 153–177). Chicago, IL: University of Chicago Press.

Bauwens, Jeanne & Hourcade, Jack J. (1994). *Cooperative teaching: Rebuilding the schoolhouse for all students.* Austin, TX: Pro-Ed.

Bell, Terrel H., & Elmquist, Donna L. (1991). *How to shape up our nation's schools.* Salt Lake City, UT: Bell & Associates.

Benard, Bonnie. (1991). *Fostering resiliency in kids: Protective factors in the family, school, and community.* Portland, OR: Northwest Regional Educational Laboratory.

Bennett, Hal. (1972). *No more public school.* Berkeley, CA: The Bookworks.

Berends, M. (1992). *A description of restructuring in nationally nominated schools.* Madison, WI: University of Wisconsin, Center for Organization and Restructuring of Schools.

Berla, Nancy. (1991). Parents and schooling in the 1990s. Parent involvement at the middle level school. *The ERIC Review, 1*(3), (ERIC Document Reproduction Service ED 340 387).

Berndt, Thomas, & Ladd, Gary (Eds.). (1989). *Peer relationships in child development.* New York: John Wiley and Sons.

Big kids teach little kids: What we know about cross-age tutoring. (1987). *Harvard Education Letter, 3*(2), 1–4.

Boyer, Ernest L. (1983). *High school: A report on secondary education in America.* The Carnegie Foundation on the Advancement of Teaching. New York: Harper and Ross.

Bracey, Gerald W. (1989). Moving around and dropping out. *Phi Delta Kappan, 70*(5), 407–410.

Braddock, Jomills H., II (1990). *Tracking of Black, Hispanic, Asian, Native American and White students: National patterns and trends.* Baltimore, MD: The Johns Hopkins University, Center for Research on Effective Schooling for Disadvantaged Students.

Brandt, Ron. (1993a). Finding Time for Collaboration. *Educational Leadership, 51*(1), 30–34.

Brandt, Ron. (1993b). On restructuring roles and relationships: A conversation with Phil Schlechty. *Educational Leadership, 51*(2), 8–11.

Bruner, Charles. (1991). *Thinking collaboratively: Ten questions and answers to how policy makers improve children's services.* Washington, DC: Education and Human Services Consortium.

Bruner, Jerome. (1960). *The process of education.* Cambridge, MA: Harvard University Press.

Burgeoning educational underclass. (1987, May 18). *U.S. News and World Report,* pp. 66–67.

Business Round Table. (1993). *Essential components of a successful education system: The Business Round Table education policy agenda.* Washington, DC: Author.

Canfield, Jack. (1990). Improving students' self-esteem. *Educational Leadership, 48*(1), 48–50.

Carnegie Corporation. (1993). Turning points revisited: A new deal for adolescents. *Carnegie Quarterly, 38*(2), 1–6.

Carnegie Council on Adolescent Development. (1989). *Turning points: Preparing American youth for the 21st century: Report of the Task Force on Education of Young Adolescents.* Washington, DC: Author.

Carnegie Council on Adolescent Development. (1992). *A matter of time: Risk and opportunity in the non-school hours. Report of the Task Force onYouth Development and Community Programs.* Washington, DC: Author.

Center for Community Education. (1991). *Linking schools and community services: A practical guide.* Rutgers, NJ: State University of New Jersey—Rutgers, School of Social Work.

Center for Research on Effective Schooling for Disadvantaged Students. (1990, November). *One-to-one tutoring: Procedures for early reading success.* Baltimore, MD: The Johns Hopkins University.

Center for Research on Elementary and Middle Schools. (1987). *Research identifies effective programs for students at risk of school failure.* Baltimore, MD: The Johns Hopkins University.

Center for the Study of Reading. (1989). *10 ways to help your children become better readers.* Champaign, IL: University of Illinois.

Center on Organization and Restructuring of Schools. (1992). *Estimating the extent of school restructuring. Brief to Policymakers.* (No. 4).

Charlesworth, Rosalind. (1989). "Behind" before they start? Deciding how to deal with the risk of kindergarten "failure." *Young Children, 44*(3), 5–13.

Children and Youth Services Division. (1991). *Positive youth development.* Salem, OR: Author.

Children's Defense Fund. (May, 1989). *Service opportunities for youths.* Washington, DC: Author.

Children's Defense Fund. (1991). *The state of America's children: 1991.* Washington, DC: Author.

Clay, M. M. (1985). *The early detection of reading difficulties.* Portsmouth, NH: Heinemann.

Clay, M. M. (1991). *Becoming literate: The construction of inner control.* Portsmouth, NH: Heinemann.

Coleman, James. (1991). *Policy perspectives: Parental involvement in education.* Washington, DC: U.S. Department of Education, Office of Educational research and Improvement.

Comer, James P. (1988). Educating poor minority children. *Scientific American, 259*(5), 42–48.

Comer, James P. (1993). *School power: Implications of an intervention project.* New York: Free Press.

Commission of Chief State School Officers. (1987). *Elements of a model state statute to provide educational entitlements for at-risk students.* Washington, DC: Author.

Community Learning Centers. (1992a). *Grant to help group seek education breakthrough.* St. Paul, MN: Author.

Community Learning Centers. (1992b). *Public school incentives.* St. Paul, MN: Author.

Conant, James B. (1950). *The American high school today.* New York: McGraw-Hill.

Corvallis Oregon Public Schools. (1989). *Student information summary.* Corvallis, OR: Author.

Council of Chief State School Officers. (1989). *Success for all in a new century.* Washington, DC: Author.

Crime report: Youths who kill hit record high number. (1993, October 13). *Fort Lauderdale Sun Sentinel,* p. C-1.

Crohn, Leslie. (1992). *Forum proceedings: Integrating education and human services: Strategies to strengthen Northwest families.* Tigard, OR: Northwest Regional Educational Laboratory.

Dallea, Georgia. (1987, February 9). For the conflicts of youth, help from a peer. *New York Times,* p. 1.

Dalton, David W. (1986). How effective is interactive video in improving performance and attitudes? *Educational Technology, 26*(1).

Davis, William E., & McCaul, Edward J. (1990). *At-risk children and youth: A crisis in our schools and society.* (Report of the Institute for the Study of At-Risk Students, College of Education). Orono, ME: University of Maine.

Davis, William E., & McCaul, Edward J. (1991). *The emerging crisis: Current and projected status of children in the United States.* Orono, ME: University of Maine, Institute for the Study of At-Risk Students.

Demos, Virginia. (1989). Resiliency in infancy. In Timothy Dugan and Robert Coles (Eds.), *The children in our time* (pp. 3–22). New York: Bruner/Mazel.

Deshler, Donald D., Schumaker, J. B., Alley, G. R., Warner, M. M., & Clark, F. L. (1982). Learning disabilities in adolescent and young adult populations: Research implications. *Focus on Exceptional Children, 15*(1), 1–12.

Designs for Learning. (1992). *Community learning centers: Design* (Draft). St. Paul, MN: Author.

Designs for Learning. (1993, October). *Community learning centers,* 1–2. St. Paul, MN: Author.

Development of accelerated middle schools. (1993). *Accelerated Schools, 3*(1), 10–15.

Donaldson, Gordon A., Jr. (1993). Working smarter together. *Educational Leadership, 51*(2), 12–16.

Dorman, Gayle. (1984). *Middle grades assessment program.* Carrboro, NC: Center for Early Adolescence.

Dorman, Gayle. (1987). *Improving middle grades schools: A framework for action.* Carrboro, NC: Center for Early Adolescence.

Draper, Robert. (1993, February). Senator Spite. *Texas Monthly, 21*(2), p. 56, 78–84, 92–95.

Durian, Greg, & Butler, Jocelyn A. (1987). *Effective schooling practices and at-risk youth: What the research shows (Topical Synthesis #1).* Portland, OR: Northwest Regional Educational Laboratory.

Duttweiler, Patricia Cloud. (1992). Engaging at-risk students with technology. *Media and Methods, 29*(2), 6–8.

Edelman, Marian Wright. (1993). Foreword. In James P. Comer, *School power* (2nd ed. 1993) (pp. vii–viii).

Education Commission of the States. (1991). *Restructuring the education system: A consumer's guide.* Vol 1. Denver, CO: Author.

Eisenberg, Michael B. & Ely, Donald P. (1993, Winter). Plugging Into the "Net." *The ERIC Review.* 2(3), 2–3.

Elam, Stanley M., Rose, Lowell C., & Gallup, Alec M. (1993). The 25th Annual Phi Delta Kappa/Gallup Poll of the Public's Attitudes Toward Public Education. *Phi Delta Kappan, 75*(2), 137–157.

Elmore, Richard F. (1983). Complexity and control. What legislators and administrators can do about implementing public policy. In L. S. Shulman & G. Sykes, (Eds.), *Handbook of teaching and policy* (pp. 342–269). New York: Longman, Greenman and Co.

Epstein, Joyce L. (1985). After the bus arrives: Resegregation in desegregation schools. *Journal of Social Issues, 41,* 23–43.

Epstein, J. & Salinas, K. C. (1990). *Promising practices in major academic subjects in middle grades.* The Johns Hopkins University, Center for Research on Effective Schooling for Disadvantaged Students, (No. 4 May).

ERIC Clearinghouse on Elementary and Early childhood Education. (1990). *Guidelines in family televison viewing.* (ERIC Document Reproduction Service ED 320 662).

ERIC Clearinghouse on Elementary and Early Childhood Education. (1993). *What should be learned from kindergarten?* Urbana, IL: Author.

Erickson, Donald A. (December, 1981). A new strategy for school improvement. *Momentum, 12*(4), 48.

Erickson, John W. (1988). *The next step.* Newport, OR: Lincoln County School District.

Estes, Nolan, Levin, Daniel, & Waldrip, Donald R. (1990). *Magnet Schools: Recent developments and perspectives.* Austin, TX: Morgan Printing and Publishing.

Fenstermacher, Gary D. (1992, February 26). *Where are we going? Who will teach us?* Presidential address, annual meeting of the American Association of Colleges of Teacher Education. San Antonio, TX.

Fine, Michelle. (1986). Why urban adolescents drop into and out of public high school. *Teachers College Record, 87*(3), 393–409.

Five sites implement community learning center design. (1993). *Community Learning Centers, 2*(1), 1–2.

Foxfire approach: Core practices. (1993). *Hands On: A Journal for Teachers, 47,* 2–3.

Frymier, Jack. (1992). Children who hurt, children who fail. *Phi Delta Kappan, 73*(12), 257–259.

Frymier, Jack, Barber, L., Carriedo, R., Denton, W., Gansneder, B., Johnson-Lewis, S., & Robertson, N. (1992). *Growing up is risky business, and schools are not to blame.* Final report, Phi Delta Kappa study of students at risk, vol. 1. Bloomington, IN: Phi Delta Kappa.

Frymier, Jack, & Gansneder, Bruce. (1989). The Phi Delta Kappa study of students at risk. *Phi Delta Kappan, 71*(2), 142–146.

Gathercoal, Forrest. (1990). *Judicious discipline,* 2nd Ed. Ann Arbor, MI: Caddo Gap Press.

Gathercoal, Forrest. (1992). *Judicious parenting.* San Francisco, CA: Caddo Gap Press.

Gibbons, Maurice. (1976). *The new secondary education: A Phi Delta Kappa task force report.* Bloomington, IN: Phi Delta Kappa.

Gilder, George. (1993). Telecosm: The Issaquah miracle. *Forbes ASAP, 114*(23), 114–123.

Glickman, Carl. (1991). Pretending not to know what we know. *Educational Leadership, 48*(8), 4–10.

Goodlad, John. (1984). *A place called school: Prospects for the future.* New York: Mc-Graw-Hill.

Goodlad, John. (1990). *Teachers for our nation's schools.* San Francisco, CA: Jossey-Bass.

Gottfredson, Gary D. (1988, April). *You get what you measure, you get what you don't: Higher standards, higher test scores, more retention in grade.* Paper presented at the annual meeting of the American Educational Research Association, New Orleans, LA.

Gregory, Thomas. (1993). *Making high school work: Lessons from the Open School.* New York: Teachers College Press.

Gross, Beatrice. (1990). Here dropouts drop in—and stay. *Phi Delta Kappan, 71*(8), 625–627.

Haberman, Martin, & Dill, Vicky. (1993). The knowledge base on retention vs. teacher ideology: Implications for teacher preparation. *Journal of Teacher Education, 44*(5), 352–360.

Hamilton, Steven F. (1990). Is there life after high school? Developing apprenticeships in America. *Harvard Education Letter, 6*(4), 1–8.

Hawley, Richard A. (December, 1990). The bumpy road to drug-free schools. *Phi Delta Kappan, 72*(4), 310–314.

Hawthorne school. (1991). Unpublished evaluation report. Seattle, WA.

Heckinger, Fred M. (1992). *Fateful choices: Healthy youth for the 21st century.* New York: Carnegie Council on Adolescent Development.

Hemming, James. (1948). *Teach them to learn.* New York: Longman, Greenman and Co.

Henry, Tamara. (1993, December 15). Computers serve as equalizers in schools. *USA Today,* p. 1.

Henry, Tamara. (1993, December 17). Violence makes victims out of 1 in 4 students. *USA Today,* p. 1.

Herndon, Ron (Director). (1990). *Partners for success [video].* Portland, OR: Western Productions.

Herrmann, Beth Ann. (ed). (1994). *The volunteer tutor's toolbox.* Newark, DE: International Reading Association.

Hilliard, A., III. (1991). Do we have the will to educate all children? *Educational Leadership, 49*(1), 31–36.

Hobbs, Beverly. (1993). *School-community collaboration as a strategy for meeting the needs of at-risk youth.* Unpublished doctoral dissertation. Corvallis, OR: Oregon State University.

Hodgkinson, Harold L. (1985). *All one system. demographics of education, kindergarten through graduate school.* Washington, DC: Institute for Educational Leadership.

Hodgkinson, Harold. (1993). American education: The good, the bad, and the task. In Stanley Elam (Ed.), *The state of the nation's public schools*. Bloomington, IN: Phi Delta Kappa.

Hollifield, J. (1988). Poor basic skills: Common denominator of a society at risk. *R&D Review, 3*(1), 2.

Holmes, C. Thomas. (1990). Grade level retention effects: A meta-analysis of research studies. In Lorrie A. Shepard & Mary Lee Smith (Eds.), *Flunking grades: Research and policies on retention*. New York: Falmer Press.

Hopfenberg, Wendy S., & Levin, Henry M. (1993). *The accelerated schools resource guide*. San Francisco, CA: Jossey-Bass.

Howe, Harold II. (Nov. 1991). America 2000: A bumpy ride on four trains. *Phi Delta Kappan, 73*(3), 192–203.

Illich, Ivan. (1971). *De-schooling society*. New York: Harper and Row.

Institute for At-Risk Infants, Children and Youth and Their Families. (1991). *Toward the development of models for evaluating teachers and educational personnel who work with at-risk students and their families: Identification of effective teaching strategies and practices for working with at-risk children and their families: A status report*. Tampa, FL: Author.

Institute for Educational Leadership. (1986). *Dropouts in America: Enough is known for action*. Washington, DC: Author.

Jennings, Wayne. (1993a). Amazing developments in education—In case you hadn't noticed. *Community Learning Center, 2*(1), 1–6.

Jennings, Wayne B. (1993b). Charter schools start in Minnesota. *Changing Schools, 21*(3), 19.

Jennings, Wayne, & Nathan, Joe. (1977). Startling/disturbing research on school program effectiveness. *Phi Delta Kappan, 58*(7), 568–72.

Joyce, Bruce. (1986). *Improving America's schools*. New York: Longman, Greenman and Co.

K–12 computer networking. (1993). *The ERIC Review, 2*(3) 1–27.

Kantrowitc, Barbara. (1993, August 2). Wild in the streets. *Newsweek*, p. 46.

Karres, Deborah. (1994, April 11). State responses to violence in public schools. *American Association of Colleges for Teacher Education Briefs, 15*(7), p. 3–5.

Katz, L. G., & Chad, S. D. (1989). *Engaging children's minds: The project approach*. Norwood, NJ: Ablex Publishing.

Kelly, Diedre, M. (1993). *Last chance high: How boys and girls drop in and out of alternative schools*. New Haven, CT: Yale University Press.

Kettering Foundation. (1989). *Growing up at-risk*. Dayton, OH: Author.

Kirst, Michael W. (1993). Strengths and weaknesses of American education. Stanley Elam, (Ed.), *The state of the nation's public schools*. Bloomington, IN: Phi Delta Kappa.

Kleinfeld, Judith, McDiarmid, G. Williamson, & Parrett, William H. (1992). *Inventive teaching: The heart of the small school*. Fairbanks, AK: University of Alaska Fairbanks, Center for Cross-Cultural Studies.

Kohl, Herbert. (1991). *I won't learn from you*. Minneapolis, MN: Milkweed Editions, Thistle Series.

Kohler, Mary C. (1992). *Involving youth in decision making.* St. Paul, MN: U.S. Department of Education.

Kolderie, Ted. (1993). The states begin to withdraw the "exclusive." *Changing Schools, 21*(3), 1–8.

Kozol, Jonathan. (1967). *Death at an early age: The destruction of the hearts and minds of Negro children in the Boston public schools.* Boston, MA: Houghton Mifflin.

Kozol, Jonathan. (1991). *Savage inequalities: Children in America's schools.* New York, NY: Harper Perennial Publishers.

Kurth-Schai, Ruthanne. (1988). The roles of youth in society: A reconceptualization. *The Education Forum, 52*(2), 113–132.

Kuykendall, Crystal. (1992). *From rage to hope.* Bloomington, IN: National Educational Service.

Lang, C. (1992). *Head Start: New challenges, new chances.* Newton, MA: Education Development Center.

Ledell, Marjorie, & Arnsparger, Arleen. (1993). *How to deal with community criticism of school change.* Alexandria, VA: Association for Supervision and Curriculum Development.

Lee, V., & Smith, J. B. (1992). *Effects of school restructuring on the achievement and engagement of middle grade students.* Madison, WI: University of Wisconsin, Center on Organization and Restructuring of Schools.

Leinhardt, Gaea, & Pallas, Allan. (1982). Restrictive educational settings: exile or haven? *Review of Educational Research, 52,* 557–578.

LeTendre, Mary Jean. (1991). Improving Chapter 1 programs: We can do better. *Phi Delta Kappan, 72*(8), 576–580.

Levin, Henry M. (1989). *Accelerated schools: A new strategy for at-risk students.* Policy Bulletin no. 6, pp. 1–6. Bloomington, IN: Consortium on Educational Policy Studies.

Levin, Henry. (1991a). Accelerated visions. *Accelerated Schools, 1*(1), 2.

Levin, Henry M. (1991b). Assessing progress in the accelerated school. *Accelerated Schools, 1*(1),

Levin, Henry M. (1991c). What are accelerated schools? *Accelerated Schools, 1*(1), 1.

Levin, Henry. (1993). Accelerated visions. *Accelerated Schools, 3*(1), 1–2.

MacIver, Douglas J., & Epstein, Joyce L. (1990). *How equal are opportunities for learning in disadvantaged and advantaged middle grade schools?* (Report No. 7). Baltimore, MD: The Johns Hopkins University, Center for Research on Effective Schools for Disadvantaged Students.

Madden, Nancy A., & Slavin, Robert E. (1983). Mainstreaming students with mild handicaps: Academic and social outcomes. *Review of Educational Research, 53,* 519–570.

Madden, Nancy A., Slavin, R. E., Karweit, N. L., Dolan, L., & Wasik, B. A. (1991). Success for all. *Phi Delta Kappan, 72*(8), 593–599.

Magi Educational Services. (1985). *New York State magnet school research study.* Larchmont, NY: Author.

Mann, Dale. (1986). Can we help dropouts: Thinking about the undoable. *Teachers College Record, 87*(3), 307–323.

Manning, Anita. (1994, Jan. 21). Gunshot kills one U.S. child every two hours. *USA Today*, p. 1.

Mark of Cain. (1990, January 15). *Newsweek*, p. 6

Martin, Dave. (1988). Wake up: The American dream is fading and our future is at risk. *The American School Board Journal, 175*(2), 21–24.

Martin, Dave. (1989). *The beginning of sorrow*. New York: Random House.

Mason Elementary School: Helping children beat the odds. (1993). *Accelerated Schools, 3*(1), 4–9.

Massachusetts Advocacy Center. (1988). *Before it's too late: Dropout prevention for the middle schools*. Carrboro, NC: Author.

McGuillie, Strike. (1993, Nov. 8). When fundamentalists run the schools. *Newsweek*, p. 45.

McMullan, Bernard F., Garrett, Cheryl, Watts, Marion, & Wolf, Wendy. (1992). *A shared responsibility: College/school partnerships serving minority youth*. Bala Cynwyd, PA: Center for Assessment and Policy Development.

McPartland, James M., & Slavin, Robert E. (1990). *Policy perspectives: Increasing achievement of at-risk students at each grade level*. Washington, DC: U.S. Department of Education.

Mecklenburger, James A. (1992). The beginning of the "break-the-mold" express. *Phi Delta Kappan, 74*(4), 280–289.

Miller, William H. (1988, July 4). Employers wrestle with "dumb" kids. *Industry Week*, p. 48.

Mitchell, R. (1989). Off the Tracks. *Perspective, 1*(3), 1–16.

Molnar, Alex. (1993). Fundamental differences? *Educational Leadership, 51*(4), 4–5.

Muncey, Donna E., & McQuillan, Patrick J. (1993). Preliminary findings from a five-year study of the Coalition of Essential Schools. *Phi Delta Kappan, 74*(6), 486–489.

Nachtigal, Paul. (1972). *A foundation goes to school*. New York: The Ford Foundation.

Nash, M. A. (1990). *Improving their chances: A handbook for designing and implementing programs for at-risk youth*. Madison, WI: University of Wisconsin—Madison, Vocational Studies Center, School of Education.

Nathan, Joe (Ed.). (1989). *Public schools of choice*. St. Paul, MN: The Institute for Learning and Teaching,

National Center for Educational Statistics. (1991). *Dropout rates decline over decade*. Washington, DC: U.S. Department of Education, Office of Educational Research and Improvement.

National Center for Educational Statistics. (1993). *Digest of education statistics 1993*. Washington DC: U.S. Department of Education, Office of Educational Research and Improvement.

National Commission on Excellence in Education (1983). *A nation at risk*. Washington, DC: U.S. Department of Education.

National Dropout Prevention Center. (February, 1990). *Mentoring programs for at-risk youth*. Clemson, SC: Clemson University.

National School Boards Association. (1989). *An equal chance: Educating at-risk children to succeed*. Alexandria, VA: Author.

Natriello, Gary. (1988). *An examination of the assumptions and evidence for aternative dropout prevention programs in high school.* Report No. 365. Baltimore, MD: The Johns Hopkins University, Center for Social Organization of Schools.

Newman, Fred. (1987). *Conference proceedings: Meeting the needs of youth at risk.* Portland, OR: Northwest Regional Educational Laboratory.

Northwest Regional Educational Laboratory. (1990). *Effective schooling practices: A research synthesis 1990 update.* Portland, OR: Author.

Northwest Regional Educational Laboratory. (1993a). *Community as classrooms.* (Northwest Report, pp. 6–7.) Portland, OR: Author.

Northwest Regional Educational Laboratory. (1993b). *The promise of tech prep: A special report.* Portland, OR: Author.

Northwest Regional Educational Laboratory. (1993c). *Schools, agencies team up for health.* (Northwest Report, pp. 1–4.) Portland, OR: Author.

Oakes, Jeannie. (1993). *Last chance high: How girls and boys drop in and out of alternative schools.* New Haven, CT: Yale University Press.

Office of Educational Research and Improvement. (1987). *Dealing with drop outs: The urban superintendent's call to action.* Washington DC: U.S. Department of Education.

Office of Educational Research and Improvement. (1992). *New reports focus on eighth graders and their parents.* Washington, DC: U.S. Department of Education, National Center For Educational Strategies.

Pabst, Diana L. (1993). To police or to protect. *R & D Review, 8*(5), 1–3.

Pallas, A. M., Natriello, G., & McDill, E. L. (1989). The changing nature of the disadvantaged population: Current dimensions and future trends. *Educational Researcher, 18*(5), 4 and 16–22.

Parnell, Dale. (1982). *The neglected majority.* Washington, DC: Community College Press.

Parrett, William. (1979). *An investigation of teachers' and students' perceptions of instructional practices in alternative schools.* Unpublished doctoral dissertation, Indiana University, Bloomington, IN.

Perfect school. (1993, January 11). *U. S. News & World Report,* pp. 46–61.

Personalizing New York City high schools: The coalition campus schools project. (1994, Winter). *Resources for Restructuring.* National Center for Restructuring Education, Schools, and Teaching.

Pinnell, Gay Su. (1990). Success for low achievers through Reading Recovery. *Educational Leadership, 48*(1), 17–21.

Pinnell, G. S., Lyons, C. A., DeFord, D. E., Bryk, A.S. & Seltzer, M. (1994). Comparing instructional models for the literacy education of high-risk first graders. *Reading Research Quarterly, 29,* 9–38.

Project Plus. (1990). *A special report on mentoring.* Pittsburgh, PA: Project Literacy United States.

Raywid, Mary Ann. (1983). Schools of choice: Their current nature and prospects. *Phi Delta Kappan, 64*(10), 684–688.

Raywid, Mary Ann. (1993a). Community: An alternative school accomplishment. In G. Smith (ed.), *Public schools that work* (pp. 23–44). New York: Routledge.

Raywid, Mary Ann. (1993b). Finding time for collaboration. *Educational Leadership,* *51*(2), 30–34.

Reimer, Everett. (1971). *School is dead.* Garden City, NY: Doubleday.

Report targets rise in teen pregnancy. (1993, Nov. 20). *Fairbanks Daily News-Miner,* p. A-1.

Riley outlines sobering facts on crime. (August 2, 1993). *Education USA,* p. 6.

Riley, Pamela. (1993). California's charter schools. *Changing Schools, 21*(3), 14–18.

Romer, Roy. (1993). Charter schools: A tool for reinventing public education. *Changing Schools, 21*(3), 1–9.

Rural Entrepreneurship Through Action Learning. (1993). *It's time to get real.* Athens, GA: Real Enterprises. [Brochure.]

Sarason, Seymour. (1971). *The culture of school and the problem of change.* Boston, MA: Allyn and Bacon.

School Restructuring Consortium. (1991, July). *SIRUS-A: Navigating by the stars. (School Improvement Resources Inquiry–USA).* A National Study of School Restructuring. Bloomington, IN: Indiana University, School of Education.

Schorr, Lisbeth. (1992). *Service integration and beyond: The challenge in integrating education and human services: Strategies to strengthen Northwest families.* Forum Proceeding, Northwest Regional Educational Laboratory.

Schorr, Lisbeth B., & Schorr, Daniel. (1989). *Within our reach: Breaking the cycle of disadvantage.* New York: Anchor Books/Doubleday.

Scott-Jones, Diane. (1993). Adolescent child bearing: Whose problem? What can we do? *Phi Delta Kappan, 75*(3), K1–K12.

Shepard, Lorrie A., & Smith, Mary Lee. (1989). *Flunking grades: Research and policies on retention.* London: Falmer Press.

Silberman, Charles, E. (1970a). *Crisis in the classroom.* New York: Random House.

Silberman, Charles, E. (1970b). Murder in the classroom: How the public schools kill dreams and mutilate minds. *Atlantic Magazine, 225*(6), 82–96.

Sinclair, R. L., & Ghory, W. J. (1987). *Marginal students: A primary concern for school renewal.* Berkeley, CA: McCutchan.

Slavin, Robert E. (1991a). Chapter 1: A vision for the next quarter century. *Phi Delta Kappan, 72*(8), 586–589, 591–592.

Slavin, Robert E. (1991b). Synthesis of research of cooperative learning. *Educational Leadership, 48*(5), 71–82.

Slavin, Robert E. (1993). Students differ: So what? *Educational Researcher, 22*(9), 13.

Slavin, Robert E., Karweit, Nancy L., & Madden, Nancy A. (1989). *Effective programs for students at risk.* Boston: Allyn & Bacon.

Slavin, Robert E., Karweit, Nancy L., & Wasik, Barbara A. (1992, December). Preventing early school failure. *Educational Leadership, 50*(4), 10–18.

Slavin, Robert E., & Madden, Nancy A. (1989). What works for students at risk: A research synthesis. *Educational Leadership, 46*(5), 4–20.

Smith, Gerald R, Gregory, Thomas, B., & Pugh, Richard C. (1981). Meeting students' needs: Evidence for the superiority of alternative schools. *Phi Delta Kappan, 62*(8), 561–564.

Smith, Gregory A. (Ed.) (1993). *Public schools that work.* New York: Routledge. 254 pp.

Smith, R. C., & Lincoln, C. A. (1988). *America's shame, America's hope: Twelve million youth at risk.* Flint, MI: Charles Stewart Mott Foundation.

Smith, Vernon, Barr, Robert, & Burke, Daniel. (1976). *Alternatives in education: Freedom to choose.* Bloomington, Indiana: Phi Delta Kappa.

Spady, William G., & Marshall, Kit J. (1991). Beyond traditional outcome-based education. *Educational Leadership, 49*(2), 67–72.

St. Paul Open School. (1993). Program guidelines. [Brochure.] St. Paul, MN: Author.

Stanford University. (1993). The development of accelerated middle schools. *Accelerated Schools, 3*(l), 10–15.

State Community Children and Youth Services Commission. (1990). *What is community action planning, Version 3.00,* p. 1–4. Salem, OR: Author.

State of New York. (1993). *Executive budget.* Albany, NY: Author.

State Policy Research, Inc. (1993a, Jan.) State Policy Reports. Vol. 11(2). Birmingham, AL: Author.

State Policy Research, Inc. (1993b, Aug.) State Policy Reports. Vol. 11(16). Birmingham, AL: Author.

Steffy, Betty E. (1993). Top-down, bottom-up: Systemic change in Kentucky. *Educational Leadership, 51*(1), 42–44.

Stern, Marilyn, & VanSlych, Michael R. (1986). *Enhancing adolescent's self-image: implementation of a peer mediation program.* Paper presented at the meeting of the American Psychological Association, Washington, DC.

Stichter, Charlotte. (1986). When tempers flare, let trained student mediators put out the flames. *American School Board Journal, 173*(3), 41–42.

Sweeney, Mary Ellen. (1993). Successful strategies for charter schools: A checklist. *Changing Schools, 21*(3), 9.

Tanner, Daniel. (1993). A Nation "truly" at-risk. *Phi Delta Kappan, 75*(4), 288–297.

Teddlie, Charles, & Stringfield, Sam. (1993). *Schools make a difference: Lessons Learned from a ten-year study of school effects.* New York: Teachers College Press.

The American Teacher 1993: Violence in America's Public Schools. (1993). New York: Metropolitan Life.

Tomorrow's schools: Principles for the design of professional development schools. (1990). East Lansing, MI: Holmes Group.

Tomorrow's teachers. (1986). East Lansing, MI: Holmes Group.

U.S. Department of Commerce. (1992). *Statistical abstract of the United States, 1992.* 112th Ed., *The National Data Book.* Washington, DC: Author.

U.S. Department of Education. (1987a). *What works: Research about teaching and learning.* 2nd edition. Washington, DC: Author.

U.S. Department of Education. (1987b). *What works: Schools that work.* Washington, DC: Author.

U.S. Department of Education. (1992). *National assessment of educational progress. Trends in academic progress: Achievement of U.S. students in science, 1969–70 to 1990; mathematics, 1973 to 1990; reading, 1971 to 1990; writing, 1984 to 1990.* Washington, DC: U.S. Department of Education, Office of Educational Research and Improvement, Educational Testing Service.

U.S. Department of Labor. (1992). *Learning a living: A blueprint for high performance.* Washington, DC: Secretary's Commission on Achieving Necessary Skills.

Viadero, Debra (Feb. 9, 1994). "Impact of reform said to be spotty and not systemic." *Education Week,* 13(20). p. 1 & 12.

Waldrip, Donald R., Marks, Walter L., & Estes, Nolan. (1993). *Magnet school policy studies and evaluations.* Austin, TX: Morgan Printing.

Wasik, Barbara, & Slavin, Robert E. (1993). Preventing early reading failure with one to one tutoring: A review of five programs. *Reading Research Quarterly, 28*(2), 179–200.

Wehlage, Gary G., Rutter, Robert A., Smith, Gregory A., Lesko, Nancy, & Fernandez, Ricardo R. (1989). *Reducing the risk: Schools as communities of support.* Philadelphia, PA: The Falmer Press.

Wehlage, Gary, Rutter, R. A., & Turnbaugh, Anne Van Til. (1987). A program model for at-risk high school students. *Educational Leadership, 44*(6), 70–73.

Wells, Amy Stuart. (1991). *Middle school education—The critical link, striving for excellence: The national goals.* Washington, DC: U.S. Department of Education, Office of Educational Research and Improvement, Educational Resource Information Center.

Werner, Emmy, & Smith, Ruth. (1982). *Vulnerable but invincible: A longitudinal study of resilient children and youth.* New York: Adams, Bannister & Cox.

What are accelerated schools? (1991). *The Accelerated Schools Newsletter, 1*(1), 1–16.

Wheelock, C. (1986). Dropping out: What the research says. *Equity and Choice, 3*(1), 7–10.

Wigtil, James V., & Wigtil, Joanne M. (1993). Counseling with at-risk students. In Ann Vernon (Ed.), *Counseling children and adolescents* (pp. 160–179). Denver, CO: Love Publishing.

Wilson, Barbara. (1993). *Celebration of teaching and teachers.* Speech at Boise State University, October 27, 1993.

Wilt, Joan. (1993). Charter schools: An entrepreneurial approach to public schools. *Changing Schools, 21*(3), 10–12.

Winter, Sam. (1986). Peers as paired reading tutors. *British Journal of Special Education, 13*(3), 103–106.

Wirth, Arthur G. (1993). Education and work: The choices we face. *Phi Delta Kappan, 74*(5), 361–369.

Young, Timothy. (1990). *Public alternative education: Options and choice for today's schools.* New York: Teachers College Press.

Young, Timothy, & Clinchy, Evans. (1993). *Choice in public education.* New York: Teachers College Press.

Zeichner, K. M. (1983, March). *Individual and institutional factors related to the socialization of teachers.* Paper presented at First Years of Teaching: What are the Pertinent Issues? University of Texas, R & D Center for Teacher Education, Austin, TX.

Zimmerman, Jack, Norris, Dia, Kirkpatrick, Jerry, Mann, Augusta, & Herndon, Ron. (1989). *Partners for success: Business and education.* Portland, OR: National Association for Schools of Excellence.

Appendix:
School Self-Evaluation Checklists for Serving Students At Risk

In order to provide schools and communities with assistance in ensuring that all students at-risk can be adequately served, four self-evaluation checklists have been included. These self-evaluation checklists include:

- School Self-Evaluation Checklist: Beliefs/Baseline Assessments
- Evaluation Profile: Preschool and Elementary School
- Evaluation Profile: Middle Level School
- Evaluation Profile: High School

These self-evaluation instruments have been developed and field tested in order to stimulate discussions in schools and communities and serve as evaluation tools. The checklists relate statements of fact, perceptions, and beliefs to the best available research on students at risk and provide a basis for school/community consensus building. They also provide a way for schools and communities to monitor baseline data and to evaluate their effectiveness in meeting the needs of at-risk youth. Each statement in the four checklists relates directly to research findings and experienced-based practice that have been discussed in *Hope At Last for At-Risk Youth*.

The first checklist focuses on beliefs and is presented in an agree—disagree format. It also includes a baseline assessment profile. The following three checklists provide a way to inventory and evaluate the degree to which a specific school is addressing the needs of students at risk.

Self-Evaluation Checklist

Beliefs

Based on a comprehensive review of research and evaluation of schools that document success with all children, the following self-evaluation was created. This checklist should provide a strong indicator of whether or not the teachers, administration, and parents associated with a school have the beliefs and dispositions necessary to guarantee success for students at risk. For personal, schoolwide or school/community assessment, please complete the following questionnaire using strongly agree (SA); agree (A); disagree (D); or strongly disagree (SD). Following the completion of the self-evaluation, small groups should discuss their responses and attempt to develop consensus points of view.

1. Teachers, administrators and parents must have a shared vision and/or agreed upon goals for addressing the needs of students at-risk.

    SA _____   A _____   D _____   SD _____

2. Teachers, parents (and students in middle and high schools) should be allowed to participate in the planning and governance of a school.

    SA _____   A _____   D _____   SD _____

3. Teachers, parents, and administrators should voluntarily agree to participate in significant school improvement or restructuring efforts.

    SA _____   A _____   D _____   SD _____

4. In order to effectively address their needs, at-risk students should be grouped into "slow learning" tracks.

    SA _____   A _____   D _____   SD _____

5. Teachers who do not agree with the shared beliefs of the majority of teachers and parents should be allowed to transfer to another school without any negative consequences.

    SA _____   A _____   D _____   SD _____

6. Some children (other than the mentally handicapped) simply can not achieve up to the learning levels of their more successful classmates.

    SA _____   A _____   D _____   SD _____

7. In order to effectively address their needs, at-risk students should be retained in the early grades until they are ready to proceed successfully.

    SA _____   A _____   D _____   SD _____

8. The majority of teachers must support any significant school improvement or restructuring effort for it to be effective.

    SA _____   A _____   D _____   SD _____

9. At-risk students should be assigned to special education so that they can receive the individual support and attention that they need.

SA _____   A _____   D _____   SD _____

10. With the exception of the mentally handicapped, all children can learn up to grade level, regardless of family situations or socioeconomic status .

SA _____   A _____   D _____   SD _____

11. Teachers, administrators, and parents must be caring, demanding, and hold high expectations for all students.

SA _____   A _____   D _____   SD _____

12. Children of poor, dysfunctional families can't be successful in school.

SA _____   A _____   D _____   SD _____

13. Traditional school organization and traditional approaches to teaching and learning must be significantly restructured in order to effectively address the needs of at-risk students.

SA _____   A _____   D _____   SD _____

14. Since at-risk students often disrupt classrooms and interrupt the orderly learning of the other students, they should be assigned to special classrooms or programs.

SA _____   A _____   D _____   SD _____

15. Students who are not progressing satisfactorily in school should be retained, regardless of grade level, until they can proceed with success.

SA _____   A _____   D _____   SD _____

16. Many at-risk students would be better served by dropping out of school and getting a job or joining the armed forces.

SA _____   A _____   D _____   SD _____

17. Parents must be significantly involved in supporting the instructional programs of the school

SA _____   A _____   D _____   SD _____

18. At-risk students should be removed from regular classrooms and placed in homogeneous groups so that their needs can be better addressed.

SA _____   A _____   D _____   SD _____

19. Different students learn in different ways and different teachers teach in different ways.

SA _____   A _____   D _____   SD _____

20. The most effective way to teach at-risk students is to create small groups of teachers and students that function as caring communities of mutual respect.

SA _____   A _____   D _____   SD _____

21. At-risk students should be pulled out of regular classrooms for part of the day so that they can receive enriched and remedial instruction in reading and/or assistance in special education.

SA _____   A _____   D _____   SD _____

22. The needs of at-risk students can be met by scheduling them into special study skills and personal assistance courses for one or two periods each day.

SA _____   A _____   D _____   SD _____

23. Every child can and must be taught to read by the end of the third grade.

SA _____   A _____   D _____   SD _____

24. The needs of at-risk high school students can best be met by scheduling them into short, intensive programs designed to transition them back into regular classrooms as soon as possible.

SA _____   A _____   D _____   SD _____

25. The needs of at-risk students cannot be met by schools alone. To succeed, parents, community leaders, and social service agencies must be cooperatively involved in the school.

SA _____   A _____   D _____   SD _____

26. At-risk students must be taught in the same way as the gifted and talented; their learning must be enriched and accelerated.

SA _____   A _____   D _____   SD _____

27. The learning of all students must be carefully, continually, and frequently assessed.

SA _____   A _____   D _____   SD _____

28. Educational resources should be reallocated to focus on the needs of at-risk students.

SA _____   A _____   D _____   SD _____

29. At-risk students should be assigned to mandatory remediation and individualized programs.

SA _____   A _____   D _____   SD _____

30. Successful programs for at-risk students must start as early as possible and support should continue until students have demonstrated a track record of success in school.

SA _____   A _____   D _____   SD _____

31. Schools have too much to do already without trying to involve the community and social service agencies into cooperative programs.

SA _____   A _____   D _____   SD _____

32. Parents are children's first teachers, and they must participate in activities that help prepare their children for school.

SA _____   A _____   D _____   SD _____

33. Disruptive students who can't behave should be expelled from school.

SA _____   A _____   D _____   SD _____

34. Effective classroom teachers can adequately address the needs of at-risk students.

SA _____   A _____   D _____   SD _____

35. Prevention programs at the early childhood, preschool, and early elementary grades are more successful and more cost effective than dropout prevention programs and alternative schools at the middle and high-school levels.

SA _____   A _____   D _____   SD _____

36. Schools can overcome the negative impact of poor parenting and dysfunctional families.

SA _____   A _____   D _____   SD _____

37. Principals should visit classrooms frequently and try to motivate teachers to be successful with all children.

SA _____   A _____   D _____   SD _____

38. Children and youth can be effective in helping each other learn.

SA _____   A _____   D _____   SD _____

39. School reform can only occur when it is mandated by the state or the local school board.

SA _____   A _____   D _____   SD _____

40. Schools should have before and after-school extended day programs to provide additional educational opportunities for at-risk students.

SA _____   A _____   D _____   SD _____

41. One-to-one tutoring is the most effective instructional program for at-risk students.

SA _____   A _____   D _____   SD _____

42. Computers should be available in technology laboratories rather than in classrooms.

SA _____   A _____   D _____   SD _____

43. Providing a number of alternative public schools that are available to students, parents, and teachers on the basis of choice tends to create confusion and complicates the orderly administration of education.

SA _____   A _____   D _____   SD _____

44. Public schools should be available to parents and their children on the basis of free choice.

SA _____   A _____   D _____   SD _____

45. Every at-risk student should have an adult mentor.

SA _____   A _____   D _____   SD _____

46. Students at every grade level should be learning about possible future careers.

SA _____   A _____   D _____   SD _____

47. The best way to prevent violence is to hire more police and juvenile authorities.

SA _____   A _____   D _____   SD _____

48. Schools should teach conflict resolution techniques to students of all ages.

SA _____   A _____   D _____   SD _____

49. No matter what is attempted, schools cannot be significantly changed or restructured.

SA _____   A _____   D _____   SD _____

50. Schools do not need to be significantly changed to address the needs of school-age youth.

SA _____   A _____   D _____   SD _____

Interpreting the Beliefs Checklist

Even though the statements included in the beliefs checklist may be overly simplistic, they are in fact based on the best available research and evaluations of successful programs.

These items supported by research include statement numbers 1, 2, 3, 5, 8, 10, 11, 13, 17, 19, 20, 23, 25, 26, 27, 28, 30, 32, 35, 36, 37, 38, 40, 41, 44, 45, 46, and 48. If teachers, parents, and administrators agree or agree strongly on a majory of these 28 items, there is a strong possibility that the school can begin to guarantee success for many children. The greater the consensus on all of these items, the greater the likelihood of successfully teaching all students.

Items that are not supported by research and that in fact have detrimental effects on at-risk students include statement numbers 4, 6, 7, 9, 12, 14, 15, 16, 21,

22, 24, 29, 31, 33, 34, 39, 42, 43, 47, 49, and 50. If one agrees with a number of these 22 statements, there exists a strong possibility that there is confusion, fundamental disagreement, or lack of understanding among the teachers, parents, and administrators in the school regarding effective education for at-risk students. It is also highly unlikely that all students will be able to succeed in school. If there is confusion, disagreement, and misunderstanding, each school should provide professional staff development opportunities which emphasize research and evaluation of effective at-risk programs, conduct extensive discussions, and attempt to work toward greater schoolwide agreement. If consensus cannot be achieved, intensive long-term development may be required. **Please complete the Baseline Assessment Profile on page 303 before proceeding.**

Evaluation Profile: Preschool and Elementary School

Please check each statement that reflects an accurate description of your school or school district. This checklist can be used individually or by groups of teachers, parents, and administrators. Discussions should then be conducted to compare individual responses and work for schoolwide consensus on as many items as possible. Once completed, the checklist should serve as a profile of the schools effectiveness in addressing the needs of students at risk. The profile can also be used to compare the effectiveness of different schools in serving students at risk.

Shared Vision/Goals

1. Does the school have a shared vision and/or agreed upon schoolwide goals? _____

2. Is the school involved in a schoolwide improvement or restructuring program that is supported by the majority of teachers and parents, i.e., programs like Success For All, Accelerated Schools, or some local independent plan? _____

3. Do teachers, parents, and the principal share the responsibility for planning, governing, and managing the school? _____

4. Does the school district encourage local control or have a policy providing site-based management? _____

5. Does the school have a planning or governance council consisting of parents, teachers, and administrators? _____

6. Does the school regularly utilize parents and other adults as classroom volunteers? _____

7. Does the school district provide alternative schools that focus on different approaches to teaching and learning? (example: Montessori schools, non-graded schools, open schools, continuous progress schools, etc.) _____

8. Does the school serve less than 500 students?   _____

9. Do parents, teachers, and administrators hold high expectations for
all students?   _____

Parents

10. Does your school have a parenting skills program?   _____

11. Does your school offer opportunities for parents to help children
prepare for school?   _____

12. Are parents encouraged to assist in the school's instructional
programs?   _____

13. If parents are unable or unwilling to assist in the school's instructional programs, are supplemental arrangements provided for these
children?   _____

14. Are parents encouraged to volunteer in the school?   _____

15. Are parents provided an opportunity to participate in school planning and governance?   _____

Early Childhood and Preschool

16. Does the school have a child care program?   _____

17. Does the school have a preschool program?   _____

18. Does the school have a kindergarten program?   _____

19. Does the school provide all-day kindergarten?   _____

20. Does the school participate in a Head Start or similar preschool
enrichment program?   _____

Curriculum and Instruction

21. Does the school qualify for Chapter I?   _____

22. Does the school qualify for a schoolwide Chapter I program?   _____

23. Does the school participate in the Reading Recovery program?   _____

24. Does the school use a one-to-one tutorial program:
   * using the Reading Recovery program?   _____
   * using trained, certified teachers?   _____
   * using trained volunteers?   _____
   * using peer tutors?   _____

25. Does the school curriculum emphasize reading, writing, story telling and communicating?   _____

26. Does the school utilize a non-graded or multi-age grouping in the early elementary grades?   _____

27. Does the school encourage cooperative learning?   _____

28. Does the school cluster computers in each elementary classroom?   _____

29. Does the school provide enriched resources for the preschool through third grade?   _____

30. Does the school have a program of frequent, continuous, and planned student assessment of reading, writing, and mathematics?   _____

31. Do all third graders in the school read at or above grade level?   _____

32. Does the school refuse to retain students in grades K-3?   _____

33. Does the school teach all children as if they were gifted and talented?   _____

34. Does the school place primary emphasis on ensuring a strong foundation in the subjects of: reading, writing, and math?   _____

35. Do students tutor one another?   _____

Social Services

36. Does the school have a free breakfast program for qualifying students?   _____

37. Does the school have a free lunch program for qualifying students?   _____

38. Does the school have some type of youth services council or committee, comprised of school and social service agencies, that addresses the needs of at-risk youth and their families using a case management approach?   _____

39. Does the school have a free meal program during the summer?   _____

40. Does the school coordinate the resources and services of social service agencies?   _____

41. Does the school participate in community partnerships?   _____

42. Does the school have a morning or afternoon extended day program for latchkey, at-risk, and other students?   _____

43. Does the school provide counselors or social workers to assist students and their families?   _____

After individual teachers, administrators, and parents have completed the checklist and through discussions have developed schoolwide consensus on as many items as possible, the profile should serve as an indicator of effectiveness in meeting the needs of students at risk. Since each item on the Evaluation Profile reflects the best available research regarding the components of school effectiveness for students at risk, the greater the number of items that accurately describe a school, the greater the likelihood that the school is effectively serving students at risk.

Evaluation Profile: Middle-Level School

Please check each statement that reflects an adequate description of your school or school district. This checklist can be used individually or by groups of teachers, parents, and administrators. Once consensus items are identified, the checklist should serve as a profile of the school's effectiveness in addressing the needs of students at risk. The profile can also be used to compare the effectiveness of different schools in serving students at risk.

Shared Vision/Goals

1. Have teachers, administrator, and parents conducted a consensus-building process that has culminated in a shared vision and/or school-wide goals?   _____

2. Is the school organization modeled more on elementary schools than senior high schools?   _____

3. Are students involved in the planning and governance of the school through some type of student council or student government?   _____

4. Does the school have a planning and/or governance committee or council that includes teachers, administrators, parents and students?   _____

Curriculum and Instruction

5. Has the school been organized into a number of small learning groups where a cohort of students and teachers work together for most of the school day?   _____

6. Does the school curriculum include a focus on the developmental needs of young adolescents (for example: healthy lifestyles, sexual and social development, communication, critical thinking, recreation, etc.)?   _____

7. Does the school curriculum include an interdisciplinary core?   _____

8. Does the school use flexible scheduling to provide longer blocks of time for core subjects and interdisciplinary study?   _____

9. Does the school offer a number of elective courses that focus on career education and exploration, recreation, and interest areas?   _____

10. Does the school emphasize cooperative learning in the classroom?   _____

11. Are students grouped into heterogeneous classes?   _____

12. Does the school have a mentor program for students at risk?   _____

13. Does the school have a counselor or social worker who assists students and their families?   _____

14. Does the school have a computer technology laboratory?   _____

15. Does the school have clusters of computers in each classroom?   _____

16. Do teachers serve as classroom counselors and advisors during a prescribed time during the day?   _____

17. Does the school involve students in out-of-school activities?
   - Field trips   _____
   - Career exploration   _____
   - Service activities   _____
   - Cross-age tutoring   _____
   - Intramural sports/recreation   _____
   - Other   _____

18. Does the school provide drug and alcohol programs for students who need them?   _____

19. Is the school involved in a schoolwide restructuring or improvement effort that is supported by the majority of the teachers?   _____

20. Do students in the school have opportunities to participate in alternative programs?   _____

21. Are there high expectations for student learning?   _____

22. Are these high expectations held for all students?   _____

23. Does the school have opportunities for students to participate in clubs and extra-curricular activities?   _____

24. Does the school have a transition program to help elementary students successfully matriculate to the middle-level school?   _____

25. Does the school have a transition program to help students matriculate to high school?   _____

26. Do students have opportunities to participate in after-school community youth clubs?   _____

27. Are opportunities provided to learn the skills of conflict resolution?   _____

Parents

28. Are parents involved in establishing school and community rules and regulations? _____

29. Are parents encouraged to be involved in the school? _____

30. Do parents participate as volunteers in the school? _____

31. Are parents encouraged to assist students with homework? _____

After individual teachers, administrators and parents have completed the checklist and through discussions have developed schoolwide consensus on as many items as possible, the profile should serve as an indicator of effectiveness in meeting the needs of students at risk. Since each item on the Evaluation Profile reflects the best available research regarding the components of school effectiveness for students at risk, the greater the number of items that accurately describe a school, the greater the likelihood that the school is effectively serving students at risk.

Evaluation Profile: High School

Please check each statement that reflects an adequate description of your school and/or school district. This checklist can be used individually or by groups of teachers, parents and administrators. Once consensus items are identified, the checklist should serve as a profile of the school's effectiveness in addressing the needs of students at-risk. The profile can also be used to compare the effectiveness of different schools in serving students at risk.

Shared Vision/Goals

1. Does the school have a shared vision and/or agreed upon schoolwide goals? _____

2. Is the school involved in a schoolwide improvement or restructuring program that is supported by the majority of teachers and parents (i.e., programs like Coalition of Essential Schools)? _____

3. Do teachers, parents, and the principal share the responsibility for planning, governing and managing the school? _____

4. Does the school district encourage local control or have a policy providing site-based management? _____

5. Does the school have a planning or governance council consisting of parents, teachers, and administrators? _____

6. Does the school regularly utilize parents and other adults as classroom volunteers? _____

7. Does the school offer a school-within-a-school or alternative programs?   _____

8. Do parents, teachers and administrators hold high expectations for all students?   _____

Parents

9. If parents are unable or unwilling to assist in the school's instructional programs, are supplemental arrangements provided for these children?   _____

10. Are parents encouraged to volunteer in the school?   _____

11. Are parents provided an opportunity to participate in school planning and governance?   _____

Curriculum and Instruction

12. Does the public school offer alternative or magnet programs specifically designed to meet the needs of at-risk youth?   _____

13. Are all students, regardless of academic levels, offered the opportunities to participate in district alternative/magnet schools?   _____

14. Does the district offer some type of teen parent program or young parent program?   _____

15. Is the teen parent program designed to provide an educational program for all teen parents in the community?   _____

16. Does the school district offer a comprehensive vocational training program?   _____

17. Does the school district or school have a 2 + 2 program in cooperation with a local community college?   _____

18. Does the school district or school participate in a partnership with local business and industry or a Private Industry Council?   _____

19. Does the school district or school participate in apprenticeship programs?   _____

20. Does the school district or school offer any program similar to the Foxfire Experience?   _____

21. Does the school district or school provide for real life, out of school programs?   _____

22. Does the school district or school have a mentoring program?   _____

23. Does the school district or school have a career education program?   _____

24. Do students in the school district or school have access to a U.S. Job Corp program? _____

25. Does the school district or school offer students a summer catch-up program or evening program? _____

26. Does the school district or school offer students a high school equivalency program? _____

27. Does the school district or school offer students the opportunity to leave high school and pursue coursework at a community college or university? _____

28. Does the school district or school provide students with the opportunity to use computers, in conjunction with classroom instruction? _____

29. Does the school district or school provide for drug and alcohol prevention programs and drug and alcohol support groups? _____

30. Does the school district or school have a health clinic available for high school students? _____

31. Does the school district or school participate in a self-esteem building program? _____

32. Does the school have an outdoor education program? _____

Social Services

33. Does the school have a free breakfast program for qualifying students? _____

34. Does the school have a free lunch program for qualifying students? _____

35. Does the school have some type of Youth Services Council or committee, comprised of school and social services agencies that addresses the needs of at-risk youth and their families using a case management approach? _____

36. Does the school have a free meal program during the summer? _____

37. Does the school coordinate the resources and services of social service agencies? _____

38. Does the school participate in community partnerships? _____

39. Does the school have a morning and/or afternoon extended day program for latchkey, at-risk and other students? _____

40. Does the school provide counselors or social workers to assist students and their families? _____

After individual teachers, administrators, and parents have completed the checklist and through discussions have developed schoolwide consensus on as many items as possible, the profile should serve as an indicator of effectiveness in meeting the needs of students at risk. Since each item on the Evaluation Profile reflects the best available research regarding the components of school effectiveness for students at risk, the greater the number of items that accurately describe a school, the greater the likelihood that the school is effectively serving students at risk.

Baseline Assessment Profile

Schools should establish baseline data to effectively monitor progress toward identifying and serving the at-risk student population. Data should be updated and reviewed on a regular basis by the school staff and community.

1. What percentage of students score at or above national averages on standardized achievement tests?   _____

2. What percentage of students qualify for free lunch programs?   _____

3. What percentage of students qualify for Chapter I services?   _____

4. What is the school's average weekly absentee rate?   _____

5. What percentage of the students qualify for special education services?   _____

6. What percentage of the students are identified as learning disabled?   _____

7. What percentage of the students qualify for bilingual services?   _____

8. What percentage of the students have received counseling or other social services for crisis intervention?   _____

9. What percentage of the students have been adjudicated?   _____

10. What is the school's weekly average number of incidents of violence or vandalism?   _____

11. What is the school's weekly average number of classroom disruptions that are referred to the principal?   _____

12. What is the dropout rate for the school?   _____

13. What is the percentage of teenage mothers in the school?   _____

14. Does the school maintain an intervention tem to support at-risk youth?   _____

15. Does the school provide a diverse array of intervention services for at-risk youth?   _____

Index